THE GOOD SHARPS

The Brothers and Sisters Who Remade Their World

Hester Grant

Chatto & Windus
LONDON

1 3 5 7 9 10 8 6 4 2

Chatto & Windus, an imprint of Vintage,
20 Vauxhall Bridge Road,
London SW1V 2SA

Chatto & Windus is part of the Penguin Random House group of companies
whose addresses can be found at global.penguinrandomhouse.com

First published in the United Kingdom by Chatto & Windus in 2020

penguin.co.uk/vintage

A CIP catalogue record for this book is available from the British Library

ISBN 9781784742133

Typeset in 11.5/14 pt Dante MT Std
by Integra Software Services Pvt. Ltd, Pondicherry

Printed and bound in Great Britain by Clays Ltd, Elcograf S.p.A.

Penguin Random House is committed to a sustainable future for
our business, our readers and our planet. This book is made from
Forest Stewardship Council® certified paper.

THE GOOD SHARPS

In memory of my father

'The good Sharps! None ever spoke of them
without *"good"* before their name!'

ANNIE RAINE ELLIS, *Sylvestra: Studies of Manners
in England from 1770 to 1800*, Vol. I (1881)

Contents

CONTENTS

Overture

When Johan Zoffany returned to London, in the spring of 1779, it was on the crest of a gilded wave. Flushed with the triumph of his reception in the Habsburg courts of Europe, the German artist could boast to his friends in the expatriate community of musicians, singers, sculptors and engravers that thrived in cosmopolitan London at that time, of the patronage of Pietro Leopoldo, Grand Duke of Tuscany, of the Duke and Duchess of Bourbon-Parma – and of the empress Maria Theresa herself. Had she not ordered him to travel from Florence to her palace in Vienna with his unfinished painting of Duke Leopoldo's family, in a specially adapted carriage? And afterwards, in recognition of his services to the imperial majesty, bestowed on him the title of Baron of the Holy Roman Empire?[1] With such testimonials, and the proceeds of his continental commissions swelled by a speculative trade in the sale of old masters, Zoffany could look forward to the revival of his English portrait practice, and a life of extravagant ease.

Perhaps, in the weeks that followed, as he fingered the exquisite furnishings of his newly acquired town house in Albemarle Street, or sauntered along the Thames by his country home at Strand-on-the-Green, Zoffany pondered on the glories of this homecoming, and compared it to his arrival in London nineteen years before. Then he had been a nobody, an obscure artist from Regensburg, whose sole claim to fame was a series of murals in the chapel and palace of the Archbishop of Trier at Koblenz.[2] Intent on plundering the rich spoils of English patronage, Zoffany spent his first months in London grubbing for work, painting clock faces, and drapery in other artists' pictures,[3] before David Garrick – the most famous actor of the day – spotted his genius for recording the ephemera of theatre. Garrick's patronage brought him to the notice of aristocrats in the actor's social circle, and a series of increasingly illustrious commissions followed.

By the late 1760s, Zoffany had become the most fashionable family portraitist in London, a reputation sealed by his employment by George III and Queen Charlotte to paint the treasures of the Tribuna in the Uffizi Gallery in Florence.[4] Here he assumed the role of a celebrity, courted alike by Habsburg dukes and English *milordi* such as Lord Cowper and Sir Horace Mann, and received the recognition of his peers in election to the *accademie* of Florence, Bologna, Parma and Cortona.[5]

Behind the constant revolutions of Zoffany's life lay a restless ambition that the rewards of an ordinarily comfortable existence did not satisfy. Impulsive, capricious and intellectually curious, the artist sought stimulation in new experience, while his delight in the material trappings of wealth demanded a steady stream of rich clients. It was a quest for adventure, and a newly acquired interest in the art and antiquities of the East, as well as the lure of the riches of the East India Company – Zoffany 'anticipates to roll in gold dust' noted his fellow artist Paul Sandby – that inspired his travels in India in the 1780s.[6] In London, the proceeds of commissions from Habsburg courts and Indian nabobs were frittered on conspicuous display, such as a retinue of servants in scarlet and gold livery in honour of the colours of the coat of arms granted to him by the empress Maria Theresa.[7]

It was on his return from Italy and Vienna in the spring of 1779, when his travels in India still lay ahead of him, that Zoffany was approached by William Sharp, a London surgeon, with a request to paint a portrait of his extended family. Fresh from the resplendence of the Habsburg court, the German artist might have looked askance at the advances of a client of a distinctly sub-aristocratic hue. But Zoffany's portrait practice had failed to live up to the glorious promise of his homecoming. Instead of a revival of royal and noble favour, he had been shunned at court – partly on account of his failure to obtain the king's permission before accepting a title from the empress Maria Theresa – while fashion now favoured the grand style of portraiture practised by Joshua Reynolds and George Romney in preference to his own more muted sensibility. In these circumstances, Zoffany could hardly afford to be contemptuous of the 400-guinea fee – a vast sum for the time – agreed for the painting of the Sharp family.

There were other reasons why Zoffany looked kindly on the Sharp commission. Patron and artist shared a passionate love of music, which each indulged by throwing musical water parties on barges on the Thames, and had friends in common such as the German musicians Johann Christian Bach and Carl Friedrich Abel. There was also a synchronicity between William Sharp's journey from middle-class obscurity to wealth and position, and Zoffany's own. Both enjoyed a remarkable talent for society, that in Zoffany's case facilitated his acceptance by groups as diverse as the patricians whose portraits he painted in the late 1760s, louche expats in Florence, and the intellectuals who met at Jack's Coffee House every Wednesday evening to discuss natural history, amongst them the naturalist Daniel Solander, Captain James Cook and Josiah Wedgwood. Occasionally Zoffany overstepped the mark, as when he offended Lord Cowper by wearing a pink coat in Rome – apparently the preserve of English earls – but mostly his social instincts were pitch perfect.[8]

A self-portrait contemporaneous with the painting of the Sharp family shows Zoffany in his studio, accompanied by his daughter Maria Theresa and the father-and-son cellists Giacobbe and James Cervetto, brushes and palette in hand, and an unfinished portrait on the easel beside him.[9] Though the artist is dressed elegantly, in a coral-pink coat – of a darker shade than that which caused offence to Lord Cowper – and yellow waistcoat, it is almost impossible to trace in the coarse, and rather brutish, features of his face, the charm and ease of manner for which he was known. The painting on the easel in the self-portrait is as yet merely background, composed of the blues and greys and yellows of a nascent sky.

It is in this way that the portrait of the Sharp family begins, with the faint shadows of a pale blue sky, and the steely mass of an approaching storm cloud. Patron and artist have agreed that the family is to be depicted on the deck of their favourite barge, the *Apollo*, embarking on a musical water party on the Thames at Fulham. As Zoffany adumbrates the contours of the sky, he contemplates a creative act that goes beyond the mere mimetic depiction of a family at play. As the novelist, or biographer, presents his characters in a narrative that fuses artifice with reality, so Zoffany constructs an image that is at once perfectly true – in the likenesses of individual sitters, in his depictions of dress, hair, instruments and water, in the lines of the nave of All Saints and the wooden railings of Putney Bridge – and yet utterly contrived, given that the Sharp family would never have piled themselves up in the manner suggested to give a concert on the water. Like a false memory, the painting has all the vividness of truth, untarnished by the dull practicalities of reality.

By the time that the Sharps, in twos and threes, some by weary carriage from Northumberland, and others a short ride from the City of London, arrive at Zoffany's studio, the artist has already sketched in their figures, and assembled the family virtually, in a triangle on the deck of the *Apollo*, with a married brother at each corner, and the remaining brother, sisters, wives and nieces in between. No doubt there is a flutter of awkwardness about the sitters as they assemble in the studio, particularly those from the north who are less sophisticated than their London relations, and there is much smoothing of dresses, and arranging of ribbons, and anxious glances in the mirror to ensure the correct tilt of a specially made hat. Zoffany, with urbane charm, puts everyone at ease, while his dog Roma assists by showing a special devotion to Frances, the least confident of the Sharp sisters, laying an affectionate paw on the train of her blue silk dress. The artist paints as he talks, apparently effortlessly, pinning down the fleeting phenomena of look and manner, in a few licks of pearly highlights, interlaced with flashes of pure vermilion.[10]

From a palette of ultramarine and Prussian blue, verdigris, lead-tin yellow, Naples yellow, ochres, red lead, lead white, vermilion and Vandyke brown, William appears on the tip of Zoffany's brush, in a dark blue coat with a red collar and gold-laced buttonholes, the luminous beauty of his face, and the deep clear blue of his eyes, holding the viewer's gaze with an air of serene command.[11] A society surgeon, William glides through the ranks of the London elite, employing his professional connections to construct an increasingly sophisticated and aristocratic acquaintance. His brother James, who forms the left-hand corner of the triangle, looks up at the sky, with legs splayed to accommodate the coils of a bass wind instrument known as a serpent. He wears an old-fashioned coat of reddish-brown, and a black tricorn hat, and seems to lack William's refinement. Yet James is a visionary, an inventor, engineer and ironmonger, who revels in the giddy pace of technological change, and with remarkable acuity exploits the opportunities it represents.

John, the eldest of the Sharp brothers, who forms the right-hand corner of the triangle, is dressed in sober clerical black. The modesty of his averted look belies the scale of his achievements at Bamburgh Castle in Northumberland, which he transforms into a revolutionary social enterprise, while also commissioning the world's first lifeboat, the 'unimmergible'. Even these endeavours are, however, overshadowed by the successes of his youngest brother Granville, who leans on a harpsichord, in a sage-green coat and black knee breeches, with an expression of almost mystical fervour on his long angular face. Eccentric, didactic and socially awkward, Granville has neither William's urbane charm, nor James's entrepreneurial flare. Nevertheless he becomes the 'father' of the campaign to abolish slavery, a passionate advocate of social and political reform, and a philanthropist of rare determination and resolve.

Granville sits by his sister Elizabeth, who stretches her slim white arms to the keyboard of the harpsichord. She is accompanying another sister, Frances, who holds a music book in her hand, and appears to be about to sing, while the long train of her blue silk dress serves as a pillow for the somnolent Roma. Judith, the third sister, sits above them in a mustard-coloured riding habit and a black hat trimmed with ostrich feathers, while her fingers curl over the strings of a long-necked lute. Barely educated and debarred by the prejudices of their time from public life, the Sharp sisters cannot hope to rival the illustrious achievements of their brothers. Yet each in their way lived as an independent woman.

This is the story of the siblings that make up the Sharp family, of whom seven are depicted in the painting (Thomas, the second eldest brother, died in November 1772, seven years before the painting was commissioned) – from their childhood in a remote rectory in Northumberland, through coming of age in London, past courtship and marriage, and the trials of later life, to the apotheoses of their various remarkable careers. Through their achievements in fields that included medicine, manufacturing and social welfare, the siblings changed the lives of thousands of people in eighteenth-century Britain. Moreover, the family were involved in many of the events and movements that defined the period, amongst them the campaign against slavery, the American War of Independence, constitutional reform, the canal movement and philanthropy. In this way, the story of the Sharps is also a mirror of the age in which they lived.

What follows is a portrait of seven individuals, and of the family as a whole – for notwithstanding their personal achievements, it is as a family that the Sharps shine brightest. The siblings remained extraordinarily close throughout their adult lives, sharing joy and sorrow, mutually supportive, delighting in joint enterprise and activity, and following ideologically consistent paths. In this, and in their capacity for shared merriment, good humour and mildly eccentric fun, the Sharps' story is a template not merely for lives well lived, but of the power of the family to enrich and sustain the individuals who comprise it.

The most characteristic, and idiosyncratic, form of Sharp family activity was the musical water party, which the siblings hosted with great verve and ingenuity on barges sailing up and down the Thames. Resembling a kind of floating *fête champêtre*, with music, dancing and elaborate picnicking, the Sharp water party was a familiar feature of London life in this period. Zoffany's celebrated depiction of the Sharps on the deck of their sailing barge the *Apollo* is the defining image of this most harmonious family.

Part One

(1721–1752)

The South West View of the City of Durham.

I

Beginnings

On a wintry afternoon in late November 1721, Thomas Sharp, a young clergyman, newly appointed to the parish of Rothbury in Northumberland, sits down to write a letter to his brother John. It is chilly in the stone-vaulted study where he works, and only the palest traces of watery sunshine find their way through the narrow aperture of the window above his desk. When he looks up, Thomas can see Rothbury spread out before him, a straggle of heath-thatched houses and unpaved streets, and beyond them a bleak expanse of moorland, where the shadows of evening are already gathering.

Thomas steels himself to return to his letter, which he is finding difficult to write. The subject is of the greatest significance to him: a proposed marriage between himself and Judith Wheler, the daughter of a Durham prebend.* Though he writes in the tones of respectful restraint to be expected of an early eighteenth-century clergyman who seeks the approval of a much older brother, Thomas's letter bears the traces of a rather less clerical passion. It was the Whelers who suggested the match, but the young clergyman has fallen in love with his proposed bride. Judith, he explains to his brother, 'will make me the most usefull & agreeable wife, of any Lady, that I have yet heard of, or seen'. Having made up his own mind, Thomas is anxious for his brother's approbation: 'I can yet determine nothing till I have consulted so near a Relation & so dear a friend, as you are.'

---

* A prebend, or prebendary, was in this period an Anglican clergyman with a remunerated role in the administration of a cathedral or collegiate church.

It is only towards the end of the letter that Thomas's feelings seep through the constraints of his carefully constructed argument. Judith's dowry will be small, he admits, but this is 'a point of no consideration, nor ever will be'. Then, in a sudden burst of self-revelation, he intimates that it is desire, rather than the prospect of financial gain, that impels him to the altar: 'Were I as little disposed to any sort of love, as I am to that of money, & could rule all my desires, as well as that of worldly interest, I should be a better & happier man.'[1]

It is easy to understand why the Whelers chose Thomas Sharp as a husband for their daughter. At twenty-seven years of age, he appeared to be a confident, gifted and high-achieving young man. Following a successful academic career at Trinity College, Cambridge, he had entered the Church, where he was the recipient of several lucrative preferments, including the livings of Ormesby in Yorkshire, and later Rothbury in Northumberland, and prebendal stalls in Southwell and Durham.[2] As the younger son of the former Archbishop of York, John Sharp, Thomas could bask in the reflected glory of his father's posthumous reputation, and patronage came thick and fast.[3] Within eighteen months of writing the letter to his brother, Thomas had been appointed the Archdeacon of Northumberland, at the almost unseemly age of twenty-eight, with responsibility for the county's clergy and maintenance of Church buildings.[4]

Yet behind the brilliant facade, and display of relentless high achievement, lay a complex individual. He was almost certainly a depressive, a point obliquely alluded to in his letter to his brother John, while he was advised by friends to refuse the living of Rothbury on grounds that the bleakness of its situation would contribute to his 'melancholy'.[5] Thomas also struggled to extricate himself from the shadow of his father, whose apparently saintly goodness threw into relief the imperfections of what he perceived to be his own flawed nature.[6] Driven by self-doubt, and the necessity of justifying his fitness for the offices he had obtained through his father's reputation, Thomas devoted himself to his clerical duties, and was an exemplary and reforming parish priest, archdeacon and ecclesiastical administrator. He also found time to publish seventy-nine works, on a wide range of subjects that included liturgical instruction, morality and abstruse points of Hebrew translation.[7]

Of the woman he loved, Judith Wheler, almost nothing is known. Her presence in the Sharp archive consists only of fragments of correspondence, and a recipe book containing instructions for 'Chocolate Almonds', 'Goosberry Tart' and 'mince pys', as well as the more medicinal 'Receipt for ye Cold', 'Dr Barnard's Syrup' and 'For ye Ricketts'.[8] Perhaps something of her character can be traced from her forebears, who included several generations of scholars, soldiers and diplomats.

Unlike the Sharps, who were small-time Yorkshire clothiers and farmers before John the archbishop propelled himself through the ranks of the ecclesiastical hierarchy, Judith was descended from landed gentry. Her mother's family was remarkable for its loyalty to the Stuart kings. In July 1643, her great-grandfather Sir Bevil Grenville, a Cornish landowner and ardent Royalist – 'a gallant and sprightly gentleman, of the greatest reputation' – was killed at the Battle of Lansdown.[9] John, his eldest son, and Judith's great-uncle, was only fourteen when he was injured at the second Battle of Newbury, but recovered to hold the Isles of Scilly for the Crown,[10] and later acted as a secret intermediary between Charles II in exile and Royalist conspirators in England. A grateful Charles II made him Earl of Bath following the restoration of the monarchy in 1660.[11]

John's younger brother Denis is said to have given up 'the richest deanery, the richest archdeaconry and one of the richest livings in England' to join the exiled James II in France, but received little thanks for his loyalty.[12] Denied the use of the Anglican liturgy, and insulted by James's Catholic priests, he fled to Corbeil, south of Paris, where he later died in poverty. His sister Bridget married Sir Thomas Higgons, a diplomat and author.[13] Though Higgons preferred life under William III to an uncertain future abroad, his three sons Thomas, George and Bevil were Jacobites of a far more ardent persuasion, and devoted their lives to the restoration of the Stuart monarchy.[14]

Grace Higgons, their sister, married the scholar and clergyman Sir George Wheler. As a boy, Wheler was adept at woodwork and built a small harpsichord, while a youthful interest in plants developed into a serious study of botany. He travelled widely, and brought home specimens, among them St John's wort, previously unknown in

England. Wheler's scholarship included one of the earliest studies of Christian archaeology, *An Account of Churches and Places of Assembly of the Primitive Christians.* The couple had eighteen children, of whom the youngest was Judith Wheler.[15]

John Sharp's reply to his brother's letter seeking approval for a marriage to Judith Wheler has not survived, so we do not know his views on the suitability of the match. But he seems to have been in favour, because seven months later, on 19 June 1722, Thomas married Judith in her father's church in Houghton-le-Spring. The Whelers had been astute in their appraisal of Thomas's qualities, as Thomas had been in the object of his love, for the marriage proved a strong and happy one. The couple's children, who are the principal characters in this story, were raised in two warm and bustling homes: the rectory at Rothbury, where Thomas wrote the letter to his brother in 1721, and a prebendal house in the cathedral close at Durham.

The household in which the siblings grew up closely resembled those of the clerical families that would later feature in the novels of Jane Austen and Anthony Trollope. Like their fictional counterparts, Thomas and Judith worried about their daughters' marriage prospects and the employment of their younger sons, fraternised with the local gentry, superintended village schools, and visited the sick. It was from their clerical upbringing that the siblings developed an attachment to the Church of England that was to be one of the mainstays of their adult life. From the Sharp side too, the siblings learned intellectual rigour, and perhaps the rigid self-discipline and commitment to duty that were such defined features of their father's and grandfather's careers.

But the siblings were also unconventional, and this sits less well with the Rothbury rectory and the serene walks of the cathedral close. It is tempting to trace their anti-establishment tendencies to Judith's forebears, and see in the unorthodoxy of Denis Grenville and his Jacobite nephews the template for the radicalism that, as later chapters reveal, characterised Granville's and James's adult lives. Whereas the philanthropic spirit that informed all the siblings' activities can be ascribed to the example of their father, the inventiveness of their charity seems to bear the genetic hallmark of the writers and free-thinkers of their mother's family.

Judith left no record of her first impressions of the rectory at
Rothbury, but they almost certainly bore no resemblance to Catherine
Morland's encomiums to the parsonage at Woodston. Unlike the
heroine of *Northanger Abbey*, Judith could not possibly have described
the drawing room of her future marital home as 'the prettiest room
in the world!' In place of the elegant facades, sloping lawns and light-
filled apartments of literary imagination, Whitton Tower had small
rooms and low vaulted ceilings. Built in the fourteenth century, the
tower was a rare example of a fortified rectory known as a 'vicar's
pele'.[16] It had four storeys, the lowest of which was a cavernous basement. The first and second floors were barrel-vaulted, and a stone
spiral staircase wound its way up one side of the house. Though the
main accommodation was in the tower, there was also a range of
domestic outbuildings including a pantry, scullery and dairy.[17]

Whitton Tower still stands, though heavily altered, on a hillside
overlooking Rothbury. The fortunes of this small market town were
transformed in the late nineteenth century under the patronage of
the industrialist Lord Armstrong, who built his great house Cragside
nearby, and following the building of the railway in 1870 it became
something of a resort. Until then, Rothbury had little to recommend
it. Bishop Pocock, who visited in 1760, recalls a 'poor town of two
streets which are not paved and the houses are mostly thatched; they
cover them with sods for warmth and thatch with heath'.[18] Today,
though the railway has gone, the town retains a quiet air of elegance
and prosperity. Fine late eighteenth- and early nineteenth-century
houses line the High Street, and there is a gentle bustle in the shops
that serve walkers and sightseers. The River Coquet curls round the
southern border of the town, and here in the summer months, by
the broad arches of a medieval bridge, children swim and play in the
shallows. A mile downstream the Coquet passes through the Thrum,
a narrow gorge named after the drumming sound of the water as it
cascades.

Though the Coquet has stretches of great beauty, the moorland
that spreads out to the north of the town has a darker feel. These are
bleak lands, windswept, with scrubby vegetation and a scattering of
poor wind-bent trees. The place retains a wildness today, and would

have seemed much wilder in the early eighteenth century when Northumberland was a remote outpost of the nation, steeped in poverty, lawless, and virtually cut off from its hinterland by the appalling state of the local roads. It was in this desolate place that Judith, for the greater part of the year, lived and brought up her family. For the children, rambling about in the tower, with the unchecked landscape of hill and moor at their doorstep, and the delights of the river – boating and fishing, and swimming in the summer – at their beck and call, wildness had its compensations. For Judith, left alone with the children for days on end as Thomas went about his business, the remoteness might have been harder to bear.

It was made even harder by the fact that she was almost constantly pregnant. During the first sixteen years of her marriage, Judith gave birth fourteen times. John, her first child, was born in March 1723. Then followed, in quick succession, Wheler in May 1724, Thomas in March 1725, Grace in April 1726 and George in March 1727. Barely eleven months later Charles was born, and after him, in equally rapid order, William in March 1729, James in January 1731, and Samuel in December 1731. Finally, now in her mid to late thirties, Judith gave birth to Elizabeth in January 1733, Judith in November 1733, Granville in November 1735, Anne in April 1737 and Frances in May 1738.[19]

Judith enjoyed an average respite of just over five months between one pregnancy and the next, though the relatively long gap between William and James (thirteen months), and Judith and Granville (fifteen months), rather distorts the figures. On three occasions she had only four months to recover from a birth, on three further occasions a mere two months, and after the births of Elizabeth and Wheler, just one month before she conceived again. To the physical demands of carrying and nourishing the unborn child was added the strain of the birth itself, repeated year after year, without pain relief, and in circumstances where – in an age when every woman knew someone who had died in childbirth – she must cope with the anxiety of knowing that the labour might be fatal to her.[20]

As if the continual pregnancy and labour, and the care of a rapidly expanding family, were not sufficient drain on her resources, Judith was also required to cope with the loss of her children. Wheler died when he was five weeks old. Grace, her first daughter, died a few weeks after her second birthday, and George, her next child, at twelve weeks. Samuel survived until he was two, and Anne until she was one. Judith, despite the devastation of such repeated loss, would not have considered herself particularly unlucky. At a time when between a quarter and a third of children did not survive their tenth birthday, infant death was an almost inevitable risk of motherhood.[21] In considering her relative good fortune, Judith might reflect on women she knew who had fared less well, for example her mother-in-law, the wife of Archbishop Sharp, who had buried fourteen of her eighteen children. Despite her loss, Judith had at least the solace of the nine children who survived (though of these, Charles, her fifth son, died in his teens).

The death of a child brought with it endless worry over the health of those who remained. For a woman like Judith, with a large family, and the experience of death to scar her, the illnesses of her children were agonising. As sickness was endemic in large families with young children, and medicines rudimentary, she would have been in an almost constant state of anxiety. In the absence of vaccination, contagious diseases such as measles and scarlet fever spread quickly through a family, so that it was not unusual for three or more children to be ill at a time. Diaries and letters of eighteenth-century mothers who faced such a predicament record the fatigue of constant attendance at multiple sickbeds, the absolute preoccupation with the sick children at the expense of all other thoughts and activities, and the emotional exhaustion of constant waiting, 'tortured with apprehension'.[22]

If Judith's role as mother was almost interchangeable with that of nurse, then she was also required to be a teacher. Contemporary society placed great store by the idea of the mother as moral guide and educator of her children.[23] In his seminal 1693 publication *Some Thoughts concerning Education*, the philosopher and political theorist John Locke argued that children were 'white paper or wax to be moulded and fashioned as one pleases'.[24] According to Locke, a mother should bring to her task not only 'sobriety, temperance, tenderness, diligence and discretion', but also the ability to respond sensitively to the 'various tempers, different inclinations and particular defaults' of her children, adapting her methods accordingly. For poor Judith, stretched to the limit by the competing demands of her ever-bur-geoning brood, Locke's edict meant that she must manage her children with apparently superhuman qualities of resourcefulness and patience, and also provide bespoke care according to individual 'inclinations' and 'defaults'.

In attempting to discharge the obligations of motherhood, Judith had only limited resources at her disposal. The living of Rothbury was small in comparison to those in more prosperous parts of the country, and though Thomas received additional income from his prebendal stalls in Durham and Southwell, a significant proportion of this was expended in hospitality. Charitable giving made further inroads into the family budget, for as well as maintaining five schools, Thomas supported individual projects such as the crenelated tower 'Sharp's Folly' that still stands near the rectory at Rothbury, which he commis-sioned to provide employment to local stonemasons.[25] His daughter Elizabeth later recalled that: 'My Dear Father with his generous mind and open hart and with his large family never over spent his incomb in any one year and often in making up his yearly account, had a balance which always immediately he gave away to chariotys.'[26]

The social isolation of remote rural parishes like Rothbury was one reason why clergy with prebendal stalls often left their parishes in the hands of a curate, and resided semi-permanently in the cathedral city.[27] Thomas, who was as conscientious in his duties as a parish priest as he was a devoted archidiaconal administrator, spent only three months of the year in Durham, and the remaining time in Rothbury. Every year, the Sharps bundled into the caravan of carriages and waggons required to transport a family of eleven and its possessions, and set off along the fifty miles of potholed, rutted roads that divided their two homes.

Imagine the scene on the morning of the annual migration to Durham, when Judith, who has been up since dawn, packing bags and dressing children, marshals her forces for the last agonising stages of departure. Outside the carters grumble as yet another bundle is presented to them, and the horses whinny expectantly and stamp their feet. As the moment of leaving draws near, the scene descends into a frenzy of chaotic activity. Children run to and fro, as something is forgotten, or lost, and bags are upended, and jump in and out of carts according to an apparently interminable negotiation as to who is to sit next to whom. It is only when the last vehicle rounds the corner of the lane that leads from Whitton Tower to the banks of the River Coquet below that Judith can draw breath, and as they clatter over the bridge into Rothbury, she begins to look forward to the pleasures of the months to come.

To children used to the unpaved, sod-thatched streets of Rothbury, Durham must have appeared to them afresh, on each occasion of their visit, as a place of almost magical grace and beauty. Built on a peninsula, carved by the wide green waters of the River Wear, the city retains even today an otherworldly loveliness. The massy towers of the great cathedral rise high above the streets, loftily perched and almost circled by the river. Everywhere there is a sense of quietness and elevation.

The cathedral close, which in Durham is called the college, lies to the south of the cathedral. At one end, a vaulted gatehouse connects the close to the North Bailey, while to the west a sloping passage known as the Dark Entry leads down to the river. It was here, at the river end of the college, that the Sharps lived, in the house belonging to the prebend of the 'tenth stall'. Built on the edge of the sandstone bluff that supports the city, the western face of the house falls sharply down to the riverbanks below. A path leading from the Dark Entry runs past the foot of the Sharps' house, following the line of the river.[28]

After the relative isolation of their life at Rothbury, the children viewed the serene precincts of the cathedral close as a hub of frenetic social activity. The Sharps knew everyone in the small world of the Durham chapter, and the families of fellow ecclesiastical dignitaries provided a welcome pool of friends.[29] In discovering old haunts, and renewing friendships, the weeks at Durham passed in a whirl of activity. Certainly in later life the Sharp children looked back to the time they spent in the city with great fondness. Much of what they loved about Durham – the great cathedral and its music, the vivacity of college society, and the wide green river – had a lasting influence on them.

2

Vocation

In later life the Sharps were exceptionally close, and it is apparent that their attachment to each other, and the pleasure that they felt in each other's company, developed in childhood. The siblings remembered Rothbury and Durham with affection, recalling with gratitude the 'two such happy homes we had been blessed with'.[1] The happiness of Thomas and Judith's marriage, and its characteristic of mutual, loving respect, provided a template from which the children learned to develop their own relationships. To this was added the experience of growing up in the noise and bustle of a large family, with its potential for numerous individual attachments, and shared jollity.

With the joy of many children came the responsibility of providing for them, and Sharp finances were limited. In a letter to his youngest son Granville, written after the boy left home to serve an apprenticeship in London, Thomas lamented: 'I cannot do for any of you so well as I could wish.'[2] It was natural that Thomas should want his sons to enter the Church, but the cost of the requisite university education meant that only the two eldest boys could pursue a clerical career. After attending grammar school in Durham, John went up to Trinity College, Cambridge, in 1740 at the age of seventeen, and Thomas followed three years later.

John and Thomas were both academic, and they relished the intellectual opportunities available at Trinity. Not for them the idleness and debauchery that characterised the behaviour of many mid-eighteenth-century undergraduates. Instead, a typical day begins early with chapel, breakfast and Demosthenes, in private study, or with their college tutor. After a lecture on Euclid, the boys dine in hall, which according to a fellow undergraduate is 'ugly, smoky and smelling so strong of bread and meat that it would be impossible for me to eat a morsel'.[3] In the afternoon, John returns to his books, but Thomas, who is less diligent, repairs to a coffee house where he smokes a pipe and reads the London newspapers. After a turn about the college quad, orders are given for supper, which is eaten with friends in one or other of their rooms. The star of these occasions is the teapot of punch, often of immense size, which the bedmaker prepares in accordance with his master's instructions. John retires early, but Thomas is expansive under the influence of drink, and talks with his friends until the early hours of the morning.[4]

Though their syllabus at Cambridge would seem highly prescriptive to a modern student, it provided a comparatively well-rounded education, and was broader in scope than that available in Oxford at the time. The enduring influence of Isaac Newton meant that the curriculum included mathematics and science, as well as the traditional classical component. This is evident in the commonplace book which John began during his time at Trinity, that shows an interest in, among other subjects, 'mechanicks, Hydrostaticks & Pneumatics … Opticks & Astronomy' and 'Medicine'.[5] Degree candidates were also expected to study theology and to know the Gospels in Greek.

Exams known as 'acts and opponencies' were taken in the second term of the third year. Rather than a written test of the sort taken today, these took the form of oral 'disputations' conducted in Latin. The candidate was required to maintain three theses, of which two were usually mathematical, in the face of counter-arguments posed by 'opponents'. At a further public 'accustomed examination', the candidate fielded questions from an audience. The persistence and quality of the questioning varied, as did the assiduity of the examinee. Briggs Cary, who took his degree in 1755, later recalled: 'I sat in the Combination Room at Peter House for my Bachelor of Arts Degree from the 13th to the 15th January in this year. NB We played at Cards all the Time.'[6]

That John and Thomas were of a more studious disposition can be assumed from their subsequent careers. Having successfully taken their first degree, John and, later, Thomas stayed at Trinity for a further three years studying for an MA, and Thomas subsequently obtained a fellowship. Both boys entered the Church, but did not turn their back on academia, taking in time the further degree of bachelor of divinity, and in John's case, the ultimate prize of doctor of divinity.

Back home in Northumberland, Thomas and Judith pondered the future of their four younger sons, Charles, William, James and Granville. Parental preoccupation with the career prospects of their children was as distinct a feature of middle-class life in the eighteenth century as it is in the twenty-first. The received view at the time was that parents were responsible for seeing 'their children well dispos'd of, well settled in the world', and that this required not only the provision of a sound moral upbringing, and a suitable education, but the discernment of a child's vocation.[7] In fact the career choices available to the Sharp boys were rather limited. Training for the law was expensive, and the army in this period was a niche occupation with little opportunity for advancement.[8] This left the option of a career in trade or commerce for which it was necessary to serve an apprenticeship.

What trade to choose was a matter of some complexity, and it was with parents like the Sharps in mind that in 1747 Richard Campbell published *The London Tradesman*. This listed hundreds of trades and professions, with information on the attributes required for a successful practitioner, the cost of training, and likely financial reward. Though published just too late to help Judith and Thomas as they struggled to decide how to establish their younger sons, the book provided expert guidance to a generation of anxious provincial parents.[9] In the absence of *The London Tradesman*, the Sharps resorted to the advice of friends and relations. A steady flow of younger sons to London in search of employment meant that the metropolis was tied to the provinces by a web of tightly knit familial connection. Judith and Thomas had relations who lived and worked in London, and their advice is likely to have been sought not only on the question of which trade to choose for their sons, but also which master the boys should be apprenticed to.

In 1743, as Thomas went up to Cambridge, his younger brothers, fifteen-year-old Charles and fourteen-year-old William, journeyed to London to begin their apprenticeships. Their sister Elizabeth recorded the event in her journal: 'My Father Dr Thomas Sharp, my mother and sist. Jud. brought my two bros. Chas. and Willm. up to town to be bound apprentices.' According to Elizabeth, 'Bro. Chas. was put to an Acadimy to prepair him for the East Indies', while William was apprenticed 'to a Surgen, Mr Phillips in Mincing Lane'.[10] Though Elizabeth does not record why medicine was chosen for William, and the East India Company for Charles, the boys' interests and inclinations would certainly have been taken into account.[11] If so, Charles's yearning for adventure was his undoing, for he died the following year in Indonesia. There is no record of the circumstances of his death, and of the death itself, only Elizabeth's rather peremptory account in a postscript to her earlier entry: 'Chas. dyed at Batavia in his passage to the East Indies some time afterwards.' It must have been a lonely and frightening death for a sixteen-year-old boy, thousands of miles from home.

The relatives who helped the Sharps choose a trade and master for William are also likely to have played a part in the negotiation of the premium. Calculated by reference to a master's reputation, and the size and potential of his business, the premium was generally seen as an excellent yardstick of an occupation's status, prosperity and esteem.[12] Thomas paid £350 for William's apprenticeship, which suggests not only that Mr Phillips was a man of repute, with a sizeable practice, but that William's prospects as a surgeon in mid-eighteenth-century London were considered to be very promising.[13]

William was fortunate in beginning his career in a period when the practice of surgery was transforming itself, both in terms of the quality of its technique, and the status of its practitioners. The early modern medical world had three types of doctor: the physician, the surgeon and the apothecary, of whom the first enjoyed social and professional pre-eminence. Whereas a physician studied 'physic' at university and was accepted as part of an educated urban elite, the surgeon, who had learned his trade as an apprentice, was categorised as a manual worker. During the eighteenth century, better training and a gradual improvement in surgical technique led to an increase in status of surgeons, while the lucrative London market generated an elite of highly respected and wealthy practitioners.

Were we to follow William on the first few weeks of his apprenticeship, his activities would bear little resemblance to those of a first-year medical student today. Instead of studying textbooks and revising for exams, William devoted his time to the company of his master, James Phillips, from whom he was expected to learn the rudiments of surgical technique. The day was spent in Phillips's carriage, bumping about the cobbled streets of London, as the surgeon journeyed between appointments in the City, the wide thoroughfares of Mayfair and St James's, and the leafy outlying villages of Chelsea, Fulham and Highgate. As a successful London surgeon, Phillips charged high prices for his services, and his clients were commensurately drawn from the ranks of the wealthy upper classes.

So we can picture William, as he accompanies his master on his round of calls, climbing the steps of a large town house in Upper Brook Street, or perhaps Cavendish Square. The footman who opens the door bows gravely, and ushers the surgeon and his apprentice into a dimly lit library, in which the blinds have been discreetly drawn, or perhaps the upstairs sanctum of a lady's dressing room.[14] Here against a backdrop of damask curtains, delicately patterned Chinese porcelain and the priceless baubles of a grand tour, Phillips is called upon to discuss the symptoms of tooth decay and venereal disease, to examine a fistula or ulcer, and to treat skin eruptions, boils, ruptures and syphilitic chancres.[15]

It was precisely the incongruity between the elegance of the surroundings, and the raw physicality of the consultation, that required a surgeon in Phillips's position to possess virtues beyond those normally associated with surgical technique. To be proficient in prognosis, and procedurally adept, was not enough: a surgeon hoping to succeed in the crowded London market must also be a gentleman, with the finely tuned social skills necessary to smooth away the inevitable embarrassment of the encounter. As he looked on from the corner of the room, making notes or perhaps passing a surgical instrument when required, William absorbed the etiquette of the upmarket medical consultation.[16]

At first, William can only lend a hand in 'making lint', 'washing rollers' and 'spreading plaisters' and other necessary preparations to a surgeon's craft.[17] Then as the months roll by, and William shows himself to be an apt pupil, he is trusted with the performance of an elementary procedure: perhaps a tooth-pulling for a less valued client.[18] The task is carried out competently, and William receives a glowing report for his bedside manner – and is entrusted with further operations, of an increasing degree of complexity. He learns to let blood, for which there is always demand, to cup with leeches, to patch fistulas and manage whitlows, as well as routine maintenance work such as cleaning, pus removal, ointments and bandaging.[19] It is only in the final years of his apprenticeship that he attempts the most difficult challenges of eighteenth-century surgery, such as the removal of bladder stones, and excision of cancerous tumours from the breast. In an age before anaesthetic, with the patient writhing and screaming on the bench, this is all about steadiness of hand, precision and speed.[20]

Though William left no account of his student days, it can be assumed, extrapolating back from his later career, that he was a model apprentice who seized every available opportunity to broaden his knowledge. No doubt, like fellow apprentice Richard Kay who recorded his training in London in the early 1740s, William attended extramural lectures on subjects such as 'Dead bodies', 'Outer Ear', 'Skull', 'Vision' and 'Aliment through Body' given by specialists such as John Girle and William Smellie.[21] His master James Phillips held the post of surgeon at St Bartholomew's Hospital, and this gave William access to a range of medical conditions, and surgical expertise, as well as unclaimed dead bodies to dissect. Besides his staunch work ethic, William possessed the self-discipline necessary to resist temptations, such as gambling and drinking, that were traditionally the undoing of London apprentices.

In later life the Sharp siblings were remarkable for their unity, which they maintained despite differences in individual prosperity and success. This has a particular resonance in view of the fault lines – ubiquitous at the time – that began to divide them in early childhood. Whereas parents in this period were advised to treat their children equally, it was an equality moderated by contemporary perceptions of birth order and gender.[22] For instance, John and Thomas were chosen, because of the accident of the timings of their birth, to follow a certain path in life, which was subsequently not available to their younger brothers. More significantly, the three surviving girls, Elizabeth, Judith and Frances, were destined, by reason of their gender, to a life of purely domestic and subsidiary significance: to the role of daughter, sister, wife and mother.

The successive departures of the Sharp boys to school, Cambridge and apprenticeship divided the siblings more than would be the case today. Bad roads and poor transport exacerbated distance: at a time when the journey from Newcastle to London took up to fourteen days, there was no coming home for the weekend. Indeed it is probable that the boys did not return to Rothbury for years at a time. The departure of the Sharp brothers weighed heavily on James, who at twelve was now the eldest of the siblings left at home. If the removal of John and Thomas to university had been painful, they at least, in their late teens and early twenties, were of a sufficiently remote age to be outside his immediate social circle. But Charles and William were his near contemporaries, and they had done everything together. Now, while Charles and William gloried in the adventure of London, and in Charles's case, looked forward to the almost unthinkable (though, as it turned out, fatal) exoticism of a voyage to the East Indies, James was stuck at home with his sisters, and Granville, who at seven, hardly counted for much.

For Elizabeth, aged ten, the parting from her brother William was particularly painful. These two siblings were exceptionally close and they remained devoted to each other throughout their lives. Now, with unfathomable depths of time and distance separating Elizabeth from the brother she adored, she drew closer to her younger sisters, Judith, aged nine, and Frances, who at five was the baby of the family. In the increasingly feminine atmosphere of the rectory schoolroom, the sisters developed a strong bond of intimacy.[23]

Though it was possible for girls of their class to attend a local school, or receive instruction from a governess, there is no evidence that the Sharp sisters were given these opportunities. Instead their mother Judith took charge of the girls' education, which took the form of a kind of Georgian home-schooling. For teaching materials, Judith dredged up the memories of her own education, which as the youngest of fourteen children is unlikely to have been substantial, perhaps employing a book or two from the Sharp library, a discarded atlas from John's or Thomas's schooldays, a French crammer, and the Bible.

Though Judith may not have expressed it as such, the education she gave to her daughters was not so much about learning for its own sake, as for the acquisition of skills requisite to the successful performance of matrimony and motherhood. Dancing, drawing and music were part of the informal curriculum because they were considered desirable accomplishments in a future wife. French and a smattering of history, geography and astronomy were included on the grounds that they contributed to genteel conversation, while also providing a bedrock of knowledge for the pupil's own future maternal educational obligations. In conformity with the prescription of contemporary advice manuals, Judith attempted to adhere to a timetable of useful and improving activities.[24]

Elizabeth, Judith and Frances, along with thousands of other genteel girls across the country, started the day with a bracing walk, before prayers and breakfast. Perhaps for Elizabeth, there would then be an hour of harpsichord practice, while Judith worked at her drawing board, and little Frances went over her letters with their mother, before they changed over, or worked on their needlework before dinner. The afternoon brought another walk, after which Judith and Elizabeth took it in turns to read aloud a passage from an improving book which, in deference to the strictures of the advice manual, was afterwards discussed or learned by heart. Occasionally, the torpor of the late afternoon might be interrupted by the visit of a neighbour: tea things were brought out, and the girls practised the art of polite conversation, which according to the conduct literature of the time was efficacious in teaching a refined and polished manner and a 'certain ease and elegance of address'.[25] Exhausted by their efforts, the girls stumbled yawning to the supper table. Then prayers said, and candle in hand, they climbed upstairs to bed.[26]

Contemplating the position of their nine surviving children in the autumn of 1743, Thomas and Judith had reason to be optimistic about their future. The cataclysm of Charles's death was yet to come, and they could imagine him, with quiet satisfaction, at the East India Company in Leadenhall Street, and William hard at work with Mr Phillips in Mincing Lane. Thomas was up at Cambridge, by all accounts doing well at his studies, while John, now in his fourth year, was clearly on his way to academic glory. James showed a practical bent, and might go into business, while Granville was too young to pose any pressing anxiety about a choice of future careers. As for the girls – their marriage prospects were too remote a problem to cause immediate concern. All in all, given the size of their family, and the limitations on their finances, the Sharps could with some justification conclude that they had managed things very well.

3

London

In 1746, James, the fourth of the surviving Sharp brothers, arrived in London, aged fifteen, to be apprenticed to Samuel Southouse of the firm Southouse & Chapman, ironmongers in Leadenhall Street. Accustomed to the quiet lanes of Rothbury, and the hushed precincts of the cathedral close, his first experiences of London must have been overwhelming. Twenty times larger than its provincial rivals, the metropolis was a vast, teeming, densely packed concentration of life.[1] Assaulted on every side by noise, smell, tumult and confusion, the city would have appeared to James almost unimaginably loud and brash. In the streets, carts jostled hackney carriages, porters with loads from the docks, and sedan chairs, while drovers herded livestock to the slaughterhouses at Smithfield and Tower Hill.

The noise was constant: the bellowing of animals, and scrape of iron wheels on stone; the cursing and shoving of carters and chairmen as waggons collided and loads upset; and over everything the cater-wauling of street hawkers trying to make themselves heard above the uproar. Packed together, the smell of unwashed bodies saturated the air, where it mingled with the stink of excrement and refuse heaps, and the pungent effluents of the tripe sellers, bone boilers, grease makers and leather tanners. In dimly lit lanes, and winding alleys, bulging upper storeys and shop signs blocked out light and air, and a heavy pall of coal smoke lingered above the houses, reducing the day to a state of semi-darkness.

This was London, a wonder city, pre-eminent in wealth, influence and prestige, not merely among its provincial rivals, but in comparison to the great cities of Europe. The seat of government, and home to the principal residences of the Crown, it combined political power with unparalleled commercial clout. Britain's burgeoning empire fuelled a rapid growth in overseas trade, and an increasingly sophisticated financial infrastructure. In addition to its commercial heft, the capital could claim, at least until 1730, to be the largest manufacturing centre in Europe;[2] while through the Port of London the city controlled the country's international, coasting and inland distribution network. Londoners carried on a vast range of trades, of which many, including the boat- and shipbuilders, coopers, sugar refiners, and warehousemen, were linked to the city's role as a maritime power. Other specialities included textile manufacture and finishing, building, leather-making, porcelain manufacture, the engineering of precision instruments such as clocks, navigation tools and watches, and cabinetmaking. The London artisan was considered an excellent workman; even the Abbé Le Blanc, a Frenchman not known for his partiality to the English, conceded that he 'is never content to work below his own standard of good workmanship', while the 'vilest workman thinks nobly of his trade'.[3]

In an age of minute social distinction, London trades were ranked as 'genteel', 'dirty genteel', 'genteelish', 'ordinary', 'mean' and 'mean, nasty and stinking', according to criteria such as wages, the requirement for artistic talent, and the relative cleanliness of the work.[4] In the 'mean, nasty and stinking' category came the grease makers and glue makers, the bone boilers and brick makers, who congregated on the South Bank and in the East End. There were also trades described as 'slavish' or 'fit only for sturdy lads', involving backbreaking labour, such as anchor and anvil smiths, or exposure to toxic materials.[5] Workers at the white and red lead manufactories in Whitechapel were known 'in a few years to become paralytic by the mercurial fumes'; braziers became deaf and hunchbacked; plumbers suffered from paralysis; potters were 'paralytic, lethargic, splenetic and toothless'; and hat-making was 'very slavish work, being continually obliged to be stooping over the steam of a great kettle'.[6]

Much of this was the consequence of the manufacture of luxury goods for the wealthy, which was a principal component of the local economy. In the early 1700s it became fashionable for the upper classes to spend part of the year in London, where they found ready access to Parliament, lawyers, doctors, shops, the marriage market and the society of their peers. This fashion delineated a new art of urban living, realised in the freshly built squares and terraces of the West End, and in the style of life carried on by its residents.[7] From November to May, the London season whirred, propelled by a relentless quest for diversion, with glittering balls and receptions, concerts and exhibitions, the theatre, the Italian Opera, firework displays and regattas. For the rich and well connected, a topography of pleasure overlaid the map of the city. There were parks to saunter in, and shop-filled arcades, and in the evening the delights of the Vauxhall Gardens with their supper boxes, and tree-lined walkways, and Italian ruins and Chinese temples all illuminated by the glow of a thousand oil lamps.

As James soon discovered, this was a golden age of consumption, when the demands of the new metropolitan elite stimulated an outpouring of luxurious imported and domestic goods. The shops of London were a modern marvel, wondered at by visitors from Europe as much for their ornate interiors and 'large plate-glass windows' as for the range and quality of their wares.[8] Elite retailers clustered in the long malls of Cheapside, the Strand and Fleet Street, and in the newly constructed streets of Mayfair. Here were the milliners, linen drapers, tailors, perfumers, goldsmiths, instrument makers, jewellers, music publishers, glass and porcelain showrooms, pastry cooks and wine and spirit merchants that catered for the wealthy. A man or woman of means in search of the finest Florentine and Genoese olive oil, caviar, mangoes, samphire, pickled walnuts, capers or anchovies, could find them at John Pott of Cornhill; while Domenico Negri, 'Confectioner of Berkeley Square', supplied dried and crystallised fruits, biscuits, ice creams and water ices.[9] No well-heeled tourist's itinerary was complete without a visit to Chevenix's at Charing Cross, where he could marvel at the intricacy of the toy* maker's buckles, trinkets, seals and snuffboxes, as well as watch chains and toothpick cases, sugar 'knippers', ink stands and smelling bottles.[10]

---

* 'Toys' in this context refers to small metal goods, rather than playthings for children.

The fabric of London has always been in flux, constantly reshaping itself to reflect the fortunes of its inhabitants. In this era, as the wealthy relocated westwards to escape the 'fumes, steams and stinks of the whole easterly pyle', the poor moved into the houses they left behind, dividing them into tenements.[11] The new squares of Mayfair and St James's became an enclave of the rich, echoing in spaciousness and ordered elegance the studied ease of their residents. For the poor, crammed together in the rookeries of Holborn and St Giles, there was only wretchedness and squalor.

The poorest areas of London were situated on the fringes of the City, where they had developed during the late Tudor and early Stuart period as a result of attempts to limit urban sprawl. When restrictions were placed on the construction of houses on new foundations, developers responded by building in places which would escape notice, such as in the courts of existing properties. Houses were so badly built that it was not unusual for them to collapse, while others remained in a state of wretched dilapidation. The author of 'Low-life', writing in 1764, described a slum scene at midnight: 'houses which are left open and are running to ruin are filled with beggars, some of whom are asleep, while others are pulling down the timber and packing it up to sell to washer-women and clear starchers'.[12] The consequence of building 'out of sight' was a labyrinthine streetscape, comprised of 'courts within courts' and 'alleys behind alleys', that invited overcrowding and degradation.[13]

It was in these communities that the gin craze of the 1720s to 1750s wreaked its most tragic consequences. In the early 1700s the government encouraged distilling as a means of providing a market for cereals when prices were low. Gin was affordable even for the poorest in society, for whom it offered temporary relief from cold, misery and hunger. In the absence of an effective system of licensing, the spirit was sold everywhere. According to a report published in 1726, in some parishes gin could be purchased in 'every fifth house', but this did not take into account those who sold it 'in the streets and highways, some on bulks set up for that purpose, and others in wheelbarrows, and many more who sell privately in garrets, sellars, backrooms and other places'.[14]

Gin fuelled an epidemic of tragic proportions. From 1720, birth
rates fell, and death rates soared: between 1730 and 1749, approximately
75% of children in London died before the age of five.[15] Though a
series of commissions and reports furnished the government with
incontrovertible evidence of the harm caused by the spirit, Parliament
vacillated, its resolve weakened by the persistent lobbying of the landed
interest. It took a concerted campaign of protest – in which Hogarth's
print *Gin Lane*, a stream of petitions to the House of Commons, and
evidence of the catastrophic mortality figures, all played their part – to
force the government's hand. In 1751 an Act was passed which, by
increasing the duty on spirits, and clamping down on its indiscriminate
sale, turned the tide on the epidemic.

When James arrives in London in 1746 to take up his apprenticeship
at Southouse & Chapman, the city is still in the thrall of gin. He does
not have to venture far from Leadenhall Street, where the ironmongery is based, to witness its ravages. Sent on an errand perhaps, by
his master's wife, to buy a yard of ribbon, or a memorandum book
for the counting house, he turns left along Leadenhall Street, past
Cornhill and Poultry, until the broad vista of Cheapside, with its
dazzling parade of shops, opens before him. Here he dawdles, nose
pressed against the plate glass of 'John Smith, Map and Printseller',
riveted by a print of a naked Venus, or a map of the world, or the
neatly stacked boxes of watercolours, Indian ink, black lead pencils
and brushes. Out of the corner of his eye he can see a pair of tur-
quoise silk shoes lined with silver lace, and a silver-gilt flowered hair
ornament with a delicate bird trembler, and other mysterious instruments of feminine allure, in the window of 'Martha Wheatland and
Sisters, Milliners & Haberdashers'.[16]

   Poverty rubs up against wealth, even in this bastion of luxury. A
street boy pesters the elegant frequenters of Martha Wheatland's
emporium, until the proprietor shoos him away. No one appears to
notice the figure slumped at the corner of Gutter Lane, but the shriek
of a drunk on Watling Street, and the incessant bawling of street cries
– 'All fire and no smoke!', 'Rare mackerel three a groat or four for
sixpence!', 'My pretty little ginny tarters!' – are harder to ignore. The

girl who sells James a notebook is dressed in cheap finery, but, as he can hardly help noticing, her breasts are almost bare: 'Will Your Honour buy a sweet nosegay or a memorandum book?' she asks him.[17]

Perhaps he returns by the river, through the maze of lanes and alleys that border the banks of the Thames from London Bridge to Limehouse. Here, amongst the crumbling tenements of St Katharine's, and Ratcliffe Highway, James sees poverty beyond anything he has witnessed in even the poorest cottage of Rothbury. As he picks his way between piles of dirt and excrement, groups of scald-headed* children watch him listlessly. One sits with a baby in her lap, while others make an attempt at play, hopping backwards and forwards over the open drain that runs down the middle of the street. A skeletal man props up the doorway of a lodging house with a bottle in his hand, gesticulating aimlessly, while sounds of raucous laughter float up from a neighbouring cellar.

Later that night, tucked up in a truckle bed under the counter in the ironmongery, James contemplates the first few weeks of his apprenticeship. For all the longed-for adventure of the journey from Northumberland, and the much-anticipated delights of London life, it has not been plain sailing. Like many of his fellow apprentices, this is the first time he has been away from home, and the swagger with which he contemplated his departure, and the bravado of his final farewells, belied an underlying anxiety. In place of the comforting ordinariness of the rectory at Rothbury, he is required to adjust to life with a family whom he has never met before, and with whom he has little in common.

As well as adapting to the routines of an unfamiliar household, James has to negotiate the personalities of his master, and his master's wife, and the older apprentices in the firm. He is the new boy at the bottom of a well-established pecking order, and must make do with the last serving at dinner, a bed under the counter in the shop, and being ordered about by everyone. Instead of casting iron in the foundry, of which he had dreamed, he is given humiliating tasks

---

* 'Scald-headed' is a term that was used at the time to describe various diseases of the scalp. Symptoms included hair loss, and pustules which dried to form scales.

such as sweeping, and carrying, and running errands. The hours are exhausting, with a working day that stretches from seven in the morning until nine at night.[18]

But James is better placed than others to cope with the challenges of apprenticeship. To start with he is a child of a large family, used to fitting in and managing a complex set of relationships. He is fortunate too in having an equable temperament, and can pull off that difficult balancing act of endearing himself to his master, while remaining on good terms with his fellow apprentices. Diligent, like his brother William, he combines assiduity with a practical mindset, and a talent for invention. It is not long before these qualities become apparent to his master, and James is given an increasing range of responsibilities.

Meanwhile the mid-eighteenth-century iron trade was almost perfectly suited to a boy of James's talents. Business was booming – at home and abroad. Exports of iron-made products quadrupled between 1714 and 1750, as British producers, protected by imperial fiat, met the demands of the expanding colonial market.[19] At home, rapid economic and industrial change stimulated an insatiable demand for iron. Growth in internal trade, and improvements in road transport, resulted in the need for more metal parts for waggons, carriages and harnesses; growth in overseas trade made necessary the supply of 'spike nails', 'deck nails' and 'sheathing nails' for the construction of ships; house builders needed roof laths and floor nails, and locks and hinges for domestic furnishing; and agricultural innovation increased the requirement for tools.[20]

The great ironmasters of the late seventeenth and early eighteenth centuries can claim to be the first true industrialists.[21] The ironmaster was responsible for the first stage of the industrial process: the transformation of ore into wrought-iron bar. The ironmonger, by contrast, presided over the secondary stages of the production cycle, and in particular the manufacture and sale of iron-made goods. The term ironmonger was used loosely: it included wholesalers who purchased bar from ironmasters and distributed it to producers; and also retailers trading in shops up and down the country. As the intermediary between ironmaster and the individual workman, the wholesaler ironmonger wielded significant power. He not only supplied the artisan with his raw material, but also marketed and distributed his finished goods.

There were few manufacturers of scale in the early eighteenth century. The typical producer of mass-market iron goods was an individual, or family, or master working with the assistance of apprentices and a few paid employees. There was intense specialisation, so that workmen invariably produced only one type of ware, while the skill required for different products varied widely. Nail-making, for instance, required the least skill, while lock makers were required to exercise varying degrees of expertise according to the type of lock required, and scythe makers were known to be the most skilful of the comparable trades.[22] Ironmongers placed orders with individual workers: for example, with the numerous families of nail makers who laboured from their cottages in the villages of the West Midlands.

Southouse & Chapman, where James served his apprenticeship, appears to have combined the wholesale and retailing function of the trade, and was thus well placed to exploit opportunities at home and abroad. A shop on the premises in Leadenhall Street sold a traditional range of largely domestic iron goods, while a manufacturing arm traded goods on the national and international market. It was on this foundation that James later built his own highly successful and innovative business, becoming in the process one of the most enterprising and respected manufacturers of his day. The trajectory of his rise from humble apprentice to wealthy industrialist stands as a paradigm of eighteenth-century energy and ambition.

4

Greeny

In April 1750, Granville, the youngest of the Sharp brothers, arrived in London with his father, to be apprenticed to a linen draper on Tower Hill. Thomas describes the first day of the apprenticeship in a letter to his eldest daughter Elizabeth, dated 25 April 1750.[1] In his account, Thomas refers to his sons by their pet names: Granville is 'Greeny', William is 'Billy', and James is 'Jimmy'. While his description conveys something of the natural anxiety of a father who entrusts his son so completely to another man's care, the letter is written with the evident purpose of reassuring anxious sisters left behind, and the tone is tender and light-hearted.

Greeny, he begins, 'went to his new master on Monday noon'. Thomas explains that he is able to give an account of the master and his family, for 'I and Billy dined there with them. And had a handsome dinner.' He is glad to report that 'I like both the master, and his wife, who is young, and seemingly a very good compos'd cheerful woman'. Moreover, the linen draper lives in 'one of the most airy and pleasant houses in all the city being a corner house looking one way upon great Tower hill and the other way upon little Tower hill, the corner of the House pointing to the Tower itself'.

The situation of the linen draper's premises is fortunate because 'it is at an equall distance, or nearly so, from Billy and Jimmy. So that they three stand in a triangle.' Thomas's description brings to mind Granville's good fortune in being the youngest of the three surviving sons to move to London. His elder brother William had no close family members living in the city when he began his medical apprenticeship in 1743, and bore the brunt of the upheaval alone. When James arrived in London three years later he had the advantage of being able to rely on William for friendship and support. By the time of Granville's arrival in 1750, James and William were young men – William was twenty-one, and James two years younger – and so were in an excellent position to guide the boy through the difficult early days of his apprenticeship.

While some elder brothers might have shirked this duty, it is clear from Thomas's account of the first days of Granville's apprenticeship that William and James were kind as well as conscientious. He recounts how 'On Tuesday morning Jimmy went & bought of Greeny a new blue apron wch. tho' it cost but a shilling, pleased Greeny much'. There appears to have been an arrangement between Thomas and the elder boys to take turns to visit Granville, for 'Billy went to see him about 11 o'clock' and Thomas followed 'in the Evening about 7'. The strategy was evidently successful, for the father reports that Granville 'seem'd in good spirits all that day, and has continued so ever since'.

Thomas finishes his letter to Elizabeth with an account of William's domestic economy. The relationship between William and Elizabeth was one of the strongest of the many bonds of attachment that connected the Sharp siblings, and Thomas's postscript shows that their friendship was as warm in early life as it was to remain when they were older. Having completed the seven-year term of his apprenticeship, William had recently taken over his former master's practice, and had set up by himself in the house in Mincing Lane. Thomas explains to Elizabeth: 'Now as Billy went to Housekeeping that self-same Day in the Evening, viz. Monday the 23rd I must tell you how he goes on; because you are intitled to know this, as you are (he says) to be his housekeeper.'

William appears to have begun housekeeping rather ambitiously, for 'On Tuesday morning he bought a shoulder of mutton for dinner' and 'his maid roasted it'. All was not well, however, for 'Mrs Reed scolds … because he used his new pewter without scouring it first'. The following day 'he had pancakes and what was left of the shoulder the day before', and 'I must not forget his frugality in making the drippings of ye shoulder of mutton on Tuesday serve to make the batter of ye pancakes on Wednesday'. That is all Thomas can report of William's housekeeping, for 'What he has had today I cannot tell now but I shall know by and by when he comes in to sit with me as he does every night'.

Commendable though William's domestic efforts were, there was in fact no need for him to self-cater. London in this period offered a multitude of opportunities for eating out, so much so that many people never ate at home. This was partly the consequence of the fact that most Londoners lived in single rooms with limited access to cooking facilities. This was a golden era of street food, when the hungry city-dweller need only stroll down his local street to be assailed on every side by the cries of hawkers advertising their wares: 'Oysters!', 'Hot cross buns!', 'Hot bad'd wardense!', 'Dutch bisket!', 'Neat's feet!' If he preferred to dine sitting down, the Londoner was equally spoilt for choice, for a thousand inns, taverns, alehouses, eating houses, cook shops, pie shops, eel-pie shops and 'ordinarys' competed for his custom.

The French traveller Henri Misson left a vivid account of a visit to a cook shop, where: 'four spits, one over another carry round each five or six pieces of butchers (never anything else; if you would have a fowl or pidgeon you must bespeak it) meat, beef, mutton, veal, pork and lamb. You have what quantity you please cut off, fat, lean, much or little done, with this a little salt and mustard upon the side of a plate, and a bottle of beer and a roll, and there is your whole feast.'[2]

A slightly less refined establishment, situated in a cellar, is described by Tobias Smollett in *The Adventures of Roderick Random*, where the eponymous hero is 'almost suffocated with the steams of boil'd beef, and surrounded by a company consisting chiefly of hackney coachmen, chairmen, draymen and a few footmen out of place, or on board wages, who sat eating shins of beef, tripe, cow-heel or sausages'.

Thomas stayed in London for several weeks before returning to the north, and wrote to Granville from his lodgings in the Temple on 15 May 1750 on the eve of his departure.[3] This is correspondence of a very different tone to that which characterises his letter to Elizabeth written three weeks earlier. He begins: 'As my coming to London was altogether on your account, so upon my leaving you there, my greatest present concern is for your well doing.' Thomas explains that, as a father, he has acquitted himself of his part of the bargain for the future welfare of his son, having 'placed' Granville 'to the best of my skill; I hope, well'. Responsibility now passes to Granville to make the most of the opportunities that have been given to him. Whether or not the apprenticeship turns out 'well' is in Granville's hands, for 'it is wholly in your power to make it so, or to make it otherwise'.

Thomas urges the boy to 'mind what I told you, about saying your prayers morning & night, and about going to Church on Sundays twice a day, & spending your Sunday innocently'. His advice extends to Granville's personal as well as religious conduct, and especially as it concerns 'your diligence in your Maste[r's] business, your respectful behaviour towards him & your Mistress, and obliging carriage towards all in the family'. Compliance will reap him a double reward, for if Granville is 'beloved & respected' by his master then this will 'tend [t]o make your apprenticeship more easy and agreeable to yourself'. Thomas explains that though he personally will continue to do all he can for his son, he will do so only in proportion to the standard of Granville's own conduct: 'While you deserve it, what is in my power to do you shall not be wanting.' If Granville complies with this advice then his prospects are bright, for 'honesty & industry with God's blessing will do great things for you'.

Though it is possible that Thomas wrote letters of this sort to all his sons as they ventured into the world, there is something in the tone and wording of the letter to suggest that it had a more particular purpose. Granville grew up to be the most remarkable member of a remarkable family, and it is apparent that at least some of the characteristics that defined him as an adult were present in the child. As a grown man Granville's idiosyncrasies included an absolute commitment to the truth as he perceived it, which he maintained stubbornly, sometimes with insufficient regard to the conventions of polite behaviour. As he later remarked of himself: 'I have never yet been afraid to do and avow whatever I thought just and right, without the consideration of consequences to myself', for 'it is a point with me never to conceal my sentiment on any point whatever ... when there is a probability of answering any good purpose by it'.[4] It was perhaps

Granville's disinclination to conceal his opinions that made his father nervous on the eve of his departure from London.

Though Thomas's letter is for the most part admonitory, with the professed purpose of reminding Granville of his responsibilities and duties, there is also something apologetic in it. For instance, towards the end of the letter, Thomas openly regrets that 'I cannot do for any of you so well as I could wish'. Though the regret is directed towards all the siblings, Granville is its most conspicuous recipient. Looking backwards from Granville's later career, and the characteristics of his adult life, it seems almost inconceivable that he should have been apprenticed to a linen draper. The incongruity between the situation, and his obvious talents and inclinations, is startling. His intellect and scholarly aptitude were seemingly apparent from a young age: as a child, he read the whole of Shakespeare sitting in an apple tree in the rectory garden.[5]

It seems that at one point Thomas, perhaps in recognition of Granville's academic interests, had intended that the boy should follow his two eldest brothers into the Church. Granville studied for a time at the grammar school in Durham, where his brothers John and Thomas had been pupils before they went to Cambridge. However, if it had once been Thomas's intention to educate his youngest son, his means were insufficient, for as Granville's biographer records: 'he was at a very early age withdrawn from the public grammar-school at Durham, before he had gained more than the first rudiments of the learned languages, and was sent to a smaller school to be instructed more particularly in writing and arithmetic'.[6] Granville would later compensate for the inadequacies of his early schooling by a relentless course of self-improvement – and by a single-minded determination to succeed, regardless of the obstacles in his path.

Part Two

(1753–1769)

A View of the River Thames *from* Chelsea.

5

Water

The scene is the Thames, near Chelsea, on a warm afternoon in May 1753. As it rounds a shallow meander in the river, a pleasure barge glides into view. A labourer, at work in the market gardens that spread westwards from Tothill Fields, catches the faintest breath of music on the air, and resting on his hoe, looks out across the water. As the barge draws towards him, he sees the features of a griffin on the prow, and beyond it the curling folds of a red standard. Then the long low sides of the hull come into view, and the decorative festoons of a dark green cabin, and a raised crimson stern. Men and women, in brightly coloured silks, stand on deck or sit with their backs to the sides of the stern. Boatmen hunch over their oars, but their strain appears to bear no relation to the gliding forward motion of the barge. Even the soft plash of wood on water, and the delicate ripples that stream past the moving hull, seem to have a mysterious life of their own.[1]

The barge passes him and pulls westwards, skirting the meandering woodland path that leads from Westminster to Chelsea. Soon the Rotunda comes into sight, and the elegant pavilions and walkways of Ranelagh Gardens, and beyond them Gough House, and the great pedimented edifice of Chelsea Hospital. By Old Swan Tavern, and the City barge houses, and the Physic Garden, and Bishop Stairs, the barge floats serene, while only the gentlest of breezes disturbs the broad canvas sails and curls the edges of the standard. Cheyne Walk approaches, and then recedes into the distance, while on the south bank the settlement of Battersea gives way to open fields. They pass

Fulham, a riverside village, and the wooded country of Parson's Green, and fashionable Hammersmith, with its mall, and row of luxurious mansions. Here finally the boatmen lift their dripping oars, and the barge drifts slowly southwards to the hamlet of Barn Elms. Tea is served, a flute plays, and the gentle hum of conversation floats across the water.[2]

In the Sharp archive there is a small, leather-bound volume that opens upwards like a reporter's notebook.[3] The words 'The Boat Book' are written in ink on the front cover with a bold hand and a flourish that curls down from the final letter. It is a memorandum book, and the notes and jottings that cover its pages are mostly in William's handwriting.[4] Now aged twenty-four, William is three years out of his medical apprenticeship, and a doctor on his own account. The Boat Book refers to a series of river excursions that took place on the Thames in the summer of 1753, and records the preparations for the expeditions and their expenses.

The excursions consisted of boating parties to one or more of the villages that lined the Thames beyond the borders of the city. The season began quietly, for the first two expeditions are simple affairs in comparison to the extravaganzas that came later in the summer. William's notes begin: 'at a court martial* held April 12 1753 – agreed that a voyage shall be made on the fifteenth inst.', and that 'the Company consist of ten viz the boats crew' and 'Messrs Lister Barnard Dodsworth' and 'Crainston'. William appears to have been responsible for provisioning the party, for his notes continue: 'To Take Tea Sugar Kitchen Tea cupps & sawcers silver cup & Cake Butter/Bread, Beef, Vinegar Salt/Tea spoons, milk ... wine & glasses'.

The second expedition recorded in the Boat Book was another exclusively male affair, this time a tea party at Wandsworth Creek. Though William expresses the purpose of the voyage as 'to Drink tea aboard the *Apollo* April 22nd 1753', this might be only half the truth, for the provision list included 'Shrubb' (a fruit liqueur made from brandy, sugar and the juice and rind of citrus fruits) and 'Cupp' (a

---

* What kind of 'court martial' is not clear: presumably it is just a colloquial reference to an informal meeting of the members of the boating club.

usually gin-based drink that was flavoured with spices, herbs, fruits and botanicals), as well as the mandatory 'Tea & Equipage'. The pleasures of the male drinking party were shortly forgone, however, for the remaining expeditions recorded in the notebook for that year involve mixed company. On 6 May: '2 Miss Coles, Mrs Hutton' and 'Miss Cotterell' joined 'Dr Merrick, Mr Hutton, Mr Hayman & Mr Wilkinson' in an excursion to 'drink tea Fulham'; while on the following Wednesday 'Mrs Lalouche, Mrs Edwards, Miss Diggs' and 'Mrs Lovibond' were members of a party at Greenwich.

As the summer progressed, the ambitions of the organising committee knew no bounds, as each new excursion surpassed its predecessors in size and elaborateness. On 13 May, a party of fifteen feasted on 'Biscuits 3 doz, Chockolate, Bread, Milk, Butter, Fowler, Ham, Beef, Sallet & Raddishes, Oil & vinegar, Ven[ison] Pye', and sipped 'Port' and 'Madeira Wine', on a stately progress to Maidenhead and Oxford. The guests on an excursion to Hampton Court on 4 June enjoyed their 'Shrubb' and 'Gooseberry Pye' with the novel luxury of 'A table cloth' and 'Napkins' while being serenaded with 'Musick' played on 'Hautboys* & Bassoon'.

William's notes give some indication of the complexities involved in planning these excursions. Even the relatively humdrum gathering of 15 April 1753 required labyrinthine organisation: William's to-do list on this occasion includes dispatching the *Apollo* to an inn at Brentford (presumably in readiness for the launch), hiring a horse, ordering bread and wine, and having a table made.[5] In addition to the logistical challenges of the day itself, much preparatory work went into ensuring that the boats were ready for the voyage. William's aide-memoire for 19 April 1753 records the following tasks: 'To have ... a Cringle for the Mast', 'a ring & cleat to every timber', 'Hooks to the awning Rails', 'Ropes to fasten on the awning', 'to Buy the awning & have it made' and 'Cushions'.

Though the notebook suggests that there was some sort of central committee directing operations – whose officials no doubt included 'Messrs Lister Barnard Dodsworth' and 'Crainston' – William appears

---

* A hautboy is a form of oboe.

to have been in overall command. Not only did he keep the accounts and order the provisions, he also owned the boats that were used for the excursions. The two vessels referred to in the Boat Book, the *Griffin* and the *Apollo*, were later part of a flotilla of boats owned jointly by the Sharp brothers, but in 1753 only William would have been in a position to fund their purchase. Whereas William had completed his training and was working on his own account, Granville and James were still serving out their apprenticeships.

William did not draft his notes with a view to posterity, or indeed with any purpose other than that of not forgetting the provisions and equipment – but they vividly illuminate his life in this period, and he emerges from the pages of the Boat Book as a successful and socially confident young man. After only three years of independent practice, and still in his early twenties, William had sufficient funds to buy and maintain two pleasure boats, and to entertain on an impressive scale. In so far as William's bachelor life can be extrapolated from the jottings of the Boat Book, it seems to have been an enviable one, in which merriment, male friendship and the society of young women, all played a significant role.

William's bachelor excursions also form part of a line of continuity between the Sharps' childhood and adult lives. Nurtured by the two rivers of their childhood – the Coquet in Rothbury, and the Wear in Durham – the siblings' affinity for water became almost a love affair in adulthood, when the family's expeditions down the Thames became one of the sights of London. For the Sharps, the river party was a glorious embodiment of much of what they held most dear in life: music, boating, conviviality, friendship and the pleasure of each other's company. The *Apollo* barge, with its red standard and dark green painted cabin, was to become the most loved and recognisable of the boats in the Sharp flotilla, and remains an emblem of the family's passion for water.

The prominence of the part played by the Thames in the story of the Sharps is perhaps as much a reflection of the river's significance in the lives of eighteenth-century Londoners as it is of the family's idiosyncratic fondness for water. The Thames in this period was the lifeblood not merely of the capital, but of the nation, transporting passengers and goods within the city, around the country, and to and from the world.[6] Today, by contrast, the metropolitan Thames has only a limited function.

The disengagement of London from its river is physically embodied in the Victorian embankments that run along the Thames's northern shore. Whereas now the steep sides of the embankment disrupt the connection between the raised thoroughfare and the river below, in the Sharps' time city and water met almost seamlessly. Then houses and warehouses stood so close to the river's edge that the water lapped against their walls. Prints from the period show boats tied to rings in the walls of riverside houses, and the gardens of mansions sloping down to the water's edge. At the riverside stairs that stand at intervals along the northern shore, water taxis cluster waiting for custom.[7]

For James, who in the summer of 1753 is twenty-two years old and in the final year of his apprenticeship, life without the Thames is almost unthinkable. Southouse & Chapman, the ironmongery where he works, depends on the river to transport its goods, and also for the supply of raw materials, such as coal from Newcastle, and wrought iron from the West Midlands and Forest of Dean. James is often Thameside these days, negotiating with custom officers on a consignment of iron bar, or supervising the dispatch of crates of nails bound for America. Standing on the quays that stretch from the Tower of London to London Bridge, James sees East Indiamen laden with oriental porcelain, rugs and tea, and the great vessels of the Eastland Company who bring timber, grain and resin from the Baltic. Collier ships, with coals from Newcastle, crowd the docks at Billingsgate waiting to unload, while coasters carrying the produce of the gardens of Kent, and fish, salt and all the myriad wares that are sold in the markets and shops that line the city's streets, compete for space in a river that is almost perpetually overcrowded.

William is less concerned than his brother with the river as a conduit for world commerce. He has patients to see, and the Thames is a useful means of transporting him about the city. If only a short distance separates one client from the next, the young surgeon walks – though the dirt of the streets, and the inevitability of being splashed by a passing waggon, makes this a risky business. For longer journeys he

can hail a hackney carriage, and submit himself to its infamously
bone-rattling form of transport. However, even this is fraught with
risks, for he invariably encounters a snarl-up in the streets: an upset
cart perhaps, with its contents strewn across the road, or a herd of
cattle run amok near Smithfield. Then thrusting coins into the hackney
driver's hand, he runs for the river, down St Mary's Hill, and Dark
House Lane, and out by Billingsgate Stairs where the watermen sit
in their wherries waiting for a fare.

A client across the river at Lambeth, say, or Battersea always requires
a boat ride. Until 1750, when Westminster Bridge is constructed, old
London Bridge, with its picturesque rows of shops and houses, is the
only built crossing on the Thames. Though Westminster Bridge eases
the London Bridge bottleneck, William still prefers the nimble wherry
– the standard water taxi of the period. Threading its way through
the lines of waiting ships, and dodging the barges that shuttle between
ship and shore, the wherry is a far more reliable form of transport
that its land-based competitors. There is a fixed schedule of fares,
from Westminster to the City, say, or from Temple Stairs to Vauxhall
Gardens, but if he is running late William opts for a two-man 'pair
of oars' rather than the more economical, but less speedy, one-man
'pair of sculls'.[8]

It was to escape these congested areas of the river, where the noise
was incessant, and the smell – of sewage and the industrial effluents
of the manufactories and workshops that lined the south bank –
stifling, that William made his excursions to the country villages that
lay scattered beyond the western borders of the city.[9] The expeditions
recorded in the Boat Book represent the beginning of a tradition of
family water parties, which in time served to perpetuate, as well as
reflect, the Sharps' social advancement. Though the extravagant
floating *fêtes champêtres* of the 1770s and 80s, which are to come,
outclass the modest tea parties of William's bachelorhood, they follow
the same pattern. Many of the essential characteristics of the later
water schemes – William's leadership role, apparently seamless organisation, favoured destinations such as Barn Elms, Fulham, Twickenham
and Wandsworth, and the winning formula of music, river, tea and
society – were established in the early years.

6

Music

Of the river excursions planned by William and his friends in the summer of 1753, three were distinct in featuring musical entertainment. Guests on the voyage to Hampton Court on 4 June were regaled by 'Hautboys & Bassoon' and 'Flutes & Vox Humana'. An elaborate two-day expedition to Deptford, Vauxhall, Chelsea, Shepperton, Laleham, Twickenham and Brentford on the weekend of 16–17 June included a 'musick afternoon'. And William's aide-memoire for an excursion to Laleham and Twickenham in August included 'Horns bitts Hautboys, Bassoon 5 books 3 Desks'.[1] There is no doubt about William's enthusiasm for these musical interludes – for he shared with his siblings a love of music that was to have a defining influence on their individual and joint lives.

The Sharps grew up in a household in which appreciation of music, and the value of a musical education, was taken for granted. Thomas, the siblings' father, was a keen amateur musician, and his extensive collection of musical manuscripts later formed the nucleus of his sons' musical library. Thomas's publication of a volume of *Rules for Tuning an Organ or Harpsichord*, and his composition of the opening double chant in *Fifty Double and Single Chants* – the earliest known printed collection of chants – published in 1765, suggest that his musicianship exceeded the proficiency of the ordinarily able amateur.[2]

Durham Cathedral also played an important role in the children's musical education. James Heseltine, the cathedral organist from 1711 until 1763, was their uncle by marriage, and as a leading figure in the musical life of the city was almost certainly influential in the development of the siblings' musical interests and taste.[3] The Sharps remained close to their uncle in later life, and at least on one occasion encouraged him to visit them in London to attend a family concert. Granville's charming invitation to this event is composed almost entirely from phrases taken from opera, songs and catches by Handel, Purcell, Aldrich and others:

> Oh the pleasures of the plains, Happy Nymphs and happy Swains – Hey down a down behold & See – Now are we met, & humours agree – Sing Merrily – now my Lads – Thus Love is Crown'd but Musick, Musick wins the Cause – Would you know how we meet – O Come & see – and – Happy Shall we be – Tis too late for a Coach but a Chaise may still bring you, to London fair City – when Innocent pastime our … pleasure Shall Crown – And may our meetings ever prove, Sacred to Harmony & Love – Ne'er trouble thy self at the times nor their turnings – but Make bright, Make bright your Warriors – Boots, and Come, Come away.
> Prithee Come or you'l rue
> So good Uncle Adieu
> G#

The siblings were also fiercely loyal to Heseltine's professional skills, comparing his organ playing favourably to that of his London rivals, as this assessment by the brothers of the service at St Paul's Cathedral in the late 1750s, makes clear: 'their Quire now is very good and had they but a Hesletine to Manage the Organ, it would no doubt be the best Choir in England, but the present possessor not having been brought up in the cathedral way, suply's it but very thinly'.[4]

Throughout their lives the Sharps delighted in making music together, both for the joy of the music itself, and for the pleasure they felt in each other's company. The siblings played their instruments together from a young age – a collection of seven part books belonging to the family that survive in the Dean and Chapter Library in Durham are a vivid example of this.[5] Containing the inscription 'Charles Sharp', 'James Sharp', 'John', 'William' and 'Thomas Sharp 1741', the books are a compilation of concertos and sonatas, some printed and others in manuscript written in an amateur and rather squiggly hand.[6]

Each of the part books contains music for a particular instrument: 'Violino Principe', 'Secundo', 'Violincello', 'Viola', 'Basso', 'Hautboy Primo' and 'Hautboy Secundo'. The printed music – which includes 'Six Overtures for Violins etc. in seven parts as they are perform'd at the King's Theatre in the Opera of *Ariadne Orlando Solarmes Aetius Porus Esther* Composed by Mr Handel' and '*Harmonia Mundi* the collection Being VI Concertos in six parts for Violins and other Instruments Collected out of the Choicest Works of the Most Eminent Authors viz Vivaldi Tessarini Albinoni Alberti never before printed' – was all published between 1728 and 1742. These dates, and the year '1741' which Thomas appended to his signature, give some clue as to the age of the children when the music was compiled. In 1741, John was eighteen years of age, Thomas sixteen, Charles thirteen, William twelve and James ten. Granville was only five, which accounts for his absence from his brothers' music-making.[7]

The Sharps' apparently limitless appetite for music may explain why several of the brothers learned more than one instrument. James is depicted with a 'serpent' in Zoffany's painting of the family, but he was also an adept on the bassoon and French horn. William was similarly ambitious – he played the organ, horn and clarinet – but it was the youngest brother Granville who was the most prolific of the Sharp instrumentalists. In the course of his life Granville learned the hautboy, clarinet, flute, double flute, kettledrums and the traverse harp. His most notable achievement was mastery of the double flute, a recondite instrument that requires the performer to play two parts of music simultaneously.[8] Opinion seems to have been divided on the success of this innovation. While the composer William Shield enthused that 'Mr Granville Sharp ... performed duets upon two flutes, to the delight and conviction of many doubters, who had conceived such an accomplishment to have been impracticable', his fellow musician, R. J. S. Stevens, was sceptical: 'the performance after the novelty of it was over, was rather disagreeable'.[9]

The traverse harp was another example of Granville's propensity for musical complexity and experimentation. According to his early

nineteenth-century biographer Prince Hoare, Granville 'constructed
(if not invented) a harp with two rows of strings, called a traverse
harp, on which he accompanied his own voice in singing'.[10] In the
Sharp archive there is an incomplete drawing of the harp that shows
the two rows of strings crossing over each other.[11] Granville also sang,
and took a technical interest in music, which he expressed in his 1767
publication *A Short Introduction to Vocal Music*, a treatise designed to
assist those wishing to learn to sing by sight.

The two eldest Sharp boys seem to have been more conservative
in their musical tastes, at least in terms of the number of instruments
they played. Thomas was a violinist, and as such was the leader of
the Sharp band during his residence in London in the 1750s. He appears
to have remained true to the violin, for there is no suggestion that he
dallied with any other instrument. His elder brother John showed a
similar loyalty to the cello, which he played throughout his life. His
passion for music is vividly conveyed in this contemporary account
of a musical gathering at John's vicarage in the Northumberland village
of Hartburn, where he was minister:

> His delight was to entertain his neighbours with musical perfor-
> mances, with the assistance of the Durham choir, many of whom
> he invited to visit him at stated periods. He himself was a musical
> performer of considerable attainments. His favourite instrument
> was the violoncello; and in the ecstasy of enjoyment he would
> throw off his coat, and fiddle among baronets and squires, and
> their lady wives and daughters, in his shirts sleeves, till ... he
> was black in the face.[12]

If symptoms of musical ecstasy were permissible in a senior member
of the Anglican clergy in the privacy of his own vicarage, they would
not have been considered appropriate in public. It is for this reason
that in Zoffany's portrait of the family, John is portrayed in quiet
contemplation, while his cello stands mutely by his side.

For all the vaunted unity of the Sharp siblings, where music was
concerned equality was tempered by what appears to have been a
pronounced gender bias. It is telling that the part books in the Dean

and Chapter Library, which convey something of the charm of the
Sharps' childhood music-making, contain no female signatures. In the
boys' defence, the absence of female participation reflects contemporary perceptions of what was acceptable in terms of a woman's role
in music, rather than any particular discrimination on the brothers'
part. There were strict rules in this period on the subject of which
instruments it was appropriate for a woman to play. The violin, for
example, was quite beyond the pale, as it was thought of as a quin-
tessentially masculine instrument.[13]

That even the forward-looking Sharps subscribed to these rules is
evidenced by the instruments chosen by the sisters. Elizabeth played
the harpsichord, and in a role entirely in accordance with contemporary
notions of women's place in society, became known 'as the family
accompanist'.[14] She is shown in this capacity in the Zoffany portrait.
Judith played the lute – again as in the family portrait – and also the
'English guitar', both fashionable instruments for ladies in this period.
Frances does not appear to have played an instrument, but she did
sing, and performed as a soloist on several occasions in family concerts.
Despite their obvious fondness for their sisters, the brothers were rather
disparaging in their assessment of the girls' musical attainment. For
example, in a letter dated 21 June 1757, Thomas suggests that it would
be 'much ... to Sister Sharp's improvement in Thorough Bass, was she
to practice from Dr Boyces Scores of Services and Anthems &c'.[15]

Sharp music-making can only fully be understood in the context of
the obvious, but still remarkable, fact that there was no recorded music
in this period. If you wanted to hear music – at least outside a church
– then unless you were one of the very few aristocrats, or members of
the royal family, who had sufficient funds to maintain their own private
orchestra, you had to make it yourself. Whereas today access to music
has no connection to the possession of musical skill, in the early decades
of the eighteenth century things were very different. Then a lover of
music was also required to be a player of music, if he or she wanted
to indulge their passion with anything approaching regularity.

This was the case even in the prosperous and sophisticated capital
city. Aside from the Italian Opera at Covent Garden and Drury Lane,
and the occasional oratorio season at the Lincoln's Inn Fields Theatre,

Londoners had little outlet for their musical enthusiasms. The great eighteenth-century musicologist Charles Burney, looking back from the later decades of the century when the concert life of London had been transformed, could muster little enthusiasm for the musical offerings of the 1750s: 'The only subscription concert at the west end of town at this time, was at Hickford's room or dancing-school, in Brewers-Street; and in the city, the Swan and Castle concerts, at which the best performers of the Italian Opera were generally employed, as well as the favourite English singers.'[16]

The 'Castle' and 'Swan' concerts referred to by Burney were organised by musical societies based in the City of London. The Castle, which was considered the grandest of the three musical clubs extant in the City at this time, was founded in the early 1720s, and like its fellow societies, operated from a private room in a tavern. Membership of the Castle was carefully monitored. While participation from 'young persons of professions and trades' was encouraged, certain categories of tradesmen – 'vintners, victuallers, keepers of coffee-houses, taylors, peruke-makers' and 'barbers' – were excluded.[17] Though it was generally the members who played at the Castle concerts, the society sometimes hired professional artists to supplement their efforts. Professional 'stiffening' was often the source of tension, as paid artists were notoriously sniffy about the quality of amateur performance. As Charles Burney once noted, 'the performers were sometimes in and sometimes out'.[18] Any deficiency in the quality of the members' playing might well have been due to a lack of familiarity with the music, as practice was not considered essential – or even advisable – for those participating in the performances. Indeed members were expressly prohibited from taking their parts home, on pain of a large fine.[19]

Given the Sharps' enthusiasm for music, it is no surprise that the Castle was the club of choice for at least one of the brothers living in London in the 1750s. We know for certain that William was actively involved in the society in 1755, when he helped organise a summer concert 'special' on the Thames. The event was advertised in the *Public Advertiser* for 5 June 1755: 'Castle Society: The Gentlemen Subscribers to the Water Concert, to be held on the 5th of July next, are desired to meet at the Half moon Tavern this Evening. At the same Time the

Ticket will be delivered.'[20] William does not give an account of the event, but it seems likely to have been a scaled-up version of his parties on the *Apollo* – complete with barge, music, dinner and drinking.

William's involvement in the scheme is evident from a small piece of card in the Sharp archive that itemises the concert's real – or more likely projected – expenditure. Headed 'Necessary Expences at Ye Water Concert', the list includes '2lb Wax Candles', '8 Tongues', '10 Doz. Rolls', 'Dinner for 80 @ 2.6d pr Head', 'Extra Performers', 'Bargemaster & Expences' and 'Wine etc.' With his experience of planning river excursions in the early 1750s, William was an obvious choice for provisioning the party, but even he must have baulked at the challenge of a 'Dinner for 80'. A second document, clipped to William's card, appears to be a copy of a balance sheet produced by the Castle's organising committee, and provided to William for his information. If this represents a final totting up of the expenses of the occasion, then William's estimate seems to have been rather optimistic. Even after the receipt of the subscriptions of the seventy-six members who participated in the event, there is a shortfall of £9 6s 8d, which the six named members of the committee – including William – divided between them. At least one of the extra expenses – 'For 2 Windows broke' – suggest that the party had been a lively one.[21]

Though the Sharps were constant in their love of music, the manner in which they expressed their devotion changed. During childhood, and adolescence, music-making took place within the family, and reflected the strong sibling bond. In the late 1740s and early 1750s, the London-based brothers participated in amateur performances in the City, in addition to family ensembles. The dilution of the family element in music-making would persist in the 1760s and 70s, when the London brothers, and William in particular, hosted concerts with an increasingly professional feel. The mutation from family, to amateur, and then gradually to an exclusively professional ensemble, mirrored the Sharps' increasing wealth and social prestige. Indeed, in later years the Sharp concert was as much an instrument of the siblings' success as it was a manifestation of it. Burnished by the aristocratic patrons of their fashionable musical soirées, the family social cachet grew exponentially.

7

Priest

In the late 1740s, while in London William and James toiled away as apprentices, and Granville was still a boy at school, John, the eldest of the Sharp boys, completed his academic and vocational training for the priesthood. After graduating from Trinity College as an MA in 1747, John was ordained as a priest in 1749, at the same time being appointed minister of Hartburn in Northumberland. Situated six miles to the west of Morpeth, the parish of Hartburn was home to approximately 260 families, of whom some lived in the village, and others in neighbouring farms and cottages.[1] The church and vicarage stood picturesquely on a strip of high ground between two streams, and they appear today much as they would have done in the time of the Sharps. Though thirteenth or early fourteenth century in origin, the main body of the vicarage dates from the sixteenth century.[2] In the 1760s John added an elegant wing to the south-east side, and it was here in the 'two very large rooms, a dining and drawing room' that he delighted to 'entertain his neighbours with musical performances'.[3]

John also set about making improvements to the vicarage gardens, and one remarkable feature of his work survives today. An arched footbridge leads from the garden to a grotto dug into a cliff face, above the stream that runs below. John designed the grotto as a changing room for lady swimmers. It has Gothic arches, and a fireplace for warming shivering bathers as they changed. A slab-roofed tunnel that leads from the grotto to the stream preserved the swimmer's modesty – and warmth – until the moment of immersion.[4] The changing room is a picturesque example of the family's fondness for water, though of a rather more energetic kind than the sedate boating parties favoured by the London siblings. The Sharps left no account of natural swimming in the burn, but I picture Judith – perhaps the girls are on an extended visit to their brother – emerging gingerly from the tunnel, adorned in an ankle-length, full-sleeved, flannel chemise.[5] It is only when she is sure that the village boys are safely out of sight, that Judith dips one exploratory toe into the freezing waters of the Hart. Whether John – attired in suitably clerical swimming gear – joined his sisters in their aquatic adventures, is not known.

Although John was the son of a clergyman, and had more experience of clerical life than other newly ordained priests, the prospect of being minister of a remote Northumbrian village was still a daunting one. The role of the cleric in eighteenth-century England was more complex and nuanced than might at first be imagined, involving social and administrative, as well as ecclesiastic, functions. John, a young man of twenty-six, fresh from Cambridge, from the moment of his admission to the ministry assumed responsibility for the spiritual and practical welfare of his parishioners. He was also required to take charge of a range of civic, charitable and educational enterprises affecting the day-to-day running of the parish.

John is conscientious, and for him the challenges of ministry appear specially daunting. In the first place, he must live up to the reputation of his father. It has been through Thomas's good offices that he has obtained the living of Hartburn – which with an annual stipend of £230 is one of the most valuable in Northumberland – and John is sensitive to charges of nepotism.[6] So he must work doubly hard – and prove to all the naysayers – that he is not only a fitting recipient of the lucrative living of Hartburn, but a man worthy of his father's estimation.

Of all his recently acquired responsibilities, those relating to the spiritual welfare of his parishioners weigh most heavily on John. The writing of the weekly sermon is perhaps a particular ordeal, especially in the early days when he has no existing body of work to fall back on. John cannot dash it off the night before, as other priests do. Nor can he risk improvising in the pulpit, with rows of expectant faces lined up before him, and the fate of the souls of the assembled churchgoers in his youthful hands. Instead he works laboriously, perhaps in the evenings by candlelight, or on morning walks by the Hart Burn, studying the scriptures, writing and rewriting, and rehearsing the modulations of his voice to make sure that his delivery is flawless.

On Sunday mornings John is up and ready long before the first bleary-eyed parishioner stumbles over the church porch. Unlike his Yorkshire neighbour the author and clergyman Laurence Sterne, who while 'going over the Fields on a Sunday to preach ... it happened that his Pointer Dog sprung a Covey of Partridges, when he went directly home for his Gun and left his Flock that was waiting for him in the Church, in the lurch', John lets nothing distract him from the task in hand.[7] Nor can he breathe a sigh of relief when the sermon is over, for his obligations to the souls of his parishioners do not begin and end in the pulpit. Clergy are under a duty to promote and deepen Christian knowledge, and that means paying particular attention to the spiritual instruction of the young. So as the organ plays its last sonorous chord sequence, and the congregation file out of church, John retreats to the vestry, and hears the parish children recite their catechism.

An eighteenth-century clergyman also bore responsibility for the secular education of his flock. John interpreted this obligation expansively, building a school in Hartburn that housed a classroom and teacher's lodgings – as well as storage space for the parish hearse. It still stands today.[8] John's administrative duties included reading out royal proclamations from the pulpit, and chairing a unit of local government called the parish vestry, whose remit included assessment of local taxation, upkeep of village roads, and support of the parish poor. Managing the squabbles of conflicting interests, and keeping the peace in the inevitably fraught and protracted weekly village meeting, required great powers of patience and tact.

If the formal duties of the clergyman were not sufficiently daunting, John also faced the challenge of living 'a godly life in the midst of ordinary daily life'.[9] The posthumous publication in 1662 of George Herbert's *A Priest to the Temple* was the first in a rash of manuals for young clergymen on the subject of pastoral care. According to Herbert, a vicar should be 'a father to his parish. A man whose doctrine could be read in his life, and whose family was a school of religion.'[10] Weighed down by the cares of his spiritual and administrative responsibilities, and the strain of leading an exemplary life, it is no wonder if John occasionally fell short of his own expectations. Punctilious to a fault, the duties which a fellow young clergyman might shrug off, or treat lightly, were to him matters of the utmost seriousness – and this inevitably increased the burden of his role.

But in spite of this, and the varied responsibilities of his ministry, John found time to perform other ecclesiastical office. In 1751, at the age of twenty-eight, he became chaplain to Joseph Butler, Bishop of Durham; the following year he was appointed Official to the Archdeaconry of Northumberland.[11] This second preferment, which required John to assist his father Thomas in the latter's archidiaconal duties in Northumberland, was a stepping stone to his appointment to the archdeaconship itself, which followed in 1762.[12] As archdeacon John acted as a senior assistant to the Bishop of Durham, with special responsibility for the maintenance of church buildings and the pastoral welfare of the clergy. He began his duties, as his father had done three decades earlier, by undertaking a visitational survey of the churches and chapels in the archdeaconry.[13] John wrote his report in the form of notes appended to his father's earlier journal of visitation, and they show a similar precision and attention to detail.

John's conscious modelling of his archidiaconal survey on Thomas's precedent is an illustration of what has been described as John's 'complex dependence' on his father.[14] Thomas had himself lived under the weight of a father's reputation: now it was the turn of his son to bear that burden. Thomas was an undoubtedly brilliant man, who excelled both as a scholar and in the exercise of his ecclesiastical duties. He was a hard act to follow, and it is evident that, at least where his clerical career was concerned, John never fully extricated himself from the mantle of his father's genius. Any tendency to comparison was exacerbated by the fact that John's career so closely followed Thomas's own. It is perhaps no surprise then that, as John Shuler suggests, 'Thomas Sharp's shadow was long cast over the archdeaconry, and John Sharp never hesitated to walk within it.'[15]

When in the early days of his career as an archdeacon John expressed the hope that 'the Clergy of Northumberland out of the regard they had for [his] Father, [would] in some measure overlook the deficiencies of his son', he was being sincere.[16] John was a profoundly modest man, without a hint of self-importance or self-regard. This is apparent from the character of his annual archidiaconal charges to the clergy, in which he strove to advise and admonish 'not in an authoritative form, but rather in a brotherly Manner'. John concluded his advice with a gentle disclaimer: 'But I don't presume to dictate to you My Revd Brethren ... but wish you all to act ... as you shall be persuaded in your Consciences after serious consideration.'[17]

Though he was a man of intellect and learning, it is noticeable that John did not publish in his lifetime. Given the extent of Thomas's scholarly output (no fewer than seventy-nine publications on a diverse range of subjects) it is tempting to conclude that John's diffidence was due at least in part to the daunting precedent set by his father. That his intellectual interests were at least as broad as Thomas's is clear from a commonplace book dating from the days of his ministry at Hartburn which contains learning on a range of classical and scientific subjects. Examples include 'A Short treatise on Light and Colours', 'Astronomical Lectures' and 'The Doctrine of the tides'.[18] John was also mechanically minded, as is evident in a technical correspondence that he carried on with his brother James on the subjects of 'axles' and 'wheels' and other aspects of locomotion.[19] The extent of John's learning is suggested in this passage from a poem by his brother Thomas, who speaks of his elder brother's intellectual attainments in glowing terms:

> In him the Sister arts united shine
> Physician, Chymist, Architect, Divine,
> Here Medels, Marbles, Butterflies we see
> Here Music, fossils, Guns, Philosophy.[20]

A collection of John's manuscript sermons, preserved in the Dean and Chapter Library in Durham, illustrate the meticulousness of their author's character. John wrote his sermons in the early years of his ministry, between 1749 and 1761. He then stopped original composition and reused or adapted his existing sermons as occasion required. The manuscripts reveal how John wrote his sermons: in rough first, and then in neat, covering alternate pages of a small booklet, with the facing page being left blank for notes and amendments. He included instructions to himself on the modulation of his voice, for example underlining individual syllables to denote stress. The sermons also cross-reference each other, with annotations such as 'insert the Fourth head of No 40 & then return to the opposite Section'.[21]

On the inside cover of the booklets, John noted the number of each sermon, and details of the occasions when he had used it. While he usually waited at least twelve months before re-preaching a sermon to the same congregation, he was not averse to rolling it out in other locations in the meantime. Some sermons were used more than others: the record is held by number fifteen, on sincerity, which he preached 205 times between 1749 and 1792.[22]

We leave John at Hartburn in the late 1750s, poring over his sermons, or negotiating the demands of fractious parishioners. He is a man who puts duty, and the conscientious fulfilment of obligation, above all other considerations. Intense, methodical and hard-working, he has great intellectual ability, but apparently lacks the confidence, or imagination, or strength of character to reach beyond the confines of his day-to-day concerns. It would be several years later, in the bleak and windswept surroundings of Bamburgh Castle, that John would realise his true and fullest potential.

8

Letters

In a journal entry for the year 1754, Elizabeth writes: 'The begining of our common letters a corospondence of 5 bros. and 3 sistrs. which lasted as long as my father and mother lived.'[1] The fact of the correspondence is unremarkable in itself: eighteenth-century siblings were expected to write to each other. However, the style of the Sharps' communication is rather different from that prescribed for sibling correspondence in contemporary letter-writing manuals. In place of formulaic salutations and conventional expressions of affection, the Sharps substituted rambunctious humour and caricature. Written in a family argot that is at times unintelligible, the correspondence is interleaved with drawings, verses, songs and a liberal smattering of the siblings' favourite comic form – 'puning' (i.e. punning).

In 1754, four of the five surviving brothers lived in London: William, James, Granville and Thomas. Of these William, as we have seen in previous chapters, was in the process of setting up a successful medical practice. James, now one year out of his apprenticeship to ironmongers Southouse & Chapman, worked for his former master as a paid employee. Granville was halfway through his apprenticeship to a linen draper on Tower Hill. Thomas, the second of the Sharp brothers, had followed John into the priesthood, and was ordained in 1750. During the period of the common letters Thomas appears to have spent part of the year in Cambridge, where he was a fellow of Trinity College, and the remainder in London as curate and lecturer at Duke's Place, near Aldgate.[2] Communal letter writing was relatively easy for the London brothers because James, and Thomas when he was in London, lived at William's house in Mincing Lane – and Granville was only a short walk away at the linen draper's house on Tower Hill. The rest of the siblings lived in the north of England: John in Hartburn, and the three sisters, Elizabeth, Judith and Frances, with their parents in Rothbury and Durham.

Though all the siblings contributed to, and appreciated, the common letters, they were of particular value to the girls. The brothers were sensitive to this, and made conscious efforts in their letter writing to entertain their sisters. The importance of the correspondence to Judith, Frances and Elizabeth is readily explicable in terms of their comparative lack of other diversion. After the relative equality of their early childhood, the siblings' lives had diverged. Whereas the boys now lived in the world as independent adults, the girls remained at home in a kind of gentle domestic thraldom. Life for them was narrow and repetitive, and aspiration had little outlet beyond the search for a suitable marriage partner.

The Sharp girls were not alone in their plight, indeed the tedium of life at home was taken for granted by genteel women in this period.[3] Life for a woman without children, or domestic responsibility, was essentially dull and monotonous, a constant round of contrived activities designed to help them get through the day. Activity was necessary, not simply as an antidote to boredom, but to prevent idleness, which was considered dangerous in young women as it invited discontent. As this late eighteenth-century father put it, in his prescription for the bringing up of daughters: 'Let them have exercise abroad and constant occupation at home ... Above all things never suffer them to be idle. The older they grow the more necessary you will find this rule to be.'[4]

In common with other young genteel girls of the period, the Sharp sisters followed a schedule, which had the dual benefit of giving structure and meaning to an otherwise purposeless day, and encouraging the development of useful accomplishments such as music and drawing. In fact, their timetable differed little from the schedule of improving activities that had characterised their girlhood education. There were still morning walks, across the Rothbury moors perhaps, or the gentler gradient of the college green in Durham, and prayers before breakfast and dinner. Elizabeth still practised the harpsichord

– perhaps wading through 'Dr Boyces Scores of Services and Anthems &c' in obedience to her brother Thomas's diktat, while Judith strummed the lute or English guitar. Frances, who had been too young to participate in the girls' schedule in the mid-1740s, was now in her late teens, and a fully-fledged member of the female cohort. She sang, rather than played, and her sisters took it in turns to accompany her.

History and geography were no longer a feature of the daily curriculum, but the girls continued to work at their French, and Judith, who was artistic, kept up her painting and drawing. Languorous afternoons were still enlivened by a visit from a neighbour, or by forays to the village school, or church, or the sickbed of a poor villager. Any lull in the day was filled by needlework, in its various forms of plainwork, knitting and embroidery. The girls had been sewing since early childhood, graduating from pin cushions to samplers, and then to the more demanding tasks of mirror frames and caskets, as they mastered an increasingly complex repertoire of stiches.[5] They chatted as they sewed, or one of the girls entertained the others by reading from a book or newspaper.

Elizabeth, Judith and Frances were more fortunate than other young women of their age because they had each other, and a sympathetic family. This did not mean that they could escape the boundaries of female respectability, but it made the restrictions easier to bear. In these circumstances, the excitement of a letter from London featured brightly. For the girls, the common letters were more than just a source of information, or entertainment, or a receptacle of feeling: they were a portal to their brothers' lives.

Imagine the perturbation in the parlour of the Rothbury rectory, when the heavy tread of the post boy is heard at the kitchen door. Frances gets there first, flying down the stone spiral staircase with her skirts in her hands, and returns in triumph brandishing the letter above her head. Resisting the temptation to open it at once, the girls return to their labours, which for Elizabeth means another attempt to perfect the complexities of Boyce's 'O Where shall Wisdom be Found?' Judith meanwhile is stitching an embroidered stool cover, while Frances struggles valiantly with her irregular French verbs. It is only in the evening, when the heavy curtains in the parlour have been drawn and the candles are lit, that the ceremony of the letter-reading commences. Mrs Sharp sits by the tea table, darning a stocking, while Judith takes centre stage in a large upholstered chair by the fire. Frances and Elizabeth perch on the arms of her chair, and lean their heads together. As Judith breaks the seal, and unfolds the ivory-coloured paper, a hush falls over the gathering. She begins: 'Dear Sisters ...'[6]

Only a few of the numerous letters written by the siblings in the period 1754–8 survive. Those that do seem to have been kept intentionally because they were seen as having a particular value. Granville copied his favourites – which are usually of his own composition – into a common-letter book.[7] A letter containing anything more than a line or two from William and James is rare, perhaps because they were busier than their brothers. Comments such as: 'Jim says he will not have Time to write this Post' are frequent in the correspondence.[8]

Certain procedural requirements applied to the drafting of the common letters. The most fundamental of these stipulated that letters should be written collectively: in other words, a London epistle was to be drafted by, or at least on behalf of, all the brothers currently resident there, while a letter from Rothbury involved the participation of all three sisters. As we have seen, the level of involvement varied, and Granville and Thomas are the authors of almost all the common letters that survive. Though it is possible that these two brothers had more time on their hands, the more likely reason for their over-representation is that they had a particular facility for the style of humorous writing favoured by the siblings. Another rule, which seems to have been enforced with more stringency, required letters to be addressed to siblings in common, for example 'Dear Sisters' or 'Dear Brothers' rather than to individuals. In a letter headed 'Letter before Action', Granville fulminates against 'the proceedings or manner of conducting or Framing of the Last Common Letter'.[9] It seems the girls had been guilty of the unpardonable sin of addressing William ('Billy') alone.

A further procedural requirement was that the letters should be read out loud, and there were also rules relating to the style and subject matter of the correspondence. The principal desideratum of the common letter, according to the examples that survive, was that they should entertain and amuse. Other functions, such as the communication of news, or the request for and provision of assistance were included in such a way as to sustain rather than impede the comic flow. The best letters, at least as determined by Granville in his choice for the common-letter book, are those in which meaning is almost obscured by comedy.

Thomas's speciality was an eccentric narration of the week's events. Take for example his account of 'a very Agreeable Concert Spirituale' in Mincing Lane, in a letter to his sisters dated 20 April 1756.[10] When one of the violinists called in sick, the success of the concert had seemed in doubt. But: 'everyone knows, that when Gentlemen are not to be had, two or three Couple of Chairs Make no Ordinary Figure in a Country Dance. And why may not a Chair Play as well as Dance? ... A Couple of Chairs were immediately removed to the Second Fiddle's place, and there set.'

All was not well, however: 'For tho' the Uppermost Chair, was so contrived, as to hold a Fiddle, point to the Book, and make a Motion with its foot, and give something of a Sound, humourously enough, yet not a Bar was right beat, and not a Note in Tune, for what Ear cou'd be expected from a Piece of Wood, you know!'

The denouement comes in the revelation that the 'Chair' in question – at least the uppermost of the two 'removed to the Second Fiddle's Place' – was the Revd de Chair, a minor canon of St Paul's Cathedral, of apparently limited musical ability.[11] His name provided Thomas with the material to indulge in what the Sharps fondly called 'puning', a comic technique much evident in the common letters.

Another of Thomas's elaborate comic riffs is found in a letter to the sisters dated 23 December 1756, in which he describes a momentous event in the life of his brother William. He begins his narrative: 'Last Thursday was the Happy Day, & on Sunday she received her first visits, together with the Compliments & Congratulations of not less than 20 or 30 Ladies and Gentlemen.'[12] Thomas is fulsome in his praise of this female acquisition to the household in Mincing Lane:

She is tall, genteel, very Pretty & not yet Eighteen, is descended from a very Ancient Family & was born in London, but has spent the best of her Time in Cornwall ... she may most truly be said (in the Vicar's words) to be such 'as will be an Ornament to yr Parlour, yr drawing Room, yr Chamber, & every Part of yr House, such as gives Pleasure to a Man's Friends to behold & Satisfaction to himself.

In addition to her feminine virtues, 'Cecilia Morgan' is also musically talented. According to Thomas, she is the 'Soul of Harmony' and 'one of the most Musical Creatures Breathing'. But disaster lay in store for the matchless Cecilia:

Scarce had she taken a survey of her new apartment, on Saturday night, when regardless of an oil-cloth whose uplifted corner stood ready to receive her footsteps, she made a trip, & like a second Amelia fell & bruised her lovely nose. With all officious-ness did I offer my sustaining arm, but to little purpose, for tho' it served to lessen, yet cou'd it no[t] prevent the fall. However this Disaster was very soon remedied, for 3 surgeons being in the House, & the whole Faculty within call, the cicatrice was soon plaister'd up ...

Thomas continues in this vein for several pages, but it would have been already apparent to his readers that the lovely 'Cecilia' was in fact William's new chamber organ – of which he was clearly inordi-nately proud.[13]

Granville also favoured the comic form over a straightforward narration of the week's events. In a letter to his sisters dated 18 October 1757, he spins the news that the girls have failed to win a prize in a recent government lottery, in an elaborate satire on the conduct of the Seven Years' War. He illustrates his narrative with a drawing of a cannon firing numbers that represent lottery tickets bought by the siblings individually (e.g. 'F Sharp') and in syndicate ('Common to 8 Sharps'). Granville's letters often take inspiration from political events, and reveal an early consciousness of issues, such as parliamentary reform, that were to preoccupy him in later life. One example dating from 1756 fulminates against 'the business of Bribery & Corruption'.[14]

Thomas stands out as the prominent voice in the common letters. Verbally dextrous, and with a ready wit, he is humorous, sardonic, whimsical and wounding in equal measure. Conscious of his superiority in this field, he can be caustic in his appraisal of his siblings' efforts. For example, in a letter to his sisters dated 22 November 1757, he criticises their plagiarising of the 'Cecilia Morgan' device to found their own comic revelation.[15] James comes in for particularly remorseless joshing, the conceit usually being that he is slow on the uptake.

Beyond these insights into Thomas's character, and the occasional reference to the siblings' interests and experiences, the common letters can be a frustrating source for the biographer. In the pages of elaborate witticisms, and apparently impenetrable in-jokes, there is little illumination of individual relationships, depth of feeling, or the innermost workings of the mind. Nonetheless, there emerges a sense of the Sharps as exuberant, playful and unconventional – and of the shared love of jollity, and common understanding, that made the sibling bond so strong.

9

Upheaval

In 1757 the sisters were able to experience their brothers' lives at first hand, rather than through the medium of the common letters, when they made a much-anticipated visit to London. Elizabeth records that her brothers were given leave by their father 'to take their 3 sistrs. up with them for 6 weeks to bro. Wm's house in Mincing Lane'.[1] Elizabeth's diary entry for 1757 is characteristic of the journal as a whole in being brief and emotionally restrained, but it still conveys something of the excitement of the visit. She is clearly touched by the efforts made by her brothers to make the stay memorable: 'The kindness of our dear bros. and great attention of all our friends are never to be forgot by us, and the very great sevility, everybody where ever we were introdused, can hardly be conceived ... Musick and every emusiment my dear bros. contrived, whilst with them.'[2]

Perhaps the chief joy of the visit to London was that the siblings – all except John – were reunited, after years spent apart. Since the early 1740s, when first John, and then Thomas, William, James and finally Granville had left the family home, the Sharps had rarely come together as a family. The difficulty of long-distance travel, and the all-encompassing nature of the brothers' employment – there was no entitlement to annual leave in the eighteenth century – all but removed the opportunity for family reunion. Now there was the prospect of six whole weeks in each other's company. It is possible that there was a little awkwardness at first, as they sat round the table together on the evening of the girls' arrival in London. After all some fifteen years had elapsed since their childhood in Rothbury and Durham – and so

much had changed. But the underlying closeness soon asserted itself:
Thomas cracked a joke perhaps, some long-forgotten story was retold,
and the dining room in Mincing Lane was soon echoing with the
sounds of renewed jollity and laughter.

No doubt the sisters' pleasure in being reunited with their brothers
was mixed with a sense of wondering admiration. Imagine Elizabeth's
pride in the success of her beloved William: he was now a respected
London surgeon, with his own practice and a large town house in
Mincing Lane. James too was going from strength to strength – there
was talk of him buying into the partnership of Southouse & Chapman.
Even Granville, the baby of the family, had grown up – he was in the
final year of his apprenticeship, and would soon be branching out on
his own.

In addition to the charm of being in their brothers' company, there
was the excitement of London itself. The shock James had felt when
he exchanged the quiet lanes of Rothbury for the raucous streets of
the metropolis was even more pronounced for his sisters. They had
led a completely sheltered existence, and had little experience of life
beyond the narrow confines of a Church of England rectory. Unlike
William and James, who had faced the maelstrom of London outside
the bosom of their family, the girls had their brothers on hand to
manage the transition. As Elizabeth makes clear in her diary, the
boys pulled out every stop to ensure that the visit was memorable.
There was music of course – at Mincing Lane, or with friends at the
Castle concert, or once or twice at the glamorous Italian Opera at
Covent Garden – and boat parties on the Thames, and services at St
Paul's Cathedral, as well as the traditional London sightseeing attrac-
tions of the Tower of London, St James's Palace and Westminster
Abbey.

After six weeks of gaiety, the girls returned to Rothbury for the
summer. The regular pattern of domestic life was upset in early June
when Judith, their mother, fell ill. Elizabeth describes what happened
in her journal: 'In this month my dear mother was taken very ill and
on the 2nd July dyed aged 57.'[3] The siblings were still recovering from
the death of their mother when there was another hammer blow. In
her diary entry for 16 March 1758, Elizabeth records: 'Dyed my dear

father The Revd Dr Thos. Sharp of a few days' illness, to the very great affliction of his whole family.' The brevity of Elizabeth's account belies the emotional impact of this second bereavement. The siblings had lost both parents within a matter of months. Elizabeth ends her account of Thomas's death with a simple statement: 'more affect. pairents could not be or more worthy'.[4]

For the sisters at least, the loss of their father had implications beyond the ordinary experience of grief. The family homes in Rothbury and Durham were tied to Thomas's clerical employment; on his death, both properties reverted to the Church. To the emotional upheaval of a double bereavement was added the strain of uprooting themselves from their childhood homes. There were also the practicalities of the contents of two houses to deal with. Elizabeth records that three of her brothers – John, Thomas and Granville – stayed in Durham after their father's funeral 'to assist us, in preparing ourselves … to settle affairs and pack up'. After shutting up the residentiary house in Durham, 'my 3 bros. and us 3 sistrs. went from thence to Rothbury to settle and pack up'. No doubt the brothers provided emotional as well as practical support for the sisters, as they paid their final farewells to 'two such happy homes we had been blessed with'.

As if a double bereavement and the loss of two homes was not sufficient for the girls to contend with, they also had to face the anxiety of an uncertain future. Thomas left £700 to each of his daughters in his will, which though a sizeable bequest, was not enough to allow them to live independently.[5] On the death of parents, single women without adequate means were thrown on the mercy of their brothers, or other male relations. In a position of absolute dependence, spinsters were subject to their brothers' goodwill, which might be extended, or withheld, at whim. A dying parent's natural anxiety for the fate of unmarried, and insufficiently provided for, daughters was alleviated in the case of Thomas and Judith by their knowledge of the siblings' love for each other. According to Elizabeth, the common letters played a role in assuring them of this: '[the] weekly correspondence both my father and mother expressed on their death beds the satisfaction it had given them being assured their daughters would be protected by their bros. and happy with them'.[6]

Having packed up the houses at Durham and Rothbury, the brothers and sisters gathered at John's vicarage at Hartburn 'to prepair for our London journey'. It had been agreed that Elizabeth and Frances would live with William in Mincing Lane, while Judith 'stayd the first year with bro. Sharp at Hartburn'.[7] In fact, Judith stayed permanently in Northumberland (apart from the occasional foray south to visit her London relations) and became a long-term resident of her eldest brother's household.

Further change occurred in the summer of 1759, when Elizabeth left Mincing Lane to live with James in Leadenhall Street. Elizabeth's relocation was the consequence of a change in James's affairs, for in July 1759 he bought into the partnership of his former masters, iron-mongers Southouse & Chapman, with a £1,000 loan. According to Elizabeth, 'Mr Southouse retired soon into the country and let him have the house to live in with an intention to visit him ocationaly.' Though the other partner Mr Chapman continued to live in the house in Leadenhall Street, it became James's responsibility to look after the clerks in the business. Communal living of this sort might seem pecu-liar to a modern sensibility, but it was in fact quite normal for a household to consist of servants, and apprentices, as well as family members. Elizabeth moved to Leadenhall Street in order to take on the role of James's – presumably much needed – housekeeper.

Though the siblings lived in separate houses, they met every evening in Mincing Lane. Elizabeth describes how the brothers and sisters gathered: 'when my Bros. bussiness's were over, to a little musick amongst ourselves, and to supper. Bro. T. when in town was there. Bro. G from Tower Hill and ourselves. I returned every evening in my long cloke and patens when necessary with Bro. James and now and then they came to us if not otherwise engaged.'[8]

I fancy that it is James who arrives last at these family gatherings, no doubt with coal dust in his hair, or a tell-tale streak of grease down one cheek. Supper comes later, but first there is music in the elegant wood-panelled drawing room where William entertains. Cecilia Morgan stands in pride of place, at the far end of the room, and around her cluster the family instruments: Thomas's violin, James's 'serpent' propped against the wall, William's horns, and Granville's increasingly eclectic collection of hautboys, clarinets, flutes and kettle-drums. Elizabeth takes her place at the harpsichord, and the family gather about her with their instruments. There is a cacophony of tuning up, and much leafing of papers, and scraping of chairs – before Thomas calls order with a rap of his bow on the music stand. Then, in the flickering candlelight of the sconces that line the walls, the music begins.[9]

With the death of their parents, the siblings assumed responsibility for preserving the unity of the family. This was challenging in view of the geographical divide between the London Sharps and their relations in the north, and the siblings made conscious efforts to surmount this by keeping up a regular correspondence. As the eldest of the London cohort, and with a house of his own, William took on a paternal role in relation to his brothers and sisters. Mincing Lane became a kind of family hub, with permanent and semi-permanent residents co-habiting in apparent harmony.

Judith's residence in the north meant that Frances and Elizabeth were thrown together more, and they seem to have become increasingly close during this period. Elizabeth lived in Leadenhall Street from the summer of 1759, in her role as James's housekeeper, but absence from Mincing Lane does not appear to have muted her fondness for her brother William. If privately she regretted that it was not William who had asked her to be his housekeeper – as he had promised when they were children – she kept this to herself. Elizabeth had a purpose to her life: in place of the schedule of contrived activities that had structured her days for as long as she could remember, she was responsible for a household, and for feeding and clothing not only her brother, but also old Chapman and the clerks. Of all the changes wrought to the lives of the siblings by their parents' deaths, this perhaps was the most significant.

IO

Marriage

The loan that had allowed James to buy into the partnership of Southouse & Chapman, and which laid the foundation for his future success, came 'by the kindness of Mrs Prowse'.[1] In her journal Elizabeth describes how she acted as an intermediary in the transaction: 'Mrs Prowse kind offer through <u>me</u>, if to offer that sum would procure a partnership, he should be welcom, and that they would not ever call for it until it was my bros. own convenience to return it. So kind and unexpected an offer was very acceptable.'

Mrs Elizabeth Prowse was the siblings' first cousin: her father, John Sharp, was the elder brother of the archdeacon Thomas Sharp. There was a fifteen-year age gap between John and Thomas, so the generations had become rather skewed. The Sharp siblings were in fact closer in age to Mrs Prowse's children (their first cousins once removed) than they were to Mrs Prowse herself. This explains why in years to come, when the families became close, Mrs Prowse assumed a quasi-maternal role towards the Sharp siblings. Elizabeth would later say of her cousin, in a heartfelt posthumous tribute: 'She [has] been as a real mother to me, and I may say to all my dear bros. and sisrs. from the time of my own dear father and mothers death, and there was nothing that lay in her power, but what she did, or would have done for any of us.'[2]

John Sharp had married an heiress, Anna Maria Hosier, the daughter of Charles Hosier, a goldsmith who 'raised his fortune in the Citty of London'.[3] The couple had two daughters, Elizabeth – who became Mrs Prowse – and Mary, and a son, John, who died at the age of thirteen in 1734. John and Anna's grief at the loss of their only son was compounded when their younger daughter Mary married a Roman Catholic lawyer. The distress occasioned to the family by the marriage is apparent in this excerpt from Elizabeth Sharp's journal: '1748 July 2 Miss Mary Sharp 2nd daughter of John Sharp Esq ... married James Booth Esq an eminent conveyancer of London ... but a Roman Catholick, much to the grief of her sisr. and her other relations.'[4]

When Charles Hosier died two years later, he left his estates to his grand-daughter Elizabeth, and – as a mark of family disapprobation – only a legacy to her sister Mary Booth.[5] Family prejudice wreaked a harsh revenge, for Mary's marriage proved disastrous. James Booth's marital behaviour roused Elizabeth Sharp to a quite uncharacteristic pitch of fervour, referring to him in her journal entry for 12 August 1767 as a 'Cruel bad husband'. When Mary's resilience to her husband's brutality and neglect reached breaking point in August 1767, she fled the marital home and sought sanctuary with her sister. Negotiations for the couple's 'compleat separation' took place at James's house in Leadenhall Street on 12 August.[6] Booth was eventually persuaded to give Mary a small annual stipend, which her sister supplemented.

Elizabeth made up for her sister's unfortunate choice of husband by marrying Thomas Prowse of Berkley House in Somerset, a country gentleman of sound religion and apparently unblemished repute.[7] Elizabeth's inheritance from her grandfather amounted to a substantial fortune, including the estate of Wicken Park in Northamptonshire. The couple had ten children, of whom five died in childhood, and lived peripatetically between their estates in Somerset and Northamptonshire, and a London town house in Argyll Street, just south-east of what is now Oxford Circus.[8]

Elizabeth Sharp makes little reference to the Prowses in her diary until 1757, when in contemplating the delights of the girls' six-week visit to their brothers in London she noted that 'the kind attention and notice of Mr and Mrs Prowse's family added greatley to our comfort and happiness'.[9] The sisters clearly made an impression on the Prowses, because soon after their departure from London, John Prowse, the eldest son, followed them to Northumberland. While there he accompanied Thomas Sharp on an archidiaconal visitation, travelling on horseback 'quite into Northumberland to see the different places'. The reason for this assiduity became clear when, on the eve of his departure, John 'made his addresses to Sisr. Jud'. All his hard work came to nothing, however, because Judith refused him. John, his tail between his legs, 'soon after haisend up to town'.[10]

Judith's refusal proved no more than a temporary setback to the growing intimacy of the families. Though relations seem to have been muted in the months following the proposal, this was no doubt due more to the deaths of the siblings' parents than to any feelings of embarrassment or animosity. The Prowses in any event had their own grief to bear, for on 17 February 1758 their daughter Susan died aged sixteen 'of an inflamation in her bowels'. Ten days later, her elder brother John – whose proposal of marriage had so recently been refused by Judith – died from smallpox.

The Sharps and Prowses met by chance a few months later in Islington, then a small village just outside the City, as the Sharp girls, still in mourning, journeyed down to London to live with William in Mincing Lane. The brothers had agreed to meet the girls' hackney coach at Islington and drive them into London in their own carriages.[11] As the girls were changing from one vehicle to another, the Prowse coach pulled up alongside. Given their multiple bereavements, it was, as Elizabeth recorded, not only 'an unexpected meeting' but 'an affecting one on all sides'.[12]

The outcome of this chance meeting was that the families, united in grief, became increasingly intimate. Frances Sharp, now a young woman of twenty, spent much of the succeeding year with the Prowses. This was at the particular request of Mrs Prowse, as Elizabeth records in her journal entry for 13 March 1759: 'Sisr. F Sharp went to Argyle [sic] Street for 10 days at the request of Mrs Prowse and afterwards returned to Argyle Street for 3 weeks more.' In April Frances stayed with the Prowses at Wicken Park; and in May she travelled to Somerset with them. Perhaps Mrs Prowse drew comfort from the presence in the household of a girl of a similar age to the daughter she had lost. Frances would also have provided companionship to the two surviving daughters of the family.

Though the most regular of the Sharp guests, Frances was not the only sibling to be shown favour by the family. In April 1759 Elizabeth,

William and James were invited to stay a few days at Wicken. The Sharps reciprocated in May by inviting the Prowses to 'a party of pleasure' on the Thames, boating from Hampton Court to Richmond Hill 'where we landed and dined at the Inn at the top of the Hill, and came down to the boat, drank tea on board, landed at Branford and returned from thence to our carages spent a most pleasant day'.[13] It was within the context of this renewed amity between the families that Mrs Prowse two months later made her 'kind and unexpected' offer to fund James's entry into partnership with Southouse & Chapman.

It was without further preamble on the subject of her relations with the Prowses that Elizabeth recorded in her diary entry for 2 March 1762 that 'Bro. John and Sisr. Sharp, and Bro. Thos. came up out of the North to Leadenhall Street'. Then, on 24 April 1762 she notes that the 'Rightings were signed at Mr Prowses for his son Geo's mariage'. The significance of these statements soon becomes apparent, for in Elizabeth's next diary entry dated 27 April 1762 she records: 'Our wedding day, at ½ after 8 at St James's Church, London, my elder Br. Dr Sharp performed the service, my Bro. W. gave me away to Mr George Prowse. His father, mother and sisr. Prowses were present as were sisr. Sharp and my dear Jud. and Fanny and 5 bros. John, Thomas, William, James and Granville.'

Not even the laconic style adopted by Elizabeth in her diary entries can quite obscure the significance of this moment in her life. Following the death of his elder brother John from smallpox, George stood heir to the considerable Prowse fortune. He was also four years younger than Elizabeth. A woman of slender means, now nearly thirty, Elizabeth can hardly have expected such an advantageous match. We know nothing of their courtship, beyond the inference that it thrived in the circumstances of growing intimacy of the families in the late 1750s. Though it was almost certainly a love match (Elizabeth after all could bring no material advantage to the marriage), the union bore the imprimatur of Mrs Prowse, whose regard for the Sharps, and for Elizabeth personally, was well established by this time.

The match was more than just financially advantageous to Elizabeth. Despite the closeness of the Sharp and Prowse families, they inhabited slightly different social spheres. This divergence in status can be traced back to the contrasting opportunities afforded to the two sons of the archbishop. Whereas the elder son John Sharp lived a life of leisured ease as a country gentleman and MP, and was able to consolidate his rank by marrying money, the younger brother Archdeacon Thomas Sharp had to work for his living, and due to his relatively limited means was required to indenture his three youngest sons as apprentices. Thomas's status was insufficiently elevated to attract wealth of the kind offered by John's wife Anna Maria Hosier, with the result that the discrepancy in the brothers' rank sharpened. This is manifest in the experience of the next generation, and most concisely in the fact that the Sharp children had to earn their living, but their Prowse cousins did not.

While William worked a twelve-hour day, negotiating London traffic, humouring fractious patients and undertaking nerve-racking surgical procedures, his cousin (and now brother-in-law) George Prowse wiled away his hours in gentlemanly repose. Though the families were closely related, they represented separate strands in a tightly woven fabric of elite society, broadly defined as 'genteel'.[14] There is no indication that the disparity in rank impeded the relationship between the families – the marriage of George and Elizabeth is proof enough of that – but it would certainly have been apparent.

Marrying George Prowse precipitated Elizabeth into a new kind of existence. Whereas previously she had worked as a housekeeper for her brother James at his ironmongery in Leadenhall Street, she now lived with her husband and his family on their country estates in Somerset and Northamptonshire. Instead of days spent superintending wayward servants, planning meals, buying vegetables, sorting linen, sewing buttonholes, and preserving, she returned to a life of genteel inactivity – though on a rather grander scale than that which had characterised her Rothbury girlhood. Prompted by a sense of duty, by her affection for the Prowses, and by the gratitude she felt for the kindness that they had shown to her own family, Elizabeth proved an exemplary daughter-in-law. This is evident from the earliest days of her marriage – in the summer of 1762 she helped nurse Mr Prowse through a serious illness, taking her turn to sit up all night with him.

Mr Prowse's recovery from ill health was celebrated by a family expedition, described by Elizabeth in her diary as 'A jaunt after my fathers illness from Berkley'. She notes the itinerary on a small card interleaved in the pages of her journal:

Aug 23	Saulsbury
	Readbridge in Hampshire
Aug 26	Southampton
	Mount Bevons and returned to Readbridge
Aug 27	Went through the New Forest to Limigton and returned to Readburn
Aug 28	Left Readburn and got to Saulsbury
Aug 29	At the Cathedral
Aug 30	Wilton, Lord Pembruks
	Longford, Lord Fokestones
Sept 1	Returnd to Berkley[15]

This was the first of many 'jaunts' that Elizabeth enjoyed with the Prowses in the 1760s, and in later years with her own family. The jaunt, as described by Elizabeth in her journal, was an early form of touring holiday. Travelling by carriage, and staying in inns or with friends and acquaintances, the party engaged in activities which would be familiar to modern tourists, such as visiting cathedrals and stately homes. Elizabeth's first expedition in 1762 was contrived in part as a change of scene for the recuperating Mr Prowse, but convalescence was only one reason and not a precondition for travel – indeed the jaunt was very much a holiday in the sense that we would recognise it today.

Genteel tourism of this kind was relatively new in the early 1760s, but it expanded rapidly in the decades that followed. Tours were designed around clusters of famous houses, such as Chatsworth, Hardwick and Kedleston in Derbyshire, Houghton, Holkham, Blickling and Raynham in Norfolk, and Longleat, Mount Edgecumbe and Saltram in the west.[16] The landscape garden was another attraction. Stowe in Buckinghamshire, Stourhead in Wiltshire and Hagley in Worcestershire, with their meticulously choreographed landscapes of vistas, grottos, fountains, temples and statuary, became celebrity attractions. By the end of the century the most popular gardens catered for annual droves of visitors with guidebooks and plans, and strategically located tea rooms.[17]

The rise in popularity of country-house tourism coincided with the ascendency of an aesthetic value system based on the notion of 'good taste'. Influential arbiters included Colen Campbell, whose 1715 architectural manual, *Vitruvius Britannicus*, prescribed neoclassical ideals of proportion, grace, symmetry and an absence of excessive ornament; and Edmund Burke, whose *A Philosophical Enquiry into the Origin of our Ideas of the Sublime and Beautiful*, published in 1757, sanctioned a more emotional response to works of art.[18] Under the influence of writers such as these, the ability to make appropriate value judgements on architecture and art became the indicator par excellence of an individual's education and social standing.[19]

Visiting country houses was considered to have a useful role in the finishing of young ladies. For Elizabeth, whose education had been insubstantial, the opportunity for self-improvement offered by country tours must have been of particular value. We know from the books that Elizabeth bought as an adult that she was keen to make up for the deficiencies of her childhood schooling. We can imagine her then touring Wilton House and Longford Castle, guidebook in hand, her head filled with ideas of the beautiful and the sublime, endeavouring to acquire, and perhaps even exhibit, the good taste which was so necessary in a lady of her newly acquired status.

In the early 1760s, when Elizabeth makes her first 'jaunt', visits to country houses are still made under the auspices of old-fashioned notions of hospitality. To view Wilton House, the Prowses need only send a servant ahead with a note to ask whether it is convenient to visit. Or perhaps they just turn up, like the Gardiners and Lizzy Bennet did at Pemberley. The housekeeper who shows them round bears little resemblance to the genial Mrs Reynolds in *Pride and Prejudice*, but is instead more like her counterpart at Stowe who provoked an outraged tourist to comment: 'NB The servant that shewed the house ignorant, and insolent.'[20] Notwithstanding the limitations of her guide, Elizabeth does her best to distinguish Van Dyke from Lely, and admire the Double Cube room.[21] But even so, like Lizzy Bennet, her eyes keep wandering through the open windows to the parkland beyond. The tour over, the Prowses hand over the obligatory half-crown to their undeserving guide, and are whisked away in their carriage to the next stop on the itinerary.

Elizabeth's elevation to the ranks of the landed gentry might have strained the unity of the Sharp family. Instead, the siblings seem to have viewed Elizabeth's good fortune as indivisible from their own. Disparity in status, as between Elizabeth and her ironmonger brother James, and prosperity, as for example between Granville and his well-to-do surgeon brother William, was never allowed to obstruct the amity of sibling relations. This was unusual enough to invite contemporary comment: one observer of the Sharps wrote that she knew of no family 'wherein more true brotherly kindness appears / While unenvying each shines in their diff[e]rent spheres'.[22]

II

Invention

On 23 February 1764, James – who was now thirty-three years old, and sole proprietor of the ironmongery in Leadenhall Street – wrote a letter to his eldest brother John.[1] Though he opens on the subject of his business affairs – 'this is the busiest time of the whole year, and I have larger orders by me to compleat than almost I ever had at any time before' – it is apparent that James has something else on his mind. It is not long before he turns to the matter which preoccupies him: 'a distemper I have got upon me which you was well acquainted with some years ago'.

The malady seems to have been of long standing, indeed 'I have been troubled with it more or less ever since the last time you was in town'. In the unlikely case that John is confused about the identity of the 'distemper', James reminds his brother of 'a Punn you made upon a Lady at the last Sunday nights Musick you was att in Mincing Lane – when you said you wished [me] Lodge there'. The love-struck James had clearly been delighted by his brother's remark: it 'was very agreeable to me, as it corresponded so much with my own opinion and also shew'd it would have your approbation'.

The 'Lodge' on which John punned – and the cause of his brother's distemper – was Catharine Lodge, the daughter of John Lodge, a packer of St Helen's, Bishopsgate Street.[2] Besides showing that the Sharps' fondness for 'puning' was as keen as ever, James's recollection of his brother's pleasantry reveals how important it was to him that John should approve of Catharine.

James's desire for his siblings' approbation in the matter of his choice of marriage partner seems unusual to a modern audience – but it would not have been thought so at the time. While love was viewed as a constituent of a successful marriage in the eighteenth century, the suitability of a match in terms of character, parity and fortune had also to be considered. Romance must be prudent, and in such circumstances it was thought natural that a man would seek the endorsement of his relations.[3]

With a family as close as the Sharps, the securing of sibling approval must have been a daunting prospect: akin perhaps to meeting the criteria for membership of a particularly exclusive club. In his letter of 23 February 1764, James identifies the most stringent of the Sharp entry requirements: that the applicant should not disrupt the harmony of familial relations. The siblings approve of Catharine because 'she appears to them as well as myself to be the person that will continue ever to keep us in the present happiness we now enjoy'.

Fortified by his siblings' approval, James now had to pluck up courage to tell Catharine of his feelings. Fortunately for James he was able to see Catharine regularly – 'I have the pleasure of going with her every day to the riding school as she learns to ride along with Fanny [Frances]'. Evidently James did steel himself to ask Catharine to be his wife, perhaps as they walked together to the riding school, or at a musical evening in Mincing Lane, for the couple married on 3 May 1764.[4] Before the proposal James had predicted to his brother that 'should I meet with success I think I bid fair for being made the happiest man living'. His confidence was not misplaced, for the marriage proved a strong and happy one.

James's resolve in the matter of his proposal to Catharine was strengthened by the knowledge that he was prospering financially. The ironmongery – which was now known simply as 'Mr James Sharp, London' – occupied two sites: the original Leadenhall Street head-quarters, which included a traditional ironmonger's shop; and a manufactory on Tooley Street. Surviving plans of the Leadenhall Street premises show two separate properties.[5] The first, identified as 'Mr Sharp's Shop' with 'Dwelling Apartments above', is the original Southouse & Chapman building. It was here that James had lived as an apprentice, sleeping in a truckle bed under the counter and running errands for his master's wife, and where Elizabeth later scoured and sewed buttonholes as his housekeeper. However, James was clearly not content to live above the shop, because at some point he built what the plans identify as the 'New House'. Standing adjacent to the old Southouse & Chapman establishment, this was an exceptionally large and elegant detached property with four storeys and a classical five-bayed facade.[6]

What the plans describe as 'Mr James Sharp's Manufactory' was located across the river from Leadenhall Street, at 133 Tooley Street. These extensive premises included a foundry, numerous workshops, an 'accompting house', a cart shed, a mill, several yards and a number of tenanted houses. Not even Colen Campbell, stringent arbiter of neoclassical good taste, could have found fault with the elegant proportions of the manufactory buildings. It is apparent from the architecture of his premises – as it is from the design of the products that he made and sold there – that James brought an aesthetic as well as mechanical sensibility to his business. Like his contemporary Josiah Wedgwood, James excelled in 'uniting art with industry'.[7]

James employed forty men in his Tooley Street premises, who together manufactured a vast range of products, including:

> Anchors of every size ... A Ship's Windlass of a particular Construction ... Iron Axle-trees ... for every sort of carriage ... Several particular patterns of Iron Windmill shafts for reducing Friction ... every Sort of Wains, Waggons, Carts &c either broad or narrow-wheeled, for West-India Planters Use are made, as well as Trucks particularly constructed for Sugar-Hogheads ... Several sorts of Street or Porter Trucks ... Bottle-Carts, Fish-Carts, Baggage-Carts or Caravans on Springs or Braces ... Navigation-Wheelbarrows – Brindley's Pattern ... Cocoa Hooks and Cotton Rollers for West Indies ... Cranes of various Constructions ... Fire Engines, to a particular Pattern ... Weighing-Engines, portable, for weighing great Weights, Horses, Cattle, Waggons &c ... Stoves for the Introduction of Warmed Air.[8]

Small-scale domestic products, for example 'iron sa[u]ce pans' and 'Teacettes', were stocked in the ironmongery in Leadenhall Street, while larger items such as wheelbarrows for canal construction, waggons for farms and carrier services, carriages for gentlemen, and dirt trucks for city refuse collectors were shipped to customers nation-wide. Increasingly, however, James relied on exports to expand his concern, confiding in 1770: 'My business has hitherto been chiefly to America and the West Indies.'[9] Many of the goods manufactured in Tooley Street, such as the 'Trucks particularly constructed for Sugar-Hogheads' were designed specifically for use in the sugar-cane plantations of the Caribbean, while 'Cocoa Hooks and Cotton Rollers for West Indies' served a similar clientele.

James's life as proprietor of 'James Sharp, London' bears little resemblance to the early days of his apprenticeship in 1746. Instead of sweeping, fetching coal and running errands, he carries the weight of managing a large concern. Though the tedium of the chores of apprenticeship are only a distant memory, and James has the run of the manufactory to experiment with his beloved mechanics, propri-etorship brings anxieties that he could not have contemplated in adolescence. For a start, he is responsible for the livelihoods of forty employees, and must cushion them against the inevitable ebb and flow of the market. As well as supervising the workforce and the manufacture of his goods, James faces the daily challenge of controlling cash flow, raising capital, chasing bad debts, managing distribution networks, and marketing. He must also spend time on design and innovation to meet the needs of a rapidly changing market.

I imagine James to be always in a hurry, from the moment that the dawn light filters through the green moreen curtains of his four-poster bed, to his final scribblings by candlelight at the mahogany Pembroke table in his study.[10] He is up and dressed in no time, and bounds downstairs to the dining room for coffee, before setting off down Leadenhall Street for the exchange. Here, amongst factors, brokers, discounters and stock-jobbers, he picks up news, negotiates a debt, raises funds on a shipload of hogheads bound for the Americas, discusses prices with an ironmaster of his acquaintance, and analyses the pros and cons of a new species of financial instrument. From this absorbing conversation, he is interrupted by the breathless arrival of a junior apprentice, who brings news of an important customer at the manufactory.

Calling out his farewells, James heads out of the exchange, down George Yard, and Grace Church Street, and Pudding Lane, and onto the quayside at Botolph's Wharf. Here among barrels of herrings and crates of salted cod he flags down a passing wherry which takes him across the heaving river with hair-raising speed. Holding his hat to his head, James runs the last few metres to the manufactory, pausing only to hail the doorkeeper who holds open the heavy clanking gates, and arrives at the entrance to the foundry barely ten minutes after the apprentice had found him on the exchange. He greets the gentleman farmer from Cambridgeshire with hearty apologies, and proceeds to a demonstration of the very latest in agricultural engineering, courtesy of a pair of horses who have been hitched up for the purpose. The last plough having been put through its paces, James says goodbye to his client, though without the satisfaction of a definite order, and hurries back to Leadenhall Street for dinner.

He is late of course – Catharine his wife expects it, and is forgiving – and after a mutton chop and a couple of glasses of claret, he retires to his counting house to work on the mechanics for a new type of chaise. Sleep overtakes him mid-calculation, but he is roused from his slumbers by a clerk seeking urgent advice on a consignment of substandard iron bar from Sweden. This leads him to an almost impenetrable paper trail of dispatch notes, orders, countermands and bills of lading, and it is only when the bells of St Mary's Axe peal the hour that he realises he is late for the family gathering at Mincing Lane. Seizing his hat, he flies down Lyme Street and Church Alley, and within what seems like a few seconds he is in the music room, fitting the mouthpiece to his serpent, and playing the opening cadences of a Handel overture.

As well as manufacturing an astonishing range of products, James also specialised. The Sharp archive contains pattern books of 'Utensils in Husbandry' with engravings of ploughs, harrows and other items of agricultural machinery identified as 'Made & sold by James Sharp, London'.[11] There is a 'A Machine for cutting Chaffer Cane tops for Cattle', a 'Hand Crane', a 'Winnowing Machine', a 'Hand Mill for

Splitting of Beans', a 'Steel Corn Mill', 'A Horse Hoe for Weeding and Earthing between the Plants in drill Husbandry' and 'A jointed Horse Rake for Couch Grass or Stubble', as well as numerous types of plough such as 'A Turn Wrest or Kentish Plow', 'Mr Ducket's Trenching Plough' and 'A Drill Plough for Single Dropping'. Agricultural machinery of this sort might today be considered of rather abstruse interest, but in the eighteenth century it was cutting-edge technology.

The period 1700–1850 witnessed an unprecedented rise in agricultural productivity. This agricultural revolution evolved hand in hand with the Industrial Revolution: higher crop yields allowed more people to be fed which led to population growth, while at the same time increased efficiency meant people could be spared from the fields to work in mills and factories.[12] Productivity was increased by two methods: by enlarging the acreage under cultivation (usually by the enclosure of previously commonly owned land), and by improving the yield per acre. The latter was brought about largely as a result of improvements to the traditional system of crop rotation, and in particular by the introduction of fodder crops such as clover and turnips.[13]

Agricultural innovation of this kind created the need for more sophisticated equipment. As fodder crops require finer soil than cereals, improvements had to be made to traditional cultivation tools such as ploughs and harrows. New crops needed new solutions: the laborious process of slicing turnips by hand for the consumption of livestock was addressed by the invention of a machine known unsurprisingly as the 'Turnip Cutter'. The rapid pace of change sparked the imagination of intellectuals and reformers across Europe. In London, the Society for the Encouragement of Arts, Manufacture and Commerce encouraged members to submit blueprints of innovative agricultural machinery, together with a scale model of the machine for display in the society's headquarters.[14]

As the engravings of his 'Utensils in Husbandry' show, James Sharp was at the forefront of innovations in agricultural machinery. The foundry at the Tooley Street premises played a vital role in his development and production of farm implements. Before the introduction of cast iron at the beginning of the eighteenth century, the village blacksmith made ploughshares and implements by hammering wrought iron into the required shape. The development of cast iron, which is manufactured in foundries by pouring liquid iron into moulds of sand, revolutionised the production of equipment not simply because the process was quicker but also because it ensured standard-isation.[15]

The technological sophistication of James's products can best be appreciated by examining the history of the machinery depicted in his pattern books. A significant proportion of his products became common on British farms only in the middle of the nineteenth century. For example, implements of the type manufactured by James as 'A Hand Mill for Splitting of Beans' were a rarity until the 1840s. Winnowing machines, such as the one advertised by James, followed a similar trajectory. Hoes of the kind described in his pattern books as 'Horse Hoe for Weeding and Earthing between the Plants in drill Husbandry' did not become widespread in British farming until seven-ty-five years later.[16]

With his developments, James adopted business strategies that were ground-breaking at the time. He utilised innovative design and manu-facturing techniques, and was quick to spot opportunities in the market. He also manufactured at scale: a workforce of forty represents an enterprise of significant proportion in a period when most ironwork production was carried out by individuals or families at home or in small workshops. In addition to employing and training specialist workers, James used techniques of division of labour, and delegated effectively. When asked in later life by George III how he found time to pursue his other interests (in this instance the construction of canals), James replied: 'I have many servants, and by placing people in their proper departments I can be spared for two or three days very well.'[17] The manufactory at Tooley Street, with its foundry, skilled workforce and standardised products, anticipated the establishment of the agricultural engineering industry by half a century.

What has been called James's 'inventive genius' is apparent in numerous sketches that survive in the Sharp archive.[18] Covering subjects as diverse as wheels, axles, 'Moving Parapets', drawbridges, cogs, various kinds of carriage, what appears to be a filing cabinet on wheels, and 'Defence Barrows', the drawings show that James was constantly experimenting. He was also adept at utilising other people's ideas. In marketing material for a winnowing machine, for example, he credits 'the ingenious Mr Ducket, of Petersham' with development of the prototype. But he is also careful to note his own contribution to the product: 'Since it came into my Hands, some useful Alterations have been made, which render it more simple, and, perhaps as compleat as it is capable of being made.'[19]

Surviving pattern books and advertisements indicate how much effort James invested in the marketing of his products. With separate French and English editions, the 'James Sharp, London' catalogues feature exquisite copperplate engravings of implements and machinery.[20] They also typically include a detailed analysis of the functioning and utility of the product, and draw the reader's attention to another of James's marketing techniques: 'NB Horses are constantly ready, at the Manufactory, to shew the Effects of the several Rakes, Ploughs, Shovels &c or to draw the different Sorts of Carts, Waggons, or Rollers, whereby Judgment may be formed of the Utility of each Machine.'[21]

Along with demonstrations of his latest products, James took every opportunity to pull strings and exploit his own and his siblings' connections. Recipients of his promotional material included the Duke of Northumberland, whom he knew very slightly through his brother John. In common with leading manufacturers of the day such as Josiah Wedgwood and James Watt's business partner Matthew Boulton, James appreciated the power of polite patronage, and made every effort to utilise it. He was fortunate in having a family who, from the late 1760s, increasingly mixed in influential and aristocratic circles.

James was the great innovator of the Sharp family. He was a visionary who understood the potential of technology to bring about great change, even while others remained sceptical. The manufactory in Tooley Street stands as a testament both to James's commercial acumen, and his considerable mechanical ingenuity. Creative, resourceful and hard-working, he was already – in his mid-thirties – a figure of considerable renown, and his star would continue to rise.

12

Wicken

Despite their liberal views, the Sharps took a barely concealed delight in their acquaintance with the upper classes. Even Granville – the most radical of the siblings – notes with relish in his journal the names of various members of the aristocracy with whom the family associated.[1] Elizabeth was no exception, and from the early years of her marriage, she is assiduous in recording her encounters with the nobility. So on 7 October 1762 Elizabeth notes in her journal that 'The Duke of Somerset visited at Berkley' while a visit to 'Lady Cork' features in an entry for September 1764. The following year, in February 1765, the Prowses 'dined at Stow. Met Lord and Lady Chatam there, I believe before he received his Title of Lord and see most of their family, there, Mr W. Pitt, the young Grinval boy who afterwards was Lord Grinval.'[2]

Elizabeth was dining at Stowe with three former, or future, prime ministers: William Pitt the Elder, later Earl of Chatham (who served in an informal capacity during the Seven Years' War, and more formally between 1766 and 1768); his son William Pitt the Younger (who served between 1783 and 1801, and again from 1804 to 1806); and William Grenville, 1st Baron Grenville (whose short ministry lasted from 1806 to 1807).[3]

1 October 1764 marked a turning point in George and Elizabeth's life. Elizabeth alludes to it, in characteristically subdued fashion, in her journal: 'Mr Prowse and I left Berkley with an intent to settle at Wicken.' She explains that whereas 'Till this time, we had lived in my Father Prowses Family as our home', the Prowses had now concluded that it was time for George and Elizabeth to have a place of their

own. Fortunately there were two estates to play with: Berkley House in Somerset remained the family seat, while Wicken Park in Northamptonshire was given to George and Elizabeth: 'My Father had given up that place for his son to live at.'[4]

Elizabeth's account of the couple's journey to Wicken in October 1764 gives a rare insight into her personal feelings. Elizabeth confesses that she is a little apprehensive about the return of domestic responsibilities, from which she has been exempt since leaving Leadenhall Street. 'My mind,' she confides, '[was] not a little filled with the care of commencing a House Keeping again.' Aside from this, the couple were in buoyant mood as they anticipated the delights of setting up home together. As Elizabeth notes: 'Got to Wicken, having had no small pleasure in forming our plans for living there (on our journey).'[5]

An early nineteenth-century print of Wicken Park, depicting an elegant house surrounded by parkland, illuminates the 'no small pleasure' felt by George and Elizabeth as they travelled to take up residence. With Tudor origins, Wicken Park House was rebuilt in 1717 in creamy limestone ashlar soon after the purchase of the estate by George's maternal great-grandfather, Charles Hosier.[6] Consisting of two storeys, with a hipped slate roof, the house was classically proportioned, with a simple facade and long sash windows facing the garden to the south of the property. Inside, a broad staircase, with slim turned balusters, led from the two-storey hall to a galleried landing. The principal reception rooms of dining room, drawing room and library were accessed from the hall.

After Mrs Prowse inherited Wicken in 1750, the family set about improving and extending the property. When George and Elizabeth took up residence in October 1764 the estate extended to 2,000 acres, and included the entire parish of Wicken with the exception of a few cottages and the Glebe.[7]

For landed gentry such as the Prowses, the country house represented a perfect counterpoint to the gaudy frenzy of the London season. Shopping, assemblies, operas and balls which scintillated in the early weeks of November, palled as the first warm days of May wafted the stink of the City over Mayfair and St James's. Now was the time to retreat to the country, where simpler pleasures could be enjoyed. For a gentleman, the country offered occupation in the form of running the estate, or pottering about the hothouses, or dabbling with agricultural improvement, while leisure hours were spent hunting, shooting and fishing. A lady, on the other hand, could play the role of Lady Bountiful, dispensing charity to the needy of the estate villages, while also entertaining her friends amidst the beauties of lake, parkland and garden.

The country house was also the medium through which a discerning proprietor could express his wealth and taste. An interest in architecture was almost de rigueur among the elite of the mid-eighteenth century, and fortunes were expended on perfecting the proportions of the family seat. The Prowses were no exception: what Elizabeth refers to as 'forming our plans for living there' included a wholesale remodelling of Wicken Park House with two new wings and a third storey to the main block. Rather than employ the service of a professional architect, George and Elizabeth relied on her father-in-law, Thomas Prowse, an amateur, who had previously designed Hatch Court near Taunton.[8] Elizabeth describes how during the Prowses' visit to Wicken in February 1765 – 'the first time after it was ours' – Thomas 'drue the plan of the New Building, to be added to the House and ordered the repairs to the old part, which roof was raised to make 3 garets and was new tiled'.[9]

Decoration of the matrimonial home was a traditional occupation for upper-class newlyweds in this period, and George and Elizabeth took to the task with gusto. Like their fellow homemakers, they pored over the catalogues of cabinetmakers, engravers, plasterers and upholsterers, and issued instructions to painters, plumbers and carpenters. No doubt there were exploratory expeditions to London, to visit 'The Cabinet and Upholstery Warehouse' of Thomas Chippendale in St Martin's Lane, or William Hallett's emporium in Great Newport Street, where Elizabeth marvelled at the card tables and writing cases, walnut commodes, sofas, candlestands and 'neat Mahogany Chairs Stuff'd in linnen'. Auction houses were frequented, and print sellers, and William Linnell's showroom in Berkeley Square where vast pier glasses, and elegant girandoles, jostled chinoiserie beds and Siena and Derbyshire marble tables. Back home, Elizabeth agonised over wallpapers, and the colour of the silk for the dining-room chairs, while George weighed up the advantages of French carpets over list, hair or painted floor cloth.[10]

The works continued for several years, and Elizabeth makes frequent reference to their progress in her diaries, for example, in May 1766 she notes: 'the new Building was begun and getting very forward'. The project was nearing completion in 1768 when, according to estate records, the parlours, bedrooms and staircase were painted and the corridors papered. Work proceeded fitfully thereafter, for it took until 1777 for the drawing room to be furnished, and the cellar was completed in 1787.[11]

Elizabeth's attachment to Wicken began in these early days of her marriage, as she and George excitedly made plans for their future there. It was to be her home for the next forty-five years, and in that time she worked tirelessly to improve the estate and the lives of the people who worked there. Wicken plays a leading role in the Sharp story, not simply as Elizabeth's beloved home, but as a place where the siblings came to be together. It is characteristic, then, that barely a week passed between George and Elizabeth taking up residence in October 1764, and the arrival of a large party of Sharps, comprising James and his wife Catharine, William, Granville and Frances. The brothers and sisters all visited regularly in groups, or pairs, or individually, or as part of a larger party. The London siblings in particular valued the estate as a place of rest and recuperation, and there was nearly always a Sharp child or a convalescent staying.

The intimacy between George and Elizabeth and the rest of the Prowse family was unaffected by their establishment of a separate home. The family still spent the winter together in Argyll Street, and the Prowses were regular guests at Wicken – often visiting for several weeks at a time. In these early years of her marriage, Elizabeth developed a deep affection for her two sisters-in-law. When in September 1766 the couple learned that Bessy Prowse was 'dangerously ill of a fever', George and Elizabeth rushed to Somerset to be with her. On arriving at Berkley House, they 'found her better to our great joy'.[12]

Life at Wicken was enlivened by 'jaunts' of the kind enjoyed by the Prowse family previously. In the summer of 1765 Elizabeth's sister

Frances – who was still living in William's house in Mincing Lane –
joined them on 'a journey to visit my eldest bro. in the north'. The
Sharps made a virtue of the slowness of eighteenth-century travel by
visiting friends and relations en route. In this way the journey became
part of the adventure, rather than something to be endured before it
started. George, Elizabeth and Frances were such enthusiastic visitors
that it took them four weeks to travel from Northamptonshire to
Northumberland. This six-day extract from Elizabeth's journal gives
an idea of their itinerary, and also of the dense network of the family's acquaintance:

July 1	At Mrs Elesleys, Mr Nickelsons, at Brumpton and Jurwarth
July 2	At Willington my cousin Middletons
July 5	Durham at Mr Whelers
July 6	Dr Bedfords

The travellers finally pitched up at John's vicarage in Hartburn on
10 July, and the party was complete twelve days later when James and
Catharine arrived from London. Not content with the exertions of
their recent journey, Elizabeth and her party spent their first day at
Hartburn on an excursion: 'To Brinkburn Abby to see the Ruen and
romantick situation'. Perhaps Elizabeth had developed a taste for the
medieval as a result of the publication of Horace Walpole's seminal
Gothic novel *The Castle of Otranto* in the previous year.[13] The remainder
of the stay passed in a whirlwind of activity as the siblings visited
childhood haunts, saw old friends, and explored local tourist attractions
such as Holy Island and 'the castle and woods of the Duke of
Northumberland'.

The leisurely pace of the jaunt continued on the journey home:
there were more stop-offs with friends ('August 5 to Scarborough, see
Mr and Mrs Gyles Earle there') and further opportunities for country-house visiting ('August 9 ... to Stamford. See Lord Exeters noble
house'). The party arrived back at Wicken on 12 August, after two
months' absence, to find that decorating works – conveniently planned
to coincide with their absence – were complete: 'The House covered

in and seelings so dryed, we were enabled to inhabit the rooms on our return.'[14]

There were also expeditions with the Prowses. In her diary entry for 11 July 1766, Elizabeth describes an expedition to the Midlands: 'My Mother and Siss, Mr Prowse and myself set out for a little jaunt to see Oxford, Banbury, Warwick, Coventry, Dunchurch ... a new part of the country to us.' The visit to Wicken of a 'Mrs Portman' later in the year provided the occasion for further excursions. The lady was clearly a country-house aficionado, for a rigorous schedule of activity was devised for her amusement: between 3 and 8 August there were visits to 'the Duke of Bedfords at Wobern', 'Lord Spencers at Althrop', 'Lord Halifaxes Horton', 'Lord Northamptons Castle Ashby' and 'Blenham'.[15] It was an itinerary which might defeat even the most indefatigable modern-day member of the National Trust.

The happy flow of family life was interrupted in October 1766 when Thomas Prowse experienced a return of what Elizabeth called 'my Father Prowses old complaints'. Prowse seems to have been a recalcitrant patient: when a doctor recommended the health benefits of a journey overseas, he absolutely refused to consent to the scheme. It was not an outlandish suggestion: the Prowses had travelled to France for the sake of Thomas's health in 1763, and the benefits of recuperation abroad were widely accepted in this period. Literary adherents included Henry Fielding, who sailed to Lisbon in 1754 in search of a cure for gout, asthma and cirrhosis of the liver, and Laurence Sterne who sought relief for the symptoms of tuberculosis in France and Turin in 1762.[16]

It is an indication of the family's regard for Elizabeth that Mrs Prowse, in the face of her husband's obduracy, and fearing for his life, turned to her daughter-in-law for support: 'my mother P. angsiety was so great, and beleaving such a journey might be of great service, that she wrote to me, to beg we would indevour by letter to perswaid him to go, and beged we would offer to go with them, which we did'.

Elizabeth must have been persuasive, because Thomas eventually consented to the trip. When the Prowses arrived in Argyll Street in advance of the expedition, Elizabeth was dismayed by the deterioration in her father-in-law's condition: 'my Father so altered, as shocked us very much'. Hasty preparations ensued and in just under a week they were ready to set out. The drive to Dover was an ordeal: the rattling of the carriage on bad roads caused the patient untold distress, and despite the growing urgency of the situation, they could proceed only at a snail's pace. Elizabeth notes: 'We had a tedious journey and much anxiety before we reached Dover.'

On arrival, the patient's condition deteriorated further. He could not be moved, so all thoughts of travel to the continent were put on hold, and the family spent December in Dover. These were difficult weeks for Elizabeth: cooped up in the dingy rooms of a seaside inn, she had to endure the constant waiting for a change in the patient's condition. She took it in turns with her mother-in-law to sit with Thomas during the night, and bore the fractious demands of her father-in-law with cheerful patience. Perhaps the only respite from the heavy atmosphere of the sickroom was the occasional hastily taken walk along the cliffs with George, where they were battered by the winter winds.[17]

One bright interlude came in the form of a visit from her brother William, who attended the patient in a medical capacity. But even the joy of seeing William was marred by the gloom of his prognosis. Neither he nor the other doctors who attended Thomas could do anything for the patient. The end came in the early morning of 1 January 1767. As Prowse struggled in the throes of death, a violent storm raged outside. Snow piled high against the walls of the inn, and water flooded through the front door 'above a <u>futt deep</u> where it was not known to come before'. At last, at half past three in the morning, Thomas Prowse died: 'to the very great affliction and disstress of us all'.[18]

As the family grieved in the weeks and months that followed, George Prowse stepped up to the responsibilities of his inheritance. In his new role as head of the family, George was assiduous in his concern for his mother's welfare. Her plight was certainly a pitiable one: having lost seven of her ten children, she now faced the grief of early widowhood. As is apparent from Elizabeth's diary, George expressed his love for his mother by ministering to her physical comforts. She was given first choice of estate for her residence: 'Berkley or Wicken which place she liked best.' When she plumped for Somerset, George and Elizabeth hurried there to superintend 'the intended alterations to the House, that they might be done and ready to receive my Mother and siss. Prowses, when they chose to go there'. The couple then made a flying visit to Wicken, once again for the purpose of Mrs Prowse's comfort: 'had the present Blue Room papered, windows altered, and a new bed, curtaning and chares fitted up to by my Mothers Rooms, as that room she sayd she prefered to any other'.[19]

But eight months after the death of Thomas Prowse, the family was met with an even greater disaster. On 20 August 1767, Elizabeth noted in her diary: 'My dear Mr Prowse was seized with a dreadful fever.' Five days later, she recorded: 'Dyed, on ye 25. Aged 30 (the very greatest shock and affliction I ever received), at 3 o'clock in the morning at Wicken.'[20] The tragedy had unfolded with bewildering rapidity. Through the torturous hours of her husband's final illness, Elizabeth had no time to prepare herself for his loss. The end, when it came, was so shocking that she may have lost all sense of reality, and it was perhaps only in the days that followed that she became sensible of her condition. At the age of thirty-four, Elizabeth was left a widow, childless, and with an uncertain future before her.

In this darkest hour of Elizabeth's life, the support of her family was of incalculable value. After recording George's death, Elizabeth noted: 'Happily for me my Mother Prowse was with me at the time.' In spite of the severity of her own loss, Mrs Prowse was able to give comfort to her bereaved daughter-in-law. And it was not long before the Sharps arrived: 'my Dear Bros. and Siss. soon with us'. It was with the emotional and practical support of her siblings, as well as surviving members of the Prowse family, that Elizabeth rebuilt her life in the months and years to come.

13

Strong

In the early 1760s Granville appeared to be the least brilliant of the stars in the Sharp family firmament. While William and James prospered, Elizabeth enjoyed the fruits of an advantageous marriage and John's clerical career bloomed, Granville seemed destined for a life of uneventful mediocrity. Of the three brothers who served as apprentices, Granville alone failed to make a success of his trade. On the expiry of his apprenticeship in 1757 he obtained employment with a rival linen producer 'which he had reason to suppose established on a large foundation'. This proved not to be the case, and 'finding the concern far more contracted than he had imagined, he soon relinquished his engagement'.[1]

In the summer of 1758, Granville joined the Civil Service as a junior clerk in the Board of Ordnance, the government department that supplied munitions and provisions to the armed forces. Britain was then embroiled in the Seven Years' War – a global conflict involving all the major European powers – so this was a busy time for the department. Granville's departure from the linen business came hard on the heels of the death of his father: if he had stuck at it hitherto to avoid disappointing the archdeacon, he was now at liberty to follow his own inclinations.[2] His choice of employment suggests a lack of professional and material ambition, in marked contrast to that conspicuous in the activities of his brothers William and James. It is indicative of Granville's attitude to his work in the Civil Service that, in all the reams of his voluminous correspondence, he makes barely any reference to it, except on one occasion when he described himself as a 'sinecurist'.[3]

The undemanding nature of the position at the Ordnance Office meant that Granville had the time and mental freedom to develop his intellectual interests: and this may have informed his choice of employment. From the early days of his apprenticeship, Granville had sought to compensate for the deficiencies of his education by a rigorous regime of self-improvement. In the absence of a formal classical education – of the kind enjoyed by his elder brothers John and Thomas – Granville mastered Greek and Latin through private study. He also taught himself French, Hebrew and 'the Syriac and Chaldee dialects'.[4] According to his biographer Prince Hoare, Granville made his 'first advances in learning' as a result of a dispute with a fellow apprentice 'concerning the Trinity, and the Atonement of Christ' – perhaps an unusual subject for teenage badinage. When the apprentice ascribed Granville's misunderstanding of the points in question to 'his want of acquaintance with the Greek tongue' which prevented him from reading the New Testament in its original text, Granville was stung into action. As Hoare noted: 'To be ignorant of the truth, was, to his ardent mind, a source of inexpressible pain; to neglect the means of acquiring a knowledge of it, insupportable disgrace.'[5]

Granville's study of Hebrew followed a similar trajectory. This time it was a Jewish apprentice who 'frequently contested with him the truths of the Christian religion' and who dismissed Granville's 'earnest reasonings' as the consequence of 'ignorance of the language in which they were written'.[6] Granville soon knew Hebrew well enough to engage in scholarly debate on the construction of various passages of the Old Testament. In 1765 he published his first work, the wonderfully abstruse: *Answer to the Rev. Dr Kennicott's Charge of Corruptions in the Hebrew Texts of Ezra and Nehemiah*. But despite his obvious intellectual talents, Granville never thought of himself as a scholar. When a professor of Hebrew at Cambridge publicly acknowledged his debt to Granville's work, Granville wrote to him explaining that he was unworthy of such an honour:

It is necessary (as well for your own sake, as for the dignity of the important office you hold in the University) that I should give you due previous caution that I am not a regular scholar, and that the little knowledge I have acquired has been taken up entirely without the instruction of any master; so that my name must not even be mentioned, as having the least degree of authority to influence either the opinions or practice of any regular scholar.[7]

Though Granville went on to publish more than sixty works, on subjects as various as teaching English as a foreign language, 'Encroachments on the River Thames', 'The State of the London Workhouse', the etymology of the word 'Jerusalem', and 'The Law of Retribution', he never quite got over the idea that he was a pretender to scholarship. As he saw it, no amount of relentless auto-didacticism could compensate for the deficiencies of his childhood education.

One day in 1765, Granville left William's house in Mincing Lane, where he had lived since finishing his apprenticeship, to walk to the Ordnance Office. William held a free surgery for the poor every morning, and Granville was used to seeing the sick and destitute who queued outside his brother's house. On this particular occasion his attention was drawn to the figure of a black boy, of about sixteen or seventeen years of age. Granville later wrote that 'the appearance of the Boy was so extremely distressful (as he seemed ready to drop down)'. Granville took the child to his brother, 'that immediate Relief might be given to him'.[8]

The boy told the brothers that his name was Jonathan Strong, and that he had travelled to England from Barbados as the property of David Lisle, a lawyer and plantation owner. Lisle had subjected Strong to a regime of brutality, in the last incidence of which he had repeatedly struck the boy about the face with a pistol. This had 'made his head swell very greatly' and 'a disorder fell on his eyes'.[9] Lisle abandoned Strong concluding that he was so damaged as to be worthless, and the boy wandered about the streets of London in a state of extreme distress: 'I could hardly walk or see my way, where I was going.' He later recalled how he had found William's free surgery for the poor: 'I meet with a man – told him my case: he recommended to Mr William Sharp in Mincing Lane, Fenchurch Street: I took his advice, and went to Mr Sharp.'[10] When Granville saw him in the queue in Mincing Lane, the boy was lame and almost blind.[11]

Strong's condition was a glimpse into a world of cruelty and repression from which an educated Englishman generally averted his gaze. The 'dead silence' that fell upon the dining room in Mansfield Park, when Fanny Price attempted to discuss the slave trade with her uncle Sir Thomas Bertram – himself the owner of a plantation in Antigua – is characteristic of prevailing attitudes.[12] Slavery was viewed by most men and women of the Bertrams' class as an unfortunate necessity which could be ignored because it was perpetrated on the other side of the Atlantic. Just like today, in the eighteenth century the workings of the global economy were only partly visible.[13] Moreover a considerable part of the wealth of the upper classes flowed directly or indirectly from ownership of plantations in the Caribbean. Though none of the Sharps owned a plantation, James's business relied on the export of goods to enterprises in the colonies. That a man like James, with liberal views and philanthropic inclinations, traded with slave-owners reveals the moral blindness of the British to the implications of their commercial dealings with the Caribbean.

The idea of slavery as an 'unfortunate necessity' was linked to the introduction to Britain in the seventeenth and eighteenth centuries of coffee, tea and chocolate, which while being wildly popular, also required sugar to make them more palatable. Sugar soon became a national obsession, and it was in these years that the British love of puddings developed. Every conceivable confection of sugary matter – 'Hot puddings, cold puddings, steamed puddings, baked puddings, pies, tarts, creams, moulds, charlottes and bettys, trifles and fools, syllabubs and tansys junkets and ices, milk puddings, suet puddings' – found its way onto the nation's dining tables.[14]

Along with the demand for sugar came the belief that its production required slave labour. Apologists for the trade argued that the toil required for the cultivation and harvesting of sugar cane was so back-breaking, that nobody would undertake it voluntarily.[15] As John Pinney, a plantation owner on the island of Nevis, put it: 'It is [as] impossible for a Man to make sugar without the assistance of Negroes as to make bricks without straw.' The conviction grew that the British economy depended on the slave trade, and from this it was a short step of reasoning to conclude that slavery was necessary.[16] The isolation

of the system on the islands of the Caribbean allowed the British to
reconcile their attachment to liberty, which defined the empire in the
popular imagination, with the repression sanctioned in their own
colonies.[17] Even among enlightened thinkers, few saw the contradiction
between freedom for whites, and the subjugation of black slaves.[18]

The system by which slaves were procured to work the Caribbean
plantations began off the west coast of Africa, where 'slaver' ships
hovered waiting to fill their holds. As slavery was a feature of many
of the chiefdoms and kingdoms of Africa in this period, Europeans
were able to tap into a pre-existing market.[19] Traders drove enslaved
Africans from the interior to the coast where they were sold to the
captains of the waiting ships. It took a British captain approximately
three to four months to fill his hold.[20] As he sailed up and down the
coast, following leads, working on hunches and competing with his
rivals, the slaves that were already in the ship suffered the horrors of
the voyage to come but in a more extreme form. The heat of the
African sun beat down on the deck, and there was no ocean breeze
to alleviate the stifling closeness of the hold.

For the voyage to the Caribbean, known as the 'middle passage',
male slaves were 'fastened together, two and two, by hand-cuffs on
their wrists, and irons rivitted on their legs'. They were 'frequently
stored so close, as to admit of no other posture than lying on their
sides'.[21] The former slave Olaudah Equiano described the conditions
below deck:

> The stench of the hold ... now that the whole ship's cargo were
> confined together ... became absolutely pestilential. The close-
> ness of the place, and the heat of the climate added to the
> number in the ship, which was so crowded that each had scarcely
> room to turn himself, almost suffocated us ... This wretched
> situation was again aggravated by the galling of the chains, now
> become insupportable.[22]

As the slaving ship neared the islands of the Caribbean, those slaves
who had survived the journey were taken on deck to be cleaned and
prepared for sale. The fit and healthy were sold first, while those of

particularly 'meagre' proportions were weighed on public scales and sold at a rate of threepence, sixpence or ninepence to the pound.[23] High mortality, and a correspondingly low birth rate, meant that there was a constant need for fresh slaves. This kept the trade in constant motion, as the owners and captains of slave ships, the middlemen on the African coast, and the host of agents and factors who managed and financed the operation all conspired to feed the insatiable appetite for human cargo.

The horrors of the middle passage and the plantations seem a long way from Mincing Lane; but for those who chose to see, Jonathan Strong was a living embodiment of slavery in the very heart of London. Granville's chance encounter with Strong opened his eyes to the reality of the slave trade. In fact there was little excuse for ignorance, as it was common for plantation owners, captains of slaving ships, army and naval officers, and government officials to bring slaves with them when they returned from overseas.[24] There were perhaps 5,000–7,000 black people living in London in the 1760s.[25] Some worked as liveried footmen or servants to the fashionable rich, while others scraped a living as musicians, sailors, haulers and stevedores. Most were desperately poor, and congregated in down-and-out areas of the city, such as St Giles, and the stinking alleys that bordered the river from St Katharine's to Limehouse.

It was not merely Strong's presence in London that betrayed the reality of the trade. Lisle's violent treatment of Strong exemplified the casual cruelty that was endemic to the system. Slavery brutalised those who participated in it, from the sailors on the slaving ships, to the middlemen working on the African seaboard, to the plantation owners on the islands of the Caribbean.[26] Lisle's behaviour shows that slave owners did not always think it necessary to modify their conduct on arrival in England, so that the savagery of the slave trade might be as visible on the streets of London as it was on the plantations of Barbados and Jamaica.

The common use of British newspaper advertisements to buy and sell slaves was also difficult to ignore. The following notice in an issue of the *London Advertiser* from 1756 is typical:

To be sold, a Negro Boy, about fourteen years old, warranted free from any distemper, and has had those fatal to that colour;

has been used two years to all kinds of household work, and to wait at table; his price is £25, and would not be sold but the person he belongs to is leaving off business. Apply at the bar of the George Coffee-house, in Chancery Lane.[27]

This more succinct example appeared in the 18 April 1769 edition of the *Gazetter and New Daily Advertiser*: 'For sale at the Bull and Gate Inn, Holborn, a chestnut gelding, a Tim whisky, and a well-made good-tempered Black Boy.'[28] The newspaper advertisement was also the resort of slave owners when their slaves ran away. This appeared in the *Daily Post* on 4 August 1720:

Went away 22nd July last, from the house of William Webb, in Limehouse Hole, a negro man, about 20 years old, called Dick, yellow complexion, wool hair, about five foot six inches high, having on his right breast the word 'Hare' burnt. Whosoever brings him to the said Mr Webb's, shall have half-a-guinea reward and reasonable charges.[29]

The task of the professional slave-hunter, who specialised in the return of runaway slaves, was made easier if the fugitive was wearing a collar. It was for this reason that a notice in the 28 September 1728 issue of the *Daily Journal* informed its readers that the runaway in question wore a collar engraved with the words 'My Lady Bromfield's black, in Lincoln's Inn Fields'.[30] Such was the market for slave collars that the goldsmith Matthew Dyer, of Orchard Street in Westminster, thought it worth his while to notify the readers of the *London Advertiser* of his manufacture of 'silver padlocks for Blacks or Dogs; collars, &c'.[31]

Following Jonathan Strong's visit to the surgery, William arranged for the boy to be admitted to St Bartholomew's Hospital. He remained there for four and a half months. Strong later described the assistance given to him by Granville in this period: 'All the while I was in hospital, the gentleman find me in clothes, shoes, and stockings, and when I come out, He paid for my lodging, and a money to find myself some necessaries; till he get me into a place.'[32]

After Strong's discharge from hospital, Granville found employment for him with an apothecary called Mr Brown, who lived in Fenchurch Street. Brown gave Strong lodgings, a uniform, and – most significantly – wages. For the next two years the former slave worked as an errand boy for the apothecary and, according to Granville, 'grew to be a good looking, Stout, Young Man'.[33]

In the relative comfort of his life as an errand boy in Fenchurch Street, Strong must have hoped that he had put the days of slavery behind him. But his freedom was to be short-lived. One morning in the late summer of 1767 Strong was attending the apothecary's wife 'behind a hackney coach' when he was spotted by his former master.[34] Lisle had abandoned the boy because he considered him so damaged as to be worthless. Now after two and a half years of recuperation, the boy was once again an object on which 'Barbadian eyes could not look without cupidity'.[35] Determined to recoup the boy's value, Lisle followed the coach 'for the purpose of obtaining intelligence of his abode', and 'having discovered it, laid a plan to entrap him'.[36]

Lisle purported to sell his former slave to a Jamaican planter called James Kerr, who stipulated that the purchase price should not be paid until Strong was safely aboard a ship bound for the Caribbean. Lisle now laid his plans for the boy's kidnap. On 5 September 1767 Lisle, with two of the lord mayor's officers whom he had retained to assist him in his task, holed up in an inn situated a short distance from the apothecary's shop. A message was sent to Strong, requiring him on a pretext to come to the inn, and he arrived to find Lisle and his accomplices waiting for him. Strong was seized and locked up in the Poultry Compter, a small prison on Cheapside, pending the departure of the ship that was to take him to Jamaica.[37] Run under the auspices of the sheriff of the City of London, the Compter was used to detain men and women charged with offences such as vagrancy, drunkenness, prostitution and homosexuality. It was not a salubrious spot: a report on London prisons published in 1776 described it as a place where 'riot, drunkenness, blasphemy and debauchery, echo from the walls, sickness and misery are confined within them'.[38]

Strong sent a desperate note to his employer, but when the apothecary arrived he was 'violently threatened' by Lisle who accused him of having 'detained his property'. Brown was intimidated and left, but not before Strong had managed to hand him a letter for Granville 'imploring protection from being sold as a slave'. On Sunday 13 September 1767 Granville, accompanied by his brother James, went to the City prison and demanded to see Strong. Having heard the boy's story, Granville 'charged the master of the prison, at his own peril not to deliver him up to any person whatever, who might claim him, until he had been carried before the Lord Mayor'.[39]

Three days later, Granville gave formal notice to the lord mayor, Sir Robert Kite, that Jonathan Strong was being detained in the Poultry Compter without warrant, and petitioned that David Lisle and James Kerr should attend court to answer for their actions.[40] The lord mayor issued the appropriate summons, and a hearing took place at the Mansion House on 18 September. James and Granville attended on behalf of Strong. Although Lisle and Kerr did not appear in person, their interest was represented by Kerr's attorney William Macbean, and by David Laird the captain of the ship due to carry Strong to Jamaica. In his written account of the hearing, Granville describes Strong's reaction to the testimony of the two witnesses for the defence: '[he] was put into extreme anguish they being, both of them, absolutely unknown to him'. As the legal argument continued, the boy 'seemed ready to sink down with fear'.[41]

Having heard the evidence from both sides the lord mayor ruled 'that the lad had not stolen any thing, and was not guilty of any offence, and was therefore at liberty to go away'.[42] Immediately the captain seized Strong's arm, claiming that he took him 'as the property of Mr Kerr'. The coroner, Thomas Beach, moved towards Granville and whispered in his ear: 'Charge him!' Grasping his meaning, Granville told the captain 'that he would charge a Constable with him for an assault if he presumed to take Jonathan Strong'. The captain withdrew his hand, and 'all the parties retired from the presence of the Lord Mayor'. After that, Granville records: 'Jonathan Strong departed also, in the sight of all, in full Liberty, nobody daring afterwards to touch him.'[43]

A few days after the hearing James Kerr brought a civil action against Granville and James, alleging that that they had deprived him of his property, and claiming damages of £200. On 1 October David Lisle turned up at William's house in Mincing Lane and challenged Granville to a duel, on the grounds that he 'had procured the liberty of his slave, Jonathan Strong'. Granville declined the challenge.[44] The brothers now turned their attention to the defence of the claim brought against them by Kerr, retaining an eminent solicitor working in the lord mayor's office to represent them, and seeking the advice of the recorder of the City, Sir James Eyre.

After consideration of the relevant legal authorities, the lawyers advised the Sharp brothers that the case against them was so strong as to make any attempt at a defence foolhardy, and suggested settling on whatever terms could be obtained. They showed Granville a copy of what was known as the 'Joint Opinion', which had been given in 1729 by the then Attorney General Sir Philip Yorke and Solicitor General Charles Talbot, both future Lord Chancellors. This was to the effect that a slave did not become free on his arrival in Britain, and that a master could compel a slave to return with him to the Caribbean. Though the opinion was not given as part of a legal judgement – it was in fact stated after a dinner in Lincoln's Inn Hall – it had acquired the force of law, and according to the Sharps' lawyers, had been confirmed on several occasions by Lord Mansfield, chief justice of the Court of King's Bench.[45]

Granville was shocked by his lawyers' advice. He could not believe that 'the Laws of England were really so Injurious to natural Rights', and concluded that Yorke and Talbot had misinterpreted the law for 'political reasons'.[46] In these circumstances, and given the pusillanimity of his own lawyers who seemed unable to look beyond the Joint Opinion, Granville concluded that the only option was to take on the case himself. 'Thus forsaken,' he recalled later, 'by my professional defenders, I was compelled, through the want of regular legal assistance, to make a hopeless attempt at self-defence.' Though he was totally unacquainted with the study and practice of law, 'having never opened a law-book (except the Bible) in my life', he began 'most reluctantly' to 'search the indexes of a law-library, which my bookseller had lately purchased'.[47]

In the months that followed, Granville devoted himself – with as much assiduity as he had previously applied to the Hebrew texts of

Ezra and Nehemiah – to a study of English law as it touched upon the question of the liberty of the subject. He was used to private study, and the relatively undemanding regime of the government office where he worked (the Seven Years' War had ended in 1763, so things were quieter in the Board of Ordnance) gave him both the time and mental energy needed for the task.

Granville's chance encounter with Jonathan Strong outside the surgery in Mincing Lane proved to be the most decisive event of his life. The drive and commitment that later characterised his campaign for justice for Strong and his fellow slaves were largely unfocused in the years prior to 1767. The Strong case harnessed Granville's energies to the pursuit of the abolition of slavery, and launched him on his career as an activist.

As Granville embarked on his study of the English law, he received a letter from his maternal uncle Granville Wheler in which he 'warmly pressed' his nephew to take holy orders.[48] Wheler went so far as to offer to resign the living of Great Leke in Nottinghamshire, which was worth £300 a year, in Granville's favour. To a man apparently well suited to the priesthood, who had been denied it only on account of his father's lack of means, Wheler's offer was nothing short of a godsend. Here was an opportunity for Granville to give up his lowly employment at the Board of Ordnance, and to embark on a career that was not only distinguished and remunerative, but befitting to a man of his scholarly inclinations.

But Granville refused the offer. In his letter of reply dated 26 November 1767 Granville explained that, though he was sensible of Wheler's 'extraordinary generosity and kindness', his uncle's confidence in him was misplaced. He could not, he said, 'satisfy myself concerning my own qualifications for the proposed honourable function'. What was more: 'even if I could flatter myself that I am at all capable of serving the cause of religion, yet I should apprehend that I might much more effectually do so as a layman, than as a clergymen'.[49]

Granville sacrificed the Great Leke living in part so that he could retain his freedom of manoeuvre. Outside the priesthood, Granville could follow the dictates of his conscience, guided only by his faith and what he believed to be just and true. While he was never shy of exploiting his connections in the Church establishment, almost persecuting the bishops of his acquaintance with his requests for their support, he did so from outside the clerical fold. With a deftness that was characteristic of the Sharps, he managed to reconcile his family's conservative clerical tradition with his own radical social and political agenda.

14

Old Jewry

In a letter to his brother John dated 9 January 1769, James wrote: 'poor Mincing Lane is no more, no more jolly doings there, and yet I hope our Musical doings are not at an end ... Brother Will has agreed for the Noblest house in the City of London.'[1]

William had lived in Mincing Lane, between Fenchurch Street and Great Tower Street, since the beginning of his apprenticeship in 1743. On the completion of his term he had taken over his master's practice and house, and it was here – as Granville embarked on his apprenticeship in Tower Hill – that William began housekeeping. In 1757, after seven years of private practice, William moved to a larger house in Mincing Lane, where he provided a home for Granville and Frances, and Thomas and Judith when they were in London.

James's nostalgia for Mincing Lane was keenly felt, for it had been the setting for many of the Sharps' 'jolly doings' of the 1750s and 60s. It was here that they had written, and received, their common letters; where the girls stayed on the occasion of their memorable six-week visit to the brothers in 1757; where the sisters found a home following the death of their parents; and where – with Miss Cecilia Morgan in pride of place – the family engaged in their much-loved 'Musical doings'. James comforted himself for the loss of Mincing Lane with the prospect of William's new residence in Old Jewry which, James confidently reported to John, was the finest house in the City of London.

The streetscape of Old Jewry was not in itself prepossessing. Tucked between 'Mr Hoffman, Tallow Chandler', and 'Messrs Chansey &

Barklet, Druggists', the entrance to William's new house hardly gave
the impression of grandeur. But once through the arched passage that
led from the street to a central courtyard, the splendour of the property was vividly apparent. A carriage sweep circled in front of the
house, flanked to the east by the fine facade of the detached mansion,
and to the north and south by a coach house and stabling. Here a
guest could leave his carriage in the capable hands of a waiting groom,
before climbing the broad steps to the front door. Once inside, even
the most seasoned observer of architectural splendours might marvel
at the dimensions of the double-height hall, while the painted murals
that adorned the walls of the magnificent staircase resembled those
painted by Hogarth at nearby St Bartholomew's Hospital. Leading
from the hall were a series of grand apartments, including a lofty
dining room, measuring forty feet by twenty feet, a drawing room,
and several smaller reception areas.[2]

It was in these sumptuous surroundings that William hosted a series
of celebrated concerts in the 1770s and 80s, which were patronised by
members of the social elite. The mansion in Old Jewry is a testament
to William's professional success – and also perhaps evidence of his
ambition. Prosperity alone does not explain the purchase, for there
were plenty of renowned surgeons who did not buy mansions in the
City, and few who hosted elegant concerts attended by members of
the aristocracy. The move to Old Jewry, the advancement of William's
career, and his fondness for social elites indicate that he was a man
with aspirations.

He was certainly the most socially dextrous of the Sharp siblings.
Like his grandfather the archbishop, William possessed qualities
that endeared him to all classes of society. The following posthumous tribute is typical: 'so cheerful his temper, so affable his
address, so considerate and universal his attentions, that all who
beheld him, loved him'.[3] There was also a refinement about
William, both in appearance and manner, that is less apparent in
his brothers. This can be detected in Zoffany's painting of the
family, where the grace of William's figure as he stands at the
tiller contrasts with James's and John's more solid forms, and
Granville's nervous angularity. Despite the intertwining of William's

and James's lives, from their boyhood companionship as apprentices in London during the 1740s to their joint management of the parties and excursions that illuminated the lives of the siblings in the 1750s and 60s, William's social circle gradually extended beyond that of his brother.

It is telling that in the early days of their musical life in London, the brothers took it in turns to host the family concerts, but that as the years went by, they were held less and less frequently in Leadenhall Street. Following the purchase of Old Jewry in 1769, James's house was relegated to a venue for smaller family gatherings. James always attended the concerts in Old Jewry, and there is no suggestion that the slight divergence of their social paths led to any diminution of the closeness between the two brothers. Still it is inconceivable that the Old Jewry concerts could have been held in Leadenhall Street – or that the cream of society would have gone there.[4]

But in spite of the evidence to the contrary, William was not considered to be an ambitious man, either by himself or by those who knew him. When asked once to name his professional rivals, William replied, 'I was never the rival of any man.'[5] If asked to account for his achievements, he might have credited hard work, good fortune and God's providence, but with the implication that he had been the recipient, rather than the author, of his success. In a similar way, there is no suggestion that William plotted his social advancement. Those who knew William spoke warmly of his grace and sensibility, but without imputation that these qualities were feigned to solicit good opinion.[6] William was a genuinely kind, compassionate and warm-hearted man.

There was a reciprocity between William's professional and social success – for his acquaintance was a fruitful source of patients, just as his patients embellished his social circle. The qualities that endeared William to his friends were of equal value to his clients. Bolstered by his connections, and his graceful and well-bred manner, William became one of the most sought-after surgeons of the London elite. Like his contemporary, the great anatomist and obstetrician William Hunter, William was fortunately placed to take advantage of the increasing prestige of the surgical profession.

Arriving in London from Scotland in the early 1740s with few contacts, Hunter built up a fashionable obstetric practice with clients including the Pitts, Lady Ossory, the Fitzroys, the Earl of Sandwich, Lord North and Queen Charlotte. Hunter and William were both entrepreneurs: free from the constraints of institutional controls, they were able to build up their practices as they wished, exploiting the opportunities available in a buoyant market.[7] Prosperity contributed to their advancement. Conspicuous consumption, as exemplified by the purchase of an expensive carriage, or in William's case a mansion in the City, was not only pleasurable, but a highly effective advertisement of professional achievement. As the contemporary verse explained: 'The carriage marks the peer's degree / And almost tells the doctors' fee.' Both men used their wealth to engage in activities – Hunter became a collector, and William held fashionable concerts – which happily elided private passions with 'symbolic act[s] of assimilation into the values of high society'.[8]

Ultimately the success of both men depended on sheer hard work. Hunter ran an anatomical lecture course six days a week from October to May, in addition to his private practice. Though William never lectured, friends remarked on his 'indefatigable industry', and an appointments book dating from 1785 – when he was in his late fifties – gives an idea of the intensity of his schedule.[9] William regularly worked seven days a week, and saw between twenty-five and thirty patients a day. As patients were generally seen in their own homes in this period, and William's clients lived all over London, much of his day was spent travelling. On Sunday 8 February 1784, for example, he saw – amongst many others – 'Mrs Garos No. 14 Bentinck St Soho'; 'Mrs [W]'s little boy, Poultry'; 'Mrs Packington, Hoxton'; '[Luteridge] at Knigthsbridge'; 'Penton Highgate'; and 'Douglas Bedford Square'.

While William was clearly a competent surgeon – his client list being proof enough of that – he was not a revolutionary one. As far as we know, his only formal contribution to the development of surgery was a paper given to the Royal Society on 12 February 1767 on the subject of a 'New Method for treating Fractured Legs'. In an age without anaesthetic or antibiotics, when all surgical intervention was fraught with risk, it is possible that William's success flowed as

much from what he did not do, as from what he did. Whereas eighteenth-century surgery has generally been derided as causing more
harm than good, research into the performance of individual surgeons
has shown low fatality rates amongst those who 'sensibly respected
their limits'.[10] That William was one of the sensible ones in this regard
is suggested in *A Discourse Occasioned by the Death of William Sharp
Esq*, the published version of the oration given at his funeral: 'in the
treatment of cases to which the most summary measures are usually
applied, he employed himself in superseding, by easy and circuitous
steps, the necessity of extreme and hazardous experiments; and in
reducing the pain and inconvenience of the sufferer'.[11]

William's embodiment of the twin virtues of compassionate sensibility, and surgical restraint – what the writer of the *Discourse* termed
his 'tender and conservative purposes' – recommended him to the
very highest in the land. A memorial plaque in All Saints, Fulham,
where William is buried, refers to him as 'Surgeon to King George
III'. Though there is no reference to William in the Royal Appointment
Books, nor any formal record of his position, the evidence of the
plaque is supported by Zoffany's painting of the family, which shows
William in the 'Windsor' livery – a uniform established by George III
in 1762. Further support for a royal connection is provided by a letter
in the Sharp archive, written by the king on 3 September 1783, in which
he complains of unpleasant symptoms caused by eating 'luscious
pork'.[12] In a letter to his sister Judith dated 18 February 1799, William
recounts how 'On Wed.y last I was command by the Queen to attend
her Majesty at the Queens Palace, with Mr Keate' to consult on
Princess Amelia's knee.[13] Several instances of favour shown to the
Sharps by George III and Queen Charlotte from the early 1770s (and
related in subsequent chapters), provide further persuasive evidence
of William's professional relationship with the royal family.

For all the celebrity of his client list, and the comfort of his own
life, William did not become desensitised to the sufferings of the
London poor. The free surgery that William ran every morning in
Mincing Lane – and which he replicated at Old Jewry – was an attempt
to reconcile his own good fortune with the desperate poverty which
he witnessed every day as he went about his work. The compassion

which informed William's care of the rich was applied with even greater value to his treatment of the poor. The surgery is an expression of the urge to philanthropic action that was common to all the Sharps.

It is hardly first light when patients begin to arrive at the door of William's surgery in Old Jewry. By 8 o'clock, when the doors finally open, the line snakes back almost to the corner of Gresham Street. All the diseases of poverty and want are in evidence there: emaciated children with bandy legs queue patiently by the side of leaden-eyed mothers, behind beggars with weeping sores, and old men shaking in the grip of typhoid fever. Women in the last stages of pregnancy lean against the walls, jostled by syphilitic sailors and a carter whose head bleeds copiously from a blow by a horse's hoof. Apart from the baby who screams at his mother's shrunken breast, and the relentless hawking and spitting of a consumptive, the patients wait their turn in silence.

The Jonathan Strong case shows that the clinic was well known in the City, and illustrates the kind of assistance that William provided there. At a time when there was almost no free medical provision the benefit to the poor of the service offered by William can hardly be overstated.[14] The Mincing Lane, and later Old Jewry, surgery anticipated the dispensary movement, which developed in the 1770s with the aim of providing free outpatient care. The first dispensary opened in Red Lion Square in 1769 (four years after Strong's attendance at Mincing Lane), and they were widespread in London by the end of the century.

William also arranged for Jonathan Strong to be admitted to St Bartholomew's Hospital, where he was nursed back to health. Today there would be nothing impressive about a routine referral to hospital, but in the 1760s hospital places were limited and tightly controlled.[15] Anyone wishing to be admitted to St Bartholomew's could do so only by obtaining the support of a patron (usually a governor) with the right to present patients. Having obtained the necessary patronage, the applicant was then required to appear before a weekly hospital 'board' where their condition was assessed. If the ailment was considered to be curable, and the patient themselves sufficiently deserving, they would be admitted, subject to the payment of a small fee to cover the cost of linen and burial if required. William's leverage on the board of St Bartholomew's derived from his position as an assistant surgeon at the hospital, which he had held since 1755.

London hospitals retained three surgeons and three physicians, and a number of assistant surgeons and physicians, to treat the patients in their care.[16] The appointments were unpaid but conferred a range of benefits on the practitioner that included professional prestige, an additional income stream in the form of paying pupils, and the opportunity to develop skills and collaborate with colleagues.[17] For William at least, a hospital post also had a charitable dimension. Since the number of positions was tiny in proportion to the pool of eligible practitioners, and posts were held for life, appointments were few and far between and hotly contested. Appointees were elected by the governors of the hospital, and candidates campaigned much as they would in a political election, canvassing the support of individual governors and exploiting social and political connections.[18] The circumstances of William's election to the post of assistant surgeon, on 27 February 1755, are recorded in an entry in the Journal of St Bartholomew's Hospital. Of the six surgeons who applied for the position, all but William 'declined the Ballot'* so that he was 'unanimously elected'.

*

On 5 September 1765, four years before his move to the mansion in Old Jewry, William had married Catharine Barwick, the daughter of a London merchant.[19] At the time of the marriage William was thirty-six – thirteen years older than his bride. Catharine remains a shadowy figure in the Sharp story, despite her close association to its principal protagonists. She left behind her little with which to flesh out the bare facts of her life, and is scarcely more than a name in the Sharp archive. Only in Zoffany's portrait of the family is Catharine placed centre stage, and even here – poised and elegant in a pale blue

---

* It was normal for applicants to withdraw from the ballot when it was clear that they had garnered insufficient support to win.

riding habit with her daughter Mary in her arms – there is an air of detachment about her.

Catharine's epitaph, inscribed on the west end of the family tomb in All Saints, Fulham, does little to illuminate her life. It appears rather to reduce her to an ancillary role, of relevance only in relation to the lives of other people:

> The Conduct of this excellent Woman
> Under the various Relations of domestic Life
> Exhibited an amiable and edifying example
> Of that meek and quiet Spirit
> Which is, in the sight of God,
> a great Prize.

A little more colour is provided by a memorandum book kept by Catharine in the first few years of her marriage. Written in a confident and well-educated hand (and with none of the spelling mistakes that litter the journal of her sister-in-law Elizabeth), the book comprises an account of the expenses arising from her marriage. These include both those incidental to the marriage itself ('Licence 1.11.6'; 'Taylor's Bill for Myself'; 'Frock, washing Frock 5.14.7'; 'George for Boots'; 'Mrs Lodge's Servants'; '4 Favours') and the cost of refurbishing William's house in Mincing Lane.[20]

Like other well-to-do brides, Catharine committed to overhauling her husband's home, substituting pretty decorative schemes for the drab domestic inefficiencies of the bachelor establishment. The notebook itemises the expense of the refurbishment and furnishing of individual rooms, including the 'Common Parlour' ('9 chairs', 'Side Board Table', '2 Dining Tables', 'Breakfast Table'); the 'Best Parlour' ('6 Stuff'd Chairs', '2 Girandoles', 'a Pair China Candlesticks', 'Shepherd Playing on a Flute to a Shepherdess'); the 'Dressing Room' ('Toilet Table', 'Hanging 2 Bells', 'Writing Box'); and the 'Kitchen' ('Pewter', 'Brass', 'Gridiron', 'Bellows').

Catharine's memorandum book, and a private ledger dating from the 1810s, suggests that she was a careful and methodical woman, rigorous in her record-keeping, and a capable manager of the family home. Since the ideal wife in this period was required to be 'as prudent and economical as she was charming and genteel', and a methodical household was viewed almost by extension as a virtuous one, Catharine's talent for order was significant.[21] As the wife of a wealthy man with a large establishment, she was required to be an expert manager. This is evident in her superintendence of the building works described in her memorandum book, involving the management of numerous tradespeople ('Tho. Smelling, Glazier', 'Hannah Buschard, Plumber', 'Tho. Seagood, Plaisterer', 'Simon Wass, Painter', 'Will Robinson, Carpenter', 'Will Tovery, Mason'), and which she was presumably required to repeat on an even larger scale following the purchase of Old Jewry four years later.[22]

Beyond the exceptional circumstance of building works, Catharine was also the full-time manager of a team of servants whose co-operation was essential to the successful running of the home. The recruitment, retention and management of domestic staff were almost universal tribulations for gentlewomen in this period. Catharine, like other women of her class, was absolutely dependent on her servants, and therefore subject to the whims and inconsistencies of their behaviour. Given the often humiliating work conditions, long hours, and poor rewards associated with domestic service it is no wonder that servants constituted an unreliable workforce.[23] For a woman such as Catharine, hardly a week went by when she was not 'reeling from a servant's flight, arranging temporary relief, procuring replacements or training new applicants'.[24] Even in periods of relative calm, the mistress of the household was required to keep a continual superintendence over her staff. And she must do all this while giving the appearance of a smoothly running home, un-beset by crises and abscondings, for 'she was expected to conceal her efforts behind a cloak of gracious nonchalance'.[25]

Spare a thought then for Catharine on the morning of a Sharp concert in Old Jewry. Up before dawn, she has, as I imagine it, barely finished dressing when the first hammer blow strikes. As her maid fastens the top button of Catharine's yellow silk morning gown, she informs her, with maddening insouciance, that the kitchen girl has absconded overnight. Later, in the cavernous basement kitchen, the

cook, wild-eyed, flings about the pots and pans, and threatens to leave
if a replacement is not found upon the instant. Catharine, desperate,
scribbles a note to her sister-in-law, and a boy runs with it to Leadenhall
Street. A temporary kitchen maid having been secured, the cook
retreats to her labours with sullen resignation.

Catharine meanwhile is negotiating a dispute between a housemaid
and a casual worker whom she has employed to do a day's ironing.
She can still hear their bickering as she retreats upstairs to discuss
flower arrangements with a waiting florist. Then a visitor is announced,
and Catharine must take tea with serenity while the sounds of
impending chaos erupt about her. The visitor safely dispatched,
Catharine returns to the fray, managing squabbles, supervising
cleaning, counting chairs, checking guest lists and greeting the confectioner who arrives weighed down by jellies and muscadine ices. The
hall is barely ready when the musicians turn up, and the only recently
restored calm disintegrates into a confusion of scraping chairs and
squawking instruments, and the babble of high-pitched voices.
Somehow – she has no idea how she manages it – Catharine is ready
when the first guests arrive, and can hang on William's arm with an
easy grace, as if she does not have a care in the world.

What little else we know about Catharine concerns the ordeal of
her constant, and almost constantly unsuccessful, attempts to have
children. In her diary entry for 30 July 1773, Elizabeth notes: 'Dear Sisr.
W safe in her bed, but with her usual ill luck. A fine child but still
boarne.'[26] The extent of that ill luck is brought home by Elizabeth's
account of Catharine's only successful delivery, on 19 April 1778: 'my
dear Bro. and Sisr. W was blessed with a little girl, which was named
Mary. I was with my dear Sisr. at this time, the only time of her
success, after 18 or 20 times she had been with child, that this great
blessing was felt most thankfully by us all.'[27]

*

A man of exceptional kindness, warmth, generosity and compassion,
William inspired love in all who knew him. He was also socially adept,
and the favour shown to him by the upper classes facilitated the Sharp

family's rise in society. Professional advancement not only cemented William's relationship with the elite, it also made him rich. But rather than being spoiled by his success, William counterbalanced wealth, prestige and the demands of an increasingly glittering social life with social responsibility. His free surgery and position at St Bartholomew's Hospital suggests the facility with which he reconciled professional aspiration with a commitment to doing good. Though William's career presupposes an element of ambition, it was not of the self-serving kind. The purchase of Old Jewry, for example, was almost certainly motivated by a desire to burnish the Sharp family concerts in the splendour of the mansion's ground-floor apartments. As such it was intimately connected to, and almost indivisible from, William's passionate devotion to music and his family, and is an example of his urge to share his prosperity with those he loved.

Part Three

(1770–1777)

A View of the PRINCES HOUSE at Kew.

Published according to Act of Parliament, by G. Kearsly, N.º 46. Fleet Street, June 1.ˢᵗ 1776.

15

Kew

As the prow of the *Apollo* noses through the wooden arch of Kew Bridge, a gust of wind whisks a sheet of music from the outstretched hand of the conductor Felice Giardini.[1] Up it whirls, round and round, until not even the sharp-sighted cabin boy can make out its shape against the flying clouds. The same gust catches the sheet of the great square canvas sail, and the barge gathers pace.[2] In dappled sun and shade, ladies in muslin dresses hang on to their fluttering hats, while the red standard strains at its tether. As the *Apollo* shoulders the tip of the small island known as Brentford Ait, Giardini takes his place between the cellist John Crosdill, and the shining flank of the harpsichord. Behind him, Redmond Simpson eases a reed into the slim neck of his hautboy, the French horns boom, and Granville trills on the double flute. When Giardini puts his fiddle to his chin, there is a moment of quiet – and then the opening notes of Handel's aria 'Volo pronto, e lieto il core' float across the water.[3]

The wind carries the music southwards, through the open window of the Prince of Wales's house which stands back from the river on the northern tip of Richmond Gardens.[4] George, the Prince of Wales, who is nearly eight, and his younger brother Frederick, are listening with only half attention to the monotonous Latin incantations of their schoolmaster. As the melody curls round the schoolroom, the boys glance up at each other and smile. In a moment, and with only the most perfunctory explanation to their tutor, the boys are running down to the river. They pass their younger brothers, William, who is four, and Edward, who is so little that he is still in long dresses, and their governess Lady Charlotte Finch, who are also hurrying towards the music. The four little princes* stand side by side on the riverbank and gaze at the *Apollo* with rapt attention.

From her vantage point on the raised red stern of the *Apollo*, Elizabeth can see the princes clearly. George, the eldest, is dressed in a moss-green jacket and breeches with white stockings, and is distinguishable by the garter that crosses his chest. Beside him, and with his arm lightly resting on George's shoulder, stands Frederick, who wears a teal suit picked out in glittering silver thread. William, in red, bounces up and down in excitement, while the long white skirts of Edward's dress stand out against the folds of Lady Charlotte's grey silk.[5] Behind them, Elizabeth can see the avenue of elms that leads from the river to the Dutch House, and the exquisite landscape of the royal gardens, and in the distance the fretted balconies of a Chinese pagoda rise high above the treeline.[6]

The boatmen steer the *Apollo* towards the riverbank, and the barge lies at anchor a few yards from where the princes are standing, Then, cupping his hands around his mouth, William Sharp asks the boys 'whether Their Majesties have any requests for the band?' There is great deal of whispering and conferring in the royal party, before George replies politely, 'If they could please play "The Miller of Dee"?' Giardini raises his bow, catches the eye of his musicians, and the song begins: 'There dwelt a miller, hale and bold, beside the river Dee / He danced and sang from morn till night, no lark so blithe as he.'[7]

The serenading of the four little princes on the banks of the Thames at Kew is recorded by Elizabeth in her diary entry for 5 August 1770. According to her account, the royal party 'stud for near half an hour, & appeard much pleased and sent to request 2 or 3 different songs they knew, which was imediately sung'.[8]

A few days later, on 8 August 1770, the Sharps embark on a second water party. Giardini reassembles his band for the occasion, and during the morning they have 'a little Rehersel' on board the *Apollo* while it

---

* The four princes are George, Prince of Wales (1762–1830), the future George IV; Frederick, Duke of York (1763–1827); William (1765–1837) who was later William IV; and Edward (1767–1820), the future father of Queen Victoria.

is moored by London Bridge. The sound of the music brings out 'a great number of boats with companey' which fan out behind the *Apollo* as it glides upriver. Every sort of vessel is there: from the opulent pleasure barge, gaudy with brightly coloured awnings, to the modest yawl, and the wherry hired by the hour. Sails billow, and boatmen sweat over their oars as they strain to keep up with the *Apollo*. The hulls of even the most modest craft are crammed to the gunnels with cutlery and china, crates of fowls, and salads, and Madeira.⁹ The river is so full that shallops jostle wherries, and parties in separate boats call to each other across the water.

Soon they are leaving the crowded waters of the City and sailing westwards, past market gardens and open fields, and the sleepy river-side villages of Chelsea, Fulham and Putney. As they approach Kew, Giardini signals his musicians to stop playing: for the Sharps have resolved 'not to have any musick till after we had passed the Gardens'. But their discretion is misplaced, for the arrival of the *Apollo* has been eagerly anticipated by the residents of the Prince of Wales's house. Somehow 'notis' has been given to the princes:

> & in a moment we see them all at the door, bowing very low, which obliged us to return and they immediately came skiping to the waterside. Three very fine boys and the Princess Royal*. My Bros. sent to the Prince of Wailes to say what they would play, & mentioned the two songs he had asked for the last time, which he seemed pleased with, & beged if it would not be two much trouble, that we would finish with a hunting Tune, with French horns.¹⁰

This time, Giardini and his band serenade the princes for an hour, before the *Apollo* continues on its way to Richmond. Here the anchor is weighed, and the flotilla clusters about the *Apollo*, while everyone takes tea. The Sharps invite the company in adjoining boats to come on board, and the ladies tuck up their dresses as they clamber in and

---

* Princess Charlotte (1766–1828).

out of the shallop that shuttles between the *Apollo* and its satellites. When the last passenger is returned to his wherry, and every teacup is stowed, the party turns homewards. As they pass Kew, Elizabeth sees George III, Queen Charlotte and the queen's brother the Prince of Mecklenburg, sitting on the river terrace under a large tree.[11] Luckily, as she recalls, there happened 'half a bars rest' which allows the performers time to take off their hats in respectful salute.

There then proceeds an impromptu royal command performance, which begins appropriately enough with 'God Save the King'. Next up are Frances and Judith singing Purcell's 'Let Caesar and Urania live', followed by Granville with a double flute concerto, accompanied by James on the serpent. Notwithstanding the quality of the professional musical contingent, the Sharps are clearly not backward in coming forward. At last the professionals are allowed a look-in: Felice Giardini begins what Elizabeth coyly refers to as the 'favoret' song. However, the mysterious melody is only halfway through when the heavens open and 'a thunder storme began with so heavey a shewer, as put everything in a hurry'.

But the Sharps are prepared for the vagaries of a British summer. James has designed an extendable 'house' which folds out from the main cabin, and in a moment it is covering the performers and their instruments. Next the family turn their attentions to the king and queen who have 'only the Tree to chelter them'. Quick as a flash, the Sharp brothers jump into the shallop, detach its removable cabin (also designed by James) and carry it up the bank towards the royal party. As Elizabeth reports: 'if the servants & attendance had not all rune for coats and clokes, could have held it over them, till it was fair'.[12]

The shower is soon over, and a carriage arrives to take the royal party home. But George and Charlotte have no intention of leaving, for the frisson of the storm has only added to their enjoyment of the music. Taking his cue, Giardini catches the attention of his musicians, and the performance resumes. An hour and a half later, the band is still playing when the ominous rumble of thunder foretells another downpour. This time the musicians strike up a second rendition of 'God Save the King', and the Sharps, their guests, and all the company on their boats, sing together in chorus. There is a final tribute to the king, and at each 'Huraugh!' George lifts his hat in recognition.[13]

The two water parties described in Elizabeth's journal entry for August 1770 continue the tradition of the river excursions recorded in William's 'Boat Book' seventeen years earlier. Though the later expeditions are far grander in scale, the 'scheems' resemble each other closely. The *Apollo* barge which carried the '2 Miss Coles, Mrs Hutton' and 'Miss Cotterell' to drink tea at Fulham on 6 May 1753 was still the vessel of choice for the Sharp expedition to Kew on 5 August 1770. On both occasions the party consisted of members of the Sharp family and their friends, though the guests who graced the deck of the *Apollo* in 1753 may not have felt quite at their ease with 'those of the highest and most distinguished rank' who were their equivalents in 1770.

Similarly, though we do not know upon what delicacies the guests dined as the *Apollo* progressed towards Kew in August 1770, we can be certain that they were as least as fine as the dinner of 'Biscuits, Chockolate, Bread, Milk, Butter, Fowler, Ham, Beef, Sallet & Raddishes, Oil & vinegar, Ven[ison] Pye' that was provided to the party of fourteen who went to Maidenhead and Oxford in May 1753.[14] Tea was served in August 1770 as it had been on the voyage to Wandsworth Creek seventeen years before, and also no doubt some equivalent of the 'Shrubb' and 'Cupp' that enlivened the party on the earlier occasion. The logistics of the 1770 schemes were at least as daunting as those involved in the river parties of William's bachelorhood, though perhaps in the flush of his prosperity he had others to assist him in the marshalling of boats, furnishings, provisions and entertainment.

The 'Hautboys & Bassoon' and 'Flutes & Vox Humana' that entertained the guests on a voyage to Hampton Court on 4 June 1753 were merely a soupçon of the musical delights of the water parties of the 1770s. Felice Giardini, who presided over the band on the *Apollo*, was one of the brightest stars of the London musical scene in the 1750s and 60s. He achieved fame first as a solo violinist, and later as director of the Italian Opera in Covent Garden, and conductor of the concert series at the Pantheon in Oxford Street. For the Sharps to obtain Giardini's services was nothing short of a coup.[15]

The Sharp papers are not forthcoming on the identity of the musicians playing in Giardini's band, but help is provided by the testimony of William Shield, another celebrated violinist and composer, who first came into the Sharp orbit as a young man living in Durham. John, the eldest of the Sharp brothers, invited Shield to the 'weekly performances of sacred music' which he hosted during his residences in the city. When the composer moved to London, John gave him a letter of introduction to his brother William, which 'proved a passport to his excellent concerts in the Old Jewry'. In his recollections of the Sharp family provided to Prince Hoare, Shield gives a glowing account of the water parties:

A magnificent barge, in which the three harmonious brothers, their relatives and friends, occasionally made extensive excursions on the Thames, attracted universal admiration. The ears of listening auditors on the crowded banks were gratified, not with common water-music, but with the more mellifluous tones of stringed instruments, produced by the expressive fingers of professors so highly excellent that I cannot withhold from you an alphabetical arrangement of their names:

Abel	Cramer	Park
Bach	Crosdill	Paxton
Barthelemon	Giardini	Simpson
Borghi	Hay	Vincent[16]
Cervetto	La Motte	

Shield's list is a litany of the finest musicians playing in London in this period, and gives some idea of the prestige associated with the Sharp concerts. Of particular note is the apparent willingness of performers of the repute of Johann Christian Bach (son of the great Johann Sebastian), Carl Friedrich Abel and Wilhelm Cramer to overcome the professional musician's instinctive disdain for 'common water-music'. If performance on water was not enough to stifle Bach's and Abel's enthusiasm for the 'scheem', then the prospect of playing with the amateur musicians of the Sharp family can hardly have been an inducement to these musical luminaries.

Professional musicians were generally patronising about the efforts of their amateur counterparts, and Judith's and Frances's rendering of 'Let Caesar and Urania live' and Granville's 'concerto on the 2 fleutes' might have been intolerable to the ears of a virtuoso. That Bach, Abel, Cramer and Giardini were prepared to play in the water schemes suggests either that the Sharps were musicians of a standard within the tolerance of their professional sensibilities, or that their fondness for the family and enjoyment of the event was sufficient to overcome their artistic reservations. Probably both came out in the Sharps' favour.

For all the closeness of the connection between the water parties recorded in William's 'Boat Book' in 1753, and those described in Elizabeth's journal entry in August 1770, the line of continuity is frustrated by the lack of evidence of water parties in the seventeen years that separate them. Beyond Elizabeth's description of 'a party of pleasure' on the river from Hampton Court to Richmond Hill in 1758, to which the Prowse family were invited; and her laconic 'We all went a Warter Party with My Bros. & Sisrs. Sharps' of 25 July 1768, the Sharp archive is all but silent on the subject.[17] For this reason, it is necessary to rely on inferences drawn from Elizabeth's description of the August 1770 expeditions.

Most notable is her comment in relation to the second 'scheem' that the music 'brought a great number of boats with companey then I ever remembered to attend our boat, they had provided themselves with provition for the day'. This suggests not only that the August 1770 water parties were but the latest of a series of similar excursions, but that the expeditions were of sufficient renown to attract the attention of a large number of followers. Since the owners of the accompanying boats had had sufficient notice of the scheme to provide themselves with provisions for the day, the Sharp water party must already have been a well-known feature of the London season.

The water parties at Kew are a vivid representation of the siblings' rise in fame and fortune since their arrival in London more than twenty years before. The virtuosity of Giardini's band, the flotilla of boats that accompany the *Apollo*, and the confidence with which the Sharps engage with royalty, suggests their burgeoning social status. During the 1770s, the family's carefully nurtured relationship with George III and Queen Charlotte strengthens further, and becomes the defining emblem of the Sharps' remarkable success.

16

Canals

At half past eleven on the morning of 15 September 1770, James arrives at the gate of Richmond Lodge, the summer home of the royal family, for a private audience with George III. A soldier in a red coat and white stockings steps out of his sentry box to nod him through, and James walks alone up the broad gravel path to the front of the house. Framed by the foliage of the Old Deer Park, and warmed by the September sun, the rosy-pink brick of the facade has a graceful aspect. As he stands at the front door, James pauses a moment to smooth the creases of his coat and wipe his feet, before tugging at the bell-rope. The page who opens the door is expecting him, and James is shown into a small library. After the bright sunshine of the September morning, it takes him a little time to adjust to the dimness of the interior. French windows, shrouded by dark green damask curtains, look out onto the garden, and the floor is covered by a richly patterned turkey carpet. Scattered about the room are the paraphernalia of an enquiring mind: a globe stands by the furthest window, there is a telescope, and various astronomical instruments of a kind that James has never seen before, and the tables are covered with maps, prints and drawings.[1]

James had requested the interview as a means of securing royal support for a project known as the 'London' canal. James was the driving force behind this new waterway, which was intended to bypass the meanders and navigational hazards of the Thames, to allow faster and cheaper access to the metropolis. The ironmonger returned to Richmond Lodge on 27 October for a second audience, and on both occasions he transcribed their conversation as soon as he got home. Appended to his transcript for the first meeting is the following caveat: 'I cannot be sure that what I have wrote are exactly the words spoken or that all the questions were in the order sett down but I am very sure the substance and purport of every question and answer was to this effect.'[2]

James does not explain how he obtained his hearings with the king, but it is apparent that he seized the opportunity provided by the Sharps' impromptu performances for the royal family at Kew. The musical delights of Giardini's band, and the charm of the water concert, seem to have made a strong impression on George III, for it was later reported to Elizabeth that 'a great personage was pleased with my bros. music upon the water and that he had often talked of it'.[3] There is nothing to suggest that James knew, or had had any personal dealings with, George III prior to August 1770.[4] Yet he lost no time in following up on his advantage: barely six weeks elapsed between the second water scheme at Kew, and James's first meeting with the monarch on 15 September.[5]

James emerges from his transcript of the audiences both as an engaging conversationalist, and a tactician of considerable skill. It is evident from even a cursory reading of the manuscript that it is James who is in control of the interview. Even so, he never oversteps the mark, and the persuasive force of his presentation is tempered by a carefully modulated deference. Meanwhile James's personality – energetic, fearless, brimming with enthusiasm – radiates from the page. The very fact of the ironmonger's ability to transcribe a lengthy conversation from memory, gives an idea of his mental faculties.

The audiences each lasted well over an hour, so it is perhaps not surprising that the discussion strayed beyond canals to subjects as diverse as engineering, navigation, wheels, barges, river encroachments and roads. Both men had a practical intelligence, and lively and enquiring minds, so it was natural that there should be a sympathy of interest between them. In the course of the September interview, for example, the king asked James about his ironmongery ('I suppose then you are very full of business at this time?'), and they considered the effect of political developments on international trade.[6] Much of the second interview was taken up by James's exposition of the mechanics of wheel size as applied to the state of the nation's roads: 'if a good-sized horse draws from a wheel of 6 foot high, and an obstacle lays before it, a part of the force will be lost in pulling downwards and pressing against the ground; but if he draws from a wheel of 2 feet high, he will draw upwards nearly by an elevation of 25, in a proper direction to pass it over the obstacle that lays before the wheel'.[7]

As the memory of the water scheme at Kew was still fresh in the king's mind, it was natural that the conversation should turn to music. Here there was an absolute affinity between the two men, for both came from musical families, and were themselves devoted to music. The Princess Royal, who as a little girl stood with her brothers on the riverbank listening to the music of Giardini's band, wrote in 1788 that 'A love of music to distraction runs through our family'.[8] The king told the author and courtier Fanny Burney at their first meeting that: 'To me it appears quite as strange to meet people with no ear for music, and cannot distinguish one air from another, as to meet with people who are dumb'.[9]

George's musical tastes were among the subjects discussed at the first audience with James in September 1770. The king began by confiding his view that the 'Old Musick particularly of Corelli' was superior to the music of the present day, which he considered 'too quick and hurrying'. To this James answered diplomatically that the present style of music was indeed very rapid, though there were in his view 'many fine compositions mixed with these movements'. There was then a consideration of the service at St Paul's Cathedral, which both agreed was 'sometimes very delightful but is frequently spoild by being done too fast'. Having considered the various merits ('I think Mr Cooper has the finest voice of any of them') and demerits ('Mr Hayes is a pleasing singer if he did not sing so through his nose') of the choristers, they concluded by agreeing that the service was too long, and that it was a pity that 'the Litany could not be done at another time'.[10]

With the melodies of the water concert still playing in his ears, the king was eager to ask after the various members of the Sharp family who had performed with Giardini on the deck of the *Apollo*. 'Pray,' he began, 'which of your Brothers plays upon the two flutes?' After considering Granville's instrumental and vocal talents, the conversation turned to James himself: 'O tis you that play the serpent is it?' The king intimated an interest in the mechanics of the instrument, and James showed him a mouthpiece which he happened to have in his pocket. The ironmonger explained that 'it is of the shape of the Trumpet Mouth piece only bigger'. This was a happy association for George, who said he loved the trumpet 'the most of any instrument whatever'.[11]

The king was also inquisitive about the *Apollo*. To his question: 'I like the Contrivance in your own Barge of lengthening out the house, how came you to think of such a thing?', James replied: 'Necessity obliged us to have something of this kind; for our Musick has the best effect in the open Air; and it was not possible to remove the Harpsichord and instruments so soon as was necessary in hasty showers but this contrivance answers our purpose extremely well.' This was not enough detail for George III, who enquired: 'Have you windows to that part that draws out can you make it quite secure from the weather?' James explained: 'We have windows fitted to each opening, and by means of corks upon the Edge, are made to take in and out very easily, and the whole made as close as the other house in any weather.'[12]

Despite the ease with which the conversation flowed on topics extraneous to the London canal, James was adept at steering the discussion to his own advantage. Royal approval for the projected waterway was a prize of incalculable value to James, and he employed a range of tactics to achieve it. Part of his strategy was to inspire George III with the revolutionary potential of canals, and he laid the groundwork by sending maps to Richmond in advance of the first interview. The ruse was successful, for when James arrived in Richmond Lodge, he was happy to note that George had 'one of the Plans I had sent then laying upon the table before him'. Later in the interview, James 'laid before His Majesty the Map of England with the line of all the Canals mark'd and ... pointed out to him how they would unite the Three great Rivers of Thames, Severn and Trent, with all which he seemed much pleased'.[13]

The goal of an integrated transport network lay at the heart of James's case for the new waterway. It was apparent to James, and to his fellow canal enthusiasts, that the country's antiquated transport system was unfit to meet the demands of the industrial and agricultural revolutions. Though many of the principal cities and towns of the country were sited on navigable rivers, smaller communities and new areas of settlement such as those associated with industrial processes founds themselves in the gaps between river and port. Transporting goods to and from such places required road carriage, which was often prohibitively expensive.[14] James recognised the potential of artificial waterways to integrate previously isolated communities into a co-ordinated national network. The value of canals was particularly apparent in the case of inland coalfields, for which they acted as a kind of 'golden key', unlocking their sooty treasures for transport 'far beyond the point of extraction'.[15]

It was in the conveyance of bulky and heavy commodities such as coal, grain, agricultural lime, wheat and building materials that canals represented such a distinct advantage over other forms of transport.[16] Carriage of these goods by water cost a fraction of the charge made by road hauliers for an equivalent distance. By the 1760s the economies of small towns and villages were dependent on coal not merely for domestic consumption but to fuel an increasing range of industries. For those without access to a traversable river, the cost of coal was prohibitive which meant that local industry was stifled, and the poor could not afford to heat their houses.

For this reason, much of the impetus behind the construction of canals was to provide affordable coal. A letter written on 25 February 1769 by a promoter of the Coventry canal, in answer to the objections of its opponents, illustrates the transforming power of the new waterways:

I beg to ask the opposers of the navigation from Coventry to Oxford, whether they think of all the inconveniences they have pointed out, are equal to the starving to death many hundreds of poor inhabitants in the Inland Counties where coals may be brought by such a navigation? ... There are many places near

Banbury, Brackley, Bicester, etc. where coals cannot possibly be
had at any price to supply the necessary demand for them, where
the strong and able poor have long subsisted by hedge-breaking;
the wood is almost gone for fuel ... and in short there are no
materials by which the poor can procure even a wretched fire.
In these parts, I believe they often perish by cold, though their
cases do not appear in print.[17]

Though the Newry Canal, completed in March 1742, and the Sankey
Brook Canal, partly opened in 1757, foreshadowed the dawning of the
canal age, it was the opening of the Bridgewater Canal in 1761 that
sparked the revolution. Built by the Duke of Bridgewater to transport
coal from his collieries in Worsley to the centre of Manchester, the
canal captured the contemporary imagination, both for the audacious
brilliance of the design and construction, and for its efficiency in
providing cheap coal to a town that had previously been reliant on
supplies brought in from local coalfields on waggon and pack horse.
The Bridgewater inspired the pioneers of the great canal construction
projects of the 1760s and 70s, including the Trent & Mersey, the Stafford
& Worcestershire, the Coventry, and the Oxford.[18]

The canal projects of the 1760s and 70s posed an engineering challenge of vast scale and complexity, and required engineers to evolve
new structural techniques. Tunnels, aqueducts, embankments,
cuttings, locks, inclined planes and canal lifts were designed and built
as the need arose. Visitors crowded construction sites to witness the
work at first hand, and tours de force such as the Harecastle Tunnel
on the Trent & Mersey became objects of wonder for the tourists
who flocked there.[19] Josiah Wedgwood's description of the flight of
locks on the Duke of Bridgewater's canal at Runcorn is characteristic
of the reverence inspired by the new waterways:

I was quite astonish'd at the vastness of the plan and the great-
ness of the stile in the execution. The walls of the Locks are
truly admirable, both for strength and beauty of workmanship
... to behold Ten of these Locks all at a view, with their Gates,
Aqueducts, Cisterns, Sluices, Bridges &&, the whole seems to

be the work of the Titans, rather than the production of our Pigmy race of beings.[20]

These engineering marvels were central to James's attempts to convince George III of the value of canals. Spreading out his plans on the library table, during their audience in September 1770, the ironmonger took George on a virtual journey: 'I shew'd him [James] Brindley's Canals, and pointed out the most material parts of the Duke of Bridgewaters canals, particularly at Barton Bridge where the canal is carried over the Navigable River, and att [Lynn] where the Canal is cut through a solid Rock ... and att Loombrook where a small River runs first upon the Ground; perpendicularly over that, upon an Arch ... over that the Canal passes.'

George never travelled beyond the south and west of Britain, so James's evocation of the industrialising heartlands of his kingdom had a particular fascination for him. James was quick to apprehend this, and seized the opportunity of the second audience in October 1770 to present the king with a 'small book' that he had produced especially for the occasion. This 'very neatly bound' volume contained material extrapolated from *A Six Months' Tour through the North of England* by the agriculturalist Arthur Young, and included 'plates describing the different parts of the Duke of Bridgewaters Canals' illuminating the feats of engineering described by James in the first interview.[21]

For James – as for Josiah Wedgwood – the experience of a canal construction site must have been exhilarating. I imagine him ankle-deep in the freshly dug earth of an embankment, or the sloughy clay of a canal bed, with the sound of pick and shovel ringing about him. Now he is peering down the mouth of a newly sunk shaft, marvelling at the technical ingenuity of a steam pump, or reeling back at the reverberating boom of a miner's gunpowder charge. Noon finds him with a gang of bronze-necked cutters, discussing the merits of Carne's cutting machine, or the relative benefits of scoops and shovels.[22] James is pleased to see his own navigation wheelbarrow in use, though a possible modification comes to mind as he watches a navvy labouring through clay with a heavy load.[23] He is still musing on the ramifications of a tilt to the axis of the wheel, when he bumps into the assistant

engineer, and spends the rest of the afternoon in pleasant contemplation of the structural complexities of a half-built aqueduct.

Given James's penchant for revolutionary technology, and the quickness with which he grasped its potential for social and economic
change, it is no wonder that he was a canal enthusiast of the most
diehard kind. He was also motivated, in true Sharp style, and to a
greater degree than was common in his collaborators, by the philanthropic potential of the new waterways. In a pamphlet dated December
1773 written in the form of an address to the Common Council of
the City of London (of which James was a member), he advocated
the construction of a canal between Moorfields and Waltham Abbey
in Essex, emphasising the importance of the project not merely to
the interests of the commercial sector of the city, but to alleviating
the plight of the poor. 'It is our Duty,' he argued, 'it is Justice; it
is the greatest of all Charity, to impart to Man the Means of earning
his Bread; it is Charity to our Country; it is Charity to Mankind.'[24]

It was his concern for the public welfare that informed James's
views on the funding and ownership of canals. He disliked the subscription model favoured by most canal promotion schemes on the grounds
that 'subscribers are always looking after their private gain instead of
the improvement of the Navigation'.[25] In his audience with the king
in September 1770, James expressed his disapproval of the methods
of ownership exercised by the owners of the newly built Birmingham
canal, claiming that they had pocketed the proceeds of an increase in
value of shares in the waterway at the expense of its users: 'if this
additional value had been expended upon the Canal instead of falling
into private pockets, it would have been much more noble than it is'.[26]
James's preferred model for the funding of canals was a system of
annuities payable against the value of future tolls.

James's involvement with the London canal dates from the late
1760s, when he attended a meeting of 'Gentlemen of Berkshire' to
consider a survey of a proposed canal between Sonning and Monkey
Island near Maidenhead, recently undertaken by the celebrated canal
engineer James Brindley.[27] James later explained to George III how in
the course of the meeting, the Berkshire gentlemen 'disagreed
amongst themselves, and in all probability the Scheme would have

ended here, as Mr Brindley was about to take his men from the Survey
and go home'. But James, who had 'heard with great pleasure of the
intended Canal', was not prepared to see the project 'fall to the ground'.
Taking matters into his own hands, he commissioned Brindley to
continue his survey to Isleworth, which was then a village outside
London, and canvassed support for the project in the City.[28]

In June 1770, Brindley presented the Common Council with a plan
for a 'London' canal, that connected to the waterway proposed by the
'Gentlemen of Berkshire' at Monkey Island, and extended for seventeen miles in an easterly direction to Isleworth. In his evidence to a
committee of the Common Council in June 1770, Brindley explained
that the 'expence of taking a Vessel of 100 or 120 tons from Isleworth
to Sunning, and back again to Isleworth is £80 and sometimes more;
which, by the Canal at the Tonnage proposed, will be £16 and may
easily be performed in fifteen Hours ... in the present Navigation of
the River, they are three weeks in going up, and near as long in coming
down, often to the great Loss and Disappointment of the Proprietor
in the Damage of his Goods'.[29]

It was at this point that James sought his audience with George III,
with a view to obtaining royal approval for the project. The king
appears to have been enthusiastic about the scheme, at least according
to the evidence of James's transcripts. But the imprimatur of the
monarch proved to be insufficient. Notwithstanding the obvious merits
of the scheme, James's relentless lobbying, and the support of the
Common Council, the London canal project faltered. A petition for
a bill to construct the canal, with two branches to the Thames at
Windsor and Staines, was presented to Parliament in 1771, but failed
to secure sufficient support.[30] In his audience with George III in
September 1770, James identified the 'chief opposition' to the project
as coming from the 'Millers and Lock holders, and the great Towns
upon the Banks of the River' who feared that 'the making of the
Canal will be the total neglect of the Old River'.[31]

Following the disappointment of the Isleworth project, James threw
his energies into the scheme to build a canal between Moorfields and
Waltham Abbey on the River Lea. His December 1773 pamphlet
addressing the Common Council attempted to persuade the governing

bodies of the City that canals offered as great an advantage to London and the south-east as they did to those areas of the country, such as the Midlands and the north-west, where they currently flourished.

In enumerating the advantages of the Waltham Abbey to Moorfields canal, James paid particular attention to the potential of the new waterway to ease overcrowding on the Thames. Things had come to a desperate pass on the river, not only on account of the increase in quantity of traffic, but because of the contraction of the river channel caused by detritus that 'is continually carried into it, by the Sewers' and by the encroachment of 'Embankments' and 'Causeways' – so much so that according to James, 'it is no uncommon thing to see whole Tiers of Ships forced from their Moorings one upon another, and seldom a Tide passes without Accidents by Vessels running foul of others'.[32]

In addition to the possibility of relieving congestion on the Thames, the new canal offered many of the benefits traditionally associated with artificial waterways, including 'a continual Supply of Provisions of every kind', the stimulation of economic activity in the areas served by the canal, and cheap passenger transport.[33]

James's pamphlet is an eloquent exposition of the value of the new waterways, and stands as a testimony both to his expertise in this area of communications technology, and his passionate commitment to its cause. A later appendix, which sets out in detail the projected toll revenue of the new canal, gives some indication of the amount of time, thought and effort which James invested in the project.[34] Given his commitment to the campaign for the two new London waterways, and his knowledge of the 'Progress of the Canal Navigations' in the country as a whole, it is no surprise that he was seen as an expert in the field by his contemporaries.[35]

During his audience with George III on 27 October 1770, James observed: 'The pains I have taken in this matter brings everybody to me who have anything to propose in this way.'[36] Indeed in the few weeks that had elapsed since his first visit to the king, James had been besieged by calls from individuals seeking assistance with their canal projects, including one 'with a plan for a Canal from Lechlade to Gloucester, which he says may easily be done', and another looking 'to continue the Canal near the River Kennet, in a direct line from Reading to Newberry, and from thence to Hungerford, Marlborough, Calne, Chippenham and ... Bath'.[37]

Given James's exertions in the cause of the development of the Waltham Abbey waterway, its failure must have come as a crushing blow. Though the details of the collapse of the project are not known, it is likely that it was the victim of the same 'ill-judged and interested opposition' that frustrated the London canal. In both cases opposition to the schemes was fuelled by the north-eastern coalmasters who feared a challenge to their monopoly in the supply of coal by sea to London and the south-east.[38] For all his efforts James could not compete with the wealth and power of the coal lobby, whose influence over the parliamentary committees charged with considering the schemes ensured that no significant amount of coal ever reached the capital via canals during the Industrial Revolution, and the coastal supply line retained its dominance for the rest of the century. In fact due to the comparatively advanced state of the road network in the south-east, as well as the power of the coal lobby, London and its hinterland remained one of the few areas of the country to be deprived of the benefit of an extensive canal network.[39]

James left no record of his feelings in the aftermath of the collapse of his beloved London canal schemes. No doubt he raged against the backward thinking and vested interests that had stymied the projects. As a born innovator, the failure of others to see the benefits of a revolutionary new technology would have been almost incomprehensible to him. But the bitterness of the failure does not detract from the efforts he made to bring about great change.

James's transcripts of his audiences with George III are one of the great treasures of the Sharp archive. The ironmonger emerges as a man of remarkable energy, dexterity and acumen. In addition, the transcripts provide a rare glimpse of the more intangible elements of the Sharps' social and professional success: the charm, charisma and affability that were so valued by their contemporaries, but which have otherwise left little permanent mark on the historical record.

17

Radical

The scene is the King's Presence Chamber, St James's Palace, on the morning of 21 November 1770. As the clock on the gatehouse strikes eleven, George III takes his place in a high-backed upholstered chair at one end of the long room. Above him extends an immense crimson canopy picked out with silver embroidery. Shafts of sunlight fall on the bare floorboards, and on the tapestries that line the otherwise plain grey panelled walls. George sits for a few moments in quiet contemplation, cupping his chin in his right hand. Though there is nothing handsome about his fleshy face and protruding eyes, the king has a steady open expression that commands respect. He wears a short-powdered wig, which is rather old-fashioned, a plain coat, and ivory silk knee breeches.[1]

A herald's peremptory cry rouses George from his reverie. In a moment he can hear the crescendo of approaching feet, and then the first members of the delegation enter from the antechamber to his right. In the vanguard comes the lord mayor, Brass Crosby, resplendent in black and gold damask, and a tricorn hat with waving black ostrich feathers. Close behind follow the aldermen Barlow Trecothick, Sir William Stephenson, James Townsend and Richard Oliver, all in scarlet robes trimmed with fur. Then, in mazarine blue, come the Common Councilmen, who gather at the far end of the chamber. The town clerk clears his throat: 'Your Majesty,' he begins. The king nods slightly, and the speaker continues: 'We the lord mayor, aldermen, and commons of the City of London, in common-council assembled, most humbly beg leave to approach Your Majesty, and most sincerely to lay again at the foot of the throne our aggravated grievances, and earnest supplication ...'[2]

As the voice of the town clerk trails away, the lord mayor approaches the monarch with bent head. He kneels, and kisses the king's hand, before returning to his feet, and leaves through the door to the ante-chamber. The four aldermen follow, and then, one by one, with awful solemnity, the blue-robed Common Councilmen kneel and kiss the royal hand. Almost the last to approach is James Sharp. As James raises his head to meet the king's gaze, George gives a slight start of recognition, and his cheeks flush. The encounter is over in a moment. James gets to his feet, and follows his fellow Councilmen out of the chamber.[3]

Given his conservative clerical background, James might have been expected to lean to the right in politics. In fact, he was a staunch radical, and his views on the prevailing political issues of the day were invariably anti-establishment. His master Samuel Southouse had been a member of the Common Council of the City of London for over twenty years, and James no doubt picked up the rudiments of political discourse around the dinner table with his fellow apprentices in Leadenhall Street. In December 1765, James was himself elected to the Common Council. For the rest of his adult life he was an active member of the assembly, serving on standing and special committees, and assuming a leadership role on matters – such as transport and communications – in which he had expertise.[4]

James could not have entered politics at a more febrile time. Late-1760s British politics was dominated by the figure of John Wilkes, and his disputed election to the parliamentary seat of Middlesex. Brilliant, feckless, charming and infamously promiscuous, Wilkes had risen from obscurity to become one of the leading lights of the political firmament. In 1762, Wilkes, while serving as MP for Aylesbury, launched a scurrilous weekly newsletter, the *North Briton*, which aimed at discrediting the ministry of Lord Bute. His genius for political invective found a ready subject in the treaty recently agreed in Paris to end the Seven Years' War, which was widely viewed as being overgenerous to the French. Ministerial hatred for the *North Briton* was to no avail, for government lawyers could find no grounds for prosecution.

But in issue 45 of the paper, published on 23 April 1763, Wilkes went a step too far, denouncing what he called the 'ministerial effrontery' of requiring George III 'to give the sanction of his sacred name' to an 'odious' treaty.⁵ The government prosecuted Wilkes for seditious libel and he fled to France, and having been convicted in his absence, was expelled from the House of Commons. In February 1768, Wilkes returned to England, and within weeks was elected to the parliamentary seat of Middlesex. Once again Wilkes was expelled from Parliament, this time on the legally dubious grounds that he was unfit to be a member. Wilkes was promptly re-elected at a by-election on 16 February 1769. There then followed a farcical cycle in which Wilkes's repeated elections to the Middlesex seat were followed by immediate expulsions.

James, like his fellow radicals, was appalled by the government's handling of the Middlesex election affair. For them, Wilkes's expulsion from Parliament represented not merely an infringement of the voter's right to elect the representative of his choice, but an example of the corruption of the legislative by an overweening executive. The Wilkes case brought to a head fears that government was exerting undue influence over the House of Commons, thereby upsetting the delicate balance of the constitution. City politicians, such as James, took a particularly dim view of ministerial interference. A proud and vigorous community of 12,000 freemen, the City put great store by their governing institutions, the Common Hall, the Common Council and the Court of Aldermen. Jealous of their right to self-governance, the City was invariably at odds with the national government of the day, and was particularly hostile to the aristocracy and leading gentry, whom they viewed as parasites vying for places and perks in the king's service.

James was an active member of the Bill of Rights Society, which was founded in February 1769 to provide financial assistance to the beleaguered Wilkes. Moreover, evidence of James's voting patterns in the Common Council show that he consistently voted on the pro-Wilkes side. On 5 May 1769, for example, he supported the motion for the calling of a 'Common Hall' to consider the ministry's decision to block Wilkes from taking his seat in Parliament. The following year

James was a member of the committee that drew up, and presented, a 'Remonstrance to the King' calling upon him to dismiss his ministers and dissolve Parliament, and spoke in favour of the measure. James's radical credentials, and his fellow councillors' regard for him, was evident during the election of the lord mayor in 1771, when he was asked to chair a meeting in support of radical candidates James Townsend and John Sawbridge. He is described in a report of the proceedings as 'an ironmonger (a Gentleman well known and much esteemed in the City)'.[6]

A man less able than James might have struggled to reconcile his political views with the demands of his increasingly elevated social life. As it was, he managed to stay true to his principles, while maintaining good relations with the aristocrats that frequented his brother William's musical soirees. By day he denounced the privileges of the governing classes to a thronged City council chamber, but in the evening he could with equal aplomb make small talk to patricians in the lofty halls of the mansion in Old Jewry. With characteristic Sharp deftness, James successfully negotiated a delicate balance between establishment and anti-establishment positions.

A potential conflict between James's political views and his family's association with the royal family came into focus on the occasion of the presentation of the second Remonstrance at St James's Palace in November 1770, when it was noted that the king 'changed countenance' as James came to kiss his hand.[7] The ceremony of the occasion belied the hostility felt towards the Crown in radical City circles. The text of the Remonstrance pulled no punches: though (in the usual way) personally absolving the king from blame, the petitioners decried 'a fatal conspiracy of malevolent influences around the throne'. The government's handling of the Middlesex election affair was likened to 'the law of tyrants, set up to overthrow the choice of the electors'. In a concluding statement, the petitioners warned that the 'various wounds of the constitution can be effectually healed' only if the king dismissed Parliament, and rid himself of the 'prevalence of evil counsellors'. As James was on the committee that drew up the November Remonstrance, we can conclude that it was an accurate statement of his political views.[8]

Given that it was only a matter of weeks since James had met with George III at Richmond Palace, and a mere three months since the Sharps had serenaded the royal family on the banks of the Thames at Kew, it is no wonder if the king 'changed countenance' when he saw James in the very different context of an overtly hostile political gathering. George III, much to his credit, did not hold James's radical politics against him. Indeed, it was reported to Elizabeth that, despite their political differences, the king admired the ironmonger, whom he considered 'a very sensible clever man'. Though he was aware of James's recent political activities as 'a bill of rights man', George was 'satisfyed he did it from Principle, and does not take it amiss'. According to Elizabeth's source, the king went so far as to say that 'he did not think that there had been such a worthy sensible man, among the Citizens of London'.[9] This endorsement indicates the impression made by James during the September and October audiences. James's qualities were so apparent to George III that he was prepared to overlook a little political waywardness.

18

Absence

Thomas, the second oldest of the siblings, has until now played a small part in the story of the Sharps. During the 1750s and 60s, while his brothers laboured to establish the foundations of what would one day be glittering careers, Thomas remained on the periphery of the Sharp dynamic. In intellectual ability he was at least the equal of his siblings, but he lacked their drive and vision. The promise of Thomas's early years, vividly rendered in the sparkling repartee of his contribution to the common letters, fizzled out in adulthood and he remained until his early death in 1772 a minor clergyman of limited attainment and means.

Thomas's early life and adolescence shadowed that of his elder brother John, whom he followed first to Durham Grammar School, and then in 1743 to Trinity College, Cambridge. Here he flourished, being elected a fellow in 1749 and later graduating as a bachelor in divinity. Thomas's intellectual life is expressed in the catalogue of his library that he produced in December 1748.[1] It was unusual for someone of Thomas's age to produce a catalogue of this type, and it shows both a passion for book collecting that was a trait of the Sharp family – his grandfather the archbishop, his great-uncle John the Member of Parliament for York, his father the archdeacon, and his brother John were all collectors and also produced catalogues of their libraries – and the broad range of his intellectual interests, which included Latin history, mathematics, logic, mechanics, optics, algebra and astronomy.[2]

The collection of scores in the catalogue suggests that Thomas shared his siblings' passion for music, and this is supported by his participation in the family music-making of the 1750s and early 1760s. Indeed in many respects Thomas can be seen as the leading light of Sharp musical performance in this period. As the violinist of the family, it was natural that he should be the leader of the Sharp band, but he also took the initiative in organising concerts. Thomas's entries to the common letters of the 1750s, at least those in which meaning can be deciphered in his characteristic flights of fancy, are full of his attempts to find performers for these occasions. In a letter dated 28 February 1758, he describes how on Saturday evening he had gone 'to the Turk's Head Concert in Greek Street Soho with Granville to secure Mr Hay, Simpson &c against the next Day'. Thomas's recruitment drive seems to have been successful on this occasion, as he later reports that 'On Sunday we had a very Grand Performance of sacred Music, & a great deal of Company'.[3]

Thomas's musical horizons were not confined to the family's concerts, however, for he was also actively involved in the societies frequented by his younger brother William. Indeed such was his seniority within the ranks of the members of the King's Arms amateur musical society that he acted as 'president' on the occasion of at least one of their concerts.[4] Thomas's involvement in family music-making seems to have declined in the 1760s, which coincides with his more protracted absences in Northumberland. He was not a member of the party which serenaded the royal family at Kew in 1770, and is in fact never mentioned as participating in one of the 'water scheems'. That his interest in music did not completely fall off after his removal from London, is evident in his composition of several hymn tunes, amongst them those with Sharp connotations such as 'Bamburgh', 'Rothbury' and 'Whitton', which were later published with works by the Revd Phocion Henley in *Divine Harmony: being a Collection of Psalm and Hymn Tunes*, in 1798.[5]

Thomas's clerical career failed to live up to the promise of his academic ability, and pales into insignificance besides the achievements of his father and elder brother. In part this was due to the accident of birth, as John appears to have been a more conspicuous recipient of their father's ecclesiastical favour. There was no equivalent of the lucrative living of Hartburn for Thomas after ordination, and it was

John rather than his younger brother who was groomed to follow in his father's footsteps in the archdeaconry of Northumberland. Thomas's first preferment seems to have been the curacy of St James, Duke's Place, in London where he served during the 1750s, and it was in this period that he lived with his brothers in William's house in Mincing Lane.[6] In 1757 he was appointed to the position of perpetual curate at Bamburgh Castle in Northumberland, where his father was trustee. As Thomas was also curate of All Hallows Staining in the City in this period, he divided his time between London and the north.[7]

Thomas's final preferment came in 1765 when he was elected as vicar of the parish of St Bartholomew the Less.[8] The method of selecting an incumbent by election, which was unusual for the Church of England, derived from the church's close association with St Bartholomew's Hospital. Just as the surgeons and physicians of the hospital were elected by a ballot of the governors, so applicants for the clerical living were required to submit themselves to the vote. This clearly acted in Thomas's favour, for he was able to rely on the leverage of his brother William who was an established figure in the hospital by this date. The connection between Thomas's election and the support of family members is suggested by a voting slip in the Sharp archive, on the reverse side of which James has sketched a wheel. The slip reads: 'Sir I take the Liberty of requesting the Favour of your Vote & interest for the Revd Mr Thomas Sharp, to succeed the Revd Mr Monro, as Vicar of the Parish of St Bartholomew the Less.'[9]

Though it was routine for one Sharp sibling to help another, the assistance provided to Thomas in this case has a distinct aspect. In supporting Thomas's application for the living of St Bartholomew's his brothers appear to be giving him a leg-up, and it denotes an inequality of status that was generally absent in their sibling relations. The reason for the assistance may well have been Thomas's financial situation, for by the late 1760s he was in debt.[10] Whether through profligacy, or simply by reason of the narrowness of his stipends, Thomas had not been able to keep within his means. At a time when his siblings were flourishing, Thomas's financial predicament must have been especially painful to him.

Though it is difficult to calculate Thomas's income during the 1750s and 60s, it was certainly more modest than that enjoyed by his elder brother John. For example, the £89 salary which Thomas earned as perpetual curate of Bamburgh Castle was significantly less than the £230 received by John as vicar of Hartburn, or the £300 which their father had commanded at Rothbury.[11] Moreover, both John and Thomas senior had valuable prebendal stalls, which might perhaps have trebled or quadrupled their income. The wealth of London brothers William and James was of a different order of magnitude: as a fashionable London surgeon, William's annual salary measured in the thousands. But in considering Thomas's propensity for debt, it is well to remember that even his relatively modest income dwarfed the tiny salary paid to Granville as a junior civil servant. Given that Thomas was a bachelor, and had comparatively few calls on his income, there seems to have been little excuse for his indebtedness. What he spent his money on is not recorded, but I like to imagine him poring over the catalogue of an antiquarian bookseller, or running his fingers along the rows of gilt-bound volumes that swell an ever-burgeoning library.

Whether driven by financial imperatives or otherwise, Thomas entered a new phase of life in 1770 when at the age of forty-five he married Miss Catharine Pawson, the stepdaughter of a Newcastle businessman, who was nineteen years his junior. In her journal entry for 22 December 1769 Elizabeth reports that: 'Bro. Tho. made his proposels to Miss Pawson of Newcastle', and that Catharine's stepfather 'Mr Stev[e]nson' has consented to the match.[12] This is significant because it is Mr Stevenson who 'promises to give a bond of 5000£ at 4 pr cent' to be settled on Catharine and '3000£ more at her mothers death'.[13]

By early 1771 Catharine was pregnant, and in a show of solidarity with their new sister-in-law, Elizabeth and Judith set out for the north in early January 'that we might see our new Sisr. Sharp'. After the usual dilly-dallying with friends and relations on the way, the sisters arrived at Durham on 23 January. From there they travelled to Newcastle 'to visit Sisr. Tho. Sharp at her fathers Mr Stevensons for a fortnight and then went to Hartburn Bamborough Castle'. When the sisters returned to Newcastle they were shocked to find their 'dear sister Thos so much in appearance worse than when we left her'. So anxious was Elizabeth that she 'desired leave of Mr and Mrs Stev[e]nson that I might desire Bro. T. to come down imediatly'.[14]

Leave was given, and Thomas hastened to his wife's bedside. Two or three days after his arrival in Newcastle, Catharine was 'brought to bed of a son, still borne on the Mar 16 and dyed herself but a fiew hours afterward'. She was buried with her son at St Nicholas Church in Newcastle.[15] In the months following his bereavement Thomas became embroiled in a financial dispute with his late wife's stepfather. Elizabeth refers to this episode in her journal entry for October 1771 as 'About this time Mr Stevenson ill conduct to dear Bro: Thos.' Elizabeth had her own speculations about the cause of the quarrel: 'I fancy a jelesey that his wives affection for him my Bro her son in law, that on her bed of illness, might be more favourable to him respecting money matters.' The dispute appears to have centred on the £3,000 which had been settled on Catharine in the event of her mother's death. Notwithstanding Mrs Stevenson's affection for her son-in-law, her husband got the better of Thomas, for according to Elizabeth 'my bro. never got any of it'.[16]

Coming so soon after the death of his wife and son, the dispute with Stevenson was too much for Thomas. On 25 November 1772 at the age of forty-seven he died in John's house in Hartburn and, as Elizabeth records 'was buryd at St Nicholas Church, near his wife and son in the following year'.[17] His early death and tragic family circumstances seem all of a piece with the disappointments of his early life. Thomas had the misfortune of being born into a family of almost uniformly high achievers, against which his own relative lack of success is thrown into stark relief. What might be viewed as an ordinarily successful, or ordinarily unsuccessful, life in a normal family, becomes a failure in the context of his brothers' attainments.

Thomas appears to have been singularly lacking in the drive and motivation – and perhaps also focus – that were so keen a part of his brothers' success. An insight into his character is provided in a letter he wrote to his sister Judith in April 1761. He begins by confessing that he is 'much behind hand in my London correspondence of late, being ... a letter in Debt to Bessy, Fran & Bro Will, & 2 to yourself' (the consciousness of being 'in debt' to correspondents to whom one owed a letter was a familiar sentiment at the time). This he claims is not due to laziness on his part, but rather to his work commitments:

> Easter was a very Busy Time with me, & since that I have received an Acct. of a Degree to be taken & Exercise to be kept, & a Latin & English sermon to be preached at Cambridge – whch has perplx'd me much, as I had no Reason to have expected all this Trouble these 3 or 4 years, but for the unreasonable ambition of one of my Juniors in College, who by taking a Degree now obliges myself & abt. 19 More to take our Degrees also, otherwise he wld. get the seniority of us, & of Course have a right to College livings before us, & was I to skip this, others wd do the like, & I sh. never have any Chance for preferment so yt I am under a Cruel necessity of all this Trouble & a great Expense at a Time when I least expected it.[18]

Complaints about the 'Trouble' that he has been put to by the 'unreasonable ambition' of another, seem out of kilter with his brothers' work ethic. In a similar way, Thomas's constant resort to comedy in his correspondence denotes a lack of seriousness which is unexpected in a family of such high moral purpose. While his brothers and sisters tend to confine parody to the common letters, Thomas never lets it rest. For example, the greater part of a letter he wrote to John on 2 February 1761 is taken up with an account of a windy walk to Bamburgh Castle in which he is accompanied by the rather rotund schoolmistress Mrs Middleton: 'yet when we came to that Dangerous Pass, where the Wind on the one Hand, by its incessant turnings and Vortical Revolutions, makes a kind of Charybdis, & the Rocks and Precipices on the other Hand, a ... formidable Scylla, we were reduced to the last extremity, & the Unfortunate Dinah, Capt M-dt-n [i.e. Mrs Middleton] tho' a broad bottom'd vessel, was oversett, Keil uppermost and her convoy (Heeling gunnel to recover her) shifted Ballast & was overset likewise.'[19]

If Thomas lay outside the Sharp magic circle, his relative failure did not alienate him from his siblings. Rather the family seem to have made every effort to help Thomas, and there is no suggestion that he was made to feel the lack of those characteristics which had made his brothers such a conspicuous success. If he grew gradually more distant from the London Sharps in the 1760s this was inevitable given his partial relocation to the north. The weakening of this bond was in any event made up for by the closeness of his relationship with his elder brother John, with whom he lived and worked at Bamburgh Castle in the 1760s and early 1770s. It is to Thomas's credit that in spite of the disparity between the brothers' income and success, he never let this come between them. Rather he appears to have been ungrudging in his love and admiration for his elder brother, which rings through in this extract from a poem he wrote in praise of John's work at Bamburgh Castle:

> Balmbrough rises still, more beauteous than before,
> Blest Pyle, that shall to they New-Founder Raise,
> As lasting as theyself, a Monument of Praise!
> But whence this Founder, arduous to excell,
> Thus daring, spight of Fashion, to do well?
> Britons behold him, Gen'rous, Wise & Just,
> Firm to his Purpose, Faithfull to his Trust,
> Keen as his Parts, unblunted as his Name,
> He plucks fresh Laurels from the Brow of Fame.[20]

Due to his early death in 1772, Thomas does not appear in Zoffany's portrait of the family. His absence is curiously fitting, for while John, William, James and Granville play starring roles in the story of the Sharps, Thomas enjoys only a walk-on part. This invisibility stands in poignant contrast to the prominence of Thomas's authorial voice in the common letters. The potential, which his brothers exploited to the full, was in Thomas's case unrealised as a consequence of personal misfortune, a lack of ambition, and perhaps also a failure to take life seriously.

19

Children

It is a remarkable fact that the eight Sharp siblings who survived to adulthood produced only four children between them. The ease with which their mother Judith reproduced during her twenty years of almost perpetual pregnancy, was not replicated in the experience of the next generation. Instead the women who came after her suffered all the agonies of protracted infertility, miscarriage and stillbirth. John and his wife Mary had only one daughter, Anne Jemima (b.1762), who was conceived after ten years of marriage. William and Catharine had one daughter, Mary (b.1778) who was born after thirteen years of marriage. James and his wife Catharine had two children, John (b.1765) who was known as 'Jack', and Catharine (b.1770) also known as 'Kitty'. Thomas's only child was stillborn, Elizabeth died childless, and Granville, Judith and Frances never married.

Of the four children born to the Sharp siblings, only three survived to adulthood. James and Catharine's son Jack died on 28 January 1771, a week before his sixth birthday. This cataclysmic event is alluded to simply but movingly in Elizabeth's diary, and it is apparent that the devastation of his loss was felt by the wider family as well as by his parents. It was natural to the Sharps that they should care for and love each other's children, and Jack had spent much of his short life in the company of his aunts. Frances in particular appears to have played a significant role in the care of her nephew, and was his constant companion in Leadenhall Street and on visits to Elizabeth at Wicken. So in her journal entry for 15 April 1768 Elizabeth notes: 'I returnd to Wicken, Sissr. F and little dear Jack with me', while her entry for

25 July 1769 records that 'Sissr. F left me and went to Town, I believe little Jack with her'.[1]

Jack's visits to Wicken were often in the summer months, when London was rife with contagious diseases such as dysentery, typhoid and putrid fever. To Jack, used to the frenetic pace and densely populated thoroughfares of the City, Wicken must have represented vistas of unimpeded space and time. Perhaps for the first few days, he misses his parents, or the charms of the ironmongery, or the manufactory in Tooley Street – but these memories are soon consumed in the delight of his new surroundings. Chief among the pleasures of Wicken is undivided adult attention: at home his mother is distracted by the demands of shop and household, but his aunts seem to have no other purpose than to gratify his every whim. When the delights of unrationed stories, hide-and-seek, jacks and the board game fox and goose eventually pall, he can sit in the cool stone-flagged dairy and watch the dairymaid paddling the butter, or run into the sunlit garden. Here old Jonathan the gardener provides silent, but comfortable, companionship, and together they roll the great lawns, or stake curling bean plants, or pick gooseberries, or visit the hothouses where the smell of ripe peaches is heavy in the air.[2] When even these pleasures cloy, he can climb haystacks in the farmyard, or looks for eggs, or feed chestnut leaves to the gentle warm-breathed cows.

Catharine appears to have been reconciled to her son's prolonged absences in Northamptonshire, for she always remained with James in London. Sometimes James and Catharine stayed at Wicken for a short period en route to some other destination, as in June 1769 when Elizabeth records that 'Bro. and Sissr. James visited us at Wicken for a fiew days'.[3] Given the amount of time they spent together, it was natural that a strong bond should form between Jack and his aunts. As neither woman had children of their own, the relationship had a particular value for them. This explains why for Elizabeth and Frances, Jack's death had a tragic resonance beyond that which might be expected from their kinship.

The serious illness or death of a child was an almost inevitable part of parenthood in eighteenth-century England. So high was the incidence of child mortality that parents led the life of a gambler, dicing with fate for the highest imaginable stakes.[4] Correspondence from the period suggests the helplessness felt by parents in the face of a child's illness. Without palliative medicine of a kind routinely available today, they were powerless to ease the suffering of their child. In the absence of adequate knowledge of the causes and process of disease, they could do little to stem its course.[5]

In an age when even a slight ailment could lead to a child's death, the mildest symptom of disorder caused alarm. Parents watched constantly for signs of disease, and letters between mothers and fathers in this period harp constantly on the subject of their children's health and physical strength.[6] Kindled by the onset of a significant symptom, parental anxiety grew to breaking point as their child's illness progressed. The ordeal of the sickbed is illuminated in the testimony of parents' journals and letters, which speak of the fatigue of constant watching, of the overwhelming relief when the danger has passed, and the descent into despair when it is apparent that the child is dying.[7]

In the weeks and months following Jack's death, his parents and aunts struggled to resign themselves to his loss. Forty years previously when the siblings' little sister Grace had died, their father Thomas had written of 'having submitted my self to the goodwill of God in the best manner I am able'.[8] It was now the turn of his children to attempt the same feat of Christian resignation. The vocabulary of faith, in which parents in this period expressed their attempts to reconcile themselves to the death of a child, should not be taken as evidence that the pain of their loss was any less keen, or that submission 'to the goodwill of God' was easier than any other form of acceptance. At a time when children died with frightening regularity, the language of Christian endurance reveals rather the devastating power of parental grief and 'the abysmal depths of misery into which men and women might sink if ever they relaxed their grip on the rafts of courage and resignation'.[9]

In his letter to Judith following the death of their daughter Grace, Thomas had reminded her of the consolation of the children who remained to them: 'I do truly bless God that he doth not deal more severely with me; that he yet reserves to me three pledges of his kindness out of double that number.' However grim such odds might seem to us today, it is undoubtedly the case that Judith with her brood of surviving sons, and later daughters, was better equipped to cope with the trauma of repeated bereavement than women who lost all or most of their children. There is also evidence that parents who lost babies or very young children found it easier to bear than those grieving for an older child. Melesina Trench (1768–1827), who lost a baby daughter and a two-year-old son within a short time of each other, wrote after the death of her son:

> The loss of my infant daughter, which seemed heavy at the time, shrinks into nothing when compared with this. She was merely a little bud; but he was a lovely blossom which had safely passed all the earliest dangers, and gave clearest promise of delicious fruit ... Oh, my child my child! ... when I saw you cold and motionless before me how came it my heart did not break at once.[10]

Jack was three years older than Melesina Trench's son when he died. His death came at a peculiarly cruel age, at a time when like Melesina his parents must have hoped that he had 'safely passed all the earliest dangers' associated with infant mortality. In recording Jack's death, Elizabeth does not explain its cause, merely noting in her diary entry for 7 December 1770 that 'little Jack' had recovered after an illness, and for 28 January 1771 that he had died. So we do not know which of the many causes of child mortality, such as smallpox, diphtheria, tuberculosis, measles, whooping cough, typhus and the various kinds of 'fever', was responsible for his death. All we have is the barest clue in Elizabeth's entry for 9 April 1771, when she notes that: 'Little Catharine Sharp enoculated, and we were much pressed to return in case any thing happend [to] little Catharine as all their spirits were much depressed by their late loss.'[11]

The procedure carried out on Catharine was an early form of smallpox vaccination known interchangeably as 'inoculation' and 'variolation'. Smallpox was one of the principal causes of mortality in this period, accounting for approximately 200,000 lives in Europe every year.[12] Highly contagious, the virus affected children disproportionately so that between 80% and 98% of its victims were younger than ten years old.[13] The tendency of the virus to congregate in facial tissue meant that those who survived were often left with disfiguring scars, and in severe instances faces were mutilated beyond recognition. Many women never came to terms with the disfigurement caused by their smallpox scars, and depression, self-neglect and suicide were common in acute cases.[14]

It was to stem the catastrophic incidence and effects of smallpox that the practice of variolation evolved in various parts of the world including China, the Middle East and Africa. The procedure consisted of the deliberate infection of a healthy child in order to prevent a natural attack of the disease. Though the patient did develop smallpox after the procedure, the symptoms triggered by the induced virus tended to be milder and less harmful than those developing naturally. Technique varied according to the culture in which it developed, so that in China powdered material from smallpox scabs was blown up a patient's nose, while in the Middle East and Africa fluid from pustules was rubbed into a cut made in the patient's arm or leg.[15]

It was the African technique that found its way to Turkey, and it was here in the 1710s that it came to the attention of Lady Mary Wortley Montagu, the wife of the British ambassador to the Ottoman Empire.[16] Lady Mary became a passionate advocate of variolation, and used her position in London society to promote its adoption among the upper classes, and from there the procedure gradually gained recognition in the country as a whole. With a mortality rate of approximately 2%,[17] variolation was one of the few success stories of eighteenth-century medicine, while its revolutionary principle of the infection of a healthy subject with viral material to pre-empt a more severe incidence of the disease, was the prototype for vaccination itself as pioneered by Edward Jenner in the 1790s.

William Sharp appears to have been an ardent variolater, at least according to the testimony of Elizabeth's diary which refers on several occasions to his performance of the procedure on family and friends. In fact Elizabeth herself seems to have been the family guinea pig, for in the course of a description of a visit to Cambridge in 1751 she notes: 'bro. W came to us there to attend us to Town to his first house in

Mincing Lane, where I was enoculated by him. I believe his first patient in that complaint.'[18] While she was particular about recording the inoculations of, for example, her husband's sisters ('My 2 Sisrs: P were enoculated') she never mentions the fact of her nephew Jack's variolation.[19] While this could be an oversight on her part, it is also possible that James and Catharine decided against the procedure.

Because some children did die after being inoculated, parents were forced to balance the risks of action and inaction. Perhaps like thousands of their fellow parents, James and Catharine agonised over the decision, and hesitated to take such a daunting step.[20] I picture them at the dining table in Leadenhall Street, or in the early hours of a stifling August morning, painfully rehearsing the arguments for and against the procedure. James is in favour – he has implicit faith in his brother William's judgement – but Catharine is tortured with apprehension. She knows of a child who died after inoculation and cannot bring herself to deliberately expose her son to a life-threatening disease. Imagine Catharine's agony, and tormented self-reproach, if Jack's subsequent death was caused by a natural bout of smallpox. It was possibly in these tragic circumstances that the Sharps chose to inoculate his little sister Kitty, at the exceptionally young age of eight months.

We do not know if the Sharp siblings lamented their lack of children. Their own childhood had been so happy, that it is tempting to conclude that it was painful for them not to be able to replicate it in the next generation. In place of the boisterous, noisy and high-spirited scenes that had characterised their own early years, Kitty, Mary and Anne Jemima were brought up in the quiet order of single-child households. The Sharp archive, in truth, contains little evidence of how the family raised their children. But it can be deduced from the strength of the sibling bond, and the frequency with which Jack, and later Kitty, stayed at Wicken Park, that the girls were reared as part of a wider family nexus. The Sharps appear to have taken the values of their own childhood, and reoriented them outwards so as to involve relations beyond the immediate nuclear family. Whatever Kitty, Mary and Anne Jemima might have missed out on for want of their own siblings, was made up for by the closeness of the Sharp clan as a whole.

20

Somerset

Yesterday the Negro cause came on before the Court of King's Bench for final decision, when Lord Mansfield in a written speech, as guarded, cautious, and concise, as it could possibly be drawn up, delivered the unanimous opinion of the whole Court.

Morning Chronicle, 23 June 1772

It is the morning of 22 June 1772. In the Court of King's Bench, Lord Mansfield, dressed in the judicial splendour of scarlet robes, a full wig, and a white fur cape and sleeves, processes down the aisle that bisects the small courtroom. As he takes his place on the raised bench at the far end of the court, only the scratch of the filacer's* pen, and the muffled cry of voices from the adjoining hall, disturbs the silence. Above the lofty courtroom hangs a row of brightly coloured standards, seized on some blood-soaked foreign battlefield, while effigies of medieval kings look on in attitudes of sorrow from niches in the walls. From his vantage point, Lord Mansfield can see the faces of the crowds in the densely packed public gallery opposite him, and the black-robed lawyers huddled over their papers. The court is so full that men and women sit in the aisles, or on the benches of grumbling court officials, or stand by the witness box in tightly pressed rows. Latecomers congregate outside, with ears pressed tight to the Gothic screen that separates the court from Westminster Hall. Tension

---

* A filacer was a legal officer of the superior courts.

grips the courtroom, as the crowds wait restlessly for the legal drama
to unfold.[1]

*

We left Granville, in the autumn of 1767, embarking on a study of
English law as it touched the freedom of the individual, in order to
defend the civil claim brought against him by the Jamaican planter
James Kerr. After several months of painstaking research, Granville
set out his conclusions in a tract called *A Representation of the Injustice
and Dangerous Tendency of Tolerating Slavery; or of Admitting the Least
Claim of Private Property in the Persons of Men, in England* which he
distributed 'among the gentleman of the law' with a view to intimi-
dating Kerr into dropping his action.[2]

Granville's tactics appear to have paid off, because James Kerr did
not pursue his claim against the brothers.[3] Instead, according to Granville,
he 'deceitfully contrived' to keep the action alive 'without daring to
bring it to an issue'.[4] Kerr was eventually non-suited for contravention
of court rules, and required to pay treble costs. Any relief felt by the
brothers was short-lived, for in the spring of 1768 the planter 'litigiously
commenced another action on his account with Mr James and Granville
Sharp'.[5] This seems to have been more bravado than serious legal intent,
for once again the claim was allowed to fizzle out. On this occasion the
brothers' satisfaction was muted by news of a deterioration in the health
of Jonathan Strong, who had never fully recovered from Lisle's mistreat-
ment of him. On 17 April 1773, Granville noted sadly in his diary, 'Poor
Jonathan Strong the first [slave] whose freedom I had procured in 1767,
died this morning.'[6] He was twenty-five years old.

Though Granville wrote the *Representation* in order to defend the
claim brought against him by James Kerr, the main body of the argument is much wider in scope. Indeed it is clear that Granville conceived
of the tract both as a riposte to Kerr personally, and as a wider challenge to the legal establishment. His primary object was the debunking
of the 'Joint Opinion' given by the Attorney General Sir Philip Yorke
and Solicitor General Charles Talbot on 14 January 1729, which held
that a slave did not become free on his arrival in England and could

be compelled to return to his master. According to Granville, the Joint Opinion was wrong because it flouted fundamental principles of the common law, and ignored previous judicial authority.

He begins his argument by rejecting the assertion that there could be private property in a slave as there was in a horse or a dog. This, Granville declares, was a 'very insufficient and defective' claim, as it was 'unnatural and unjust' to make such a comparison between a man and an animal.[7] Being 'undoubtedly either man, woman or child', a slave was subject to, and received the protection of, the laws of England.[8] He dismisses the idea that slaves were not 'in consideration or contemplation' when the laws of England were made, arguing that the statutes in question 'are so full and clear, that they admit no exception whatsoever, for all persons'.[9]

Granville does not confine himself to an analysis of the law, but also argues against slavery on ethical grounds: 'A toleration of Slavery is, in effect, a toleration of inhumanity.'[10] He condemns the moral blindness of the British public, whose passivity has allowed slavery to gain a foothold in the country, and warns his readers of the moral contagion of the trade. For in circumstances where 'the uncivilized customs which disgrace English colonies become so familiar in England, as to be permitted with impunity, we ourselves must insensibly degenerate to the same degree of baseness'.[11]

Bolstered by the mostly favourable reviews of the lawyers to whom he had sent a copy of the manuscript, in 1769 Granville published the *Representation*. What had begun as a defence to a legal action became through the unanswerable logic of its argument, and its trenchant call to arms, a manifesto for the liberation of slaves in Britain. In the years that followed Granville put the theory of the *Representation* into practice by actively assisting in the liberation of kidnapped slaves. Further, by bringing these cases to court, he sought to enforce a change in the law in line with the propositions contained within his treatise. As his reputation as a friend to the black population of London was now established, he was in constant demand to assist former slaves who had been abducted by their masters.

One example was the case of a former slave called Thomas Lewis. On the night of 2 July 1770, Lewis was seized on the order of his erstwhile master Robert Stapylton, in the garden of a house fronting the Thames at Chelsea. The assailants dragged Lewis backwards into the water, tied his arms and legs, gagged him with a stick, and took him by rowing boat to a ship bound for Jamaica. Fortunately for Lewis, the incident did not go unnoticed. The house next door to that in which Lewis had been living at the time of his abduction was occupied by Mrs Banks, the mother of the celebrated naturalist and botanist Sir Joseph Banks. Mrs Banks's servants had heard his cries of distress, and the next morning they told their mistress what had occurred.

Mrs Banks lost no time in calling on Granville Sharp, whom she knew socially, as well as by reputation.[12] Granville sprang into action, and obtained a warrant for the return of the abducted slave, which was delivered to the ship in Gravesend where Lewis was being held prior to its departure for the Caribbean. But the warrant arrived too late: the ship had been cleared to sail, and the captain (who may have been involved in the conspiracy) disdained to take any notice of the document. Undaunted, on the following day Granville obtained a writ of habeas corpus on Lewis's behalf, which was sent down to Spithead on the Solent. Luck was on Lewis's side, for the ship had been detained by contrary winds, and the writ was served. The captain released Lewis, and he was brought safely back to London.[13]

Lewis's kidnapper Robert Stapylton did not pursue the matter further. But Granville and Mrs Banks had the bit between their teeth, and were determined to make an example of the case. With the assistance of a solicitor, Mrs Banks initiated proceedings against Stapylton and the two watermen who had assisted in the kidnapping. The law moved with extraordinary speed, for on Tuesday 10 July 1770 a grand jury indicted the three men on charges of assault and false imprisonment. Anxious to spare Mrs Banks the expense and stress of a contested court hearing, Granville urged her solicitor to compromise the action, on terms that charges would be dropped if Stapylton publicly acknowledged that Lewis was not his slave and paid the costs of the action. The defendants rejected this offer and instead successfully petitioned for the case to be transferred to the Court of King's Bench.[14]

In addition to increasing the likely costs of the proceedings, the removal of the action to the King's Bench had the important consequence of bringing it to the attention of the chief justice, Lord Mansfield. Born William Murray in March 1705 at Scone Palace near Perth, he left Scotland at the age of fourteen to pursue a career in England, providing the occasion for Samuel Johnson's quip 'Much can be made of a Scot, if caught young.'[15] As a junior barrister, Murray practised oratory in front of a mirror, coached by his friend the poet Alexander Pope, and spent his spare time translating Horace, Sallust and Cicero into English, retranslating it into Latin, and learning whole volumes of their work by heart.[16]

After a brilliant career at the bar, Murray was appointed Solicitor General in 1742, two days later being returned as MP for Boroughbridge, and in 1754 was elevated to the position of Attorney General. In the House of Commons he was known as 'silver-tongued Murray', having earned a reputation for polished and cerebral oratory.[17] In November 1756 Murray was appointed chief justice of the Court of King's Bench, a post which he was to hold for the next thirty-two years. For his judicial work, particularly in the fields of marine insurance and nego-tiable instruments, Mansfield is considered to be the 'founder of the commercial law of this country'.[18]

For the hearing before Lord Mansfield, the barrister and parliamen-tarian John Dunning was briefed to represent Lewis.[19] Despite being a fervent admirer of Lord Mansfield, Dunning was politically at odds with his mentor on most of the serious issues of the day.[20] In March 1770, for example, he defended the London petitioners (James Sharp amongst them) in a long speech in the House of Common (described by a reporter as 'one of the finest pieces of argument and eloquence ever heard') and he was also a trenchant critic of the government's policy towards America.[21] Described by one commentator as 'the ugliest man of his day', with a 'short and stumpy' figure, a 'sallow' complexion and 'a snubbed nose', Dunning 'laboured under an affec-tion of his nerves, which occasioned his head to be in a state of perpetual oscillation'.[22] As for his voice, this was described as being 'almost repulsive'. Nevertheless, he was a powerful advocate, and spoke with such 'rapid fluency', in 'sentences complex, complete, exquisitely grammatical, delivered rat-a-tat-tat' that he was the terror of the court reporters.[23]

On Tuesday 19 February 1771 Granville and Thomas Lewis travelled to Westminster Hall to attend the trial of Robert Stapylton. As they waited for the hearing to come on, Granville sat in a coffee house adjacent to the hall and scribbled some last-minute arguments. I imagine him at a long central table, hunched over his memorandum book, with an untouched bowl of coffee by his side. The thin contours of the philanthropist's face are wrapped in thought, and his long bony fingers move rapidly across the paper. Thomas Lewis, who sits near him, cannot comprehend how Granville is able to concentrate in the uproar of the coffee house. Dogs fight on the dirty sawdust floor, lawyers wrangle in the booths that line the wall behind them, and the shriek of the boiling cauldron rises high above the clamour. Beside them, jobbing attorneys solicit for custom, while waiters in filthy linen aprons pour streams of coffee from elevated pots. The air is thick with tobacco smoke, and the stench of unwashed bodies mingles with the odour of cooking fat exuding from the chop house next door.[24]

At last the hearing is called – and Granville and Lewis hurry through Westminster Hall to the Court of King's Bench. According to a newspaper report, the courtroom was so noisy that Dunning, croaking and wheezing as always, struggled to make himself heard above the din.[25] He began by outlining the facts of the abduction, which he referred to as a 'gross and outrageous assault', before pouring scorn on the defendant's claim to ownership of Lewis. Simply because Lewis has 'a darker complexion than the defendants', Dunning contended, they 'have taken it into their heads to say he was not under the protection of the laws of this Country, and that they have a right to treat him as their property', as 'a horse or a dog to carry him where they pleased and do what they pleased with him'.[26] Dunning ridiculed the notion that one man could own another: 'the laws of this Country admit of no such property'.

According to Dunning, the legal issue of slavery became relevant only if the defendant could prove that Lewis was his property as a matter of fact. He then called Thomas Lewis, with the intention of disproving that claim. As drawn out by Dunning's adroit examination, Lewis's account of his eventful life tended to suggest that he was a servant rather than a slave.[27] The defendant's arguments to the contrary fell on deaf ears, for in directing the jury to consider only the factual issue of property in Lewis, Lord Mansfield expressed the opinion that the defendant had failed to prove his ownership of the former slave. The jury accordingly returned a verdict of 'No property!' Before dismissing the parties, the chief justice addressed a few prophetic words to Dunning on the subject of the legality of slavery on British soil: 'There are a great many opinions given upon it; I am aware of many of them; but perhaps it is much better that it should never be discussed or settled. I don't know what the consequences may be, if the masters were to lose their property by accidentally bringing their slaves to England. I hope it never will be finally discussed.'[28]

In the *Representation*, Granville had shown that the question of the lawfulness of slavery on British soil involved the competing claims of two fundamental principles of English law: the right to personal liberty, and the sanctity of property rights. Granville argued that a slave had as much right to the protection of the common law as any other subject of the Crown, and was therefore equally entitled to his personal liberty. He also rejected the notion of a legal right to property in a human being. Convinced of the validity of this reasoning, Granville sought the sanction of judicial authority. But as ardently as Granville endeavoured to corner Lord Mansfield in the Lewis case, the chief justice with equal pertinacity tried to evade the issue.

In developing the law of commerce, Lord Mansfield was guided by what he considered to be an overriding need for stability and predictability. He once declared that 'The great object in every branch of the law, but especially in mercantile law, is certainty'.[29] In the field of slavery, certainty for Lord Mansfield was the law expressed in the Joint Opinion, so that a master could bring a slave to Britain safe in the knowledge that his property would not be taken away from him. It is apparent, however, that the chief justice saw the flaws in the legal argument represented in the Joint Opinion. Hence the alacrity with which he directed the jury in the Lewis case to a finding of 'No property!', to avoid the necessity of determining whether such property could exist in law.

In the weeks that followed the Lewis trial, Mansfield compounded his fault in Granville's eyes by refusing to pass sentence on Stapylton.

At a hearing on 17 June 1771, the chief justice prevaricated by retro-
spectively casting doubt on the validity of Lewis's testimony: 'Ever
since that trial I have had a great doubt in my mind, whether the
negro could prove his own freedom by his own evidence.'[30] When
Dunning made a second attempt to persuade the judge to pass sentence
during a hearing on 28 November 1771, Mansfield responded that as
Mrs Banks had Lewis 'in her possession', there was no need for her
to prosecute the case further.[31]

Incensed by what he viewed as the judge's moral cowardice,
Granville was doubly intent on forcing a final resolution of the wider
legal issue which both Lewis's and Strong's cases had brought into
focus. He did not have to wait long. On 13 January 1772, Granville
noted in his memorandum book: 'James Somerset, a Negro from
Virginia, called on me this morning to complain of Mr Charles Stewart.
I gave him the best advice I could.'[32] Somerset told Granville that after
being sold into captivity as a child in Africa, he was transported by
slave ship to Virginia. Here he was bought by a Scottish trader called
Charles Stewart who later worked for the British government as a
high-ranking customs officer. Over the next few years, Somerset
became his master's most trusted manservant.

In 1769 Stewart obtained permission for leave of absence from his
duties, and arrived in London with Somerset on 10 November 1769.
Nearly two years later the slave absconded. Though Stewart was
considered by those who knew him to be warm-hearted and generous,
his response to the flight of the man with whom he had lived for
years on terms of friendship, was unmitigatedly harsh. He had been
kind to Somerset, and seems to have viewed his former slave's departure as an act of betrayal. In any event, rather than washing his hands
of the affair, he appears to have determined that Somerset should be
punished for his supposed ingratitude. Stewart retained slave-catchers,
who after a fifty-six-day search apprehended Somerset and incarcerated
him in a ship, the *Ann and Mary*, bound for Jamaica. Stewart was well
aware of the kind of life that awaited his former manservant on the
plantations.

Two days after his capture, on 28 November 1771, Lord Mansfield
granted a writ of habeas corpus in favour of Somerset, in reliance on

affidavits sworn by three individuals who are thought to have been Somerset's godparents. James Somerset was duly brought before the chief justice, and the cause of his detention on the slave ship was explained by lawyers acting for Stewart. The absconding slave was nonetheless temporarily set free, and bound over to the next legal term when the facts at issue could be properly aired. It was at this point that Somerset asked for Granville's assistance.

As well as Granville's concern for Somerset's predicament, it was immediately apparent to him that this was an ideal case for a deter-mination of the issue of slavery on British soil. There was no dispute, as there had been in Lewis's case, as to the relationship between the parties. Somerset admitted that he had been Stewart's slave, and there were no other factual grounds that could allow Mansfield to wriggle out of a substantive judgement. Buoyed by the prospect of a rematch with the elusive chief justice, Granville lost no time in pursuing his objective. Within two months of the final hearing of the Lewis case, the campaigner had embarked on the prosecution of a cause that was to resolve once and for all the issue of the legality of slavery on British soil.

Meanwhile, Granville made preparations for a battle that would be expensive, as well as time-consuming. On 29 January 1772, he recorded in his memorandum book: 'Gave cash, £6. 6s. to Mr Hughes, clerk to Mr Priddle, to retain two counsel in the case of Somerset.'[33] Though this was a significant part of the modest salary he earned at the Board of Ordnance, Granville noted that 'Money has no value but when it is well spent; and I am thoroughly convinced that no part of my little pittance of ready money can ever be better bestowed'.[34] In the event, all five of the barristers who appeared for Somerset waived their fee.[35] Comprising many of the leading figures of what today would be described as the 'Human Rights Bar', Somerset's legal team included the radical lawyer and parliamentarian John Glynn, Francis Hargrave (who had corresponded with Granville on the subject of slavery at the time of the Strong litigation), James Mansfield (no relation to the chief justice) and James Alleyne. At the helm was leading counsel William 'Bull' Davy, who was known for his quick wit, self-confidence and expert cross-examination.[36]

Conspicuous by his absence from Somerset's legal team was John Dunning, who had represented Thomas Lewis. Dunning's passionate denunciation of slavery in those proceedings had won him plaudits, not least from Granville who referred to the barrister's 'diligence and adroitness' in a letter to Mrs Banks. Granville hoped to retain Dunning on behalf of James Somerset, but he was thwarted by the prompt action of the defendant Charles Stewart. Engaging in a tactic that is still familiar today, the defence team snapped up the famous barrister before Granville had a chance to intervene. Granville never forgave Dunning for acting for Stewart, which he viewed as an act of apostasy.[37]

But in doing so he misunderstood the role of the advocate. A counsel cannot pick or choose which cases he takes, according to his sensibilities. Otherwise causes which are unpopular, or unsavoury defendants, would have no one to represent them. Instead the law has developed the so-called 'cab-rank rule' which determines that counsel must take the cases that are given to them without regard to the facts.[38] In the event it was the defendant, rather than Granville, who had a right to be aggrieved because Dunning seems to have purposefully underperformed. In place of the forceful eloquence that was characteristic of his advocacy, Dunning appeared weak and ineffectual.[39]

The Somerset trial provoked considerable public interest. The *General Evening Post* noted that 'the great cause depending between Mr Stewart, and Somerset, the black, is at present one of the principal topics of conversation', while the *Gazetteer* referred to 'the much talked of cause of Somerset'. Public sympathies were with Somerset, and this explains the censure heaped on Dunning in the contemporary press. 'Vindex' in the *Gazetteer* decried what he called 'the casuistry of the venal lawyer'. Antipathy to the defendant increased in the course of the trial when it was discovered that his costs were being paid by 'the West Indian interest', the name given to the informal lobby group representing the rights of plantation owners.[40]

The Court of King's Bench, in which the case of Somerset was heard, sat in the south-eastern corner of Westminster Hall. Since its construction in the eleventh century, the great lofty hammer-beamed hall had stood at the heart of British justice.[41] It was here that the trials of William Wallace, Thomas More, Guy Fawkes and Charles I had taken place. In the eighteenth century, the four royal Courts of King's Bench, Common Pleas, Chancery and Exchequer all stood within the hall, separated from the main body of the building by screens. The courts were unlit, except in the winter months when candles were used in the afternoon, and unheated until 1794. The solemnity of the courtrooms contrasted with the hurly-burly of the hall outside, where stalls of booksellers, toy sellers, instrument makers, haberdashers and seamstresses ran higgledy-piggledy along the walls, and a thicket of taverns and coffee houses crowded just beyond its doors. Lawyers, litigants, witnesses, sightseers and salesmen thronged the wide-open spaces of the hall, making such an uproar that witnesses in court sometimes strained to be heard.

The proceedings opened on 24 January 1772, the second day of the Hilary term.[42] Lord Mansfield and his three 'puisnes', or associate judges, sat on raised benches at the southern end of the court. Beneath them sat the chief clerk and his assistants, the clerk of the Crown and the clerk of the papers, and the filacers who processed writs, and with them the marshal, criers and ushers. The hearing was simply a skirmish before the battle proper, consisting of the formal return of the captain of the *Ann and Mary* to the writ of habeas corpus. Somerset's lead counsel, 'Bull' Davy, asked the judges' permission for the case to be put over to the Easter term to allow counsel to prepare their submissions. Lord Mansfield refused this request, but did at least postpone the hearing until 7 February, which gave the lawyers a fortnight to prepare. The next two weeks were spent in consultation with Granville, whose exhaustive knowledge of the relevant areas of law was of invaluable assistance to his counsel.

On the Wednesday before the reconvened hearing, Granville delivered an iron muzzle to Davy at his chambers in the Temple. In an accompanying note, Granville explained that:

The instrument is called a Mouth Piece and many wholesale ironmongers in town keep quantities of them ready in order to supply the merchants and planters orders for the West Indian Islands. They are used on various occasions, sometimes for punishment ... and sometimes to prevent the poor wretches from gnawing the sugar canes. And sometimes they are used to prevent the poor despairing wretches in slavery from eating dirt (in order to commit suicide).[43]

There could be no more graphic reminder of the significance of the impending litigation. Granville concluded:

It is an Iron Argument, which must at once convince all those whose hearts are not of a harder metal, that men are not to be entrusted with an absolute authority over their brethren.[44]

On 7 February 1772, the proceedings reconvened in Westminster Hall, this time with each side bringing the full complement of their legal teams. Interest in the trial meant that the courtroom was crowded almost to bursting. Such was the competition for places in the public gallery that hopeful spectators went away disappointed. The diarist John Baker arrived with friends 'too late' to get a seat, and 'could hear nothing thro' the crowd'. The party left disconsolately, and went instead to the Court of Chancery, whose charms must have quickly palled, for they stayed only '1/2 an hour'.[45]

Anyone who did squeeze themselves into the Court of King's Bench on 7 February 1772 might have noticed one conspicuous absence. Granville did not attend the Somerset trial, for fear that his presence would antagonise Lord Mansfield. It was an act of considerable self-denial – after years spent campaigning on the issue of the legality of slavery on British soil, the temptation to be there at its final resolution must have been overwhelming. Instead he stayed away – maybe returning to one of the nearby coffee houses to wait for news.

As there was no factual dispute between the parties, counsels' submissions were confined to the legal issue of whether the defendant had the right to remove Somerset from the country against his will. Davy spoke first, stating his intention to show 'That no man at this day is, or can be, a Slave in England'.[46] Having established that villeinage, once recognised by the common law as a status akin to slavery, was extinct, Davy turned to the leading precedent of 'Cartwright'. In this sixteenth-century case, the defendant had brought a slave from Russia 'and would scourge him', but the judge ruled that 'England was too pure an air for Slaves to breathe in'. Davy voiced the rhetorical hope that 'the air does not blow worse since'.[47] Having spoken for two and a half hours, according to the correspondent of the *General Evening Post*, Davy sat down and passed the baton to his colleague John Glynn.

Glynn's submissions were rather shorter than his predecessor's, lasting what the correspondent termed 'above an hour comfortably', and they tended to substantiate the points made by his fellow counsel rather than breaking new ground. On the subject of villeinage, Glynn remarked that at least the remit of that ancient bondage had been clearly understood. Modern slavery, by contrast, was an entirely arbitrary institution: 'Is it confined to complexion? Is it confined to a particular quarter of the world? Upon what principle is it that a man can become a dog for another man?'[48]

On the subject of alien jurisdictions, Glynn agreed with Davy that the laws of Virginia could have no force in Britain. Consequently, as soon as Somerset arrived in Britain, he 'cease[d] to be a slave'.[49]

At the conclusion of Glynn's submissions, Lord Mansfield postponed the proceedings yet again, this time to Saturday 9 May 1772. It was now the turn of James Mansfield, the third advocate on the Somerset team, to take to the floor. He mocked what he caricatured as the 'mighty magic air of the West Indies' on which the defendant relied to found an absolute right of property in his slave, echoing his fellow counsel's arguments against the importation of colonial laws.[50] According to Mansfield, it was impossible that Somerset should forfeit his inalienable right to liberty without the introduction of a form of property unknown to the English constitution.

After another adjournment to 14 May, the young Francis Hargrave got to his feet. In a speech that the correspondent for the *Morning Chronicle* described as 'one of the most learned and elaborate' ever heard, Hargrave bolstered the arguments of his fellow counsel with a huge body of case law. 'It is almost impossible to imagine,' the correspondent continued, with only the slightest hint of weariness, 'what a number of precedents, apposite to the case in point, this gentleman had, with uncommon pains, gleaned from the law books.'[51]

Notwithstanding the volume of precedents, and Hargrave's rather dull style of delivery, his argument was punctuated by applause from the public gallery, and when he sat down he was given a standing ovation. Perhaps Granville was prowling outside the courtroom at this moment, and hearing the ovation, felt comforted that the case was going well.

It was now the turn of James Alleyne to rise to his feet. He was in the unenviable position of being the last of Somerset's counsel to speak, and to the difficulty of following a lauded performance was added the near impossibility of finding anything new to say. Nevertheless, Alleyne performed with aplomb, so much so that the correspondent for the *Morning Chronicle* thought his submissions equal to Hargrave's, though 'on very different principles'. Whereas Hargrave excelled in legal erudition, Alleyne's speech was a 'graceful eloquent oration, delivered with perfect ease, and replete with elegant language, classical expression, and pertinent observation'.[52]

This was the conclusion of Somerset's case, and it was the turn of counsel for the defendant to take to the floor. As a kind of warm-up act for Dunning, his junior James Wallace opened, arguing that it would be absurd and unjust to divest Stewart of his property simply because he had brought it from one country to another. Playing on what he knew to be Lord Mansfield's preference for aligning law with custom, Wallace claimed that it was 'a known and allowed practice in mercantile transactions if a cause arises abroad, to lay it within the kingdom'. So that in the present case 'a contract in Virginia' could not be 'denied' in London. Lord Mansfield craved certainty in the law, but, Wallace argued, how could there be certainty if a contract made in one country was not honoured in another?[53] An antagonistic public gallery murmured disapprovingly.

Then Wallace turned to precedent, and after a cursory examination of cases involving an 'act of trover',* referred the bench to the Joint Opinion. It must have been with some confidence that Wallace called the chief justice's attention to the authority in question, not merely because it had the reputation of established law, but because its authors

---

* An act of trover seeks to recover the value of personal property that has been wrongly taken or disposed of by another person.

had been the personal friends and mentors of Lord Mansfield. But if Wallace had hoped for an unconditional endorsement of the Opinion, he was cruelly disappointed. He had misread his court, and Lord Mansfield responded witheringly that the 'case alluded to was upon a petition in Lincoln's Inn Hall, after dinner; probably, therefore, might not, as he believes the contrary is not unusual at that hour, be taken with much accuracy'.[54]

When Dunning stood up to take over from his fellow counsel, he did so in the knowledge not only that 'much the greater part' of the public gallery wished to find him 'in the wrong', but that the bench were moving against him too. Mansfield's dismissal of the Joint Opinion left the defence in tatters, and it must have been with relief that he accepted the chief justice's suggestion of a yet further adjournment to the following week. Before rising, Lord Mansfield made this statement: 'If the merchants think the question of great consequence to trade and commerce, and the public should think so too, they had better think of an application to those that will make law [i.e. Parliament]. We must find the law: we cannot make it.'[55]

The statement was plainly addressed to the 'West Indian interest', and was a thinly veiled warning that the judgement was likely to go against them. Lord Mansfield explained that in his judicial capacity he could only 'find the law', and the law did not support the defendant's case. If the 'West Indian interest' wished to bring slaves to Britain with impunity, then it must petition Parliament to legislate to that effect.

On 21 May Dunning rose reluctantly to his feet to make the final submissions in the case. As has been noted, the barrister was 'dull and languid', and there was a listless quality to his arguments. Rather than attempt to resurrect the Joint Opinion, Dunning confined his advocacy to matters of policy, claiming that a decision in favour of the plaintiff risked massive economic disruption. Dunning estimated that there were 15,000 slaves in England, each of whom was worth in the region of £50. According to leading counsel, a finding for the claimant would result in the loss of property to the approximate value of £700,000.

At the conclusion of the defendant's case, it was expected that Lord Mansfield would give judgement immediately. Instead the judge informed the court that 'we are neither inclined nor prepared to decide on the present question; the matter will require some deliberation before we can venture an opinion on it'.[56] This was surprising, as Mansfield's damning of the Joint Opinion, and his response to the arguments put forward by the defence, indicated that he had made up his mind on the legal issue. The real reason for the postponement became apparent when he explained that the 'difficulty' faced by the tribunal did not lie 'in the question itself, as in the probable consequences resulting from it'. Lord Mansfield then reiterated Dunning's claim that a decision in the claimant's favour would lead to a massive loss of property.

In a further indication of where the land lay, the judge repeated his earlier opinion that 'An application to Parliament' was the 'best, and perhaps the only method of settling the point for the future'. He then offered an escape route to the defendant: 'I remember 5 or 6 cases similar to this,' he mused, 'but they were either compromised, amicably adjusted, or given up by one or the other parties: perhaps the present may end in like manner.' And if this was not sufficiently blatant, Mansfield went on to remark that 'It is not improbable that Mr Stewart may decline insisting on a decision in the present instance'. Then, with obvious reluctance, Lord Mansfield concluded: 'If the parties will have judgement, *fiat justitia, ruat coelum* [let justice be done though the heavens may fall].'[57]

In spite of the judge's admonitions, the cause was neither 'compromised' nor 'amicably adjusted', and when the court reconvened for the final hearing on 22 June 1772, Lord Mansfield delivered his judgement. Though he must have known through the reports of his legal team that the odds had shifted in their favour, still Granville kept away. As recorded by the court reporter, Capel Lofft, Mansfield's decision was short and almost certainly extempore. Having summarised the captain's answer to the writ of habeas corpus, and dismissed the Joint Opinion, Mansfield came to the heart of the matter. 'So high an act of dominion,' he stated, as that of a master forcefully removing his slave abroad, 'must be recognised by the law of the country where it is used.' Moreover, the 'state of slavery is of such a nature' that it can only be sanctioned by 'positive law'. Indeed 'in a case so odious as the condition of slaves' the law must be 'taken strictly'. This being the case, Mansfield ruled that 'Tracing the subject to natural principles, the claim of slavery can never be supported ... No master ever was allowed here to take a slave by force to be sold abroad because he deserted from his service, or for any other reason whatever; we cannot say, the cause set forth by this return is allowed or approved of by the laws of this kingdom, and therefore the man must be discharged'.[58]

According to the *London Chronicle*, as the words 'the man must be discharged' reverberated round the packed courtroom, a group of black men and women who sat together in the gallery 'bowed with profound respect to the Judges, and shaking each other by the hand, congratulated themselves upon the recovery of the rights of human nature'. A few days later, the *London Packet* reported that more than 200 former slaves had gathered 'At a public house in Westminster, to celebrate the triumph which their brother Somerset had obtained over Stewart his master. Lord Mansfield's health was echoed round the room, and the evening was concluded with a ball.'[59]

Unlike Granville, James Somerset had attended every day of the trial. It is easy to forget, in the drama of the proceedings, that what had been at stake was not just a point of abstruse legal principle, but a man's life. Had the judgement gone against Somerset, he faced years of back-breaking toil on a Jamaican sugar-cane plantation. The relief that he felt as Lord Mansfield made his ruling is beyond comprehension. Later, as the crowds dispersed outside Westminster Hall, Somerset made his way to Old Jewry, where Granville was waiting for him. In an entry in his notebook dated 22 June 1772, the philanthropist records simply: 'This day James Somerset came to tell me that judgment was today given in his favour.' After a synopsis of the judge's reasons, he concludes: 'Thus ended G Sharp's long contest with Lord Mansfield, on the 22nd of June, 1772.'

Opinion differs as to the precise scope of Lord Mansfield's judgement. Some commentators take a restrictive approach, suggesting for example that the decision amounts to no more than that 'habeas corpus applied to blacks as well as whites'.[60] It is certain that Lord Mansfield himself wished to contain the remit of his judgement to its narrowest possible extent, maintaining on several occasions that it 'went no further than to determine the Master had no right to compel the slave to go into a foreign country'.[61] The contemporary press was more expansive in its interpretation. According to the *Middlesex Journal* of 23 June 1772, Lord Mansfield ruled that 'every slave brought into this country ought to be free, and no master had a right to sell them here'. The *Morning Chronicle* proclaimed: 'Tyrants, no more the servile yoke prepare, / For breath of slaves too pure is British air.'[62]

This was premature, for although the Somerset ruling was followed in habeas corpus cases involving slaves, the air remained decidedly impure for years to come. There were still instances of slaves being bought and sold in Britain after 1772, and in contradiction of even the narrowest of the interpretations of Mansfield's judgement, fugitives were occasionally hunted down and returned to the Caribbean. But though the Somerset ruling did not eliminate slavery on British soil, it was nonetheless a milestone on the road to abolition. As well as its practical impact on the lives of individual slaves saved from transportation, the case caught the public imagination. Somerset's case levered the issue of slavery out of its hiding place of moral apathy and ignorance, into the open, where it became the subject of controversy and debate.

Moreover, the trials of Lewis and Somerset constitute the 'earliest campaign in England for the abolition of slavery and the slave trade'.[63] It was the beginning of a struggle that would culminate thirty-five years later in the Slave Trade Act of 1807, which prohibited the slave trade in the British Empire, and subsequently in the abolition of slavery itself, under the terms of the Slavery Abolition Act 1833. The Somerset case also had a profound influence in America. It was widely believed, for example, among the slave community in the Southern states that the case had abolished slavery in Britain, leading to attempts by individuals to find freedom there.[64]

The significance of Granville's contribution to the cause of anti-slavery has been acknowledged by its leading participants. Thomas Clarkson, the architect of abolition, noted in his 1808 history of the movement that 'Mr Granville Sharp is to be distinguished from those who preceded him by this particular, that, whereas these were only writers he was both a writer and an actor in the cause. In fact, he was the first labourer in it in England.'[65]

William Wilberforce, in a letter to Granville dated 17 April 1792, paid this tribute to his correspondent: 'When I call to mind that I am addressing the gentleman who led the way in this glorious struggle wherein we are engaged, I think I feel towards you somewhat of the respectful reverence of a son; whilst I am sure, I am conscious of all the affection of a brother.'[66]

What Granville depicted as his 'long contest with Lord Mansfield' was hardly an equal encounter. The chief justice, bolstered by the powerful forces of state, legal precedent and the West Indian lobby, was a stately Goliath to Granville's puny David. Two hundred and fifty years later, Somerset remains one of the great landmark cases of British legal history. The importance of Granville's role in the proceedings can hardly be overstated. Not only was he the driving force behind the litigation, and the related cases such as Lewis's that preceded it, but it was his exhaustive legal research that underpinned the claimant's argument. The judgement represents the culmination of his campaign for the liberation of slaves on British soil, and has earned Granville the reputation of being the first great abolitionist.

21

Welfare State

John, the eldest of the Sharp brothers, lived all his life in the north of England. During the 1760s and early 1770s, while William and James prospered, and Granville embarked on his campaign for the liberation of slaves, John pursued his clerical career as vicar of Hartburn, Prebend of Durham and Archdeacon of Northumberland. Though he undertook his ecclesiastical duties with scrupulous attention, it was for his work as trustee of the Lord Crewe Trust, and in particular for the development of a pioneering social enterprise at Bamburgh Castle in Northumberland, that he is best remembered.

Bamburgh Castle sits on top of a precipitous outcrop of rock on the coast of Northumberland, sixteen miles north of Alnwick. A natural fortress, the site has been occupied continuously since the Iron Age, and rose to particular prominence in the Saxon era when it was the royal palace of a line of Northumbrian chieftains. An early chronicle describes 'Bebba' as a 'most strongly fortified city', accessible by a gateway 'hollowed out of the rock and raised in steps after a marvellous fashion'. Of the many wonders of this lofty kingdom, the chronicler singles out 'a church of extremely beautiful workmanship' that contained, 'wrapt in a pall, the right hand of St Oswald the king still incorrupt', and at the highest point of the city, 'a spring of water, sweet to the taste and most pure to the sight, that has been excavated with astonishing labour'.[1]

In 1758, all that remained of Bamburgh's splendid past were the remnants of a Norman castle, consisting of a dilapidated keep and curtain walls, and three baileys – the East Ward, the West Ward and

the Inner Ward. At low tide a broad swathe of beach separated
Bamburgh from the sea, and sand dunes flecked with grasses and
pools of water lined the shore, but at high tide the waves reached to
the edge of the rocks on which the castle stood. It was a place of
wild and majestic beauty, battered by wind and the relentless crashing
of the sea, and cut off from the interior by poor roads and the lawless-
ness of the country. Bamburgh was as bleak and inhospitable a spot
as any in England at this time, but it became, by reason of what John
called 'the peculiar situation of this castle and accidental circumstances', the backdrop to an extraordinary philanthropic endeavour.[2]
Over the course of twenty-five years, John established a range of
charitable institutions at the castle, including schools, medical facilities,
a lifeboat station and a subsidised food distribution, that together
constituted a miniature welfare state.

The story of the Bamburgh Castle charities begins with Lord Crewe
(1633–1721), the Prince Bishop of Durham, who bequeathed his estates
in Durham and Northumberland to a charitable trust. By the terms
of his will, dated 24 June 1720, Crewe specified that after payment of
certain named beneficiaries, any surplus income was to be used for
charitable purposes at the discretion of the trustees.[3] When one of
the original trustees died in 1736, the siblings' father Thomas Sharp
took his place. Notwithstanding his other duties, Thomas found time
to be an exemplary trustee, repairing 'decayed tenements', inspecting
the trust's mines, and augmenting poor church livings.[4] When Thomas
died in 1758, his eldest son John, whose career closely mirrored his
own, was elected in his place. So carefully had the trust been managed
that by the date of John's accession to the trusteeship, the annual
income was running at a surplus. This was too large to be absorbed
by the needs of the named beneficiaries, and John had the idea of
investing the surplus funds into a charitable operation based at
Bamburgh Castle, which was owned by the estate.

Though John was answerable to his fellow trustees for the work
carried out at the castle, they invariably followed his proposals. As he
was the most energetic and resourceful of the trustees, it was natural
that they should accede to his requests. But rather than imposing his
will on trustee meetings, John took a gentler line, introducing his

schemes by way of suggestion, and then making them permanent by a process of default. In 1766, for example, John asked the trustees for a grant of £30 to buy corn which could then be sold to the poor at a subsidised rate. The payment was approved, and the following year an annual grant of £100 was established.[5] John recorded the decisions of the trustee board in a memo book, and was careful to note his own requests for funds. In his record of the meeting of 9 October 1766, for example, John concludes his account of an agreement that 'all Coals to be used in about the Castle of Bambrough shall be delivered gratis at some of the working collieries of the Trustees at Sunderland', with the following statement: 'NB this order was obtained at my request.'[6]

John later claimed that no theory had been involved in the Bamburgh scheme, rather it had evolved piecemeal, and in response to a range of obvious needs. It was characteristic of John to downplay the importance of his own vision for the project. But I imagine him during the early days of his trusteeship, scrambling on the rocks that lead from the castle to the sea, or picking his way through the ruins of a neglected gatehouse, with his head filled with dreams of what he might achieve there. He sees a ship struggling in heavy seas, and lies awake into the night, unable to rid himself of the tormenting image of a drowning sailor. In the morning, as he paces along the rain-washed battlements, the sight of a disused cannon sparks his imagination. He roams through the echoing castle rooms, and pictures rows of desks and the expectant faces of children, and granaries stuffed with sacks of ripened grain. Sometimes it is anger that moves him, as when he encounters a family of paupers begging on the road between Beadnell and Seahouses, or a distraught woman outside a cottage at Budle who cannot pay for a doctor to attend her dying child. Then he wanders alone for hours along the Bamburgh seashore, raging against the injustices of the world, and pledging himself to the task of bettering the lives of the poor.

John describes the inception of his work at Bamburgh in a letter to his friend John Ramsay, written in the 1780s. 'In 1757,' he begins, 'a part of the old tower being ready to fall, my father in the last year of his life got it supported, merely because it had been a sea mark for ages, and consequently as such beneficial to the public.' Given John's regard for his father, it was natural that he should continue the work that Thomas had begun, and his record of trusteeships meetings in the early years of his tenure contain constant reference to requests for money for repairs to the castle. Funded by grants from the trust, and also by his own personal contributions, John supervised the renovation of the curtain walls, battlements, rampart and gate tower.[7] The old courtroom on the ground floor of the keep was restored to its original function as a venue for holding manorial courts, and living apartments were created in the upper storeys of the tower, for the use of the trustees and the minister of Bamburgh church.[8]

John's first substantial innovation at Bamburgh was the founding of a school for local children. His account of the initiative – 'The children wanted education, therefore schools were necessary; and where so proper as under the eye of the trustees?' – underplays the scale of the achievement.[9] Children from poor homes in this period suffered from a chronic lack of education. Schools, where they existed, were usually beyond the financial reach of the worst off, and the education provided there tended to be of such a low standard as to be almost worthless. The problem persisted well into the next century: the Children's Employment Commission of 1833 found that a mere 10% of children had satisfactory schooling, and 40% had none at all.[10]

John began modestly, with a small school situated in the courtroom, when it was not in use for official business. William Peacock is mentioned as a schoolmaster at the castle in a memorandum of a trustee meeting in February 1760. He was soon joined by a female colleague, Dinah Middleton, who was installed as a schoolmistress in May. This pair must have led a spartan existence, at least until 23 March 1761 when it was 'agreed & ordered that the Schoolmaster & Schoolmistress at Bambrough Castle shall have Coals allowed for the Use of their schools' and also that 'a Bed & Bedding shall be provided for the Use of the Said Schoolmaster & that Dr Sharp be requested to provide the same'.[11]

Things were on the up, however, for in September 1762 it was reported to the trustees that three rooms in the castle had been fitted up for the use of the school, and as living quarters for the school-

A contemporary of the Sharps wrote that she knew of no family 'wherein more true brotherly kindness appears / While unenvying each shines in their diff[e]rent spheres'. Johan Zoffany's celebrated portrait brilliantly conveys the spirit of this most harmonious of families.

Cabin boy Dick Spikeman and boat master William Lee stand at the far left of the painting. James, with serpent, sits next to his daughter Kitty. Granville leans on the harpsichord by Elizabeth. Frances is next, and then John and his wife Mary. On the raised stern sits James's wife Catharine, in a black shawl, and William's wife, also Catharine, who holds their baby daughter Mary. Judith is playing the lute. William stands at the tiller, and to his left is John and Mary's daughter Anne Jemima.

Painted at the same time as *The Sharp Family*, *Self-Portrait with his Daughter Maria Theresa, James Cervetto, and Giacobbe Cervetto* (1780) shows Zoffany at work.

Archdeacon Thomas Sharp, father of the siblings, was an extraordinary man in his own right.

Whitton Tower was the Sharps' childhood home. A rare example of a fortified rectory, it still stands on a hillside above Rothbury in Northumberland.

This bird's-eye view of the Thames, looking eastwards from what is now Somerset House to the Tower of London, was printed in 1750. Sharp family water parties took place on less congested stretches of the river to the west of the city.

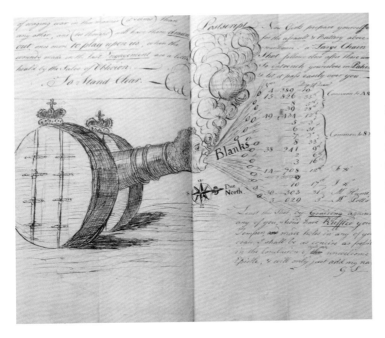

In a letter to his sisters dated 18 October 1757, Granville breaks the bad news that they have failed to win a prize in a recent government lottery: 'many Airy castles . . . even as far off as Northumberland have been demolished in a moment'.

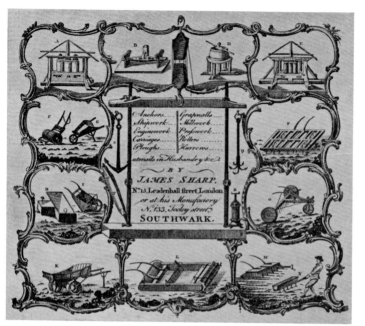

This exquisite trade card features the range of equipment that James produced in his manufactory in Tooley Street. Lines included pioneering agricultural machinery and his famous 'rolling carts'.

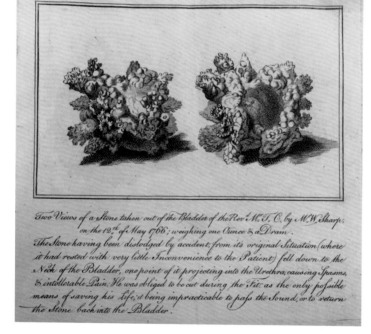

Two Views of a Stone taken out of the Bladder of the Rev.ᵈ M.ʳ T. C. by M.ʳ W. Sharp, on the 12.ᵗʰ of May 1766; weighing one Ounce & a Dram.
The Stone having been dislodged by accident, from its original Situation (where it had rested with very little Inconvenience to the Patient) fell down to the Neck of the Bladder, one point of it projecting into the Urethra, causing Spasms, & intollerable Pain; He was obliged to be cut during the Fit; as the only possible means of saving his Life; it being impracticable to pass the Sound, or to return the Stone back into the Bladder.

William performed this delicate operation to remove a bladder stone without anaesthetic. The surgeon's subsequent loss of sight was thought to be linked to the anxiety he felt when carrying out such procedures.

A man of exceptional warmth, generosity and compassion, William inspired love in all who knew him.

'[It] is a point with me never to conceal my sentiment on any point whatever': Granville could be candid almost to the point of rudeness.

WICKEN PARK.

Elizabeth resided at Wicken Park in Northamptonshire from 1764 until her death in 1810, during which time she worked tirelessly to improve the lives of the estate's inhabitants and workers.

Above: The location for Zoffany's *Queen Charlotte (1744–1818) with members of her family* is perhaps the same favoured 'Bench under a large Tree' on which the king and queen were sitting when they were serenaded by the Sharp family band in August 1770.

Left: The Sharps' relationship with George III, who is depicted here in a 1771 portrait by Zoffany, was the pinnacle of their social rise.

John established a revolutionary social enterprise at Bamburgh Castle. In this remote coastal part of Northumberland, he provided education and healthcare for the poor, and commissioned the world's first lifeboat.

James Hayllar completed *Granville Sharp (1735–1813), The Abolitionist, Rescuing a Slave from The Hands of His Master* in 1864, half a century after Granville's death. It highlights the lasting legacy of the man known in his own day as the 'father' of abolition.

In *A View in Hampton Garden with Mr and Mrs Garrick Taking Tea* (1762),
Zoffany evokes the idyll of a residence on the banks of the Thames. The
Sharps would have enjoyed these views when they visited in September 1777.

The Sharp family flotilla is shown here on the Thames near Barnes. The *Union*
yacht takes centre stage, while the *Apollo* barge – with its distinctive standard
(embroidered by Judith) and raised red stern – is towards the left of the painting.

mistress.[12] The provision of purpose-built classrooms established the separation of the school into two distinct entities, a school for boys and a school for girls. The boys were taught Latin, English, writing, navigation, arithmetic 'and other Branches of Mathematicks'. The curriculum in the girls' school consisted of reading, writing, arithmetic, plainwork, fine-work and knitting.[13]

In his account of the founding of the school, John noted that there was no more proper place to provide education than 'under the eye of the trustees'. He might as well have said under his own eye, for John almost certainly assumed responsibility for the curriculum, and for maintaining educational standards. He was particularly concerned to engage qualified and effective teachers, and it is noteworthy that by 1772, there were two schoolmasters at Bamburgh, a headmaster who taught the boys Latin and English, and a 'second master' who was responsible for writing, navigation and mathematics.[14] This separation of duties allowed John to retain specialist teachers, such as the mathematician John Dial who joined the school in 1772.

A place at the school was open to children whose parents earned no more than £10 a year.[15] This threshold seems to have been strictly observed, though a few places were open to scholars whose parents paid for their attendance. In his *Account of the Uses to which the Old Roman Tower in Bambrough Castle is at present appropriated*, dating from about 1780, John reported that fifty boys and fifty girls attended the castle schools. These numbers were elastic, however, for in a report on the castle provided in advance of the bishop's visitation in 1782, John stated that sixty boys and sixty girls were taught in the schools, as well as about fourteen whose fees were paid by their parents.[16] Attendance was closely monitored, with children who were 'absent above Six Days in a Quarter without Leave except only in Case of sickness or extreme bad weather' being excluded for six months.[17]

The Bamburgh school brought with it all the problems associated with an institution of this sort. One of the crosses which John had to bear was the chronic alcoholism of his second master, John Dial. A brilliant mathematical scholar, and a master of the technical and theoretical science of navigation, Dial's prospects were clouded by what was politely called a 'jovial disposition and fondness for company'. In a letter to John dated 26 October 1773, the second master expresses remorse for his behaviour during supper in the courtroom:

> I am so much ashamed of it, that it has never been out of my mind since, nor can I get the better of it do what I will. I am heartily sorry for my misconduct and humbly Begg Dr Sharp's Pardon, as well as the other two gentlemen that were then at supper; and I here firmly promise that I never shall be guilty of such an unmannerly, unmanly and audacious Crime as get myself as intoxicated with liquor again.[18]

John was a compassionate employer, for though Dial continued to alternate between periods of sobriety and drunkenness, he remained at Bamburgh until 1787. The mathematician's final years were mired in poverty and addiction, and he died in Horton in 1816 'in very indigent circumstances'.[19]

There can be no doubt that the Bamburgh school transformed the lives of the thousands of children who were educated there in the second half of the eighteenth century. They were the lucky beneficiaries not merely of an education, but of an education of a quality far higher than that ordinarily available to children of their class. Because of the unique properties of the curriculum, the students were equipped not only with a thorough knowledge of arithmetic and writing, but with skills such as navigation and needlework, that would enable them to find work. In later years John added to the educational provision at the castle with the establishment of a public lending library.

Six years after the opening of the first school at Bamburgh, John launched his 'corn charity' for the provision of subsidised food.[20] The corn was bought from tenant farmers on trust land, under the terms of their lease, and in later years peas, beans, oats and barley were also supplied. Prices were fixed regardless of the cost of supply, with wheat at 4s 6d per bushel, peas and beans at 3s 1d, meal at 4s, barley at 2s 6d and oats at 2s.[21]

At times of scarcity, or when corn prices were particularly high, the charity was inundated with purchasers. On 7 December 1782, for example, George Hall, the manager of the corn charity, noted that he had served 120 people and that several went away empty-handed when supplies ran out.[22] So great was the need that it was usual for 'numbers of poor to be at the Castle by the hours of five, four, three and sometimes even two in the morning, on a supposition of first come first served'.[23] Some had come great distances, as according to John, 'In a Year when Corn has been dear this Charity has been extended through a Tract of country near 40 Miles in length for no Persons who are Poor are excluded.'[24]

As with the Bamburgh schools, the corn charity was restricted to users below a certain poverty level. Tickets of entitlement were provided to prospective customers on production of a note of recommendation from a local vicar or landowner. However, the system was open to abuse, as recorded in a letter to John from Ralph Dods of the local village of Beadnell, who complained that no account was taken of the size of an applicant's family, and that unscrupulous types bought corn only to sell it on at a profit.[25] Thereafter the system seems to have been tightened up, with the details of purchasers, such as their name, place of residence, occupation, number of family and circumstances, kept in a register.

Sale days were held twice a week, and were advertised by the hoisting of a small 'Jack' on the east turret. Transactions took place in the sale room in the keep, which housed chests for different kinds of corn and for meal, and from here the queue of customers snaked down into the ward.[26] It could be disorderly at times, at least according to Ralph Dods, who complained that there is often 'such a throng and jostling' that 'Coercives' are required to 'quiet the tumult'.[27] Corn was supplied to the sale room by an efficient system consisting of a crane from the north turret worked by a horse, which hoisted supplies to the granaries on the upper floor of the keep, and from where it was conveyed into the sale room via an iron spout. Equipment such as a malt mill, a barley mill and hand querns were available at the castle for the use of purchasers. Another element of the charity was the supply of free meat to the poor at Christmas.[28]

John's efforts to reduce the devastating effects of shipwrecks date from the early 1760s. He explained what motivated him in a letter to

John Ramsay: 'The number of wrecks on this particular coast of vessels that had run for Holy Island harbour in a storm and failed of getting into it, and the melancholy sights from the castle of persons wrecked on the islands and starving with cold and hunger, together with the savage plundering of such goods &c, as were driven on shore.'[29]

The incidence of shipwrecks at Bamburgh, and the hazards of travel generally in this period, are illustrated in the correspondence between John and his manager George Hall dating from the early 1780s. Hall wrote to his employer on an almost daily basis when the latter was absent from Bamburgh, and his letters often contain references to shipwrecks. On 6 January 1783, for instance, Hall describes 'a very melancholy accident' involving a vessel 'struck upon the outer islands and in half an hour went to the bottom' while 'Four of the Ships crew six men passengers two women and two children went to the bottom with hir'.[30]

Later in that year, on 19 November 1783, Hall reports that 'Yesterday forenoon in a strong gale wind from the North a poor unfortunate sloop foundered betwixt the Megstone and the House Island and all hands suffered'. According to Hall, 'There is yet a part of hir mast above water upon which was one of the poor unfortunate sufferers for about half an hour after she went down but impossible to give him any assistance.'[31] Such was the frequency of shipwrecks that it was quite usual for bodies to be washed up on the beach at Bamburgh, and Hall often refers to finding bodies 'much wasted' in the days following a storm. On 27 December 1783, for example, he relates how 'Last night one of the poor men were [sic] found on the sands with his head of[f] but no otherwise wasted'.[32]

In February 1765, John made a passionate appeal to the trustees to assist him in preventing needless loss of life: 'Whereas in the late storms at sea some mariners and passengers who suffered shipwreck in the night time on the coast within the manor of Bambrough having got safe to shore afterwards perished by the severity of the weather before they could find any house, and others lost their life for want of proper accommodations when on shore.'[33]

His pleas did not fall on deaf ears, for the trustees sanctioned two measures that were to play a significant role in John's efforts to combat the impact of shipwrecks. The first was that 'two men shall be hired to ride along the coast during the night time during every great storm to give what assistance they can to ships in distress'.[34] The patrol became a regular feature of Bamburgh life in the years that followed, and is often referred to by George Hall in his correspondence with his employer. In a letter dated 9 December 1784, for example, Hall informs John that during a recent storm 'Ned Todd and I patrolled from 12 o'clock till day light'.[35] The patrols were used in conjunction with a signal gun, which was fired during fogs.[36]

On 1 February 1769 the trustees approved the purchase of equipment for raising ships stranded on the Bamburgh coast.[37] In the years that followed John assembled an armoury of implements that included screws, chains, grapples, boat hooks and sea tongs.[38] The value of this equipment is attested to by George Hall, who often reports its use in his correspondence with John. On 28 December 1777, for instance, he records that a Mr Burn has desired the loan of screws to raise his ship at Holy Island,[39] while on 19 March 1784 he informs his employer that 'The sloop that was on Shorston Sands are [sic] repaired in Sunderland Harbour and are now fitt for sea the owner returnes thanks for the assistance of our screw Black Hanpacks etc.'[40]

John also provided equipment for use in assisting ships in trouble. On 15 February 1772 he persuaded the trustees to fund the purchase of three pumps, while the stores at Bamburgh also included 'A suffi-cient Number of Cork Jackets for the use of such Persons as venture of in Boats to the assistance of Ships in distress'.[41] That attempts of this sort were made to rescue beleaguered vessels is evidenced in a letter from George Hall dated 19 February 1783. 'Yesterday Half past Eight,' he reports, 'a brig Run on the Swedmen for which the 9 pounder were two times fired. We immediately Launched our Big Boat and went to their assistance it being moderate weather.'[42]

It was for the purpose of assisting ships in trouble that John obtained his most revolutionary item of equipment. In September 1788 he approached Lionel Lukin, a coachbuilder in Covent Garden, with a view to purchasing a specially adapted lifeboat.[43] As well as being a fashionable London manufacturer, Lukin was a man of mechanical ingenuity whose inventions included a raft for rescuing people trapped under ice and an adjustable reclining bed for patients. In 1784 Lukin began experimenting with modifications to a two-masted Norwegian yawl, and on 2 November 1785 obtained a patent for an 'improved method of construction of boats and small vessels, for either sailing or rowing, which will neither overset in violent gales or sudden bursts of wind, nor sink if by any accident fill with water'.[44]

Lukin's 'unimmergible' featured buoyant gunwales, airtight and watertight compartments, and a false keel made of cast iron. Lukin submitted his design to luminaries such as the Prince of Wales, the dukes of Portland and Northumberland, and Admiral Lord Howe who apparently gave him strong verbal approbation, but could not be induced to take the matter any further. The coachbuilder then lent his unimmergible to a pilot in Ramsgate, but heard no more of it beyond that it had been used to cross the Channel in conditions inimical to ordinary vessels.

It was at this point that John approached Lukin with a request to use his design at Bamburgh. Rather than using a Norwegian yawl, the idea was to adapt a North Country flat-bottomed fishing 'coble' suited to the shallow shores of the Northumbrian coast. John arranged for a coble to be sent down to London, where Lukin modified it according to his original specification. On its return to Northumberland, the vessel played a key role in subsequent rescue attempts. The modified coble is thought to be the first operating lifeboat, and Bamburgh the first lifeboat station, in Britain.

In his first heartfelt plea to the trustees on the subject of shipwrecks in February 1765, John had spoken of the tragedy of those who died through want of shelter. To combat this senseless waste of life John suggested that survivors should be offered accommodation at the castle. The trustees were amenable to this proposal, and afterwards beds were always maintained at Bamburgh for the use of those who got safely to shore. Help was also given to individuals who survived a wreck but did not need to stay at the castle. For example on 6 January 1783, Hall reported that he had provided assistance to survivors including 'victuals and drink and a small mater money to set them on thir road'.[45] Those who died as a result of calamity at sea were also treated with respect. Rigorous procedures were applied to the treatment of bodies found on the beach at Bamburgh, including inspection of clothing for clues of identity, and attempts to contact the next of kin. The dead were covered with a shroud – usually a sheet from one of the beds kept for the shipwrecked which was then replaced – and buried in a coffin made by the castle carpenter.

According to John, the beds kept in readiness for beleaguered seafarers represented 'the beginning of our little infirmary, which soon suggested the idea of a general dispensary for the poor'.[46] The genesis of the general dispensary is set out in John's submissions to the trustee meeting on 20 August 1772, in which he argues forcefully for the introduction of free medical provision for the poor. John grounded his arguments on the absence of alternative facilities for those of limited means. The nearest provider of free medical care was the Newcastle infirmary, which was fifty miles away on poor roads, and therefore beyond the reach of all but a tiny minority of Bamburgh residents. For those who could not travel to Newcastle, there remained the option of paid medical services from the local doctor. This was unfeasible for many in the community, who John describes as being 'so very necessitous, that they can neither pay a surgeon for attendance or advice, or be at the necessary expence of Druggs when sick'.[47]

The trustees at the August 1772 meeting agreed to fund the services of a surgeon, who was to attend for three hours every Saturday morning. His duties were specified as being 'to give advice, administer medicines, dress the sores of all such poor Persons as shall apply for such assistance' and also to 'perform operations' if required. Back-up was to be provided by John Robson, whose responsibilities included 'baking in the mortar'* and providing assistance to the doctor when required, and also Mrs Raston whose remit was bookkeeping, making up medicines, scraping lint, and cleaning the surgery.[48]

The surgery was an immediate success – so much so that the medical team were unable to cope with the inundation of patients. In his report to the trustee meeting of 29 October 1772, John explained that: 'by the great increase of the number of patients at Bambrough Castle,

---

* This presumably refers in some way to the use of a pestle and mortar, traditionally used in pharmacies to crush ingredients for a prescription.

the Surgeon cannot get his business dispatched in three hours as first expected, but is obliged to attend the whole day every Saturday, and sometimes a part of the proceeding [i.e. preceding] and following day'.[49] John's solution was to extend the length of the shift worked by the surgeon, and the trustees accordingly rubber-stamped a proposal that the doctor attend throughout the day on Saturday. He was rewarded for his extra hours with higher pay and bed and board on Friday and Saturday nights.[50]

Over the next few years the Bamburgh medical charity became a multipurpose institution. In his *Account of the Uses to which the Old Roman Tower in Bambrough Castle is at present appropriated*, John divided the medical services provided by the charity into three distinct categories – 'A General Dispensary for the Poor', 'A General Surgery for the Poor' and 'An Infirmary' – but there seems to have been a certain amount of fluidity in the nomenclature of the different parts of the organisation.[51] As a whole the charity provided a service similar to that of a modern GP's practice, with certain additions, such as surgical procedures, more commonly associated with a hospital. The castle housed both a surgery, which was located in one of the lower rooms, and a dispensary – but it is not clear which of these was the equivalent of the GP's attendance room. Possibly the surgery was used specifically for surgical intervention, while the dispensary was more akin to what we would understand as a surgery today.

The term 'dispensary' brings the Bamburgh charity in line with the movement for free outpatient provision that was a feature of the late eighteenth century. The first dispensary opened in Red Lion Square in London in 1769, and in the years that followed a rash of other similar institutions were established across London.[52] Founded just three years after the Red Lion Square prototype, Bamburgh provided a cutting-edge service and in many respects fits the model of the London dispensaries.[53] However, it was in fact a unique experiment in medical provision. Dispensaries were exclusively urban institutions, whereas the Bamburgh charity was situated in a rural backwater fifty miles from the nearest large town and can certainly lay claim to being the first provincial dispensary. Further, while standard dispensaries were funded by subscription (which tended to restrict their freedom of manoeuvre – both in terms of the funds available, and the opinions, beliefs and prejudices of their subscribers), John had a free rein in his management of the castle charities. Under his visionary direction, the Bamburgh dispensary provided services that were beyond the scope of even the most sophisticated hospitals in large towns, and were also more inclusive.[54]

The Bamburgh charity was primarily an outpatient service. Though there were beds in what John refers to as the infirmary, these were reserved for the victims of shipwreck and 'for some particular Cases'.[55] An example of a particular case – and of the power of the Bamburgh charities to transform individual lives – is found in the correspondence of Mr Cockagne, one of the castle surgeons. In a letter to John dated 13 January 1787, Cockagne recounts the story of a sixteen-year-old girl called Patience Burrow, who had recently been discovered in a state of extreme distress in a village near Bamburgh. It seems that after the death of her parents Patience had attempted to walk from Warwickshire to Scotland in search of an uncle, though 'she did not know whether he was dead or alive'. She had been 'six months upon the way', during which time she had sold all her clothes.

Patience was discovered 'literally Naked' and in such a condition that according to Cockagne she 'would have perished in a very few hours from cold hunger and disease'. On examination she was found to be suffering from 'the Venereal Disease in the Most Shocking Manner The Labia Pudenda in a state of Mortification – the Itch to a great Degree – a Violent Cough'.[56] The girl was admitted to the infirmary, where she gradually recovered. On 14 February 1787, some four weeks after her admission, Cockagne reported that Patience was almost completely cured.[57] The girl was helped back on her feet, given money for clothes, including a flannel bed gown, a petticoat, two pairs of stockings and a pair of shoes, and was later assisted to find employment.

The surgeon at Bamburgh had at his disposal the latest range of surgical tools, including incision knives, lancets, trocars, catheter syringes, needles, a variety of instruments for the teeth, and splints of different sizes for broken legs. There was even an infirmary chair for the use of reducing dislocated shoulders, and a special bed for patients with broken legs. The non-surgical staff were equally well equipped, with weapons in their armoury such as 'a stile & Worm Tub', a case of elastic vegetable bottles, and apparatus for making artificial pyrmont water. Medicines were prepared in a 'convenient Laboratory' where the equipment included 'Furnace Retorts Receivers &c Five Mortars of different sizes with Marble Slabs Searces and other Utensils necessary in an Apothocaries Shop'.[58]

The facilities boasted a suite of baths, comprising a 'cold bath, extremely cold, the Water of which is raised from a Well above 24 Fathom deep', a 'hot bath with thermometer' and a 'tumbling' bath 'upon which either spring or seawater is received upon the head'.[59] Even the most outré of treatments was available at Bamburgh. Those with sufficient sangfroid could submit themselves to electrical equipment that gave a 'Shock with certainty to any degree required'. There were also two sets of apparatus for the recovery of drowned or suffocated persons, though the efficacy of this particular equipment is not recorded.[60]

With such facilities at their disposal, the medical team at Bamburgh were able to treat a considerable range of ailments. Patients seen in 1777–8 complained of over ninety separate disorders, from common coughs and colds to more defined conditions such as 'Erysipelas' (an acute skin swelling), 'Anasarca' (a swelling or oedema) and 'Hemiplegia' (cerebral palsy). The most common ailments recorded are gastrointestinal disorders such as vomiting and diarrhoea and other stomach complaints including biliousness.[61] Bamburgh also provided midwifery services (in 1795, for example, thirty-two women were attended while giving birth in their own homes)[62] and public health initiatives such as the inoculation of local children against smallpox. In April 1786, it is reported to John that 'the offer of Inoculation Gratis to all the Poor of Bambro and the Neighbourhood' has been 'made Publick at the Church Door on Sunday last by the Clerk'.[63]

In common with the other charities at Bamburgh, medical treatment was provided only to those who could not afford it elsewhere. There was no defined catchment area. In his *Account*, John notes that the 'Charity is open to all who apply for assistance whether English Scotch or Foreigners, on their bringing a Certificate of their Poverty properly attested'.[64] This document attesting to lack of means had to be signed by the vicar and two churchwardens of the applicant's parish, or in the case of dissenting parishioners, the signature of a minister and two elders of their meetinghouse. The charity made things easier for prospective patients by producing blank certificates onto which the relevant signatures could be written.[65]

There is no suggestion that this requirement blunted the keenness of those wishing to use the medical services at Bamburgh. Rather the figures suggest that huge numbers of people benefited from the facilities at the castle in the decades after 1770. By 1775 annual admissions numbered in the 600s, and in the following year 1,009 patients were seen. Patient numbers rose dramatically at the end of the decade, and in the 1780s the infirmary experienced a sustained period of high demand. On several occasions annual admissions exceeded 2,000. To put these figures in context, the York dispensary, serving a prosperous city of 17,000 inhabitants, served around 900 people a year in a similar period. Similarly, while 10,866 patients visited the Newcastle dispensary between October 1777 and September 1790, in the same period 22,213 people sought treatment at Bamburgh.[66]

Visiting Bamburgh in 1799, John's niece Mary described the castle as 'an absolute town within itself'.[67] After centuries of decline, Bamburgh had been restored to an existence as complete as the Norman bailey of its previous incarnation, or even the great city of 'Bebba'. I think of it as a place of constant, noisy, diverse activity. Every morning 130 children traipse through the gatehouse to school, and return again in the evening. During the day, between lessons, they play outside in the open spaces of the wards, and the sound of their shouts and laughter rings about the castle. On Saturdays the sick make their way in ones and twos up the steep path to the inner gateway, pausing now and then to catch their breath, and by early morning the queue of waiting patients curls down from the dispensary into the yard outside. Sale days bring hordes of people to the castle, pushing and shoving for places in a long line winding from the keep. Carts piled high with supplies roll through the narrow aperture of the gatehouse and into the inner ward, their wheels bumping and scraping on stone flags. Farmers heave sacks of corn to the foot of the granary, jostled by sailors returning from the reclamation room laden with the long clanking rings of ships chains. In the sale room purchasers nearing the front of the queue hear the soft tantalising whoosh of grain as it speeds down the iron spout into the chest below, and above it the staccato ring of masons' hammers resounding on the walls outside. On stormy days waves crash against the castle rock, and the wind howls, and the long low boom of the cannon rings alarm to passing ships.

For six months of the year John lived at the castle with his wife Mary and their daughter Anne Jemima, in the apartments created for the trustees on the second and third floors of the keep. Mary might have been forgiven for preferring the tranquil walks of the cathedral close at Durham, and the comfort of her vicarage at Hartburn, to lodgings above the sale room at Bamburgh. Nevertheless, and to her credit, Mary seems to have enjoyed life at the castle. In a letter to the London Sharps in 1770, she describes Bamburgh in muted, but none-theless convincing, terms as 'far from being disagreeable to myself'.[68] Like many of the women in the Sharp story, Mary is an elusive figure in the family archive. An analysis of her character depends almost entirely on Elizabeth's posthumous description of her as a 'most exc[ellent] good woman, wife & mother, of a most sweet disposition, an affect[ionate] Sisr to all her dear husband's family, & truly friendly & affable to all that knew her'.[69] Mary certainly played a role in the Bamburgh charities, though in what exact capacity is not known. One rare piece of evidence is contained in a letter dated 30 November 1782, in which George Hall reports to John that 'the ox was killed I had six mor applications most of which told me they had a Grant from Mrs Sharp'.[70]

In common with most Sharp endeavours, John obtained assistance for the Bamburgh project from at least four of his siblings. Thomas was given the living of Bamburgh in 1757, doubtless through family influence, and lived in apartments on the second and third floors of the keep, for part of the year. It is noted in the record of trustee meetings that Thomas contributed £80 of his own money to renovate the minister's lodgings, and he also played a part in managing castle affairs during John's absences.[71] Notwithstanding that the brothers lived cheek by jowl with each other at Bamburgh for months at a time, they remained on excellent terms. According to John, the brothers 'always lived in the utmost Harmony and never have had any little Bickerings or quarrels'.[72]

William played a significant role in the development of the medical charity. The Mincing Lane surgery can be seen as a prototype of the Bamburgh initiative, as it was for the dispensary movement as a whole, and William acted as an advisor to the infirmary. Letters between the brothers show that the surgeon was frequently consulted on matters such as the recruitment of staff and purchase of equipment. It was William, for example, who suggested the use of 'vegetable bottles' in the dispensary, which he assured his brother would be 'of very great benefit to many in your infirmary'.[73] He was also a generous donor to the charity. In October 1772 William sent a sedan chair to Bamburgh 'for the use of the hot bath and also for carrying such patients as are weak', and in the following year he donated a carriage for transporting the incapacitated.[74]

Granville was a correspondent of the physician and abolitionist John Coakley Lettsom who established one of the earliest dispensaries in London, and it is thought that through this channel Lettsom was consulted on the Bamburgh project.[75] Granville also played an advisory role in the renovation of the castle. Several of his drawings, including specifications for a door and windows, a plan of the castle, and a sketch of the White Tower at the Tower of London remain in the Bamburgh archive.[76] Granville also provided advice on the defence of the castle, corresponding at great length with his brother on the subject of guns, powder, shot, the militia, brass mortar and fireworks. James was an additional source of expertise on the construction side of the project. As well as drawing at least ten plans of the castle, he advised on matters such as the building of a windmill, fireproofing, and the utility of an 'Iron Closet'.[77]

Though many others played a role at Bamburgh, John was the architect of the project. It was his vision and energy that transformed the crumbling Norman ruin into a hub of charitable endeavour.[78] Bamburgh was not only his life's work, but an expression of himself, reflective of his personality as much as his beliefs. Time-keeping was a particular preoccupation, expressed in the regular use of the castle bell, as well as a system of signals and flags. But the charities also reveal a bold and imaginative aspect of John's character which is not apparent in his closely-written sermons and punctilious archidiaconal reports. What he created had no precedent, and its realisation demanded not merely the capacity for hard work, but also flair and a passionate resolve to improve the lives of his fellow men. As John Ramsay highlights in his poem 'Bamborough Castle', John was a man 'Whose labours, and even the pastimes of whose leisure hours / Breathe the love of human kind'.[79]

In a letter to his sister Judith dating from 1770, John describes Bamburgh as 'a Child of my own' and concludes: 'my attachment to the castle is such, that I can never give up my just right to it but with my life'.[80] Given John's devotion to Bamburgh, it was natural that he should be at pains to protect its future. His will provided for the payment of an annual sum to fund the upkeep of the buildings, and he also bequeathed his valuable book collection to the library.[81] But in spite of John's efforts to provide posthumous support for the charities, his death in 1792 marked the start of a gradual decline. The various enterprises languished, and a report by the Charity Commissioners in 1863 was unsparing in its condemnation of the castle institutions, concluding that they tended 'rather to produce mendicancy than to relieve distress'.[82] It is a sad testament to John's extraordinary personal contribution to the project that it could not thrive without him.

22

Canal Voyage

The Sharps were great innovators, so it perhaps comes as no surprise that they invented the canal holiday.[1] It was natural that James should wish to explore his beloved new waterways, and he was fortunate in having a family who relished travelling by water. Elizabeth refers to several expeditions in her diary, for example on 20 August 1772 ('Went a Canal Scheme to Coventry') and 7 September 1775 ('Left Sisr. F and Kitty at Wicken. Bro. and Sisr. James came down to them and took them a canal scheme'), but it is an excursion in August 1774 to which she devotes her particular attention.[2]

Elizabeth's narration of the events of the scheme begins on 15 August 1774 when she notes: 'A canal voige. 8 bros. and Sisrs. and Niece Catharine went by water.'[3] She then proceeds to an account of each day of the journey, noting in particular how many miles were travelled, where they spent the night, and the various wonders of canal engineering that they saw along the way. In all the party travelled 454 miles, of which 170 were by land and 284 by water. The scale of the expedition, the size of the party and the importance afforded to it in Elizabeth's diary suggests that this was their most ambitious venture.

The extent of that ambition is evident when it is considered that the journey, which began in Northamptonshire, and continued through Warwickshire, Staffordshire, the West Midlands, Worcestershire and Derbyshire, incorporated travel on all of the five great new canals of England – the Oxford, the Coventry, the Birmingham, the Trent & Mersey and the Staffordshire & Worcestershire. As several of these

were only half built, and the canal network of the country was as yet
not fully integrated, the travellers could not pass from waterway to
waterway in a seamless progression. Instead they were required on
several occasions to remove themselves from one canal and journey
by land to the next. Nor could the family remain on the same vessel
for the entirety of the journey, for a barge could not be taken from
one canal to another unconnected to it. Other challenges included the
provision of food and accommodation, the recruitment of crew, and
the hiring of horses to pull the barges.

Rather than being daunted by these logistical hurdles, James seems
instead to have viewed the excursion as an opportunity to exercise his
considerable powers of ingenuity. The lynchpin of the scheme was
James's invention of a 'travelling house' which could be installed on
a working barge to provide it with the amenities of a pleasure boat.
James described this contrivance to George III during their audience
in September 1770: 'I mentioned my having made a Covering or house
with Windows, which I carried with me in [my] post Chaise, and sett
up in any Coal Boat that could be got upon the Canals where we
went, which afforded me an opportunity of seeing many things I could
never have seen without.'[4]

A catalogue of the family boats, which survives in the Sharp archive,
describes the travelling house as a 'Boat House upon Wheels fitted to
the Common Coal Barges used upon Canals'.[5] It was presumably a
larger version of the 'House on the little Boat' which James and
William conveyed to the riverbank to protect the king and queen from
the rain in August 1770. Though James does not explain how precisely
he 'carried' the cabin on his post-chaise, the fact that it had wheels
suggests that it was pulled like a modern-day caravan. Alternatively,
the cabin may have been collapsible in the manner of the extending
'outside House' on the *Apollo* – which was drawn over the performers
during the August 1770 shower – making it possible for the contraption
to be carried on top of a carriage.

Whatever its precise mechanics, the 'travelling house' allowed the
family to travel in comfort on every canal in the country, while also
solving the problem of travel by land between unconnected waterways.
At the end of a section of canal, the contraption was simply removed

from the barge to which it had been attached, and transported by carriage to the next embarkation point. Further detail of the portable house is provided by an eyewitness to the Sharps' embarkation on the Oxford Canal, who describes it as: 'most neatly built: the curtains to the sash windows of silk, and silk streamers at the head and stern'.[6] It is characteristic of James that his design for the house did not sacrifice elegance to functionality, so that the family could travel on coal barges in the style to which they were accustomed on the *Apollo*.

This left the issue of eating, drinking and accommodation, for ingenious though the travelling house was, it was not large enough to furnish all the party's needs. Instead the family slept at inns along the way, whose kitchens may also have provided hampers of provisions for the midday meal. That picnicking did take place in the travelling house, in spite of its limited dimensions, is suggested by this list of expenditure for the voyage, which is found in a small leather-bound 'Boat Book' similar in layout to that kept by William in the 1750s:

> For a table set of Queens ware
> Given to Servants
> 2 Cruits
> Lanthorn
> Washing
> Tea
> Sugar
> Peper
> Chocolate
> Chocolate Pott
> Tongue
> Carriage of Horns
> 2 Hams
> Given the Peggys
> To Molly
> The two other maids[7]

The inclusion of two horns suggests that the Sharps could not forgo musical accompaniment even on a coal barge. What with the horns, Molly, the two other maids, the servants and the crew, the barge must have felt very crowded at times, though it is possible that the maids stayed with the carriages and only attended the party in the evening.

The party set out on 15 August 1774, travelling by land from Elizabeth's house at Wicken to the Oxford Canal near Daventry. A correspondent for the *London Packet* described their departure from Braunston: 'Mr Sharpe soon after arrived, and some gentlemen on horse-back; in the rear were his and the surgeon's chariots, and likewise their sisters, all filled with smart ladies, who alighted and went on board Mr Sharpe's barge, most neatly built.'[8]

The correspondent also noted the presence at one end of the barge of 'servants in smart liveries, guarding a hamper of wine, and nine chests of what I conceived to be plate, pastry and confectionery'. Even allowing for journalistic licence, it is apparent that the Sharps were not prepared to submit themselves entirely to the vagaries of the inn kitchen. The family set off with fanfare, and spent the day on the Oxford Canal travelling northwards towards Coventry.

The first points of interest that Elizabeth notes in her diary are: 'Newbolt and Rugby and passed the Tunnell 130 feet' and 'Brinklow Acquadoct 8 arches'. Due to a rerouting of the canal in the early nineteenth century, the meandering course taken by the Sharps' coal barge in August 1774 is now no more than a depression in the fields through which it used to pass.[9] The tunnel which so impressed Elizabeth and her companions as they passed through its long dark vault, is derelict. Its southern portal can be seen in Newbold churchyard on the northern outskirts of Rugby, closed up with corrugated iron. The aqueduct at which Elizabeth marvelled survived the early nineteenth-century changes but its magnificent twenty-two-feet span arches are forgotten and almost choked by the brambles and weeds that grow unchecked between their piers.[10]

Next Elizabeth records: 'Colepit Field left the Oxford Canall and got into the Coventry Canal 33 miles.' Whereas today travellers pass seamlessly from the Oxford to the Coventry Canal at Hawkesbury Junction near Nuneaton, in the early 1770s the canal enthusiast faced a more challenging transition. At this early period of the canals' existence there was no junction between the two waterways, due to a dispute over tolls. For the Sharps this failure of connectivity meant that the passengers, the crew, the travelling house and all its contents had to be removed from the coal barge on the Oxford Canal, transported by carriage the short distance to the Coventry Canal, and reassembled on the vessel that was to carry them for the next stretch of the journey.

No doubt James is in charge of operations, and stands on the prow of the coal barge co-ordinating the removal of the passengers, and the chests of confectionery, and the French horns. From his vantage point, he can see the canal winding into the distance, and cows grazing on the meadows that line its banks. William, emollient as always, smooths ruffled feathers over an upset crate, and offers his hand to the ladies as they step gingerly from barge to towpath. Meanwhile, in the travelling house, Elizabeth superintends the packing of the queensware, while Frances minds her little niece Kitty, and the two Catharines bundle the hams in strips of unbleached linen. Granville is nowhere to be seen, but is later discovered sitting on the grassy bank with his head in a tract on the common-law doctrine of *Nullum tempus occurrit regi.** Even his equilibrium is disturbed by the shouts of the bargees as the travelling house is manoeuvred off the coal barge, and hangs temporarily suspended over the water's edge. With silk window curtains askew, and silk streamers hanging limply, the house totters precariously up the bank, manhandled by the sweating crew. With one almighty effort, the house is heaved onto the top of James's post-chaise, and held fast with ropes.

Undaunted the Sharps proceeded northwards on the Coventry Canal: 'Nun Eaton to Atherstone lay 10 miles.' Atherstone marked the end of the Coventry Canal at this date, so once again the family was required to up sticks and reconvene in their carriages to travel 'By land to Tamworth. Lay at Wicknor Bridge 23 miles.'[11] Here the

---

* The name of the doctrine translates as 'No time runs against the king', meaning that the Crown is not bound by statutes of limitations, a subject on which Granville later published his own tract.

Sharps joined the Trent & Mersey Canal and 'Passed near Litchfield Armitage, a Tunnell cut through the Rock 180 feet' which can still be seen, though rather less picturesquely, by a pub car park on the A513 south of Rugeley. After a night spent in an inn at Sandon, the family continued northwards on the Trent & Mersey passing what was then the village of Stone before arriving at 'Burslem see the manufactory Mr Wedgwoods and lay at Newcastle under Lime 89 miles in all'.[12]

For James the visit to the Wedgwood manufactory was one of the highlights of the expedition. Indeed such were the attractions of the establishment to a man of James's tastes that it is likely that he planned the itinerary precisely so as to include it. Burslem was one of a cluster of six villages in north Staffordshire that were later known as the 'Five Towns' and now form Stoke-on-Trent.[13] Already an established centre of pottery manufacture, the area rose to new prominence after Josiah Wedgwood established his manufactory there in the 1760s.

Born into a family of potters, Wedgwood quickly earned a repu-tation for innovative glazes and designs, and with the assistance of his partner Thomas Bentley built up a business supplying ceramics to a fashionable clientele in London, the provinces and Europe. Wedgwood perfected a type of ceramic known as 'creamware', which later became known as 'queensware' after he had won Queen Charlotte's approval for a tea set, candlesticks and fruit baskets 'with a gold ground, and raised flowers upon it in green'.[14] This was the origin of the table set of queensware which the Sharps bought for their voyage.[15]

It has been said of Wedgwood that he was 'the greatest man who ever, in any age or country, applied himself to the important work of uniting art with industry'.[16] It was perhaps this characteristic, more than any other, that endeared him to James, who himself adhered passionately to the principle of the compatibility of style and practi-cality. James would have viewed the manufactory at Burslem with an almost religious devotion, not only because it was run inventively and utilised the latest technology, but because of the beauty of the prod-ucts that were made there. Named 'Etruria' after a style of ceramic manufactured by Wedgwood, the works stood on a seven-acre site on the banks of the newly built Trent & Mersey Canal. I picture James wandering about Etruria in a state of almost trance-like exaltation, exclaiming over the esoteric delights of a marl mill, or a boiler house, and marvelling at the biscuit oven, the enamel kiln and the dippers store. A scale bat stove takes his particular fancy, and he spends so long conversing with the operative that the Sharps in desperation send a search party to look for him.

After a night at Newcastle-under-Lyme, the Sharps set out to complete what was then the last leg of the Trent & Mersey Canal. Travelling northwards they soon came to what Elizabeth described as 'Hare Castle Hill. Went into the Tunel a mile 1700 yds. but when finished will be 1 mile and ¾ the arches all brick.'[17] When Brindley surveyed the canal in the 1760s it became apparent that the sandstone ridge north of what is now Stoke-on-Trent could not be avoided. Instead he dug what was then one of the two longest tunnels in the country. At the time of the Sharps' visit in August 1774 construction was still in progress, and it was perhaps only through James's connection with Brindley that the family were given permission to enter the completed section of the tunnel.[18]

This adventure led to further complication for the Sharp party, for the passage was too narrow to accommodate a towpath. Instead the barge was propelled by men called 'leggers' who lay on planks attached to the roof of the boat and 'walked' it through by pushing on the sides of the tunnel with their feet. Barges continued to be propelled through the tunnel in this fashion after it was completed, while the redundant tow horses were led over the hill to the northern end of the tunnel on what is still called Boathorse Road. It was because of the delays caused by this method of propulsion that in the 1820s Thomas Telford built a second tunnel at Harecastle, and for many years the two operated in conjunction. Now only Telford's tunnel remains in use, while Brindley's lies abandoned, barred and almost sinking into the rushes that grow in profusion around its mouth.

As Harecastle Hill marked the end of the Trent & Mersey at this date, after emerging from the tunnel the family turned back towards Stafford. Having spent one night at Stone, and another at Sandon, they left the canal at Haywood Junction, just east of Stafford, rather than continuing on the route of their outward journey. It was here that the party joined the Staffordshire & Worcestershire Canal for the first time on their voyage. The junction between the two canals was already in operation at this date, so the coal barge moved seamlessly from one to the other.

Cruising southwards through the Staffordshire and Worcestershire countryside, the Sharps passed Tettenhall and Kidderminster before arriving at Stourport, which Elizabeth described as 'a Basson that covers 3 acres and locks down into the Severen'.[19] An inland port that serves the junction of the Staffordshire & Worcestershire Canal with the River Severn, Stourport was a small village before the construction of the canal in the late 1760s. Today the intricate weaving of canal and basin, the locks, bridges and elegant proportions of the Tontine hotel remain much as they did when the Sharps visited in 1774. Having admired the 'Great works done in 5 years' in the canal town, the Sharps retreated back up the Staffordshire & Worcestershire Canal to Wolverhampton.

Next Elizabeth records: 'See Mr Boltons works and lay at Wolverhampton, in all 200 miles.'[20] Rather than returning to Heywood Junction, the Sharps left the Staffordshire & Worcestershire at Wolverhampton and proceeded in an easterly direction along the Birmingham Canal. It was here that the family made their visit to 'Mr Boltons works' which rivalled even the glories of Etruria as the high-point of James's tour of the industrial Midlands. Matthew Boulton had begun his working life as a manufacturer of small metal goods such as buttons, buckles, snuffboxes and pins, but rapidly expanded his business to produce a large range of ornamental products.

In 1761 Boulton bought the lease of a thirteen-acre site at Handsworth, then a mile and a half north of Birmingham across the Staffordshire border. Over the next few years he developed the site, which he called 'Soho', to create one of the most advanced manufacturing centres in Europe. Running the business on a knife edge to free up capital for investment, Boulton installed every conceivable species of machine to work the metals, alloys, stone, glass, enamel and tortoiseshell that were used in the manufactory.[21] He developed advanced management techniques, including the division and specialisation of labour, and new processes such as fusion plating. Both Soho and Etruria attracted numerous visitors who marvelled at the futuristic splendours on display, but whereas Wedgwood resented the loss of time represented by their intrusion, Boulton delighted in showing off Soho: 'I have lords and ladies to wait on yesterday, I have Spaniards today; and tomorrow I shall have Germans, Russians and Norwegians.'[22]

Agog with the wonders of Soho, the Sharps retreated westwards along the Birmingham Canal and rejoined the Staffordshire & Worcestershire at Wolverhampton. They then proceeded in a northerly direction to Heywood Junction where, rather than continuing along the Trent & Mersey in the direction of the Potteries as on their outward journey, they travelled south. After a night at Wolseley Bridge, the family 'Stayd Sunday there, drank tea at Mr Ansons Shugborough'.[23] For those members of the party who preferred their tourism to be a little more picturesque than that which to date had been the subject of their itinerary, the visit to Shugborough must have come as something of a relief.

Set in an exquisite landscape four miles east of Stafford, Shugborough Hall is as near perfect an example of the English stately home as it is possible to conceive. For the Sharps, fresh from the coal barge and the manufactory floor, the beauty of the setting must have seemed the more remarkable. Though the estate had been in the hands of the Anson family since the beginning of the seventeenth century, it was Thomas Anson who set about transforming a medium-sized country house into a neoclassical mansion complete with flanking pavilions, rococo plasterwork and ionic columns. Inspired by his grand tour, Anson employed James 'Athenian' Stuart to design a series of classical follies which are dotted about the landscape. So as their carriages roll through the Shugborough parkland, the family perhaps catch sight of a perfectly formed Doric temple, or a Chinese house on an island in a canal. At a bend in the road, a picturesque ruin comes into view, or a Tower of the Winds, or tumbling cascade, while a triumphal arch appears suddenly on the skyline.[24]

In his brief account of the canal voyage, Granville notes that the family 'Drank Tea with Mr & Mrs Anson' which suggests that they were the recipients of a degree of hospitality beyond that normally accorded to country-house visitors.[25] Following Thomas Anson's death in 1773, the estate passed to his sister's son George Adams who consequently changed his name to Anson, and it was presumably this 'Mr Anson' and his wife who entertained the Sharps. Granville does not record where they drank their tea, but it is possible that they sat in the splendour of the red drawing room, with its exquisite decorative ceiling and tall windows looking out over an ornamental lake.

Tea at Shugborough was the last event of note in the family's itinerary, for they were now homeward bound. After a brief diversion up the easterly section of the Trent & Mersey Canal towards its junction with the River Trent, the Sharps 'Left the Canal at Cavendish Bridge'. The rest of the journey back to Wicken was made by carriage, via Loughborough, Leicester, Harborough and Northampton.[26] Having left Wicken on 15 August 1774, they returned almost two weeks later on 30 or 31 August. Elizabeth ends her record of the adventure with this summary of its merits: 'A most pleasant jour. 9 Bros. and Sissrs and Niece Catharine Sharp.'

This quiet satisfaction hardly does justice to the canal voyage, but Elizabeth's record of the journey is testament enough to its glories. When the family set out with their travelling house and nine chests of pastry, they were treading a path that had no precedent, but is now a way of life. Though the modern-day narrow-boat enthusiast does not have to contend with half-built tunnels and unconnected junctions, their experience of the joys of the canal holiday is essentially the same. In fact it is on the rural stretches of the waterways, where there is no sound but birdsong and the soft chug of the motor, and nothing to be seen but the trees that line the dark water and the meadows beyond, that one comes closest to the Sharps' experience of being. In this state of timelessness, the gulf between their lives and our own recedes to a vanishing point.

23

America

Account in the *Gazette* of the Battle at Charles Town, near Boston; and letters with large demands of Ordnance stores being received which were ordered to be got with all expedition, I thought it right to declare my objections to being any way concerned in that unnatural business.[1]

Granville Sharp, 'Extracts from Memorandum
Books No. 1', 28 July 1775

For Granville, assistant to John Boddington, Secretary of the Board of Ordnance, Friday 28 July 1775 begins like any other day. After breakfasting in his brother William's house in Old Jewry, where he is still a long-term resident, he hurries along Cornhill and Leadenhall Street and down Mark Lane with his head filled with the intricacies of the law of retribution.* Anyone who happens to notice the slight, rather stooping little figure make his way through the grimy thoroughfares of the City would not have associated him with the hero of Somerset's case, or the vanquisher of Lord Mansfield. Instead he looks like a junior clerk, mild, a touch eccentric perhaps, but with the unmistakable air of subordination that one might expect of the lower ranks of the eighteenth-century Civil Service.

Granville arrives in the minuting department of the Board of Ordnance, in the upper storeys of the White Tower in the Tower of

---

* Granville wrote a tract on this subject in 1776.

London, just as the bracket clock on the mantlepiece chimes the hour. Hanging his hat on a peg on the door, he takes his place at a long table in the centre of the stone-flagged room. Beside him sit four or five other clerks, dressed in drab coats and short greasy wigs, each with his head bent low over a pile of papers. The stool on which Granville perches is opposite an arched window, and looking up from his work he can see Devereux Tower, and the Chapel Royal, and Legge's Mount, and the labyrinthine streetscape of the City beyond. Only a little light filters through the small leaded windows, and the clerks write by candlelight.

Granville works quickly, with neat movements and a minimum of show. Occasionally, without being aware of it, he hums a tune under his breath – perhaps 'The Trumpet Shall Sound' which the Sharps played at their sacred-music concert on Sunday last – but the other clerks are fond of Granville, and tolerant of his oddities, and nothing is said.[2] Having filed yesterday's correspondence in the munitions bundles, checked the accompting book and reported to Mr Boddington, Granville turns to the bag of letters that arrived that morning from America. He is not apprehensive of anything in particular as he breaks the seal on the first letter – he is too busy thinking of the law of retribution for that – but the contents of the opening paragraph bring the colour flooding to his cheeks.

The letter which Granville read on that fateful morning in July 1775 had been dispatched from America several weeks earlier. Hard on the heels of the skirmishes between British and colonial forces at Lexington and Concord in April 1775, and the Battle of Bunker Hill in Charlestown, Massachusetts, on 17 June 1775, the correspondence contained an urgent request for military reinforcement.[3] These were the opening weeks of the American Revolutionary War, and as a clerk in the minuting department of the Board of Ordnance, Granville was intimately concerned in the supply of arms to the British army.

Though armed conflict between Britain and her colonies had been unthinkable even in the months leading up to the war, the seeds of the conflict were of a much longer standing. Since the establishment of the first permanent settlement at Jamestown in 1607, the relation-ship between Britain and her American colonies had been ill-defined and unstable.[4] British policy towards America see-sawed between intervention and neglect.[5] When periodically the value of the colonies became apparent to the government at Westminster, it attempted to tighten its control. In periods of laissez-faire, Americans seized the opportunity to develop a dynamic political culture, and to strengthen the legislative powers of their colonial assemblies.[6]

This ambiguity led to competing interpretations of the Anglo-American relationship. While the British clung to the doctrine that sovereignty resided in the 'Crown in Parliament' at Westminster, the colonists argued with increasing force that power should be shared with the periphery.[7] Differences were exacerbated by failure to comprehend each other's point of view. Time and again in the events leading up to the war, the British were genuinely bemused by colonial reaction to measures which they considered to be reasonable and fair. The incendiary Stamp Tax of 1765, for example, was part of what Westminster considered to be the entirely unobjectionable policy of making the Americans pay for part of the costs of their defence.[8] What was considered reasonable in London, however, could be interpreted in Boston as arbitrary and high-handed. In an atmosphere of mutual distrust, views hardened, driving even moderate American opinion into the fold of those contemplating outright rebellion.

The famous Boston Tea Party on 16 December 1773 – which involved Americans, some of them disguised as Native Americans, boarding East India Company ships in Boston harbour and pouring the contents of 200 chests of tea into the sea – was viewed by the colonists as an appropriate response to the imperial diktat embodied in the Tea Act passed by Parliament earlier that year. The colonists saw this as another violation of their right to be taxed only by their own elected representatives, not the British government ('no taxation without representation'). On the other side of the Atlantic, there was only incomprehension that a measure intended, at least in part, to benefit Americans by reducing the cost of tea, could have merited such insolence.[9] The feeling in Westminster was that this time the colonists had gone too far, and as the actual perpetrators of the Tea Party could not be apprehended, Parliament passed a series of coercive Acts that only had the effect of uniting American opinion against the imperial power. As relations deteriorated, local militia stockpiled weapons, and it was efforts made by the British military commander General Gage to forestall this process that led to the first shots being fired at Lexington and Concord in April 1775.

In the years preceding the outbreak of hostilities, as relations between Britain and America soured, Granville had become a staunch advocate of the right of Americans to an independent legislature. By 1772 he had formally rejected the doctrine, adhered to by even the pro-American faction at Westminster, of parliamentary sovereignty over the colonies. Outraged by the implementation of punitive measures after the Boston Tea Party, in 1774 Granville published his views in a tract called *A Declaration of the People's natural Right to a Share in the Legislature; – against the attempts to tax America, and to make Laws for her against her Consent.*[10] The first edition of the *Declaration* was produced as a pamphlet in Boston, Philadelphia and New York, and in essay form in Virginia and New York newspapers. Two hundred copies reached the convenors of the Continental Congress in 1774, with the assistance of Benjamin Franklin (with whom Granville had corresponded), and according to Granville a further 7,000 copies of the tract were 'struck off by one single Printer at Boston'.[11]

Granville's opposition to the war was also linked to his friendship with individual Americans, which had flourished in the course of his anti-slavery activities. By the early 1770s Granville was a figure of standing in abolition circles in America, both as the author of *A Representation of the Injustice and Dangerous Tendency of Tolerating Slavery*, which had been reprinted in Philadelphia, and for his work on the Somerset case.[12] In May 1772, as the Somerset litigation reached its climax, Granville began a correspondence with Anthony Benezet, an influential Quaker abolitionist. As Benezet was himself the author of several anti-slavery tracts, and the promoter of abolitionist initiatives such as a free school in Philadelphia 'for the education of Black People', there was an immediate sympathy between the two men.[13]

Through his friendship with Benezet, Granville was put in touch with other Quaker sympathisers, and assumed the role of unofficial London agent for the abolitionist cause in America.[14] Granville proffered advice on how best to present petitions to Westminster from anti-slavery colonial assemblies such as Virginia and Philadelphia, suggesting to Benezet in a letter dated 21 August 1772 that the mediation of Lord Dartmouth, the 'lately appointed secretary for the colonies', might assist 'with the King and Council' were he 'to be applied to from your side of the water, by way of memorial accompanying the petition &c'.[15] Later that year, in response to a request from an American correspondent 'to inquire for an answer to the Virginia Petition', Granville replied despondently: 'I waited on the Secretary of State, and was informed by himself, that the petition was received, but that he apprehended no answer would be given.'[16]

After opening the letter from America on the morning of 28 July 1775, Granville proffered his resignation to John Boddington. He had resolved that he could no longer stain his conscience by assisting in the prosecution of a war against his friends and fellow countrymen. Boddington comes out of the affair very well, for rather than ordering Granville back to his desk, which might in the circumstances of impending national emergency have been thought reasonable, he advised his assistant 'to ask leave of absence for 2 months as the Board would take it more kindly than an abrupt resignation'.[17]

Granville took his advice, and writing that day to Sir Charles Cocks, Clerk of the Ordnance, he received 'a very polite answer' sanctioning a period of two months' leave.[18] As Great Britain descended into war, Granville made the most of his sabbatical, at least according to the evidence of his journal which records a water scheme, a journey with James to Reading in connection to the City Committee of Thames Navigation, and a protracted visit to Northumberland.[19] He also found time to 'to be private' and was 'employed without interruption in preparing several Tracts'.[20]

On 26 September 1775, a few days before the expiry of his leave of absence, Granville wrote two letters. The first was to John Boddington, expressing his anxiety about what he called 'my own particular situation'. Notwithstanding George III's issuing of the Proclamation of Rebellion on 23 August, there had been no relaxation of the philanthropist's views on the conflict during his absence.[21] Instead, as he confided to Boddington, 'my opinions on that subject are established'. This being the case, he could not 'return to my ordnance duty whilst a bloody war is carried on, unjustly as I conceive, against my fellow subjects; and yet, to resign my place would be to give up a calling, which, by my close attendance to it for near eighteen years, and by my neglect of every other means of subsistence during so long a period, is now become my own profession and livelihood'.[22]

Granville also wrote to his brothers William and James on 26 September 1775, and though the correspondence has not survived, it appears to have set out his predicament in terms similar to those used in the Boddington letter. James replied on 5 October 1775, expressing wholehearted support for Granville's decision to delay his return to the Board of Ordnance: 'We very much approve, here, of your asking a farther leave of absence.' Indeed, as James saw it, a few more months away from the office would be of positive benefit to Granville: 'It will give you a little leisure, which you so very much want.' Moreover, a further delay 'may give some chance for a turn in public affairs'. If, however, 'it should be otherwise' and Granville found it necessary to give up his employment, then he could be assured of his family's support:

> I will now speak for my brother William as well as for myself – we are both ready and willing, and God be thanked, at present able, to take care that the loss shall be none to you; and all that we have to ask in return is, that you would continue to live amongst us as you have hitherto done, without imagining that you will, in such a situation, be burthensome to us, and also without supposing that it will then be your duty to seek employment in some other way of life; for if we have the needful amongst us, it matters not to whom it belongs – the happiness of being together is worth the expense, if it answered no farther purpose.[23]

The warmth and generosity of this letter is still moving, 250 years after it was written. It is remarkable, not merely on account of the offer of unconditional financial support, but for the sensitivity with which James frames his beneficence. With such support behind him, Granville could well afford to have the courage of his convictions.

Boddington replied to Granville's letter of 26 September, by coun-
selling him against stating the reason for any request for further leave
of absence. If Granville expressed anti-war sentiments, then in
Boddington's view 'no Public Officer under the Crown would think
himself at Liberty to grant any indulgences considering the present
circumstances of the Times & situation of affairs'.[24] Granville heeded
this advice and successfully applied for a further three months' absence.
Yet another period of leave was granted in March 1776, but the patience
of the Board was wearing thin.[25] On 10 April 1777, twenty-one months
after the start of his first sabbatical, Granville noted in his journal:
'This morning I called on Sir Charles Cocks, and resigned my post in
the Ordnance; Mr Boddington having acquainted me that matters
were so circumstanced in the office at present, that Sir Charles did
not think it prudent to grant me any longer leave of absence.'[26]

Freed from the constraints of employment, Granville could devote
himself to activism. During the course of the War of Independence,
which lasted from 1775 to 1783, he published twelve tracts on subjects
as diverse as the 'Free Militia', the iniquity of pressing seamen into
forced service in the navy, the reformation of Parliament, the
common-law doctrine of *Nullum tempus occurrit regi*, and 'a Plan for
the gradual Abolition of Slavery in the Colonies'. Granville also found
time to give English lessons to the Pacific islander Omai, who following
his arrival in England in 1774 aboard HMS *Adventure*, achieved celebrity
status in fashionable London society.[27]

Granville was not a lone voice in his opposition to the American
war. The conflict polarised opinion in Britain, with one side supporting
military action, and the other calling for an immediate end to a conflict
which they blamed on the pig-headedness and incompetence of the
British government. For those on the left of the political spectrum,
the conflict represented a lurch towards authoritarianism comparable
to the John Wilkes/Middlesex election affair.[28] In their view, the
Americans were simply defending the rights of British subjects everywhere in the face of an overpowerful executive. As the war progressed,
Granville found himself allied to radicals such as John Cartwright,
John Jebb, Capel Lofft and the Duke of Richmond, who would later
come to prominence as founding members of the Society for

Constitutional Information, the intellectual wing of London political dissent in the 1780s.

Despite his proximity to the London radicals, Granville differed from his comrades in his interpretation of the American war. Whereas they traced the conflict to corruption in the British state, Granville argued from first principles. In his view, the imposition of parliamentary authority over colonial affairs was unconstitutional as it deprived British subjects of rights and liberties guaranteed under the common law, and was therefore akin to slaveholding. For Granville, then, his support for the Americans was an extension of the crusade against slavery.[29]

Granville's refusal to participate in a war of which he disapproved reveals the youngest Sharp brother at his most principled. He was a conscientious objector, and his stand against the war effort was venerated in radical and pro-American circles.[30] Nevertheless, Granville owed his plaudits almost as much to his brothers William and James as he did to his own powers of fortitude, as it was their generous offer of support which allowed him to give up his day job and commit to full-time activism. His endeavours in the years following the Somerset case show that, rather than being a single-issue campaigner, he was concerned more broadly with the rights of the individual under the law. This was to be the overarching philosophy of his activities in the months and years to come.

Part Four

(1777–1813)

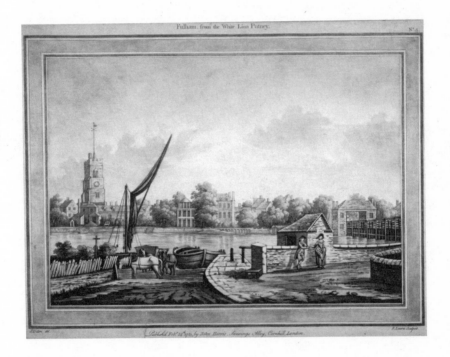

Fulham, from the White Lion Putney.

24

Union

The scene is the Thames near Windsor, on 1 September 1777. A thin layer of silvery-yellow cloud spreads across the pale blue sky, and a faint breeze touches the leaves of the elms that line the Eton bank. The horses that stand in their shade lazily flick their tails against the buzzing flies, and a fisherman sits drowsy over his untouched line. Through the stillness of the warm afternoon, a pleasure yacht plies its course about the meanders of the river. Lulled by the sweet tones of the hautboy, and the gentle murmur of conversation, the somnolent fisherman barely hears its approach. Only the flutter of the white awning, and the colours of the silks of the men and women who throng the deck, catch his eye. Then the large square ivory sail comes into view, and the slightly raised stern, and the railing that extends around the main deck. Beneath it runs a line of dark green cabins trimmed with white, burgundy and gold, each with a window framed by fluted pilasters. The yacht glides past him, leaving a stream of ruffled water in its wake.[1]

In 1777, William, now in his late forties, took possession of the *Union*, a 'most capacious and elegant pleasure yacht', which he had commissioned to serve as a summer home.[2] The extravagance of the purchase demonstrates the wealth that William had accumulated over his now long-standing surgical career. In contrast to the other boats of the family flotilla, the *Union* was custom-built, with amenities such as cabins and a 'Convenient Cook Room' that made it possible to sleep on board.[3] It seems to have been William's intention that he and his wife Catharine and daughter Mary should live on the *Union* for several weeks of the year. Granville records that William made an annual excursion on the yacht, 'traveling up the Rivers Thames, Wey & Kennet'. Several plans and illustrations of the *Union* survive, including a yellowing copy of her 'Particulars and Conditions of Sale', dating from 1786, which records that she was 70 feet in length at her 'extreme', and 13 feet 6 inches wide.[4]

A guided tour of the *Union* yacht – no visitor could escape one – began in the stern, where the admiring guest was shown the broad dimensions of the 'Steerage' or 'Orchestra'. Serving interchangeably as a store, a hall, as part of a dining room, and wet-weather accommodation for the Sharp band, the Orchestra contained amongst other things nineteen brass hat hooks and a mahogany dining table.[5] Next came the 'State Room', which according to a report in the *Morning Post* of 15 September 1777 was 'furnished with uncommon taste and magnificence'.[6] James's daughter Kitty, who stayed on the *Union* as a little girl, remembers that it was painted a light stone colour.[7] Opening the doors between the Orchestra and the State Room served to turn the space into a commodious dining room where, according to the correspondent of the *Morning Post*, 'upwards of twenty persons' could sit in comfort. The State Room was also used as a living room on days of inclement weather, and contained amongst other things four 'Sopha' bedsteads with striped cases, and a cast-iron stove.[8]

To the right of the State Room began a row of three elegant bedchambers, of which the first was 'Mr & Mrs Wm Sharp's cabin'. Here the visitor marvelled at the ingenuity of a canopied sofa bed, and the pretty white dimity upholstered furniture, before continuing to the equally magnificent 'Mr & Mrs James Sharp's Cabin'. After a cursory examination of the less splendid, but eminently practical, 'Spare Cabin', the party progressed to the service areas of the yacht.[9] First the 'Convenient Cook Room', whose amenities included a German range, a gridiron, a muffin stand, a pair of steak tongs and a pot hook.[10] Then, in short order, the 'Butler's Pantry', the 'China Closit', two 'Store Closits', a 'Linin Closit' and a 'Pantry'.[11] No tour was complete without an inspection of the two state-of-the-art water closets, while washing facilities included a 'bottle, bason, and two soap dishes'.[12]

Such was the flexibility of the accommodation on the *Union*, that Kitty remembered '23 Persons sleeping on board'.[13] Even this number did not represent maximum capacity, for in a separate document she records:

> Sleeping accommodation – for 24 persons
> 4 swinging cots in the Steerage for single Gentlemen
> 4 Sofa Beds in the State Cabin
> 3 Double Sofa Beds in the other Cabins
> 3 Births for men servants in the Passage
> 2 Births for 2 people each in the Kitchen
> 3 Boatmen's Births the foreCastle[14]

It must have been a little squashed on the yacht when full capacity was reached, but then resort could be made to the wide-open space of the deck. This measured forty-eight feet, and 'when covered with the elegant Awning, forms a spacious Ball Room'.[15] The awning is visible in a painting of the Sharp flotilla, still in the possession of the family, in which the newly built *Union* takes centre stage. Set on the Thames near Sir Richard Hoare's house at Barn Elms, the painting depicts an imaginary water excursion and shows all eight of the boats owned by the family. The *Union* is shown with guests grouped picturesquely under the awning, presumably enjoying the fresh air and beauty of the passing landscape.[16]

A series of pencil and red ink sketches in James's archive provide further detail of the exterior of the *Union*. The drawings, which appear to be rough workings, show that the yacht was modelled according to classical principles, and reveal the intricacy of the detail of its design.[17] It is apparent from these documents that James played a key role in the design of the *Union*, and the project shows both his mastery of the technical details of boatbuilding and his aesthetic sensibility. That James was given this responsibility is an example of the siblings' reliance on each other, and shows that William had an absolute faith in his brother's taste and technical understanding.

If the origins of the *Union* lay in the 'travelling house' that transformed a coal barge into a pleasure boat on the canal voyage of 1774, then it surpassed even the headiest aspirations of the Sharps who took part on that journey. It was with no half measures that the brothers set out to overcome the deficiencies of the portable cabin. Though the spirit of the *Union* was true to the canal expedition, it was in fact more country house than travelling house, as this contemporary newspaper report makes clear:

> [the yacht] comprehended all the advantages of the most finished country villa, besides many which were peculiar to itself. It had all the accommodations of a house, and was free from the inconveniences of bad neighbourhood for its scite could be changed at pleasure; it had not only the richest, but also the most various prospects; and it was a villa free from house-duty and window-lights; it paid neither church tythe nor poor's rate; it was free from both government and parochial taxes; and it not only had a command of wood and water, but possessed the most extensive fishery of any house in England.[18]

James's involvement in the *Union* went beyond his contributions to its construction. The naming of one of the two principal bedrooms 'Mr & Mrs James Sharp's Cabin' suggests that he enjoyed if not equal usage rights, then at least something approximate to it. In part this is a token of the exceptional closeness of the two brothers, which had flourished from the days of their apprenticeship in London. So hand in glove were William and James that the greater part of the Sharp story has as its central pivot the relationship between them. It was William's and James's capacity for common enterprise that provided the impetus for the family's most characteristic endeavours, and they were also the bedrock of the network of sibling solidarity.

In fact the naming of the second-best cabin is evidence that the brothers' relationship extended to a close financial interdependence. Excerpts from family correspondence suggest that William and Granville entrusted their financial affairs to James, and invested heavily in his businesses. This involved a certain amount of monetary entanglement, and also explains why the brothers held some assets in common. Thus although it was almost certainly William who bought the *Apollo* in the early 1750s, by the early 1770s the brothers referred to the flotilla as being owned by them jointly. Similarly, though William commissioned the *Union* for the use of his own family, when it was sold in the late 1780s it was advertised as 'the property of the late James Sharp'.[19]

★

The twelve-day maiden voyage of the *Union*, executed with typical Sharp panache, took place in the late summer of 1777. It is a mark of the significance of the expedition to the Sharps that both Granville and Elizabeth kept records throughout. A letter written by Frances to her sister Judith in Northumberland, during the early stages of the voyage, provides further picturesque detail. She begins her account: 'I am retired to my own Room on board the charming *Union* yacht to scribble a few lines to you & to tell you how we are getting on & how often we wish to have you of our Party – for it is really quite delightful.'[20]

Granville begins his description by listing the participants in categories according to their role on the expedition.[21] The Sharp contingent – comprising William and Catharine, James and Catharine, their seven-year-old daughter Kitty, Elizabeth, Granville and Frances – are 'Guests', whereas visitors to the *Union* during the course of the voyage (among them Sir William Dolben, Lady Howe and the Earl of March) are the 'Company'. Musicians fall into three different categories. There are the Sharp instrumentalists, William (clarinet), James (serpent) and Elizabeth (harpsichord); members of the household who are not labelled 'Guests' – for example, William's and James's versatile butlers ('Cha. Colehouse' and 'Nich. Shofline' respectively) who play the violin and French horn in addition to their domestic duties; and eight professional musicians who are taken 'up by the way at the Orange Coffee House'. The latter comprise three clarinettists, a bassoonist, a violoncellist, two players of the French Horn, and one of the Hautboy. Completing the party are the crew of three 'Yachtmen', three 'Watermen' and a 'Mr Truss' who 'took charge of the Vessel during the Voyage'. There is also the 'House-Steward' ('Thos Child') and his assistants ('Jn Barrow' and 'Henry Final').

The entire group numbers twenty-eight, which exceeds by four the maximum capacity for sleeping on the *Union* recorded by Kitty Sharp. Further confusion is created by Frances's notes on the first meal on board the yacht: 'we sat down to Dinner in the State Room Eighteen with great Ease & sixteen in the Kitching'.[22] While the superfluity of diners in Frances's account must refer to members of the 'Company' who were not invited to sleep on board, the excess in Granville's figure is explained by the departure of several of the musicians in the early stages of the journey. Frances interrupts her description of the second day on board by explaining this: 'I should have tolled you all the band left us, but Mr Kirman Simpson & Miller.'[23]

Even with the departure of the professional musicians it would have been snug on board the *Union* during the twelve-day cruise. While William and James and their wives enjoyed the privacy of their elegant bedchambers and Frances and Elizabeth were comfortably housed in the Spare Cabin next door, Granville roughed it in a less salubrious quarter of the boat. Presumably his berth was either a swinging cot in the Steerage, or a sofa bed in the State Room, where the remaining spaces were taken up by an assortment of musicians, guests and members of the household. With those left over tucked into the passageway and kitchen, while the crew lay hugger-mugger in the forecastle, a night on the *Union* was not for the faint-hearted.[24]

Frances continues her narrative with an account of the launching of the *Union* on the 29 August 1777: 'we came on board on Friday morning at Kew Bridge at Eleven oclock'. Notice has been given of the embarkation, and the river teems with brightly coloured barges, yawls and wherries who are to accompany the *Union* on the first day of her expedition. The band strikes up, anchors are weighed, and the yacht glides through the wooden arches of old Kew Bridge, with the pleasure craft streaming out behind her. The fleet sails upriver, past the royal gardens at Kew and the Old Deer Park, while on the north bank the parkland of Syon House gives way to open country. At Twickenham, the *Union* casts anchor by the riverside lawns of Marble Hill, and the pleasure boats cluster about her. An invitation is extended to the passengers on the accompanying vessels to come on board, and a rowing boat ferries the ladies in broad-brimmed hats, and gentlemen in silk stockings, backwards and forwards between the *Union* and her flotilla. As the band plays, the Sharps show their visitors the deck and cabins.

The party returns to Kew, where they dine, and tea is served to the 'all the company in the boats'. They are still taking tea when the king and queen are sighted taking their places on the bench under the oak tree where Felice Giardini serenaded them seven years before. The musicians tune up as the tea things are hurriedly cleared away, and then the band launches into the opening bars of an extempore royal recital.[25] According to Frances it is almost dark when the last notes float across the water, but even so 'the King went on with us to the End of the Gardens, where we put down our Anker for the Night, & light our Candles & began to prepar for super & bed – to the great Entertainment of the King & Queen who stayed a great while as they could see what we were about'.[26]

Nor was the king's curiosity abated by these nocturnal observations, for the following morning Frances was woken up 'about Eight oclock by being tolled the King was come on to the tow path to see us, he staid agreat whille but not long Enough for us all to get up & Dressed & our House set in order to ask him on board, & we were tolled afterwards that he came down at seven oclock & finding us all shut up went away & came again a little before Eight'.[27]

Plans for the second day were checked when it began to rain at eleven in the morning, and it continued drizzling all day.[28] But the Sharps, after a lifetime of boating, were accustomed to the caprices of the British summer, and did not let a spot of drizzle spoil the enjoyment of their day. Others were less stalwart, for according to Frances 'we had not much company but Entertained our selves with reading & work & music'.[29] One musical enthusiast did brave the elements, however, for both Frances and Granville report seeing a lady with an umbrella listening to the music from a bench on the towpath.[30] Her constancy was rewarded by an invitation to spend the day on board, and the Sharps were gratified to discover that their new guest was 'Lord Howes sister & a very agreeable woman'.[31] Their enthusiasm was no doubt enhanced by the knowledge that Admiral Lord Howe was currently commander-in-chief of the North American Station, a supporter of a negotiated peace with the colonists, and a respected member of the establishment.[32]

In spite of the weather, the party reached Shepperton in good time, and here they moored for the night.[33] The next day, Sunday 31 August, passed quietly with church and a walk along the towpath to Weybridge.[34] On the following morning, the *Union* weighed anchor as the family was eating breakfast.[35] The weather had cleared so there was an inundation of 'Company', including a Mrs Gowland, and her friends Mr and Mrs Ford of Barbados, who came on board at Staines. Presumably Granville took the opportunity to lecture the Fords on the iniquities of the slave trade. In the afternoon the party took up 'the mistress of a boarding school her assistant & 22 young ladies & carried them up about a mile'.[36]

As they approached Windsor, the family spotted Lady Holland on the towpath, wheeling her son, the little Lord Holland, and her daughter, Miss Fox, in a garden chair. It would not have escaped the Sharps' attention that the recently widowed Lady Holland was the sister-in-law of the great Whig politician Charles James Fox.[37] At Datchet they took up the Dowager Baroness Onslow, and drank tea by Windsor Castle.[38] As they did so, the party could see the steep incline of the castle slopes and the elevated North Terrace, while above them soared the great Round Tower. Cows grazed on the grassy bank by the King's Engine House, and dragonflies darted about the shallows.

It was 'while we were at Tea', Frances reports, that 'we were tolled the King & Queen were coming down' – once again. By now the Sharps were used to the demands of their royal audience, and the musicians were soon hard at work. However, on this occasion, the band played only one piece of music before the concert was interrupted. As 'God Save the King' reached its rousing climax, William rowed to shore in a small shallop, and extended an invitation to the king and queen to come on board. The offer was accepted, and clambering into the shallop with appropriate royal dignity, the monarch and his consort were soon transported safely to the waiting yacht. After the obligatory guided tour, the party sat on deck and 'Brother James & Granville brought up Tea to their Magisteys'. The tea party seems to have been an unqualified success, for Frances reports to her sister that the king and queen were 'much pleased' and 'very affable'. At last, the royal party 'got into the little boat again & went a shore to their Carriage'.[39]

The excitements of the day came to a suitable climax at Windsor Bridge, where the *Union* was heralded by a double salute of eight guns.[40] The events of 2 September seem staid in comparison to those of the day before, but there was still plenty of society, and the distinction of another gun salute, this time courtesy of Sir John Mills, at Bisham Abbey. Wednesday 3 September followed a similar pattern, with visitors of the ilk of Sir John and Lady Griffin and Lady Louisa Clayton. In the evening the party reached Reading, where they were 'attended by a great concourse of people' and moored above the highest lock at the foot of Mr Homer's Garden.[41]

The following morning marked the beginning of the return journey to Kew, and after a brief diversion up the River Kennet, the *Union* set its course towards London. The first two days of the homeward leg passed uneventfully, with a familiar round of calls from the gentry of the neighbourhood. On Thursday 4 September the party moored for the night above Henley Bridge, and Dr Curtis – 'a great lover of Music & plays Corello an hour every night', Granville noted with approbation – and his daughter came on board. After a visit from Lord and Lady Villiers, the party landed at 'Mr Freemans Island'.[42] Friday night was spent at Maidenhead Bridge, and the party was still at breakfast when the first contingent of 'Company' arrived. The day continued in familiar vein, until at Windsor Bridge the yacht was again honoured by a volley of gunfire. The Sharps spent the night peacefully a little below Datchet Bridge.[43]

Sunday 7 September was the first day of the grand finale of the maiden voyage, and it began fittingly enough with the party landing at Lady Onslow's riverside Gothic villa in Old Windsor, after breakfast. Here there was a tour of the gardens and hothouses, and an elegant dinner, before the Sharps reciprocated by showing Lady Onslow the interior of the yacht. Then: 'when it began to grow dark we had some

Sacred Musick introduced by an Overture in wch as in most of the other pieces His Royal Highness the Duke of Cumberland played the 1st violin. Mess' Bomgarten Simpson & Waterhouse of his Royal Highness's band also assisted ... the Performance of Music lasted about an Hour after wch all the Company retired; and we embarked again for the night.'[44]

A report in the *Morning Chronicle* dated 10 September 1777 confirms that the concert of sacred music took place in 'a large octagon room belonging to her Ladyship'.[45] Monday 8 September held fresh excitement, for after a visit from Lady Onslow and Lady Holland, the party spent the day watching the horse racing at Egham from the deck of the yacht.[46] The light was fading as the *Union* sailed down river to Hampton, where the party retired for the night.[47]

Tuesday morning began with a visit from the celebrated actor David Garrick, who 'went on board the yacht & drank chocolate with us'.[48] After a social call of a rather less starry kind from a Mr and Mrs Wood and a Mr and Mrs Biddle, who presented the Sharps with some fine large fish, the party moored at the foot of Garrick's garden.[49] Having admired the graceful riverside lawns, and the octagonal temple dedicated to Shakespeare, the party took on board the actor's wife, Eva Garrick, and her niece.[50] After the Garrick party went ashore at Hampton Court, the Sharps proceeded to Twickenham where they were visited by Lady Shelburne, Lady Litchfield and Sir George Pocock. Finally, on the evening of 9 September the party disembarked at Kew Bridge, and the *Union* returned to her moorings at Oliver's Island.[51]

★

In the inaugural voyage of the *Union*, the Sharp water scheme assumes its most exalted form. The elegance and sophistication of the yacht itself, and the glamour of the company that attended it, sets the journey apart even from the *Apollo* excursions of the early 1770s. It is no wonder that Granville and Elizabeth chose to record the event, and in particular every last name of the 'Company' who participated in it, in such close detail. For William, the instigator and presiding spirit, the expedition has the air of a triumphal progress.

Though the logistics of the *Union* expedition seem daunting to an unseasoned observer, they did not deter William, who had twenty-five years of experience to draw on. Nevertheless, Elizabeth's journal entry for 6 August 1777 is a reminder that the apparent effortlessness of the Sharp water parties belies the weeks of work that went into their preparation: 'I went up to Leadenhall Street to prepair for a voige in the yought, it then lay above Westminster Bridge, where we went often on Board to get everything necessary for our voige.'[52]

There remains the tantalising question of how the 'world of Company' that the family received on the yacht, and the 'boats of well Dressed Company' that attended their embarkation, knew about the expedition. A clue is given in this extract from the *Morning Chronicle*'s account of the concert at Lady Onslow's: 'Mr Sharpe and his company being entertained by Lady Onslow at her house, many ladies and gentlemen had cards of invitation to go on board.'[53] If the Sharps sent invitations and itineraries to friends and acquaintances prior to their departure, this explains why so many were primed for the occasion. Others perhaps – for example the mistress of the boarding school and her twenty-two young ladies – had no invitation but were on the riverbank fortuitously.

The family's celebrity acquaintance received further embellishment the following year, when the Sharps hosted a party on the *Union* for the ambassadors of several European states. The event was almost certainly held at the request of the government, and the prime minister Lord North was present for part of the proceedings. Granville describes the party with evident relish in his memorandum book. The *pièce de résistance* came in the afternoon when 'Lord & Lady North Mr & Miss North ... and others came on Board & Drank Tea'.[54] This gathering is another remarkable example of the facility with which the Sharps maintained their association with social and political elites, whilst also subscribing to a reforming agenda.

Taken together, the ambassadors' party and the maiden voyage of the *Union* represent the pinnacle of the Sharp family's social success. The guest list on both occasions gives an idea of the breadth of the siblings' acquaintance in high society. It also shows the importance that they attached to these connections – not only because they valued friends in high places, but also perhaps because of the leverage such contacts gave them in pursuing their ideals. Meanwhile the family's integrity and ingenuous good nature softened the edges of their aspirations, so that they were never accused of social climbing. Looking back from the giddy heights of a tea party with the king and queen, or breakfast with David Garrick, the Sharps' early days on the Rothbury moors, and as junior apprentices in London, must have seemed a very long way off indeed.

25

Elizabeth

> Though I have passed the greatest part of the summer agreeably, and enjoyed the pleasures of the country in an eminent degree; yet I cannot help esteeming the few days I continued at Wicken Park, the seat of Mrs Prowse, among the most delightful of my life.[1]

This is the opening of a letter from a 'Gentleman in Northamptonshire' to his 'Friend in London', published in the *General Evening Post* on 4 October 1777, in which he extols the joys of a recent visit to Wicken Park. Of the many pleasures afforded to him there, the writer highlights the presence of 'Mr Sharp, and his amiable family', who were 'on a visit to their benevolent relation at Wicken'. Such were the delights of the gentleman's country sojourn that, he confesses almost apologetically to his correspondent, 'I cannot help relating to you the circumstances which furnished your friend so much entertainment.'

He begins his story on the previous Tuesday evening. Dinner is not long over, and the company are still sitting round the table in the damask-papered dining room when an announcement is made that 'the labourers with the harvest home* would soon arrive'. Granville suggests 'that they make up a little party of festivity' for the occasion, and immediately the tranquillity of the post-prandial table erupts into

---

* Harvest Home (also sometimes called Ingathering) was a traditional rural festival celebrating the last day of harvest.

a ferment of activity. Elizabeth sends urgent orders to the kitchen for
bowls of syllabub, and bread, cheese and ale for sixty people, Granville
marshals the guests, and Elizabeth's versatile butler hurriedly takes
up a gleaming French horn. In ten minutes the entire company are
gathered in marching order in front of the house, and in a few minutes
more they have caught up with the last waggon piled high with hay
and laughing children.

A procession is organised, led by the footmen in livery and powdered
wigs, and the ladies, still in their rustling evening silks, close behind.
Then comes the marching band, first William and Granville on clarinet,
James with his trusty serpent, the ingenious butler on the French
horn, and another guest at Wicken, the professional musician Redmond
Simpson on hautboy, bringing up the rear.[2] Behind them roll the
waggons, overflowing with sweetly smelling hay, and finally the
sunburnt sweating labourers in wide-cut shirts and breeches. To the
sonorous tones of the march from Handel's *Scipione*, the procession
moves slowly down the winding country lanes. At part of the estate
known as Great Leys, where the stacks are to be made, the procession
forms a circle. There is a moment of quiet, before William, Frances
and Kitty – standing a little apart from the rest – sing unaccompanied
the traditional tune 'Harvest Home', their voices drifting through the
clear early-evening air. Everyone joins in the chorus, and the festivities
wind up with a toast to Elizabeth, drunk alternately by the ladies and
gentlemen in syllabub, and in large mugs of ale by what the correspondent terms 'the happiest set of peasants in England'.

This was not the only memorable event recorded by the
Northamptonshire gentleman, for a few days later Elizabeth hosts a
fête champêtre for the local gentry. The family band is again the star of
the show, and as the guests arrive in their carriages the melodious
cadences of a Bach sonata, or a virtuoso hautboy solo by Redmond
Simpson, waft across the gardens. In the interval, the company repairs
inside where an elegant breakfast of coffee, chocolate, fruit, pastries
and sweetmeats is arrayed in the dining room, the library and the
hall. After breakfast, the guests wander about the gardens, which have
been specially decorated for the occasion. There are swings hanging
from the boughs of stately horse chestnuts, cushions in shady dells,

and festoons of flowers weaved into the branches of a spreading oak tree. The *fête* concludes with a dance, and more music from the Sharp band, before the company departs in their waiting carriages.[3]

The *fête champêtre* was the last of the rural delights afforded to the letter-writing Northamptonshire gentleman. 'The next morning,' he concludes, 'I was obliged to leave this engaging party.' He did so 'with a heavy heart', and confessed to 'fancying myself in some respects in a similar situation to our first parents, so finely described by Milton when they departed from the happy garden'.[4]

Elizabeth – the 'Mrs Prowse' of the correspondent's report – had remained at Wicken Park in Northamptonshire since the sudden death of her husband George Prowse ten years previously. In the aftermath of George's death, it had been arranged between her mother-in-law, Mrs Prowse, and herself that Elizabeth would stay at Wicken and take over the management of the estate. As there were no surviving male members of the Prowse family (George's elder brother John and his father Thomas both predeceased him), there was no obvious alternative candidate for the position. The regard which the family felt for Elizabeth, and the closeness of her relationship with Mrs Prowse, also played a part in the decision. Elizabeth had been an exemplary daughter-in-law, and she now sought to repay the trust placed in her by devoting herself to the management of the Wicken estate.

Elizabeth's tenure at Wicken was formalised five years later when, in return for giving up her jointure,* and agreeing not to remarry, she secured the estate for life.[5] Whereas in 1767 there had been no rival contenders for the proprietorship of Wicken, by 1772 the position was rather different. In the five intervening years, George's sister Bessy Prowse had married Sir John Mordaunt, and the couple had a son.[6] As the Mordaunts were now the heirs to Wicken, it would have been appropriate for them to take over the running of the estate. Instead Mrs Prowse took the unusual step of giving Elizabeth a life interest in the property. That she did so is an endorsement of the competency of Elizabeth's stewardship of the estate in the preceding five years.

---

* A jointure is an estate, or property, settled on a woman at the time of her marriage, which provides for her in the event of her husband's death.

Elizabeth's journal contains repeated examples of her bond with the Mordaunts. She enumerates their visits to Wicken, and her own to the Mordaunt estate at Walton Hall in Warwickshire, and marks the births of the Mordaunt children, their childhood illnesses, and the dates of their inoculation against smallpox. Elizabeth also made efforts to develop the relationship between the Sharps and the Prowses and Mordaunts, so for example in January 1774 James and Catharine accompanied her on a visit to the Prowse estate at Berkley.

Elizabeth's fondness for the Mordaunt family is expressed with particular poignancy in a diary entry dated 17 September 1778, in which she records the receipt of a letter from her sister-in-law Bessy asking her to care for the three youngest Mordaunts during an outbreak of 'infectious fever'. Elizabeth is distraught because she cannot accede to this request, explaining that 'my dear little Mary Sharp [William and Catharine's infant daughter] was to leave me in a week to be enoculated, and as the illness was catching, I durst not receive them on her act'. As she concludes in her diary entry: 'I dont know that I ever felt sore hurt at any thing, than not being able to receive them when offered at so distressing a time.'[7]

During her forty-year stewardship of the Wicken property, Elizabeth implemented a wide-ranging series of reforms that included agricultural modernisation, the overhaul of tenancy agreements, landscaping estate parkland and woodlands, and material improvements to the living conditions of the poor. The level of her commitment is apparent in the pages of three estate ledgers that survive in the Northamptonshire Record Office.[8] Though the ledgers are almost entirely Elizabeth's work, the entries in the opening pages of the first volume, which dates from May 1768 (just nine months after her husband's death), are in the handwriting of her brother James. At this challenging period in Elizabeth's life, when she assumed responsibility for the running of the estate while still grieving for her husband, it is unsurprising that she should turn to her siblings for support. James, as an experienced businessman, was ideally suited to this task, and the May 1768 ledger shows that he planned the layout of the account books, and even ruled the lines on which the expenditure was recorded.

Elizabeth soon learned the ropes, for by the summer of 1769 only her handwriting is present. I picture her in the library on a damp February morning, meticulously cross-referencing the home farm accounts with her own records of the sale of wool, cheese and livestock. Then she turns to estate expenses, and in her careful, spidery hand transcribes the cost of thatching a cottage, or installing a water pump, into the neatly ruled pages of her ledger. Punctilious to a fault, Elizabeth occasionally found it necessary to draw attention to a blemish in her record-keeping. For example in 1776, when she forgot to charge hay produced on the home farm to the stables, where it had been consumed, she wrote in her ledger: 'next year I must be more particular & have an account what is used in that stable'.[9]

But it was not only for her fastidiousness that Elizabeth won plaudits, for she was also a successful innovator. With a zest for reform equal to that of her brothers, Elizabeth took steps to improve Wicken in line with the latest theories of estate management. Though the groundwork had been laid by her father-in-law Thomas Prowse, who purchased almost the entire parish so as to be able to enclose the common land, it was Elizabeth who consolidated these changes through her various reforms.[10]

Within a few months of taking over the estate, Elizabeth reached an agreement with her tenant farmers to replace their precarious yearly tenancies with long-term leases. This was with a view to encouraging investment, and further inducement was offered in the form of a rebate of half of the first year's rent, and by promising to help pay for improvements.[11] In this Elizabeth was as good as her word, for entries in the estate ledgers show that she personally funded a range of work on the tenant farms including ditching, hedging and fencing and paid for items such as grass seed.[12] Elizabeth also showed reforming zeal in her management of the home farm, where from the late 1760s she made systematic attempts to improve the quality of the soil and increase the land under cultivation. During the winter of 1772, for example, she marled areas of parkland to the north of the house, and subsequently drained, burned and ploughed part of the estate known as the Great Leys.[13]

Elizabeth's achievements on the estate are thrown into relief when it is considered that, not only did she lack any experience of farming or business, but was also barely educated. In fact it is at times difficult to reconcile the misspelt and simplistic pages of Elizabeth's journal with the enterprise shown by her in managing Wicken. Conscious of her lack of expertise in agricultural practice, she read widely in this area. Her personal accounts suggest that she was a voracious reader, for she purchased books on a broad range of subjects including poetry, literature and history, as well as practical material relating to the management of the estate. In the pages of works such as *Hints to gentlemen of landed property* (1775) by Nathaniel Kent, and *A Six Months' Tour through the North of England* (1770) by Arthur Young, Elizabeth drew both inspiration for future improvements to the estate and approval for prior changes such as the move from yearly tenancies to longer leases.[14]

But it was not only in the pages of books that Elizabeth found stimulation for her agricultural innovations, as she also learned from those around her. On a visit to the Prowses at Berkley House in Somerset in 1770, for example, Elizabeth observed the quantity and quality of the cream, butter and cheese produced locally. Noting that the herd at Berkley was fed cabbages in addition to more traditional foodstuffs, Elizabeth experimented with the feed given to the herd at Wicken. By 1772 she was growing cabbages, which were given to the cattle with a view to increasing their yield and reducing the consumption of grass and hay. Though Elizabeth meticulously recorded the number of cabbages grown at Wicken, and the quantities of milk, cream and cheese produced before and after the introduction of the new feeding regime, the increase in yield was not as high as she had hoped.[15]

In addition to undertaking a wide range of agricultural reforms, Elizabeth also made improvements to Wicken's gardens and parkland. In 1771 she laid out gravel walks to the north-west of the house, and seven years later created a ha-ha between the gardens and the stables.[16] During the 1770s and 80s Elizabeth laid out four new ridings through the woods bordering Wicken Park, which served both to delineate the house's woodland setting, and to complement the network of ridings criss-crossing the neighbouring estate owned by the Duke of

Grafton.[17] Elizabeth marked the construction of the first riding, in Lilby woods, in July 1772 with a musical party: 'In this month we had our musick in Lilby Rideing, that being completely Finished, about 50 Ladys & Gentlemen Drank Tea with us, & had musick. All my Bro. and Sissrs. with me for a week at that time.'[18]

Elizabeth's developments at Wicken Park were underpinned by a commitment to the social welfare of her tenants. Just as William used his medical knowledge to help the poor of London, John employed the resources of the Lord Crewe Trust to fund a variety of social enterprises at Bamburgh Castle, and Granville drew on his understanding of English law to promote the freedom of slaves, so Elizabeth took advantage of her position at Wicken to improve the lives of its residents and workers. Elizabeth sought to reconcile her own wealth and privilege with the poverty of others by working actively on their behalf. The estate ledgers show that her philanthropy ranged from ad hoc gifts of small amounts of money, to long-term initiatives such as the provision of schooling and subsidised food.

Elizabeth's personal accounts record numerous instances of charity. Her donations in late 1774, for example, include money given to 'a boy at the gate', for the 'care of the child with the hare lip', and to 'the children who dined here from ye school'.[19] This was a form of giving traditionally associated with the lady of the manor, but Elizabeth also exceeded the expectations of her role by trying to address the underlying causes of poverty. She began by improving the housing of the poor, with a programme of works on estate cottages that included rethatching and glazing.[20] Shocked by the want of sheets and blankets, which she described in her diary as 'beyond beliefe', Elizabeth spent £12 in the winter of 1774 providing supplies of linen to her tenants.[21] Elizabeth's attempts to improve the living conditions of the Wicken poor appear to have been effective, so that by the late 1770s she was spending less on relief payments.[22]

Elizabeth also paid for the children of her tenants to attend a village school. Whether she established the school is not known, but the example of her brother John at Bamburgh must at the very least have been influential in determining the type of education provided there. By the mid-1770s Elizabeth was spending £30 a year on the schoolmaster's wages, contributing to the cost of shoes and clothes for the pupils, and making one-off payments such as 'school books gave the children at the school' which she recorded in October 1776.[23] Elizabeth was also instrumental in setting up a Sunday school at Wicken, which opened in the spring of 1788.

Another initiative reminiscent of the work of John at Bamburgh was the provision of subsidised food and firewood. Also influential here was the agriculturalist Nathaniel Kent, who drew attention to the disadvantage to labourers of having to buy small amounts of food at local markets rather than at lower prices in their own village.[24] Elizabeth's response was to sell most of the produce of the home farm directly to her tenants at reduced rates. In 1778, for example, cheeses made on the farm were sold at a rate of 2½d per pound rather than at the market price of 4d. She sold beef to the poor every winter at subsidised prices, and in the particularly severe winter of 1783 the meat was given for free.[25]

While the charitable activities of the lady of the manor were traditionally confined to the period when she was residing on the estate, Elizabeth's operated throughout the year. This was significant as, in common with other country landowners, Elizabeth spent the winter months in London, staying alternately with her brothers William and James. Elizabeth lived at Wicken during the summer, and hosted innumerable parties of family and friends, who came to escape the heat and dirt of London, to convalesce, or simply to enjoy the pleasures of the country. Her diary was often jam-packed, as in the weeks following the maiden voyage of the *Union*, when she entertained in succession 'some of my friends', 'some of my niece Mordaunts', her brother William and his family, and finally 'on ye 11 [October] my mother P, Miss Jinkins, Bett, Sophia, Mary and my N. Mordaunt' who 'stayed to ye 24'.[26]

The close relationship that developed between Elizabeth and her nephew Jack in the course of his short life, was replicated following his death with his surviving sister Kitty. Elizabeth clearly delighted in the company of the little girl, whom she referred to as 'my dear Kitty', and her account books record the various treats and presents that she gave to her. During a visit to Wicken in the summer and autumn of

1774, when she was four years old, Kitty was the recipient of 'two balls', 'a box', various 'toys' and a 'Riding dress'.[27] In her accounts for the following year, Elizabeth notes the purchase of 'little books for Kitty Sharp' as well as some 'shoes' and a 'toothbrush'.[28]

Following her birth in April 1778, William and Catharine's daughter Mary joined the annual summer pilgrimage to Wicken, and she too spent much of her childhood in the company of her aunts. Mary's residences at Wicken often coincided with visits by the Mordaunt family, for example in May 1792, when Elizabeth records that 'My 3 niece Mordaunts, Kitty, Charlotte and Susan came & stayed seven weeks with us', and this served to ensure that the warm relationship between the Prowse and Sharp families extended to the next generation.[29]

The Wicken account books show, too, that the musical life of the Sharp family could flourish even in the absence of its menfolk. Entries such as 'to Mr Laley for Tuneing ye Harpsichord', and 'for a luten string' are repeated on numerous occasions over the years.[30] On 16 March 1780 Elizabeth found herself in the avant-garde of musical fashion, when she received a 'fortepiano' as a present from her sister-in-law 'Miss Prowse'. Purchased from a 'Mr Nivit' on the advice of Elizabeth's brother James, the piano cost £16 16s 0d. There may have been some delay in transporting the piano from London to Northamptonshire, as it was not until 17 August that Elizabeth paid a farmer's son two shillings for delivering the instrument to Wicken Park. Three months later, on 24 November, a 'Mr Buckinger' charged her 10s 6d for tuning the piano.[31]

As well as the private solace of the keyboard, Elizabeth was as willing as her brothers to engage in musical entertainment of a more gregarious sort. The celebratory concert at Lilby Riding in July 1772 was not the only event of its kind. In her accounts for 12 September 1774, for example, there is a payment 'to the Men & Boys in ye Wood when we had Musick, 4s' and this ties in with Granville's record of a family visit to Wicken in the previous month: 'Had Music in the Wood near Wicken before a very large Company.'[32] Nor was the *fête champêtre* described by the Northamptonshire gentleman unique, because Elizabeth describes similar festivities in a diary entry for 27 September

1777: 'about this time we had a fait Champator at Wicken our usual band & Neighbours invited'.[33] A further report, on 21 June 1770 – 'Coome and Cove, my 2 servts playd the French Horn in the woods' – suggests that Elizabeth followed her brothers' example of employing servants who were also musicians.[34]

As proprietor of Wicken Park, Elizabeth possessed a degree of influence and autonomy that was exceptional for a woman of her time. The meticulous pages of the estate ledgers reveal the extent to which she exploited that opportunity. From the grief-filled, uncertain days of August 1767, Elizabeth refashioned herself as the accomplished and enterprising manager of a large country estate. Moreover, it is apparent that she shared many of the characteristics that made her brothers such a conspicuous success, and in particular a capacity for hard work, rigorousness, compassion and an instinct for reform. Her commitment to the social welfare of her tenants stands out as her most significant achievement. It also explains the Northamptonshire gentleman's patronising appraisal of the residents of Wicken as the 'happiest set of peasants in England'. Given Elizabeth's efforts, it would be surprising if this had not resulted in more than ordinarily harmonious landlord–tenant relations.

26

Zoffany

It has been drizzling all day, and now as the drear of the winter afternoon fades imperceptibly into the darker shades of evening, the rain falls heavily. Rivulets stream down the windowpanes of the library at Wicken Park, blurring the parkland beyond. The day has receded so quickly that the housemaid, bustling about her duties in the upstairs bedrooms, has forgotten to draw the heavy velvet curtains, or to light the candelabra that hangs above the writing desk. In the premature twilight of the December afternoon, only the glow of the fire in the grate and a solitary candle on a lacquered side table relieve the darkness of the library. Apparently unaware of the gathering shadows, an artist stands by the fire at a makeshift easel, painting on a mahogany drawing board. In front of him sits an old man with a fine chiselled face and long white hair, resting his left hand on the handle of a spade. He is perfectly still, and but for the muffled sound of falling rain, and the rustle of a log falling in the grate, nothing disturbs the silence of the half-lit room.[1]

In the autumn of 1779, as we have seen, Johan Zoffany was at work on his painting of the Sharp family. For William, the engagement of an established society painter, albeit one of slightly faded reputation, at significant cost, was a marker of worldly success. It was a common aspiration of the professional classes, as well as those of more elevated station, to record their likenesses for posterity, so much so that foreigners often commented on the popularity of 'phiz mongering' in Britain.[2] Moreover the portrait, which was to be exhibited at the Royal Academy in 1781, acted as a public representation of the Sharps engaging in an activity for which they were well known. It was also the repository of family memory. In a pre-photographic age, the painting represented not only the likenesses of the individual family members, but the relationship between them, the unity of the family as a whole, and their proximity of interest and feeling.

Zoffany was an obvious choice for the commission, on account of his mastery of family portraiture, and in particular a form called the 'conversation piece'. Originating in the painting of family groups in sixteenth-century northern Italy, the genre was later imported into the countries of northern Europe. During this time certain conventions were established, for example that the sitters, who were generally members of the same family, should be engaged in an activity that was customary to them, while also being linked to each other by motifs and actions that identified their relationship. A conversation piece was also typically a work of 'artificial reality', meaning that the setting was partly or wholly a product of the artist's imagination rather than a faithful reproduction of an interior or landscape. By the middle of the eighteenth century, it had also become necessary for the sitters to be portrayed in a relaxed and animated style, with none of the rigid formality characteristic of seventeenth-century family portraits.[2]

Though Zoffany arrived in England as a history painter, versed in the decorative historical and religious art of the late baroque and rococo of southern Germany, he quickly mastered the conventions of the conversation piece. In fact his contribution to the genre owed much to the techniques that he had learned as a young artist in Regensburg, and in particular to the traditions of Dutch art which were widely admired in Germany at that time. The intricate meticulousness with which Zoffany depicts the lustrous fabrics of eighteenth-century costume, and his attention to detail, is reminiscent of the work of Dutch and Flemish artists. Continental influence is also apparent in the high finish of Zoffany's paintings, and his use of brighter colours than those favoured by British portraitists.[3]

As well as Dutch and Flemish influences, Zoffany brought to bear his own distinctive characteristics as an artist. In addition to a facility for capturing the likeness of his sitters, which was widely praised at the time, Zoffany seemed able to convey a sense of individuality and character.[4] The 'fidelity to nature' which was a feature of the German artist's depiction of costume was also apparent in the grace and naturalness of his figures.[5] With a skill honed painting scenes from Shakespeare and comic opera, Zoffany was able to animate his images, replacing the stiff artificiality of earlier examples of the genre with a sense of fluidity and barely suspended motion.[6]

It was usual for conversation pieces to be constructed from individual sittings, and Zoffany appears to have used this method with the Sharp portrait. He painted directly onto the canvas, altering poses as required at a later stage of the creative process.[8] Elizabeth's account of family sittings suggests the complexity of a process that required numerous likenesses to be taken and combined.[9] Indeed the Sharp painting represented a particular challenge for the artist as it comprised fifteen individual sitters, many of whom lived outside London. Dick Spikeman, who is depicted in the Sharp painting as a cabin boy holding a music book, was still alive in 1848. He recalled sitting for Zoffany, and remembered in particular how long it had taken to complete the painting because of the difficulties involved in organising sittings for every member of the family. A further complication, according to Spikeman, had been the reluctance of the boat master, William Lee, to participate in the process.[10]

In a journal entry dated 12 November 1779, Elizabeth notes: 'Sisr F and the children left me, as all the party was siting to Zopheney for the Family Picture, and when I go to Town am to be aded to the party.'[11] On 29 November she confirms that 'Sisr Jud and I set out for London and my picture was aded to the Grupe'.[12] After that Elizabeth is silent on the subject until December 1780, when she records that 'Near Xmass zopheney came to finish my picture and Bro. G came down with him in order to have it finished for the expition in the Spring'. As it was almost unheard of, except in the case of royalty, for sittings to take place outside the artist's studio, the conclusion must be that Zoffany was desperate to finish the painting in time for the forthcoming exhibition.[13]

But by some logistical error, the artist arrived at Wicken before the family portrait. While he waited for it to turn up, 'the weather being

bad no temtation to go out', Zoffany amused himself by painting
Jonathan Jackman, an elderly gardener, who had worked on the estate
for sixty years. Elizabeth does not relate the circumstances in which
Zoffany chose Jackman as his model, but I like to imagine him watching
the ancient retainer as he stoops over his spade in the frosty recesses
of the walled kitchen garden. The artist has his paints of course, but
no canvas other than the Sharp portrait that is in transit from London,
so Elizabeth supplies him with an 'an old Mahoganey Drawing Board'
and perhaps an easel from the schoolroom.

When the Sharp painting eventually arrived, Zoffany was still at
work on his portrait of Jackman, and Elizabeth reports that the artist
'would have been glad to have had him come up to Town to have
finished it'. However, Elizabeth could not consent to Jonathan travelling to London, as he was 'compleatley 80 on one of the days he sat',
and 'such a journey might have nocked him up'. Regretting the loss
of his subject, Zoffany told Elizabeth that 'could he have had time to
have finished' the portrait of Jonathan, he 'believed it would have been
one of his best pictures'.[14]

It was customary for patron and artist to hold preliminary discus-
sions on issues such as setting and the use of accessories. The artist
was given varying degrees of latitude, according to the level of detail
specified by the client. In the absence of relevant documents relating
to the Sharp painting, it is difficult to determine what part, if any,
William played in the creative process. It is certainly possible that it
was the surgeon who suggested the *Apollo* as a setting for the painting.
However, as Zoffany was familiar with Sharp water parties, and was
himself the owner of a pleasure barge, the idea could equally have
come from him. Given the close association between the Sharps and
the *Apollo*, in the minds of both the family and the general public, it
was a straightforward choice.

The same could not be said of the composition of the painting.
Having determined on the *Apollo* as an appropriate setting, the artist
faced the unenviable task of placing fifteen sitters and their musical
instruments on the deck of a barge, in such a way as to convey the
harmony of the family and the character of individual relationships,
in poses that appeared natural and unforced, and with the verisimili-

tude required to persuade the viewer that the family are playing music together on a boat on the River Thames. To solve the problem of composition, Zoffany resorted to the 'artificial reality' that was a feature of the genre. Whereas the river, the deck of the *Apollo*, the family members and their instruments are all real, it is inconceivable that the Sharps would have chosen to make music together bunched up in a small patch of deck below the stern. The positioning of the family is an artifice required to ensure that the figures fit into a relatively small canvas, while also allowing sufficient detail to convey individual character and likeness.

The sitters are arranged in a triangular shape with a married brother – William, James and John – positioned at the three corners, while the near side of the triangle is formed by the four members of the family who live in the north of England. Six of the figures – William, his wife Catharine and their daughter Mary, James's wife Catharine, Judith, and John's daughter Anne Jemima sit on the raised red stern of the barge. Beneath them, their heads forming a gently undulating serpentine line, sit the remaining members of the family.[15] An axis forming a right angle to the sides of the triangle leads from the neck of Judith's lute to the cello and violin in the foreground.[16] Within the rigid geometry of this structure, there is a profusion of circles, ellipses and ovals, such as the oval that curves around the heads of Granville and Elizabeth, and another circling the clasped hands of the two Catharines.

William stands at the apex of the triangle, in a position appropriate to his role as patron. He wears the 'Windsor' uniform established by George III, consisting of a dark blue coat with gold buttons and a red collar.[17] Behind him billows a crimson silk standard bearing 'the Arms of Mr & Mrs Wm Sharp – & of Mr & Mrs James Sharp, in separate Shields, tyed together with a Blue Riband Held by a Spread Eagle'.[18] Below William sits his wife Catharine, dressed in a pale blue silk riding habit and a white silk gold fringed waistcoat. Her right hand stretches out and rests gently on the arm of her sister-in-law.[19] The skirts of Catharine's habit are hidden by the folds of the dress of her daughter Mary, who sits on her lap with a kitten in her arms.

Mary looks up at her aunt Judith, who is resplendent in a mustard-coloured riding habit and a black hat trimmed with ostrich feathers. Standing between Judith and the curling line of the standard is John's daughter Anne Jemima, who wears a laced red and blue bodice, and a hat trimmed with pink roses. Her parents, John and Mary, are positioned below the raised stern, John in the foreground in clerical black, and Mary in a flowered pink gown with Dresden sleeve ruffles. John sits at the shoulder of his youngest sister Frances, who wears a blue silk *robe à l'anglaise*, and holds a book of music in her hand, as if about to sing. To her right, her slim white arms stretched to the keyboard, sits Elizabeth in a sacque dress of rich reddish-brown and a white satin hooded mantle. Granville leans towards her, his fingers curled round the music manuscript which he holds for her to read. He wears a sage-green coat and waistcoat with black knee breeches.

James sits in the foreground in a brown woollen coat, with the coils of a black serpent spread between his knees. His daughter Kitty stands beside him, dressed in a sprigged white cotton gown with a broad pink sash, and pointing one tiny slippered toe from beneath her skirts. Catharine, her mother, sits above Kitty on the raised stern, wearing a pale lavender silk dress and a quilted satin petticoat, with a black laced shawl about her shoulders. The boat master William Lee, and the cabin boy Dick Spikeman, stand in a small boat alongside the *Apollo*.

The family sits amongst their instruments. Granville holds aloft his famous double flute on which he played duets 'to the delight and conviction of many doubters, who had conceived such an accomplishment to have been impracticable',[20] while Elizabeth sits at a small harpsichord.[21] The long curved mouthpiece that James pulled from his pocket to show George III during his audience in September 1770 emerges from the black sinuous coils of his serpent, next to the cello which John played in an 'ecstasy of enjoyment' at his vicarage in Hartburn.[22] Judith plucks the strings of an elegant theorbo (a plucked stringed instrument of the lute family), and William's French horns lie on the polished surface of the harpsichord.

A dog lies at the foot of the painting, with one paw resting affectionately on the train of Frances's blue silk dress. This is Zoffany's dog Roma, who apparently grew fond of Frances when she sat for the artist.[23] Roma is depicted in an identical pose in Zoffany's portrait of John Wilkes and his daughter Mary, which is contemporaneous with the Sharp painting. It is possible that the dog is a kind of signature, or alternatively a symbol of the artist's presence on the canvas. Perhaps Zoffany wishes to convey the idea of his participation in the water party, and that he lies there listening to the music.[24]

The barge is pictured on the Thames at Fulham. On the north bank, All Saints Church stands by a small house with bow windows, while a toll house and the southern end of old Fulham Bridge mark the Putney side of the river.[25] The Thames flows diagonally across the painting, and the impression is given that the *Apollo* is being rowed upstream, in the direction of the viewer, towards the rural villages to the west of London that were so often the destination of Sharp water parties.[26] Above them dark storm clouds spread across a lowering evening sky, and the wind swells the sheets of the crimson standard. Rain threatens, and perhaps the family will soon have recourse to the ingenious awning that was employed when a thunderstorm interrupted the impromptu royal performance at Kew.[27]

Zoffany's hurry to finish the painting for the Royal Academy exhibition proved to be a largely wasted effort. If he had hoped that *The Sharp Family* would restore his former reputation, he was to be sorely disappointed. The critics who viewed the portrait at the exhibition in the spring of 1781 were almost unanimous in finding fault with it. The principal ground of complaint was the composition of the painting. Horace Walpole, while acknowledging that the figures were 'natural, and highly finished', lamented what he termed to be 'a great want of keeping on the whole'. Mauritius Lowe, reviewing the portrait for the *Earwig*, agreed with him: 'the parts are finely finished; but the effect of the tout-ensemble is abominable'. The critic of the 2 May 1781 *Morning Herald* described the painting as being 'jumbled together without the smallest attention to harmony the flats and sharps of one of the most musical families of Great Britain'.[28]

In a variation of the general critique, the *Public Advertiser* of 2 May 1781 pronounced that 'there is something repulsive in the Colouring, something not to say it at all profoundly, which reminded us of a

Turkey Carpet'. By now the painting was fair game, and the *Morning Herald* critic who previously denounced the jumbling of 'flats and sharps' thought it worth his while to return to the subject, though this time satirically, in the 4 May edition of the paper:

> Mr Zoffany in his Musical Family has given us the critical turn of the barge grounding on a shoal near Fulham. The sudden shock stops the concert, one of the Mr Sharps very naturally waves his hat for assistance from the shore – the Ladies dread a general leak. The Thames Committee brother has his eyes fixed towards the heaven, asking forgiveness for not having removed the shoals. At the same time a serpent is gnawing at his breast as an emblem of a hurt conscience. One Lady, to restore harmony, is handing to another Handel's water-piece, but she does not look at it thinking water parted from the Barge more applicable.[29]

As late as 1920, the authors of a biography of the artist refer to the painting as 'of course, overcrowded' and the grouping 'so artificial and so insecure ... that the general effect of the composition is marred'.[30] It is only relatively recently that critics have acknowledged the ingenuity of Zoffany's design. What once was described as a muddle, and 'a style of grouping that it is impossible to dwell on without pain', is now lauded for its 'panache' and 'sheer originality'.[31] The twentieth-century writer John Kerslake explains that it was the originality of the composition that floored contemporary critics: 'Want of "keeping" loses much of its force if one can accept that the viewer is virtually taken onto the deck of the *Apollo*, on the near side of the circle centred on Roma. A real close-up, almost unprecedented in English painting.'[32] Standing on the deck of the *Apollo*, within touching distance of Roma's soft fur, and the luminous blue silk of Frances's dress, the viewer is drawn into the Sharps' world.

For its ingenious composition, and for the exquisite rendering of the family's costumes, and the gleaming surfaces and curves of their musical instruments, *The Sharp Family* is now celebrated as one of Zoffany's finest conversation pieces. Since even the most damning of contemporary critics admitted that the likenesses of the siblings were well drawn, it can also be relied on as an accurate record of the appearance of the principal characters in this history. The portrait offers a representation of the Sharps at the height of their social success, the harmony of its composition an apt metaphor for the strong family ties that bound them together. In its vast exuberance and intricate visual counterpoints, the painting stands as one of the most vivid depictions available to us of the ambition, energy and elegance of the English eighteenth century, as embodied in one family.

27

Zong

It is a little after nine on the morning of 19 March 1783, in William's mansion in Old Jewry. From his study on the ground floor, Granville can hear the maids clearing away the breakfast things in the parlour across the hall, and the thud of the front door as his brother leaves on his rounds. Catharine has retreated upstairs to her dressing room to pore over the weekly accounts, and Mary is reading aloud to her governess in the schoolroom. Dipping his pen in a silver inkwell, Granville returns to his tract on the antiquity of free parliaments, which he is anxious to finish. As he writes, the sounds of a London morning drift through the open window above his desk. A boy sweeps the yard of next-door Grocers' Hall with short rhythmic strokes, a coal heaver shovels his load into a neighbouring cellar, and a hawker on Gresham Street cries repeatedly: 'A pudding! A pudding! A hot pudding!'[1]

Granville is in the process of underlining a particularly significant passage of his work when he is interrupted by a knock on the door. Immediately, and without waiting for the footman to announce him, a man enters almost at a run. Granville recognises him as his friend Olaudah Equiano, a former slave and fellow campaigner in the anti-slavery movement.[2] As the footman retreats, closing the door behind him with slightly disapproving ceremony, Granville motions his visitor towards a seat, but Equiano is too disturbed to take his ease. With his hat in his hand, and striding from one end of the room to the other, the abolitionist embarks on a tale of such numbing brutality that even the hardened campaigner Granville Sharp can scarcely believe his ears.

Equiano's account begins at Cape Coast in West Africa, on 18 August 1781. A slaving ship, the *Zong*, owned by the Liverpool-based Gregson syndicate, is departing for Jamaica with 442 slaves in her hold. There is also, unusually for a slaving ship, a passenger on board. Robert Stubbs had arrived in Africa in early 1781 to take charge of Fort William at Anomabu for the Royal African Company, but had been relieved from duty on account of his 'litigious Disposition, neglect of Duty and contempt of Authority'.[3] Stubbs joined the *Zong* as a means of escaping from what had become an invidious situation.

In the course of the passage across the Atlantic, the captain Luke Collingwood fell ill, and the passenger Robert Stubbs assumed control. On 21 November 1781, three days after sighting Tobago, it was discovered that several of the ship's water casks were only half full.[4] Six days later Jamaica came into view, but due to a navigational error it was mistaken for the French territory of Saint-Domingue. By the time the crew realised their blunder, the *Zong* had sailed 120 miles to the west of Jamaica.[5] By now there was only enough water for four days' journey, and it was estimated that it would take ten to fourteen days to reach their destination.

On 29 November, it was suggested to the crew that in view of the water shortage: 'Part of the Slaves should be destroyed to save the rest and the remainder of the slaves and the crew put to short allowance.'[6] The crew agreed unanimously to this solution, and at 8 p.m. fifty-four women and children were pushed overboard 'singly through the Cabin windows'. Two days later, forty-two male slaves were dispatched from the quarterdeck, and a further group of thirty-eight were jettisoned in the days that followed. Ten jumped overboard rather than submit to their fate, and one managed to climb back on board.

Though there is no exact record of the number of slaves who were sent to their death, a figure of 132 was accepted at a subsequent court hearing, not including the ten men who jumped from the ship.[7] In a painful insight into the atmosphere below deck as the murderous intent of the crew became known, the first mate James Kelsall recalled that slaves 'begged they might be suffered to live and they would not ask for either Meat or Water but could live without either till they arrived at their determined port'.[8]

The *Zong* massacre might have been forgotten, had it not been for the greed of the Gregson syndicate. Anxious to recoup the value of the murdered slaves, the Gregsons brought a claim against their insurers demanding compensation. A hearing held in the Guildhall in March 1783 hinged on whether underwriters were liable under the terms of a standard maritime insurance policy.[9] The claimants argued that just as the jettisoning of inanimate goods was permissible to save a vessel and its crew, so in the context of the emergency existing on board the *Zong* at the end of November 1781, it was necessary for slaves to be thrown overboard to safeguard the lives of others. 'Necessity' was the mantra repeated over and again in the course of the claimant's argument.

Robert Stubbs was the only witness to give evidence at the hearing, and what is known about the voyage is largely based on his testimony. Though the ship's mate James Kelsall gave a statement to the Gregson syndicate, which mostly tallies with Stubbs's version of events, he was not called to give evidence. Given Stubbs's reputation as a 'wicked and treacherous character', he is hardly the most reliable of witnesses.[10] In any event, it was in the interests of both men to distance themselves from the crime. Stubbs, for example, took care to throw responsibility for the murders onto Luke Collingwood, even though the captain had been considered too ill to continue in his post. In the absence of the ship's log it was open to both witnesses to distort evidence of sailing times and water supplies, to sustain the argument of 'necessity'.[11]

The strategy proved successful, for the insurers were found liable to indemnify the syndicate for the value of the murdered slaves. Notwithstanding the evidence of mass slaughter, there was no suggestion that action should be taken against the perpetrators.[12] The judgement was reported in the *Morning Chronicle* on 18 March 1783, and it was this that brought the atrocity to the notice of Olaudah Equiano. On the following day, Equiano outlined the facts of the case to Granville at Old Jewry.

Incensed by what he had heard, Granville set himself to the task of seeking justice for the murdered slaves. With all thoughts of the antiquity of free parliaments temporarily forgotten, the reformer spent the next few weeks scurrying about the streets of Westminster and Mayfair, lobbying bishops, petitioning Members of Parliament and retaining lawyers to support him. He wrote long discursive letters to senior members of the government, liberally sprinkled with apocalyptic language and underscored in red ink. Assisted by the apparently inexhaustible resource of the Sharp address book, Granville thought nothing of buttonholing grandees at Old Jewry concerts, or lecturing aristocrats on their responsibilities to the victims of the massacre.

On 22 March 1783, Granville instructed solicitors to bring a prosecution for murder in the Admiralty Courts against the Gregson syndicate.[13] At the same time, the philanthropist turned his attention to a development in the insurance litigation. Rejecting the finding of the court at Guildhall, the underwriters had refused to pay compensation and were now intent on a retrial. The issue of whether or not a second trial was permissible was listed for hearing in front of Lord Mansfield in the Court of King's Bench on 21 and 22 May. Though the hearing fell far short of the murder prosecution that he so ardently yearned for, Granville recognised it as an opportunity to present the iniquities of the case to a wider audience.

As he made his way through the crowds of litigants, witnesses, importuning lawyers and sightseers in Westminster Hall on the morning of 21 May, Granville must have recalled the moment, eleven years earlier, when he had heard of the victory in the case of James Somerset. Then he had absented himself from the hearing for fear of antagonising Lord Mansfield. Today he would be present, emboldened perhaps by his previous victory in his long duel with the chief justice, and by the years of relentless campaigning that had followed it. Accompanied by a shorthand writer whom he had hired for the occasion, Granville passed through the Gothic screen that divided the Court of King's Bench from the vast hall beyond, and took his place on a bench behind the insurers' lawyers.

As the Solicitor General, John Lee, opens on behalf of the Gregson syndicate, Granville is already fidgeting in his seat. By the time Lee reaches the crux of his argument, to the effect that the *Zong* slaves were property and therefore expendable, the campaigner is scrawling impassioned notes on pages torn from his memorandum book and thrusting them at the insurers' lawyers. Finally, Lee sits down and is replaced by Mr Heywood who argues on behalf of the applicants. This is much more to Granville's way of thinking, and he can relax a little as counsel for the underwriters dismiss the Gregsons' claim as a fraudulent attempt to recoup their loss. However, it is the second part of Heywood's submissions, in which the barrister claims to represent 'millions of Mankind and the Cause of Humanity in general', that really interests Granville. These are arguments in the development of which the reformer has been directly involved, and he nods his head strenuously in approval as Heywood denounces the actions of the crew: 'To say that wantonly or by Ignorance a Capn may throw 132 lives overboard is a Proposition that shocks Humanity.'[14]

At the conclusion of the argument, Lord Mansfield voiced his disquiet at the assertion, apparently undisclosed at the previous hearing, that the last group of thirty-eight slaves 'were thrown overboard a Day after the Rain'.[15] As this went to the very heart of the claimant's case, the judge ruled that a retrial was appropriate. 'It is,' he said, 'a very uncommon Case and I think very well deserves a re-examination.'[16] Here the legal trail goes cold. There is no evidence that a retrial took place, and though official documentation may have been lost, it seems improbable that the determination of such a notorious case would have passed unnoticed. Given the sensitivity of the proceedings, and that Granville had made no secret of his intention to bring a prosecution for murder, it seems more likely that the Gregson syndicate decided to cut their losses, and the claim was not pursued.

This was a victory of sorts – and in the weeks following the hearing, Granville redoubled his attempts to launch a criminal prosecution. On 2 July 1783 he wrote to the Lords Commissioners of the Admiralty, in whose jurisdiction criminal proceedings would have to be brought, urging them to bring murder charges against the crew of the *Zong*. He enclosed with his letter a series of documents supporting his assertion of the necessity of a criminal trial, including a transcript of the proceedings in the Court of King's Bench, and his own 'An Account of the Murder of One Hundred and Thirty-two Negro Slaves on Board the Ship *Zong*'.[17] In his covering letter, Granville explained that he had included the 'Account' in case the other documents were too long for the Lords Commissioners to read.[18]

Granville uses the 'Account' to express his outrage that the *Zong* case should have been treated by the legal system as a pecuniary claim rather than as a bloody affront to 'the fundamental right to "Life & Liberty"'. Appealing to the sympathies of his readers, Granville describes the collective trauma of the slaves as they waited to be thrown into the sea. He rejects the plea of 'necessity' on the grounds that 'there can never be a necessity for the wilful murder of an innocent Man'. In a passionate concluding statement, Granville draws a link between the responsibility of the individual perpetrators of the *Zong* massacre, and the collective guilt of the country as a whole. The only pleas of necessity that can be legally admitted, he argues, are '1st a Necessity, incumbent upon the whole Kingdom, to vindicate our National Justice by the most exemplary punishment of the Murderers', and '2nd the Necessity of putting an entire stop to the Slave Trade'.[19]

On 18 July 1783, Granville wrote to the prime minister the Duke of Portland enclosing a copy of his letter to the Lord Commissioners, and his 'Account'. He explained that though the 'punishment of that murder belongs properly to the Admiralty', it was his wish 'by the horrible example related in the enclosed papers, to warn Your Grace, that there is an absolute necessity to abolish the Slave Trade'.[20] Neither the Admiralty nor the Duke of Portland replied to Granville's communication, and no prosecution was ever brought against the perpetrators of the massacre.

In spite of this failure, Granville's attempts to obtain justice for the murdered slaves played a crucial role in disseminating the facts of the *Zong*. He sought to mobilise support for his campaign by distributing copies of the 'Account' among abolition sympathisers, and by sending it to newspapers and to well-disposed representatives of the Church of England such as the bishops of Chester and Peterborough. From there the story was picked up and reproduced in different forms across the country. In Manchester, for example, the *Zong* came to prominence in 1787 as a result of letters written by local radical Thomas Cooper, which were published in *Wheelers' Manchester Chronicle* and later as a pamphlet.[21] It was serendipitous that the litigation coincided with the decision of the London Society of Friends, in July 1783, to embark on a concerted campaign against the slave trade. Three months earlier, Granville had responded to a request from Quaker activist William Dillwyn for material useful in the fight against slavery by providing details of the *Zong* case. Thereafter the narrative proved a vital tool for the Society of Friends' anti-slavery propaganda subcommittee, which dedicated itself to publicising the abolitionist cause.[22]

From these beginnings the narrative of the *Zong* reverberates through the history of the anti-slavery movement, powerful both as a description of the 'indescribable' and as an 'authentick specimen' of the horrors of the trade.[23] The outrage of the *Zong* massacre, which Granville did so much to intrude into the public consciousness, memorialises not only the slaves who lost their lives, but the victims of innumerable acts of capricious, sadistic or merely routine violence who have no other record.

28

Glee

Even in the broad dimensions of the great hall in Old Jewry, there is little room for manoeuvre. Earls in brocaded waistcoats rub shoulders with bishops in purple cassocks, and the ostrich feathers of a splendidly attired dowager countess tickle a bespectacled jurist down from Oxford. There are ermine-trimmed mantles, and silk twill breeches, gorgeous gold-fringed velvet coats, and headdresses threaded with pearls. Lit by the light of a hundred candles, the room is a sea of shimmering threads, and crisp muslins, iridescent silks and lustrous satins. Gilt mirrors reflect the light onto the delicate tracery of the white and gilded walls, and the intricate plasterwork of the ornamental ceiling. Even the broad treads of the staircase, and the pipes of Miss Cecilia Morgan that stands on the other side of the hall, glitter in the candlelight.

From his vantage point to the left of the entrance porch, William greets his guests with his usual amiability. Catharine, beside him, is a model of composure, notwithstanding her anxieties about the evening. In the midst of a throng of recently arrived guests, Granville has cornered the Bishop of Lincoln, and is lecturing him on the benefits of a free militia. James meanwhile is engaging Lady Lake in an interesting discussion on the merits of the new waterways, while Elizabeth – a little hesitantly at first – converses with Lord Pembroke on her recent visit to Wilton House. As the longcase clock in the corner chimes the hour, William steers his guests to the chairs that line the hall on either side of the organ. There is a little delay as the male members of the party rummage about for their music, and clear their throats, and swop seats. Then, to the 'One, two, three!' of conductor Joah Bates, 152 earls, bishops, lawyers and politicians launch into the opening verse of the glee 'Amidst the myrtles as I walk'.[1]

The London Sharps divided the musical year into two parts, dedicating the warmer months of April to October to music on the water, and the chillier season of November to March to a more traditional style of performance. No formal record of Sharp recitals from the 1750s and 60s survives, and what is known of them is gleaned from correspondence. However, in November 1773, William's wife Catharine began a 'Visiting Book' for concerts at Old Jewry. Between 21 November 1773 and 10 March 1783, Catharine records the details of twenty-eight concerts, of which twenty-six, featuring sacred music, were held on a Sunday.[2] Though Catharine's list is not exhaustive – her use of the expression '*in all recollec.*'[3] suggests that it is a rough guide, and there is evidence from other sources of concerts that do not feature in the book – it provides nonetheless a vivid account of Sharp music-making in this period.

Catharine compiles a guest list for each of the twenty-eight concerts recorded in the book. After a relatively slow start at the end of 1773, when performances on 21 November and 5 December attracted an audience of thirty-four and fourteen respectively, the pace quickened. On 19 December, forty-seven guests attended, and by 13 February 1774 the Sharps could boast an audience of fifty-four. Numbers then remained constant at around the fifty to sixty mark. At least 400 different individuals attended a Sunday concert in the period November 1773 to March 1783.[4] The guest list endorses the claim that Sharp concerts were attended by 'those of the highest and most distinguished rank', with aristocratic patrons including Lord Exeter, Lord Guernsey, Lady Hamilton, Lady Mills, Lord and Lady Paulett, Lady Pole, Lord and Lady Parker, Lady Onslow and Lord Sandwich. On 13 February 1780, the attendance of the Duke of Cumberland – sometime star of the sacred-music performance in Lady Onslow's octagon-shaped music room – brought the Sharp concerts to a suitably exalted social climax.

Catharine also names the musicians at the sacred-music concerts. Some 200 individuals performed at Old Jewry during the period covered by the Visiting Book, with an average of thirty musicians per concert.[5] In common with the membership of Felice Giardini's band on the

Apollo, these included many of the most accomplished performers of the day. Singers such as John Beard, La Motte and Sarah Harrop, the violinist Antonin Kammel and the cellist John Crosdill were joined on at least one occasion by the celebrated Italian mezzo-soprano castrato Gaspare Pacchierotti.[6] That musicians of this calibre were prepared to play in Sharp concerts, both at the Old Jewry and on the rather less formal stage of the *Apollo*, is a testament both to the exemplary musical standards maintained on these occasions, and once again to the esteem in which the family was held.

The burgeoning of the Sharp concert series during the 1770s and early 1780s mirrors the flourishing of musical life in London in this period. The arrival of the Italian violinist Felice Giardini (later maestro of the *Apollo* band) in 1751 marked the beginning of what the musicologist Charles Burney called 'a memorable aera in the instrumental Music of this kingdom'.[7] Giardini's extraordinary virtuosity thrilled his audiences, who were used to the stodgier fare of British violinists. On debut at a private concert, Giardini 'threw into the utmost astonishment the whole company', while his first public performance provoked applause 'so loud, long, and furious, as nothing but that bestowed on Garrick had ever equalled'.[8]

Giardini acted as a shock to the musical life of the capital, revolutionising expectations of instrumental performance, and whetting the appetites of his audiences for higher standards and greater variety.[9] Impresarios met this need by establishing public subscription concerts, which successfully combined skilled musicianship, with a reputation for exclusivity. At the vanguard of this movement was the former opera singer Teresa Cornelys, who hosted the first of many concert series at her mansion in Soho Square in the season of 1760–1. From 1765, direction of the Cornelys concerts passed to Johann Christian Bach and Carl Friedrich Abel, whose collaboration held sway over the musical life of the capital until the launch of a rival series at the newly built Pantheon in Oxford Street in 1774.[10]

Though there was theoretically public access to concerts, exclusivity was maintained by the operation of a subscription system. Applicants for Teresa Cornelys's assemblies in the 1760s, for example, were required to apply to a vetting committee of aristocratic ladies. Cost provided another layer of social screening. Ticket prices at the Pantheon were set with the specific purpose of excluding the middle classes, while only the very wealthiest could afford the violinist and impresario Johann Peter Salomon's concerts featuring Haydn himself in 1791. Programming for the recitals was heavily weighted towards modern symphonic music, with Haydn symphonies being a particular favourite.[11] As the series predated the establishment of a body of acknowledged orchestral masterworks, there was a constant demand for new music – so much so that the subscription concerts stood accused of perpetuating an 'ephemeral novelty-culture'.[12]

One significant consequence of the flourishing of music in this period was an increasingly sharp divide between, on the one hand, professional orchestral concerts, with music of the highest quality, and on the other, amateur societies relegated to the 'practice or amusement' of their members.[13] Societies such as the Castle and the King's Arms, which had played such a large part in the musical life of the Sharp brothers in the 1750s and early 1760s, struggled to survive in this new polarised environment. The growing complexity of modern music played a part in this transition, as only the ablest and most dedicated of amateurs could come close to the virtuosity of the professional. From the late eighteenth century, concert culture became an almost exclusively passive experience.

This development was reflected in the Old Jewry concert, which from the early 1770s adopted a far more stringent approach to the quality of its performance. Whereas in the 1750s and 60s, amateur members of the family ensemble played alongside their professional equivalents, from the early 1770s the instrumentalists were always professionals. Gone were the days when Granville could entertain a rapt audience with a sonata on the double flute, or James perform a violoncello concerto on the serpent. Perhaps in the rarefied atmosphere of the Old Jewry mansion, it was no longer considered appropriate to sully the quality of the music with amateur contribution.

But the Sharps were not bound by fashion – as is apparent in their very individualist approach to programming. On six occasions in the Visiting Book, Catharine records the details of the music played at an

Old Jewry concert, including the names of soloists. On Sunday 16
January 1774, for example, the audience were treated to:

> Overture *Esther*. [Handel]
> Anthem Bishop. Blessed are all they &c
> Hear my prayer. Henley
> Worthy is ye Lamb. Handel
> Concert. Tibie [flutes]
> In thee O lord. Weldon / Verse by Waring & Soper
> Quarteto. Kammel / By Hackwood. Simson. Parkinson. G. Paxton.
> The Trumpet shall sound. Handel / By Webster – Vinicomb. Trumpet.
> Hallelujah. Handel[14]

Analysis of the six recorded programmes reveals what the musicologist Brian Crosby calls 'a certain monotony and preference for the
well-established item'. Handel's 'Hallelujah', for example, was
performed at all six concerts, his 'Worthy is the Lamb' on five occasions, and his overture to *Esther*, William Boyce's 'If we believe that
Jesus died' and John Soaper's 'Sanctus' on four.[15] The rather antiquated
flavour of the Sharp recital was noted by Elizabeth Harris, who
attended a concert at Old Jewry on 7 February 1779:

> Yesterday we din'd at Lady Shaftesbury, from thence to a concert
> at Mr Sharpes Old Jewry when I heard old anthems inumerable,
> such as I have heard old Biddlecomb, and old Pennycote sing in
> the Cathedrale at Salisbury forty year ago. Sir William Hoare
> said it would frighten Pacchierotti that he would think he was
> gott among a sett of barbarians. We were more humaniz'd in
> the second act then Pacchierotti and Ademberger* sung part of
> the Stabat Mater.[16]

In their rejection of the novelty culture of the symphonic concerts,
the Sharps showed that they were prepared to plough their own furrow

---

* Presumably the German tenor Valentin Adamberger, who is known to have sung at
the King's Theatre in London during the 1778–9 season.

in the musical world of eighteenth-century London – whatever the peppery Elizabeth Harris might say. In any event, the Sharps had the last laugh in the matter of their rather antique taste in music. Founded in 1776 with the express aim of promoting music more than twenty years old, the influential Concert of Ancient Music gave an aristocratic imprimatur to Sharp archaism. Controlled by a group of like-minded directors – nearly all of whom were peers – the Concert dedicated itself to the preservation of traditional musical values, exemplified by composers of the late baroque, and by Handel in particular. Exclusivity was maintained so successfully that the Concert became almost synonymous with nobility, and the participation of George III set the seal on its prestige.[17]

Despite the professionalisation of London concert life, there remained some opportunity for informal musical expression. Two of the twenty-eight concerts in the Visiting Book took place on a weekday, rather than a Sunday, and consisted of a secular programme of 'glee' singing. A form of part song, usually scored for three or more voices and performed without accompaniment, the glee was wildly popular in the late eighteenth century, when several 'Gentlemen's Glee Clubs' were established. The popularity of the form is evident in the numbers attending the two Sharp glee evenings. An astonishing 326 people crammed into the Old Jewry mansion for the first recorded concert on 5 May 1775, while 322 were present on 10 April 1783.[18] Though women accounted for the majority of the attendees on both occasions, only male guests were permitted to sing.[19] Details of the organisation of the concerts, such as whether the performers practised beforehand, or knew in advance what they would be required to sing, are frustratingly absent.

The glee recital on 10 April 1783 is distinct from the twenty-seven other performances recorded in the Visiting Book because of the survival of four printed programmes for the event.[20] Guests on that evening included the 9th Earl of Exeter, who employed Capability Brown to landscape the deer park at Burghley House, and the 10th Earl of Pembroke, owner of Wilton House which Elizabeth and the Prowses visited in August 1762. Of the various barons, baronets, knights and countesses who graced the occasion, the 2nd Baron Vernon and

Dorothea, Lady Eden, had the distinction of being painted by Gainsborough. Intellect was represented by the composer, musician and musicologist Charles Burney, and the jurist Dr Bever, while the Church was embodied in the form of the Bishop of Lincoln. There was musical talent in plenty, not least the famous soprano Sarah Harrop – whom Angelica Kauffman painted as the lyric muse Erato – and her husband, the conductor Joah Bates. Other notable guests included the abolitionist Sir William Dolben, and Sir Roger Newdigate, whose bequest supports the Newdigate Prize for poetry.

The splendour of the concert, and the apparently exceptional measure of printing programmes for the occasion, lends support to the theory that this was the last recital held at Old Jewry. Certainly there is no record of a concert after this date.[21] If the glee evening of 10 April 1783 was the family's musical swan song – it was certainly a magnificent one. Fusing the twin pleasures of friendship and performance, in the sumptuous ground-floor apartments of the Old Jewry mansion, it is a glorious finale to four decades of Sharp music-making.

29

Mortality

In the spring of 1783, James was fifty-two, and at the peak of his career. Since buying into the Southouse & Chapman partnership nearly twenty-five years earlier, he had transformed the ironmongery into an international concern specialising in technically sophisticated products. Innovative and with apparently boundless reserves of energy, James had earned a reputation in the City as a principled man of business. Over the course of his career, James's interests ranged from turnip cutters and dust carts to the economics of canal ownership and the mechanics of moving parts. Perhaps most remarkable is the facility with which he reconciled commercial aspiration with a devotion to the common good. The London canal schemes are the outstanding example of this: James's ardent support for the new waterways combined a clear-sighted appreciation of the economic benefits of the technology, with an understanding of its power to revolutionise the lives of ordinary men and women.

Of James's many entrepreneurial strengths, arguably the most significant was his skill in commercialising other people's ideas. In the 1760s this had taken the form of adaptation of agricultural machinery, such as Mr Ducket's ingenious winnowing machine. From the early 1770s, James's attention turned to the commercialisation of a vehicle known as the 'rolling cart' which was distinctive in having broad cylindrical wheels similar to a modern steamroller. The prototype was a 'waggon upon Rollers' designed by David Bourne, which was mothballed after a trial organised by the Society of Arts ended in failure.[1] James modified the design, rectifying a fault in the positioning of the shafts.[2]

The background to rolling carts was the appalling state of the country's roads.³ The beauty of the new technology, according to James's voluminous marketing material, was not only that it enabled travel on roads that were impassable to ordinary vehicles, but that it smoothed out existing ruts. The cylindrical wheel was versatile, and could be used with equal utility in agricultural carts, garden rollers and carriages.⁴ By late 1770, rolling carts in their various forms had become a significant venture for James.

Picture the manufactory in Tooley Street on a busy morning in October 1770. James is in his element, negotiating with a dustman for the sale of a job order of refuse carts, arranging a contract for the supply of timber from Northamptonshire, and inspecting the positioning of a pivot on the underside of a partially constructed garden roller. Every now and again an idea occurs to him, and pulling his memorandum book from his coat pocket, he scribbles a diagram or a few hastily computed figures. In the far corner of the yard, a trial of the latest prototype is under way, and James is pleased to see that the sixteen-inch rollers glide over the stone flags without damaging them. Meanwhile the foundry hums as each component is cast with perfect precision.⁵

In the early part of 1772, hopes for the success of the product were boosted when legislation was passed exempting carts 'upon Rollers of the Breadth of Sixteen Inches' from weight restrictions applicable to other vehicles. In order to obtain maximum leverage from what amounted to parliamentary approval for his product, James embarked on a public trial on Elizabeth's estates in Northamptonshire. The accompanying marketing campaign included an open invitation to 'The Nobility, Members of Parliament, and others who may think it worth their while', to view the rolling carriages at work, on the road from Stoney Stratford to Northampton.⁶

Another example of James's skill in commercialising existing designs is the 'American stove', which he manufactured from the late 1770s. In this case, the prototype was the invention of the American polymath Benjamin Franklin, who developed the stove in 1741. According to James, various difficulties connected with the original technology, including the expense of installation, discouraged potential purchasers. His modifications were designed to address these drawbacks, while also increasing the efficacy of the heating mechanism.[7]

The stove answered the inefficiencies of the open fireplace, which had monopolised domestic heating arrangements for centuries. Heat did not disappear up a wide chimney flue, as it did in a traditional hearth, but was instead retained within the internal cavities. As very little heat was lost, the American stove was far more fuel efficient than its old-fashioned counterpart. Here James could speak from personal experience: 'My common room, I know, is made twice as warm as it used to be with a Quarter the Wood I formerly consumed there.' Lauding this early form of green technology, James left others to compute 'how much Money will be saved to a Country by its spending Two-thirds less of Fuel; how much Labour saved in Cutting and Carriage of it; how much more Land may be cleared by Cultivation ... how much healthier thick-built Towns and Cities will be, now half suffocated with sulphury Smoke'.[8]

Benjamin Franklin was less enthusiastic about James's adaptation of his design. In his autobiography, Franklin noted that while he had declined to patent his invention: 'An Ironmonger in London ... after assuming a good deal of my Pamphlet, and working it up into his own, and making some small Changes in the Machine, which rather hurt its Operation, got a Patent for it there, and made as I was told a little Fortune by it.'[9]

Though Franklin exaggerates the 'little fortune', James was certainly prosperous. The optimism with which he had viewed his prospects on the eve of his marriage in February 1764 was not misplaced. An idea of James's means in his later years can be deduced from the fact that he owned three different types of carriage: a coach, a post-chaise and a phaeton. In addition to the expense, not to say extravagance, of running three carriages, James maintained two houses in the City. An inventory from the early 1790s of the New House and the dwelling apartments above the shop in Leadenhall Street suggests the comfort with which they were furnished. Individual items include 'an elegant cut glass epergne', 'Turkey and Wilton carpets', 'a set of Dining

Tables, Card and Pembroke', 'ten India japanned dressing boxes' and 'an elegant enamelled china table service containing ... sixty-two table plates'.[10]

James continued to juggle his numerous commercial ventures with an active political career. As a leading radical in the Common Council of the City of London, he campaigned on issues such as electoral reform and the reduction of executive power. James was profoundly influenced by his brother Granville's political thinking, and during the 1770s and early 1780s supported his opposition to the American war. The ironmonger spoke at a meeting of American merchants in January 1775, moved resolutions in the Common Council against the coercive measures imposed on the colonists after the Boston Tea Party, and in 1778 spoke in Council in support of a motion for conciliation with the Americans.[11]

Though 'ill-judged and interested opposition' had thwarted his ambitions for a canal from Monkey Island to Isleworth, and from Waltham Abbey to Moorfields, James played a role in the construction of the Oxford Canal, of which he was shareholder, and was also an energetic member of the Thames Navigation Committee. Established in the early 1770s, following the failure to obtain parliamentary approval for the London canals, the committee had jurisdiction over the Thames below Staines. As a Thames Navigation Commissioner, James took steps to relieve the difficulties of navigating the river. Measures included buying up individual tolls with a view to establishing a single charge, dredging the river to narrow and deepen the channel, and the building of an uninterrupted towpath.[12]

*

On 10 July 1783, Elizabeth wrote in her journal: 'On this day my Bro. James came ill to Wicken my sisr. and Catharine with him, and

---

* An epergne is an ornamental centrepiece for a dining table, often used for holding fruit or flowers.

stayd a month.'[13] Elizabeth does not identify her brother's illness, but Granville, in a diary entry dated 22 August 1783, notes: 'I went on to Wicken where I found my poor Brother James very ill of a Paralytic Disorder.'[14] If the Sharps had hoped that James would recuperate at Wicken, they were to be cruelly disappointed. By September it was apparent that there had been no improvement in his condition.[15] At this point, according to Elizabeth, the family decided to take James to Weymouth, in the hope that sea bathing might provide a cure.[16]

On 10 September 1783, a large Sharp party, consisting of James, his wife Catharine and daughter Kitty, William, his wife Catharine and daughter Mary, Mary's governess Miss Wrather, Elizabeth, Judith, Frances and Granville set out together for Weymouth.[17] They arrived on 26 September, and hired a house adjoining the hotel.[18] Once again hopes of a recovery were dashed, as 'the baithing did not seeme to agree'.[19] By 22 October, James had grown so much worse that the family determined to go home.[20] The misery of the homeward journey, as day after day they rattled over poor roads with the dying man propped between them, was for Elizabeth a painful echo of the journey she had made to Dover with her father-in-law seventeen years before. On the evening of 1 November 1783, nine days after leaving Weymouth, the family reached Maidenhead Bridge. 'When we got to Madenhead,' Elizabeth writes, 'we dispaired the getting him home.'[21]

By now James was in such a desperate condition that the brothers could barely lift him out of the carriage. On the following day, the family attempted another stage of the journey, but were held up when one of the carriage horses became unmanageable. As the horse ran amok in an attempt to free himself from his harness, the coach careered backwards and forwards across the road, throwing the family off their seats. Eventually the horse was brought under control, but a replacement had to be found, which caused a further agonising delay. As Granville records: 'we were in the most horrible dilemma that can be conceived my poor Brother being then a Dying Man'.[22]

The party finally reached Leadenhall Street in the evening of 5 November 1783. Granville describes how 'my poor Brother being in extremis – I lifted him out of the Chariot & carried him myself into his own House. We had great difficulty to get him carried up stairs.'[23] James died at '22 minutes past 5' on the following morning. He was fifty-two years old. In her diary entry for that day, Elizabeth records 'our very great greef, from so great a loss to his family, and us all. He was a most affect. Husband, Father and Bro. and had strict good principles and a most benevolent and upright mind, charitable and beloved by all that knew him.'[24]

The funeral was held at 'St Mary Axe Church at Evening Prayers' on 12 November 1783, with 'a very full congregation'.[25] James was buried in a vault 'near his son John'.[26]

The Sharp archive contains a transcription of two short obituaries of James, which appeared in London newspapers on the day after his death. The first begins:

Yesterday Morning at five o'clock died, at his House in Leadenhall Street, Mr James Sharp, universally respected, and esteemed equally for the strength of his understanding, as for the benevolence, charity and goodness of his Heart. To this Gentleman this kingdom is principally indebted for the Establishment of Inland Navigation, as well as for many useful inventions, and improvements in husbandry, Fire Engines, Stoves, and other branches of mechanics, calculated for the benefit of Mankind in general.

The second includes this passage: 'His extensive Dealings as a Merchant were ever marked with probity, unalloyed by the most distant appearance of avarice.'[27]

The vibrancy of James's character, and the energy with which for so many years he had thrown himself into his activities, makes his death peculiarly shocking. It is painful to imagine a man of such vitality lying paralysed on the seat of a post-chaise. To die in his prime – when there was still so much for him to do, see, invent and enthuse over – was a tragedy.

As for the Sharps – they never quite recovered from James's death. For nearly forty years, since the arrival of William and James in London in the 1740s, the brothers had been the bedrock of the family. They were the joint authors of the jolly doings that illuminated the sibling circle, and their mutual love and respect formed a pattern for the family as a whole. James's death left a void, and without him pleasures lost their sweetness. Granville's biographer records: 'the surviving brothers took no longer any delight in their boats; and the yacht was put up for auction'.[28]

30

Independence

In the story of the Sharp family, it is the brothers who play the leading roles. However unfair this might seem to a modern reader, it is almost inevitable in a period when women were expected to confine their interests and activities to the home. Without education or training, or professional or commercial opportunity, the sisters had little hope of emulating their brothers' achievements. This imbalance is reflected in the Sharp archive, which is weighted in favour of extraordinary public endeavours, for example Granville's campaign for the rights of slaves, and John's work at Bamburgh, rather than the seemingly unremarkable events of female domesticity. Confined to the interstices of their brothers' history, the talents and capabilities of Sharp women remain a subject of tantalising possibility. Perhaps, in another age, the brothers' success would have paled into insignificance beside the more glorious achievements of their sisters.

Yet there are exceptions to this tale of arrested development. Elizabeth, as we saw earlier, through marriage and then the early death of her husband, became the proprietor of a large estate. In her capacity as manager of Wicken, Elizabeth enjoyed a degree of influence and autonomy, far exceeding that which would have been available to her as a married woman. The survival of the estate ledgers, and her own journal, means that Elizabeth is a significant presence in the Sharp archive, in contrast to the almost spectral absence of her sisters.

Catharine, James's widow, was also able to play a role in the public sphere. Following her husband's death in November 1783,

Catharine ran the ironmongery business, with Granville's assistance, until February 1792.[1] Though Granville's biographer Prince Hoare maintains that Granville 'undertook the entire management' of the business, Granville himself refers to it as 'Sister James's Trade', while also acknowledging his own role in assisting her.[2] Granville and Catharine apparently ran the manufactory together, dividing responsibility, and contributing their own particular skills and experience.

It was not out of the ordinary for a widow to carry on her husband's business. Indeed, the wife of a shopkeeper or tradesman was considered to be under a positive duty to learn her husband's trade, not only so she could help him in the day-to-day running of the business, but to enable her to take over in the event of his illness or death.[3] In her *Advice to the Women and Maidens of London*, an anonymous seventeenth-century female manual writer implores her readers to lay aside their needlework and instead 'apply themselves to the right understanding and practice of the method of keeping books of accompts, whereby either single or married, they may know their estates, carry on their trades, and avoid the danger of a helpless and forlorn condition, incident to widows'.[4] The particular responsibilities of the tradesman's wife included managing the shop, buying raw materials, and supervising apprentices and employees, and Catharine may have had similar duties.[5]

In the days preceding James's death, Granville examined the 'J Sharp, London' accounts and concluded that that there was likely to be 'a very handsome balance'.[6] But rather than selling or winding up the business, as might have been expected, Catharine chose to run it herself. Evidence of her involvement in the ironmongery prior to 1783 throws light on this decision. Time and again, when offered the chance of travelling with James on matters connected with the trade, or staying in London or Wicken with her children, she chose the former. In a journal entry dated 7 July 1770, for example, Elizabeth notes that whereas 'Sissr. F, and little Catharine [i.e. Kitty] went down with me to Wicken', James and his wife 'went into Lankshire'.[7] In January 1774, Catharine accompanied her husband on a journey to Bath and Bristol 'where the Rolling Carriages had been'.[8]

Catharine may also have acted out of loyalty to her husband. The manufactory at Tooley Street represented a large part of James's life work, and was the backdrop to many of his most notable endeavours. Rather than putting a peremptory stop to the activities of the iron-mongery, it was open to Catharine to perpetuate his achievement. Perhaps, as she mourned the loss of her husband, Catharine drew solace from her work, and felt a nearness to James that would have been extinguished if she had sold up and moved away.

Catharine left no account of her management of the company, but I think of her among the pans and kettles in the ironmongery in Leadenhall Street. Now it is her, and not James, who is up at first light, stock-checking, taking orders and superintending her assistants. She is just overseeing the sale of a ship's windlass when a messenger boy arrives hotfoot from Tooley Street. This time it is Catharine, rather than her husband, who hurries along Lyme Street, and down Botolph Lane, and hails a wherry at Billingsgate stairs. The gentleman farmer from Lincolnshire, who is waiting a little impatiently to be shown the latest range of rolling carts, is at first surprised to be dealing with a woman. Two hours later, after an exhaustive review of the benefits of the new technology, the farmer is left in no doubt as to the female proprietor's mastery of her affairs.

After dinner with Kitty in Leadenhall Street, Catharine retires to the accompting house for a drowsy perusal of her accounts. She is just putting the finishing touches to a marketing booklet for a weighing engine when Granville arrives with a bundle of papers. Brother and sister-in-law are still ruminating on the relative advantages of Swedish and American pig iron when Granville is called away to a madrigal practice in Poultry.[9] Alone in the quiet evening light, memories of James steal upon Catharine, and it is only with effort that she returns to her work. It is past nine o'clock when she finally blows out the candle, and walks through the night to the New House, where Kitty is waiting for her.

Frances and Judith did not have the opportunities of Elizabeth and Catharine, yet each in some degree lived as an independent woman. Both lodged in the houses of one or other of their married brothers, but this was not inevitably detrimental to their freedom. It was common in this period for an unmarried woman to live with her brother's family, providing services such as childcare, nursing or house-hold management, in return for board and lodging. The experience of spinsters living in these circumstances differed markedly according to their means. Those with a private income sufficient to cover personal expenditure, and to contribute to the costs of the household, might enjoy a relatively autonomous existence. Those without private money, however, suffered the indignity of an absolute dependence on their kin, and were vulnerable to exploitation.[10]

Frances and Judith had both inherited £700 from their father, and this was later supplemented by other legacies. In 1792, Elizabeth records that 'Sisr Jud had at this time £1,800 and Sisr F £1,200 cash of their own'.[11] The income from the original £700, though it was not enough to sustain an absolute independence, was at least sufficient to cover the sisters' personal expenditure. While it is unlikely that Frances or Judith contributed to the costs of their board or lodging, they did perform reciprocal duties traditionally associated with a spinster. Frances acted as a carer for Jack, and then Kitty, and stayed with the children at Wicken Park. Judith too assumed a quasi-parental role, this time in relation to John's daughter Anne Jemima. The arrangement was beneficial to both parties, as the parent was relieved of the more onerous duties of childcare, and the aunt reaped some of the benefits of parenting.

In later years, Frances spent most of her time at Wicken Park, where she acted as a companion to Elizabeth. Although she is largely absent from the Sharp archive, there is some suggestion of a spirit beyond the purely domestic. On 2 January 1763, Elizabeth noted in her journal: 'Sisr F Sharp returned from the North', describing how she 'road down on a double horse, had one horse to carry her Port Mantue and 2 boys Wm. Cochayne and Richd. Walter to attend her'. Elizabeth explains that her sister took the journey 'for her health and visited her friends in the way'. So dense was the network of Frances's acquaintance that during the six weeks of her journey from Northumberland to London, she 'lay but one night at an Inn'.[12]

The Sharp papers also offer a few tantalising glimpses of Judith's character and talents. Intellectual interests are suggested by a letter dated 15 October 1757, which addresses Judith, then aged twenty-three, on subjects including 'Chinese writing', 'the copper coin' and 'asbestos or arcadian stone'. Her correspondent includes a fragment of a Chinese newspaper, as an example of the script.[13] That Judith had artistic ability is evidenced by the survival of two exquisite ink and watercolour drawings, the first titled *Chimney Piece in the Room at Hartburn built by Dr J. Sharp*, and the second *A Door of the Ionic Order for a Room at Hartburn built by Dr John Sharp*.[14] An inventory of William's house from the early 1800s lists several of her works, including *Mrs Jud. Sharp by herself chalks* and *Head in Red chalk old man 2 by Mrs J Sharp*.[15] Judith's creativity is further attested to by the crimson standard shown in Zoffany's painting of the family, which is referenced as 'The Work of Mrs Judith Sharp, in Patchwork and Embroidery'.[16]

Judith's individuality is evident in her portrayal in the Zoffany painting. In contrast to the more muted tones and attitudes of her sisters and sisters-in-law, Judith's attire is striking and almost flamboyant. The strength of her character is apparent in a correspondence with John dating from May 1770, on the subject of the right to inhabit Bamburgh Castle. It is the eve of their brother Thomas's marriage, and Judith calls on John to give up his residence in the castle so that the newlyweds can have a home of their own.[17] Though she calls in aid the 'joint opinion of my Brothers & Sisters in London', it is apparent that Judith herself is the author, and chief instigator, of the scheme to remove John from Bamburgh.

Perhaps the most revealing passage of the correspondence is contained within the final paragraph of John's letter dated 14 May 1770: 'I was in hopes Dear Jud, that the Building at Hartburn, undertaken at your instance, would have reconciled you to the Castle for that was my chief motive for undertaking it at present.' If John built the vicarage extension at the bidding of his sister Judith, then the ink and watercolour architectural drawings in the Sharp archive presumably represent part of her design for the project. The archdeacon's hope that the works at Hartburn might have 'reconciled' Judith to Bamburgh provides a further insight. If Judith disliked her annual residence in the castle, this might explain why she was so anxious for John to renounce it in favour of his brother Thomas.

A notable feature of Judith's adult life, and one which illuminates her character, is her decision to remain single.[18] In 1757, at the age of twenty-three, Judith turned down a marriage proposal from John Prowse, the eldest son of the Prowse family.[19] It took some gumption to refuse an offer which was not only advantageous to herself, but enjoyed the approval of both families. John's subsequent early death, and Elizabeth's marriage to his younger brother George, put Elizabeth in a position of wealth and status exactly equivalent to that which her sister had forfeited. If Judith regretted her decision, she showed little inclination to atone for her mistake. In March 1772, she turned down a second offer of marriage, this time from a clergyman called Dr Kent.[20]

Judith's decision to remain single is significant, not only because it deprived her of benefits traditionally associated with marriage, such as a home, security and children, but because it amounted to a rejection of conventional ideas of female aspiration. The absence of alternative opportunities for women meant that marriage was their only route to what has been called 'adult privilege'.[21] In a world where a chasm of status divided an unmarried woman from her more fortunate married counterpart, spinsterhood was viewed as 'a miserable predicament', rather than 'a heroic freedom'.[22] It is no coincidence that the quest for a suitable marriage partner was the dominant theme of novels in this period.

In contrast to most unmarried women, who were single by default, Judith voluntarily deprived herself of the status of a married woman. Perhaps, as she contemplated lifelong union, Judith concluded that the risks of marriage outweighed the potential benefits. Among the factors that might have influenced her was the consideration that there was almost no escape route from an unhappy marriage in this period. Divorce was so rare as to be irrelevant, while non-legal separation exposed women to social stigma and the risk of losing children and property to a vindictive husband.[23]

The formal quality of eighteenth-century courtship meant that women often knew little of their prospective husband's character before a marriage, and would learn the truth only when it was too late. If John Prowse turned out to be cruel, or manipulative, or Dr

Kent an inveterate drunk, then there was nothing that Judith could do about it – she was stuck with him. In these circumstances, autonomy might be best served in the comfortable household of a compliant brother, rather than in the untested waters of matrimony.

Elizabeth's achievements at Wicken, and the glimpses of Judith's and Frances's character that can be gleaned from the Sharp archive, suggest that they were women of courage, talent and conviction. Deprived of the educational and professional openings provided to their brothers, they nonetheless seized the opportunities that were given to them to play a traditionally male role. With typical Sharp finesse, the sisters pushed conventional notions of female autonomy to the limits, while staying within the bounds of genteel respectability.

31

Visionary

After his resignation from the Board of Ordnance in April 1777, Granville never again returned to paid employment. Instead, he devoted the remaining thirty-six years of his life to individual acts of charity, and participation in movements for social and political reform. The yellowing pages of his memorandum book, and the bundles of his impassioned correspondence, reveal the extraordinary range of Granville's causes and the time and energy that he invested in them.[1]

The inaugural meeting of the Society for the Abolition of the Slave Trade, which was to be the driving force in the campaign against slavery, took place in James Phillip's printing shop in George Yard, in the City of London, on the afternoon of 22 May 1787. Of the twelve men present, nine were Quakers, and three, including Granville and Thomas Clarkson, were Anglicans. Granville, in acknowledgement of his role as 'father of the cause in England', was asked to chair the new society.[2] But he refused, and in a letter to his brother John dated 3 November 1787, explained that though it had been thought proper to appoint him to the chairmanship, he had 'never yet been in Chair, nor attended the Meetings; but have only signed the Letters that have been sent to me'.

Though Granville may be downplaying his role, there is an obvious disjunction between the sentiments expressed in this letter, and his proven commitment to the anti-slavery cause. Clarkson took a charitable view of Granville's refusal of the chair, arguing that it arose from a feeling 'either that he had done nothing extraordinary to merit such a distinction' or because he was 'fearful lest the acceptance of it should bring a stain upon the motive, on which alone he undertook it'.[3] While humility may have contributed to his decision, Granville had other reasons for disassociating himself from the work of the committee.

The question soon arose as to the remit of the society, and in particular whether the campaign should be for the abolition of slavery, or for the more realistic target of the abolition of the slave trade. Nine of the ten committee members present voted in favour of the less ambitious, but more realistic objective, while Granville was alone in supporting the broader goal.[4] As the opinions of the other members coalesced, Granville stood up, and 'with a loud voice, a powerful emphasis, and both hands lifted up towards Heaven', exhorted his colleagues to reconsider their decision. He did not hesitate, he said, 'to pronounce all present guilty before God, for shutting those, who were then slaves all the world over, out of the pale of their approaching labours'.[5]

Though Granville accepted the committee's decision, and later endorsed the motions for the abolition of the slave trade introduced into the House of Commons by William Wilberforce, his relationship with the society remained strained. He felt it to be his duty 'not to give the sanction of his entire approbation to an undertaking which fell short of his own conception, and which he considered inferior to the real demands of humanity'.[6] Rather than focusing his energies on the work of the committee, Granville ploughed his own furrow, writing anti-slavery literature, such as the March 1797 tract *Serious Reflections on the Slave Trade and Slavery* (published in 1805), and lobbying senior members of the Church of England. In March 1779, for example, Granville informed his brother John: 'I have called upon all the Bishops that are in Town, & are not invalids; & have had the honour of being admitted to 17 out of the whole number, & I have the pleasure to find that they all seem inclined, to oppose the Slave Trade, but some are very zealous against it.'[7]

Granville's conduct as a committee member of the Society for the Abolition of the Slave Trade expresses the complexity of his relationship with the movement. Though abolitionists lauded him as a founding father, subsequent commentators have faulted Granville for his failure to capitalise on the Somerset case. He is accused of neglecting to publicise the horrors of slavery, of not being sufficiently single-minded in his campaigns, of choosing the wrong targets, and of failing to exploit the 'years of anxiety, division and introspection' during and immediately after the American war.[8]

While this critique seems unduly harsh, Granville's fractious relationship with the Society underlines his failings as a campaigner. Granville acted in all things according to the strictures of the Bible, which he venerated as a guide to everyday life as well as an unambiguous source of law and prophecy.[9] Religious and moral absolutism, and what he called 'the consciousness of unquestionable Evidence on my side', deafened Granville to contrary opinion.[10] He could be intolerant and aloof, as well as 'humane, compassionate and principled'.[11] Compromise, such as was required of him on the question of the remit of the society, was anathema to Granville. Rigid in doctrine, and with 'the most inflexible of human wills', he was often incapable of the pragmatism necessary for a successful political movement.[12]

Granville's detachment from the Society for the Abolition of the Slave Trade was exacerbated by his dislike of the religion professed by the majority of its members. Convinced of the validity of biblical precept, and of the status of the Church of England as the only true repository of Christian faith, Granville was actively intolerant of dissent.[13] He was implacably opposed to Catholicism, and despite his friendship with Anthony Benezet, did not hold back from disparaging the opinions and practices of Quakers.[14] In a letter to John dated 19 July 1787, Granville implies that he has agreed to join the Society 'for the honour of the Church of England', and in spite of his reluctance to co-operate with those he considers guilty of religious aberration.[15]

Despite these failings, Granville's contribution to the history of British abolition is unassailable. 'It is upon the pillars built by Mr Sharp, and him only, that the superstructure was raised,' Clarkson wrote, notwithstanding the recalcitrance of his former colleague.[16] What Prince Hoare described as the 'undeviating track of extreme rectitude' was as much the secret of Granville's success as it was the cause of his relative failure.[17]

★

In the years following Somerset, Granville worked in tandem with Olaudah Equiano, and organisations such as the Sons of Africa – a small abolitionist group composed of free Africans – to support the black community in London. The arrival in the early 1780s of a group of former African American slaves, freed for their part in assisting the British war effort, swelled the ranks of the unemployed. In addition to supporting individual members of the community, Granville contributed to the work of the Committee for the Relief of the Black Poor, which was founded in the harsh winter of 1785–6 to provide food, clothes, housing and medical assistance to those in need.

Though the work of the charity was invaluable, it provided only short-term assistance to the unemployed. In the early 1780s, prior to the establishment of the committee, the desire for a permanent solution to the difficulties facing the black community had evolved into an idea for a settlement for former slaves on the West African coast. In 1783, the botanist Henry Smeathman published a plan for a colony on the Sierra Leone estuary, which he had visited while collecting specimens for the botanic gardens at Kew. Granville, who had independently devised a scheme for the settlement of freed slaves in Africa, greeted Smeathman's proposals with enthusiasm. Together they set up a committee to promote the colony, whose members included Henry Thornton, a member of the evangelical 'Clapham set', and secured government support.[18]

The appeal of the Sierra Leonean project went beyond the immediate philanthropic objective of giving land and work to impoverished black Londoners. Advocates of the scheme expatiated on the symbolic value of returning former slaves to their ancestral homeland, where they could build a free and thriving society. While these arguments weighed heavily with Granville, it was the opportunity to put into practice his ideas for a perfect society that had a particular resonance for him. Published in 1786, Granville's *A Short Sketch of Temporary Regulations (Until Better Shall be Proposed) for the Intended Settlement on the Grain Coast of Africa near Sierra Leone* sets out his blueprint for a visionary utopia.[19]

In forming his plans for the perfect society, Granville drew inspiration from the ancient system of frankpledge. Though he traced its origins to Old Testament Israel, and England under King Alfred,

Granville's scheme was largely his own invention.[20] The community was to be entirely self-governing, with an administration composed of elected headmen representing groups of ten families, called tithings, and larger communities of a hundred families, called hundreds. Labour replaced cash as the unit of exchange, with the value of a commodity determined by the amount of labour needed to produce it.

In April 1787, 411 settlers arrived on the West African coast and purchased land for a settlement on the south bank of the Sierra Leone estuary. The settlers started building a village, which they called Granville Town, but the advent of the rainy season soon put a stop to their work. Already weakened by the voyage across the Atlantic, many fell victim to disease and an unyielding climate. By September 1787, eighty-six of the original party were dead, and another fifteen had left the settlement. Further depreciation followed, so that by the beginning of 1788, only 130 of the original emigrants remained.[21]

The survivors attempted to implement Granville's scheme of self-government, dividing the community into tithings, and electing leaders to represent them. Progress stalled in December 1789, when the local Temne chief burned Granville Town to the ground.[22] Undaunted, forty-eight of the original settlers built a second Granville Town, two miles to the east of the earlier settlement. In 1793, 1,200 former American slaves, who had lived in Nova Scotia since fighting for the British in the Revolutionary War, arrived in Sierra Leone. This new contingent built a settlement on the site of the first Granville Town, which they called Freetown, and the original settlers joined them there.

Disputes between new and old emigrants led to the imposition of a traditional form of colonial government, consisting of a governor and a two-member council.[23] In 1794, the French attacked Freetown, flattening the newly built houses, desecrating the church and slaughtering livestock. Though the town was rebuilt, a rebellion by Nova Scotia settlers in 1800, and a series of assaults on Freetown by exiled rebels in collaboration with a local Temne chief in 1801 and 1802, left the settlement on the verge of collapse. The British government stepped in, and in 1808 Sierra Leone became a Crown Colony.[24]

The assumption of Crown control marked the end of the road for campaigners like Granville who had dreamed of an autonomous community of freed slaves. The difficulties faced by the settlers stemmed from the discrepancy between the reveries of London-based philanthropists and the reality of life on the Sierra Leone peninsula. In choosing a location for the scheme, insufficient thought had been given to factors such as climate, soil, the prevalence of disease and the attitudes of neighbouring tribes.[25] Ill-conceived, and poorly planned, it is no wonder that the emigrants fell victim to a catalogue of disasters.[26]

Although Granville was not alone in supporting the Sierra Leonean venture, its deficiencies illustrate his tendency to sacrifice practicality to the pursuit of a noble ideal. Even as the project crumbled, Granville clung to his utopian vision, sending a shipload of watering cans to the peninsula with a note that they were to be used to water the settlers' gardens 'where plants might grow as symbols of the increased level of the town's civilisation'.[27] That Sierra Leone survived, and ultimately flourished, was due to the exceptional resilience, and versatility, of its settlers who overcame repeated setbacks to establish a 'vital community of freed slaves upon which the subsequent history of the settlement would be built'.[28]

Granville's numerous causes included parliamentary reform, female penitentiaries, the 'Caribees of St Vincent', and the Bridewell and Bethlem Hospitals. Skills honed in his early crusades were utilised in campaigns to abolish the practice of pressing seamen into service during wartime, the restoration of the Episcopalian Church in the former American colonies, and the extension of London parish relief to all applicants regardless of their place of origin. Granville's religious preoccupations found a practical outlet in membership of the Society for the Propagation of the Gospel, and he was also a founding member and the first chair of the British and Foreign Bible Society, and the first chair of the Protestant Union, which was established in 1813 with the specific remit of opposing Catholic emancipation.

The array of Granville's interests is also apparent in his later published writings. Some themes are familiar, for example *Extract of a Letter from Granville Sharp to a Gentleman in Maryland, respecting the extreme Wickedness of tolerating the Slave Trade* reflects a long-standing preoccupation with the evils of slavery, while works of biblical construction hark back to his early work on the corruptions of the Hebrew texts of Ezra and Nehemiah.[29] Doctrinal studies include the frankly titled *Remarks on an important Passage, Matt. XXI. 18, which has long been perverted by the Church of Rome in Support of her vain Pretensions to supreme Dominion over all other Episcopal Churches* of 1812, while a dissertation on free will published in 1801 concludes with the unnerving 'Postscript on Eternal Punishments'.[30] Less controversial themes include teaching English as a foreign language, duelling, encroachments on the River Thames, and the state of the London Workhouse.[31]

The Sharps' pride in Granville's achievements is expressed in Elizabeth's careful recording of his publications in her journal, while reverence for their younger brother's vocation disposed the siblings to tolerate his various eccentricities. For example, no objection was made to Granville's habit of buttonholing the family's grand acquaintances. The campaigner always viewed a Sharp party as an opportunity to canvass support for his latest scheme, and he lobbied shamelessly. The candour of Granville's conversation is noted by his friend and biographer Prince Hoare, who recalls that the 'expression of his sentiments was wholly free from disguise'.[32]

Although Hoare avoids any direct censure of his subject, even his gentle critique discloses the pitfalls of engaging in discussion with Granville. The campaigner invariably adopted a didactic tone, which tended to impede the natural flow of conversation. Moreover, he made no concession to the circumstances of the encounter, and was as likely to lecture his victim at a water party on the *Apollo* as in Westminster Hall. Ground down by the campaigner's diffuse and seemingly interminable argument, and copious biblical allusion, the guest at a Sunday-night Old Jewry concert might have sought any opportunity to escape to the opposite side of the room. Meanwhile anyone foolhardy enough to express a contrary opinion received short shrift.[33]

In the foreword to his account of Granville's life, Hoare refers to the wish expressed in various obituaries, that a future biographer 'should draw a veil over some peculiarities of Mr Sharp's character'. Though Hoare does not specify the nature of these peculiarities, they

almost certainly included Granville's increasingly fervent millenari-
anism. Of the various prophecies that occupied his mind, the most
potent was a deduction from certain passages in the books of Daniel
and Revelation, in which he identified a 'scarlet-coloured beast' as the
Church of Rome. Granville published his conclusions in an 1805 tract
called *An Enquiry whether the Description of Babylon contained in the
eighteenth Chapter of Revelations, agrees perfectly with Rome as a City, etc;
with Prefaces, and an Appendix, addressed to the Roman Catholics.*[34]

Looking back over Granville's life, two aspects of his character
appear to have particular significance. He was clear-sighted when
others groped about in a fog of apathy and self-interest, and he was
fearless in the face of power. While most eighteenth-century Londoners
might have considered slavery to be unsavoury, few felt the injustice
keenly enough, or were sufficiently resolute, to do anything about it.
Granville was one of those rare individuals who is able to break free
from the inertia of the status quo, and effect great change. Incredulous
of the inactivity, and moral blindness, of others, he devoted his life
to righting what he saw as social and political wrongs. His campaign
for the freedom of slaves on British soil is the shining example of this.
Undaunted by the scale of the undertaking, and by the might of the
forces ranged against him, Granville achieved his victory in the
Somerset case through sheer force of will. His later campaigns tended
to be less successful, in part because of his attachment to utopian
ideals. Nevertheless, the Somerset case remains a testament to the
power of the individual campaigner, and the capacity of a single man
or woman to alter the course of history.

32

Fulham

In 1780, William purchased the lease of Stourton House in Fulham, which was then a country village. Just as in his bachelor days he had journeyed westwards in the *Apollo* to escape the pungent smells and incessant noise of the congested reaches of the river, so in retirement William sought a retreat in the sweet air and tranquillity of Fulham. Standing on the banks of the Thames, and surrounded by orchards and market gardens, the village comprised several streets of fine brick houses.[1]

To own a property on the river beyond the western fringes of the capital had long been a token of prosperity and success. In 1724, Daniel Defoe spoke of this stretch of the Thames as being 'so full of beautiful buildings, charming gardens and rich habitations of gentlemen of quality that nothing in the world can imitate it', and the presence of the king and queen at Kew from the mid 1760s provided further embellishment.[2] As David Garrick delighted in the lawns sweeping down to the river at his villa at Hampton, and Zoffany gloried in his riverside house at Strand-on-the-Green, so William could take an equal pride in the broad proportions of his estate in Fulham.

An eighteenth-century advertisement for Stourton House described it as 'A compleat modern Brick House consisting of four Rooms on a Floor'.[3] Through the tall windows that lined the south-facing elevation of the dining room, there was an uninterrupted view of the river, and on hot days the family sat in the long shady portico of the front facade. The pleasures of the garden included a long avenue of elms, and an orchard 'planted and stocked with the best of fruits'.[4] On the

banks of the Thames, by the steps that led down from the garden
into the river, William built a beautiful cottage for his daughter Mary.[5]
Connected to the main house by an underground tunnel, the cottage
is shown in Zoffany's painting of the family, adjacent to All Saints.

In the years following William's purchase of Stourton House, it
was used by the family as a holiday home rather than as a permanent
residence. The commute from Fulham was too long to permit William
convenient access to his patients, so the family continued to live in
Old Jewry. This arrangement came to an end in the autumn of 1786,
when according to Elizabeth: 'Bro. W. very ill of his eye and spasms.'[6]
Though he recovered, William lost the sight of one eye, and most of
the vision in the other, with the result that he gave up his business
and the Old Jewry mansion.[7] William's eye condition was thought at
the time to be linked to the extreme anxiety he had felt during the
performance of difficult operations.[8]

Though blindness and chronic ill health deprived William of much
of the advantage of his retirement, he bore his misfortunes with
cheerfulness.[9] In a letter to his sister Judith dated 18 February 1799,
William describes how, during the long winter evenings, he has amused
his hands by making netting for his fruit trees: 'Mrs Cottin tempted
me to make another trial of it, for I had attempted it before, but gave
it up upon account of the difficulty of seeing the [thread]; but by
perseverance now I found it possible to nott by feeling, with very little
sight, much less than I supposed must be necessary.'[10]

I picture the family in the drawing room of Stourton House, on a
warm September evening in 1799. In one corner, William sits with his
netting, painstakingly feeling for the delicate threads, while Catharine's
head is bent over her embroidery. Their daughter Mary, now a young
woman of twenty-one, is practising her harp in the colonnade, and
the cascading notes drift through the open windows. The rattle of
cups on the housemaid's tray disturbs Mary from her musical reverie,
and she joins her parents in the drawing room for a discussion of their
forthcoming social engagements. As Catharine pours the tea, there is
much talk of the Fulham Association's military ball, which is to be
held at a neighbour's house on the following Tuesday. William relishes
the prospect of a visit to the Italian Opera – they are showing Thomas

Arne's *Artaxerxes* – while Mary looks forward to hosting her own dance later in the season. As the light fades over the river, Mary reads aloud the opening verses of Wordsworth's 'Tintern Abbey'.[11]

Aside from netting, William's favourite hobby was the manufacture of homemade wine. The taste for 'Shrubb' and 'Cup', that had inspired his provisioning of the bachelor tea parties of the 1750s, persisted in later life in experimental productions of 'Orange Wine Mr Allen's Method', 'Lemon Water', and 'Small Beer from Raisin Wine'. Correspondents such as 'Cooper Willyams' and 'Mr Randal Apothecary of Dean Street, Soho' sent William recipes for currant wine, and his papers include numerous records of oenological ventures such as 'An Account of wine made of Malaga Raisins – to make two Hogsheads March 1799'. William shared his enthusiasm with his sister Judith, on one occasion reporting to her: 'I have the chagrin to tell you that all the good wine you made me two years ago is drank up, except a very few bottles kept in order to know hereafter, how it keeps'.[12]

Mary was her parents' only child, and her preciousness was felt the more keenly because she had been so long sought for. Elizabeth, in her account of Catharine's delivery of Mary on 19 April 1778, noted that it was 'the only time of her success, after 18 or 20 times, she had been with child, that this great blessing was felt most thankfully by us all'.[13] The adored child of wealthy parents, Mary grew up in a milieu very different from that which had characterised her father's childhood. In place of the boisterous good-humour of the rectory at Rothbury, Mary was nurtured in an atmosphere of culture and refinement, in the manner of a rare and delicate plant.

Whereas Frances, Judith and Elizabeth had to make do with whatever education their mother, exhausted from numerous pregnancies and childbirth, could give them, Mary had the benefit of the undivided attention of a governess. As we have seen, a Miss Wrather accompanied Mary, then a girl of thirteen, and nine other Sharps to Weymouth in September 1783, in the hopes that sea bathing would assist in James's recovery. In later years, Miss Ansted assumed the role of governess, and in accordance with contemporary ideas of genteel behaviour, Mary remained friends with her after she had left the family's service.[14] On 20 June 1798, for example, Mary records the receipt of 'a letter from Ansted who is at South End', while six months later on 27 January 1799, she notes that 'My Mother, Ansted and I walked to Lady Hammond's and Lady Lonsdale.'[15]

Miss Wrather and Miss Ansted between them nurtured in Mary the habit of self-improvement. On 14 July 1798, Mary recorded in her diary: 'Began Spencer's *Fairy Queen*', and in the evening of the same day, 'began the Marques de Boulle's memoirs concerning the Revolution.' Having raced through Spencer's voluminous work, she noted approvingly on 7 August 1798: 'Finished *The Fairy Queen* with which I have been even more entertained than at the first perusal.' As well as books, Mary was also an art lover. On a tour of the West Country in 1798, she eulogised Salisbury Cathedral as 'the most perfect piece of Gothic architecture I have ever seen', and was bowled over at 'Sir Richard Harris's place' by 'a shockingly fine ... Rembrandt of Elisha raising the Widow's Son'.[16]

Mary was also sensitive to the delights of the picturesque landscape. On 6 September 1798, she noted in her diary, 'We had a delightful journey to Sidmouth over the most romantic mountains imaginable, with fine views opening before us at every step, sometimes of the sea, sometimes of rich vales interspersed with charming villages and adorned with cornfields and meadows extending to the very tops of the hills.'[17]

Rather than being simply a passive connoisseur of beauty, Mary also painted, wrote poetry, and played several instruments. Assistance was provided by a Mrs Gaitshore, who taught her painting, and an Italian singing master called Corri. Mary's literary ambition is reflected in an unpublished book of poetry, with titles such as 'The Pleasures of Pity', 'Ode to Anxiety', and the politically conscious 'Ode on the Abolition of the Slave Trade'.[18] A surviving extract from Mary's diary, for the period 1798–90, bears no resemblance to her aunt's journal. In place of Elizabeth's plodding, barely literate, but always ingenuous catalogue of family activities, Mary harps on 'floating clouds that served to chequer the most beautiful scenes imaginable'.[19] The Romantic sensibility of the *Lyrical Ballads* by William Wordsworth and Samuel Taylor Coleridge, published in 1798, had clearly made an impression on the young Mary.

On 20 May 1800 Mary married the eminently eligible Thomas Lloyd Baker of Stouts Hill, a Gothic revival house near Uley in Gloucestershire, with whom she had several children. In spite of the disjunction between Mary's polished refinement and the artless sincerity more generally characteristic of the Sharps, she was loyal to her relations. Her devotion to Wicken is expressed in a twenty-two-page eponymous poem, which begins:

> The scenes where first my infant bosom glowed
> With young delight, where wakened every sense
> To Nature's beauties and life's truest joys,
> My mind's (though not my body's) natal place,
> Fain would I sing. Assist the fond design,
> Fairest of Muses, sage Mnemosyne
> O bring thy golden tablets . . .[20]

Though James's death forestalled many of the joint activities that had illuminated the Sharps' lives since their childhood in Rothbury and Durham, it did not loosen the ties between the siblings. There were no more water parties, and nothing resembling the adventure of the canal voyage that had enlivened family life before 1783, but the Sharps remained close. Wicken Park was still a gathering place, and it was here in the summer months that William, Catharine and Mary, James's widow Catharine and their daughter Kitty, Granville and some-times Judith and Anne Jemima came to stay. In the winter months, Elizabeth stayed in London, at first alternately with James's widow in Leadenhall Street, and William in Old Jewry, and later always in Fulham. The fostering of relations between the London and the northern Sharps is especially apparent in these years. Judith and Anne Jemima were frequent visitors in Fulham, as well as Wicken Park, and the London siblings reciprocated with visits to the north.

A particularly memorable expedition took place in the summer of 1785, when the London Sharps visited Northumberland and Scotland. The Sharps did not travel light, at least according to Granville, who describes a convoy of three carriages, each with their own 'out rider', nine servants, twelve horses, and 'a large Newfoundland Dog'.[21] The first stop on the itinerary was 'Mr Beachers' where, according to Kitty, 'a Party of 24 very old friends & their children sat down to supper'.[22] After the relatively humdrum quality of Mr Beacher's hospitality, Granville proceeds to an excited recitation of the family's more aristocratic hosts. Preoccupations of this sort seem to have dulled Granville to the delights of his surroundings, for he refers to Berwick, Edinburgh, Glasgow and Carlisle only in passing.[23] The party stayed at Durham, Hartburn vicarage and Bamburgh Castle, and John, Mary and Anne Jemima joined the rest of the family for the journey into Scotland.

The expedition seems to have been undertaken partly as a memorial to James. Kitty, for example, gives an account of a special visit to Alnwick Castle:

Members of the Sharp Family who were conducted by the Duke of Northumberland and Lord Algernon Percy in 1785 to the Top of Breseley Tower* to see the Beacon made at the Manufactory of James Sharp (my father) and put up in 1781

Dr Sharp Wife & Daughter	3
William Wife & Daughter	3
Widow & Daughter of James	2
Mrs Prowse	1
Mrs Judith & Mrs Frances	2
Granville	1
	12[24]

Even on a fine August morning, it is windy at the top of Brizlee Hill. The women wear shawls over their thin muslin dresses, and the wind tugs at their bonnets. Standing in groups of three or four, the

---

* Presumably Brizlee Tower, which is situated on Brizlee Hill, overlooking the parkland of Alnwick Castle. It was built for the 1st Duke of Northumberland in 1781, probably to the design of either Robert or John Adam. What Kitty describes as the 'Beacon' is a cast-iron fire basket positioned at the top of the tower, surrounded by a viewing platform. Bamburgh Castle can be seen from the top of the tower.

party surveys the ornate six-storey tower, and converse admiringly on
the subject of its proportions, and the beauty of the view from the
projecting balcony. Though they are accustomed to mixing with
members of the upper classes, the Sharps are a little subdued in the
presence of a host of such exalted status. Only John, who knows the
duke personally, is completely at his ease, and the two men stand a
little apart from the party and discuss the impact of the continuing
drought. Meanwhile Lord Percy is entertaining the ladies with a
description of a recent court levee. Catharine and Kitty stand by
themselves a few yards further down the hill, from where they can
see the cast-iron fire basket at the top of the tower. The pilgrimage
to Alnwick has been painful for Catharine, and she struggles to hold
back her tears.[25]

The next blow fell in April 1792, when John died in Durham. Little
is known of the circumstances of his death, except for these notes
made in Granville's memorandum book: 'April 23rd Monday – This
Even I set out in the Newcastle Coach from the Blue Boar in Holborn
for Durham on account of the dangerous illness of my dear Brother
the Rev. Dr John Sharp.' Granville arrived in the city in the early
afternoon of Wednesday 25 April, just in time to see his eldest brother,
who died three days afterwards.[26]

John was buried in Durham Cathedral, in a vault adjoining the
tombs of his mother and father.[27] Following John's death, his widow
Mary left Hartburn vicarage, and the apartment at Bamburgh Castle,
and moved to a house in the South Bailey, which Elizabeth describes
as 'a most pleasant one & a most sweet situation as any in Durham'.[28]
In 1798, Mary herself died, and Anne Jemima set up house with her
aunt Judith. The two women lived comfortably together, and found
solace for their loss, both in the comforts of their home, which included
a large garden, a summer house, a hothouse and a 'Rabbit House',
and in the conviviality of Durham society.[29] When Elizabeth visited
in the autumn of 1804, she was obliged to refuse invitations to 'dinners,
balls & great routs', contenting herself with 'tea drinking in their
family way'.[30]

Frances died in September 1799, while staying with the Prowse
family in Berkley in Somerset. In a diary entry for August 1799,

Elizabeth records: 'Dear. Sisr F taken ill & took to her bed on ye 29.'
Four days later, on 2 September 1799, Frances was dead, and according
to Elizabeth 'was buryd at Berkley on ye 7'. Elizabeth described her
sister's death as 'a great greef her loss, to myself, & that it happened
from home' but the words hardly do justice to her bereavement.[31]
Through their shared childhood in Rothbury and Durham, as young
women in London, and during the long years of her widowhood,
Frances had been her sister's constant companion, and her loss must
have come as a bitter blow.

Ten years later, on 20 March 1809, Judith died at Durham at the
age of seventy-five. When news of her death reached London,
Granville (now seventy-three), hurried to Durham by stagecoach, and
Elizabeth followed him the next morning anxious, as she said, 'to be
soon with my dear niece Sharp as soon as possible on her great ...
loss'.[32] Elizabeth's description of Judith's elaborate funeral ceremony,
which included an anthem specially composed for the occasion, gives
an idea of her sister's standing in the community.[33] Anne Jemima had
now lost her beloved aunt, as well as her parents, and had no other
family in Durham. Though previously there had been 'much talk of
Jemima going to be married to Mr Parker', nothing came of the match,
and Elizabeth took the view that her niece never inclined to it.[34] Anne
Jemima remained single, and lived in the house in the South Bailey
with a companion called Mrs Paxton.[35]

In February 1810, Elizabeth herself died after a short illness, while
staying with her brother in Fulham. Her death prostrated the eighty-
year-old William, who was already riven with anxiety over the failing
health of his daughter Mary. According to the Fulham clergyman John
Owen, who later gave William's funeral oration, 'The stroke, which
severed from him unexpectedly his beloved sister, appears to have
given a shock to his bodily frame, from which it never recovered.' For
all William's efforts at resignation, it was clear to Owen that the
surgeon's grief for 'a loss, the magnitude of which those only can
estimate, who know how much he loved that excellent sister' was
'rather stifled, than subdued'.[36] Elizabeth's death severed the exceptionally close bond between William and his sister that had been
constant since childhood.

Owen remembers how, one evening shortly after Elizabeth's passing, William 'repeatedly felt his daughter's pulse, at that time accelerated to a high degree of fever; and finding, upon taking his leave of her for the night, that its quickness was in no degree abated; he retired in silence to his chamber; and then broke forth into an agony of grief'. When this paroxysm, which continued for many hours, had subsided, 'his nature seemed exhausted'.[37] William died shortly afterwards.

William and Elizabeth were buried side by side in All Saints in Fulham. An inscription on the south side of their tomb reads:

Here lie the remains of
Elizabeth Prowse of Wicken Park Northamptonshire
who died Febry 23 1810 aged 77
and of her Brother
William Sharp Esq of Fulham House[*] in this Parish
Who died March 17th 1810 aged 81
Endeared to their Family Connexions and Society
By an amiableness of Character which has seldom been
equalled
And to each other by a degree of mutual attachment
Which has never been surpassed,
'They were lovely in their lives,
And in Death, they were not divided'

Granville, the last of the siblings, lived on until the summer of 1813, when his health suddenly deteriorated. As he lay dying in Stourton House, where he had lived since his brother's death, Granville 'continued frequently to look at the family portraits, which hung round the room, with the most earnest and affecting expression, as if tracing the resemblances, and then naming them, one by one – "My dear Father", "My good Mother", "My dear brother William"'.[38] He died at about four o'clock in the afternoon, on 6 July 1813.

---

* Stourton House was also known as Fulham House.

Granville was buried by his brother and sister in All Saints. The inscription on the north side of their tomb reads:

Here
By the remains
of the Brother and Sister whom he tenderly loved
lie those of
Granville Sharp Esq
at the age of 79,* this venerable Philanthropist
Terminated his Career
Of almost unparalleled activity and usefulness,
July 6th 1813;
leaving behind him a name
That will be cherished with affection & gratitude
As long as any homage shall be paid to those principles
Of Justice, Humanity and Religion,
Which for nearly half a century,
He promoted by his Exertions,
And adorned by his Example

Granville's death brings to a close the story of the Sharps. It is, at its very heart, the story of a loving family. From the days of their child-hood in the rectory in Rothbury and the cathedral close at Durham, the siblings were bound together by immutable ties of companionship and practical and emotional support. They integrated their lives so closely that it is almost impossible to disentangle the achievement of one from the contribution of the others. Of numerous examples, Granville's journey on the road to the emancipation of slaves began at the free surgery for the poor that William ran in Mincing Lane, and it was James who helped him prosecute the case against Jonathan Strong's kidnappers two years later. Granville inspired James to campaign against the American war, while John's social enterprises at Bamburgh Castle were the model for Elizabeth's charitable endeavours at Wicken Park.

---

* Granville was in fact still seventy-seven at the time of his death. He is also commemorated in a memorial tablet by the sculptor Sir Francis Chantrey in the south transept of Westminster Abbey.

This network of mutual aid was underpinned by the siblings' attachment to a common value system. Instinctively radical and freethinking, they had a rare ability to see beyond the conventions of their class and age. So much so, that their views and activities must, on occasion, have astonished those around them. The family therefore trod a precarious path between establishment and anti-establishment positions, as determined to maintain relations with the upper classes, as they were to bring about reform. The siblings' deft social skills were key to the reconciliation of these otherwise conflicting loyalties.

The Sharps were a family of pioneers, whose trailblazing achievements included developments in agricultural engineering, social welfare, colonial legislative independence and healthcare.[39] James in particular possessed an unerring facility to seek out, and embrace, ground-breaking technologies. The clear-sightedness with which Granville perceived the corrupting evil of slavery is akin to the acuity with which James recognised the potential of canals to revolutionise the economy of Britain. Even Frances and Judith managed to push the boundaries of female autonomy.

Sharp philanthropy was practical, rather than theoretical. Instead of simply bemoaning the absence of medical provision for the poor, William ran a free surgery from his City mansion. John preferred the tangible benefits of medical care, schooling, lifeboats and subsidised food to elegantly written diatribes against the injustices of contemporary society. Similarly (though he certainly produced his fair share of what now seems impenetrable prose) Granville's pursuit of justice in the Somerset case represents the triumph of action over mere words. The Sharps transformed the lives of tens of thousands of men, women and children across England and the empire.

It comes as no surprise then that the family was often referred to by their contemporaries as the 'good Sharps'. But they were certainly not po-faced. Instead the siblings had an apparently unique ability to balance moral seriousness with a capacity for fun. The image of Giardini's band playing for the little princes at Kew, and the family's adventures on board the *Union*, rise from the faded pages of Sharp correspondence, and the misspellings of Elizabeth's diary, with a vibrancy that is remarkable in a 250-year-old document. But the eccentric charms of the water schemes, and society glitter of the performances in Old Jewry, can obscure the family's very real musical accomplishments. Not only were they serious amateur musicians in their own right, but they contributed – through the calibre of their famous Sunday evening concerts – to the development of the musical life of late eighteenth-century London.

The qualities that so endeared the Sharps to their contemporaries – warm-heartedness, amiability, a gentle eccentricity and ingenuousness – are ephemeral. We can never know quite what it would have been like to be buttonholed by Granville at a glee concert, or walk with James through the manufactory in Tooley Street, or stand windswept on the deck of the *Apollo*, or have supper with the siblings in Mincing Lane. But for that we have our imagination.

Coda

It is the morning of 8 June 1837. A widow dressed in black crepe stands by the fire in the drawing room of Clare Hall, in Hertfordshire. Twenty-five miles away, William IV, the last Georgian monarch, lies dying in Windsor Castle. Britain stands on the brink of a new age.

The widow is gazing at a portrait of her family, which hangs above the mantlepiece. As her eyes rest on one, and then the next well-remembered face, on the folds of an old-fashioned silk gown, and the gentle touch of an outstretched hand, she smiles to herself. Her gaze rests last of all on a girl in a sprigged white cotton dress, who stands in the foreground of the painting with one tiny slippered toe pointing from beneath her skirts.

Of the fifteen people depicted in the portrait, twelve are members of her close family. In the fifty-six years that have elapsed since the completion of the painting in 1781, all of those twelve have died: her mother and father, two cousins, five aunts, and three uncles. The widow is, as she reminds herself, the only survivor.

Standing to the right of the fireplace, the widow inserts her hand between the back of the painting and the wall. Her fingers search about until they feel the rough edges of a wad of paper, which she slides slowly from behind the portrait. At a writing desk at the far end of the room, she unfolds the crumpled pages and smooths them out on the surface of her desk.

There are two pieces of paper. The first begins: 'The Persons represented in Zoffani's Picture of the Sharp Family are'. The sitters are listed numerically. Number 1 is 'Dr John Sharp, Archdeacon of Northumberland &c &c &c in full Canonicals', while numbers 14 and 15 are 'William Lee Boat Master' and 'Dick Spikeman Cabin Boy, supposed to be alongside the *Apollo* in a small Boat bringing Music Books'. The girl in the white dress is number 9, 'in Pink and Black

feathers'. As well as the human sitters, there is also '16 Zoffanis Favorite
Dog, Poma [*sic*]'. The setting of the painting is described as 'the
Thames between Fulham and Putney', and there are also details such
as the 'Crimson Silk Flag' which is the work of 'Mrs Judith Sharp, in
Patchwork and Embroidery'.

The second piece of paper refers to the cost of the painting. It
begins: 'My impression is – that 200 Guineas were paid to Zoffani
when the Picture was began in 1779 – and 200 Guineas more when it
was finished 1780 or 1781.'

The widow opens a drawer, and takes from it a sheet of paper and
a nib pen. Dipping the pen in an inkwell, she begins to write in the
same delicate hand that covers the pages on the desk. She writes:

The two Pieces of Paper Enclosed, were detached from the back
of the Family Picture at Clare Hall, by Catharine [i.e. Kitty], the
Daughter of James Sharp, – the only Survivor of the Thirteen
Persons of whom the Group is composed June 8th 1837 – upon
sending the Picture to be cleaned by desire of the Proprietor
Thomas Barwick Lloyd Baker, the Grandson of William Sharp,
for whom the Picture was painted by Zoffani 1780.[1]

When the ink is dry, she carefully folds the paper over the documents she removed from the painting, and places them in her desk.

★

Catharine 'Kitty' Sharp was only nine when Zoffany took her likeness
for the family portrait, but the girl who stands in the middle of the
canvas in a white sprigged dress was already an accomplished musical
performer. In later life, she recalled how 'at four or five years old she
was placed on a table to sing to the Duke of York' and that 'one song
was always required of her' at family concerts.[2] According to the
Visiting Book which records details of Old Jewry concerts between
November 1773 and April 1783, Kitty sang a solo of 'O L.d in whome
I trust. Henley' at the recital on 19 March 1775, when she was four

and a half years old. The following year, on 24 March 1776, she sang another solo, this time 'Anth. Kent / My song shall be'.[3]

It might be imagined that a child of Kitty's precocious abilities would have delighted in the attention her talents elicited. Instead, Kitty seems to have shunned the limelight, confiding in later life that the one song that was required of her at each concert had the effect of destroying 'the pleasure of the evening for her'.[4] It takes little effort to feel for the young girl, as she sat waiting to perform, torn between the anxiety to please her family, and her terror at the coming ordeal. And yet it is also easy to understand the delight which the Sharps took in Kitty's talent, and how the joy of hearing her perform desensitised them to the girl's emotions. A much younger cousin, who heard Kitty sing in later life, remembered: 'Few ever had the power of giving so much pleasure in that way – I shall never forget her rich, clear voice and the exquisite taste of her performance vocal and instrumental – often extempore.'[5]

Kitty left no substantive records of her life, and what we know of her has percolated through the memoirs and correspondence of other members of the family. She lived with her mother, Catharine, at first in the family home by the ironmongery in Leadenhall Street, and then, when Catharine retired from the business in 1792, at Clare Hall in Hertfordshire.[6] At the age of forty-six, Kitty married Andrew Bowlt, the perpetual curate of Bamburgh Church, who was eleven years her senior.[7] Bowlt had built the modest Glebe House in the village, and it was here, rather than in the minister's apartments in the castle, that he and Kitty lived after their marriage. A sale catalogue dating from 1835, which records among other appurtenances '5 cows; 2 horses; 12 sheep; and 2 pigs', suggests that Kitty's life at Glebe House was rather less refined than that enjoyed by her cousin Mary Lloyd Baker on her husband's estate in Gloucestershire.[8]

In later life Kitty adopted the role of family archivist, and devoted herself to a careful ordering of Sharp papers and belongings. For example, her 'Catalogue of Records of Bamburgh Castle during the Trusteeship of the Sharps' contains almost all that is known about John's work at Bamburgh, including the memorandum book in which he recorded the decisions of the trustees, a 'Parchment Accomp Book', family letters and a miscellany of plans, drawings, 'Rules and Regulations', 'Signals', 'Prayers' and accounts of wrecks, guns, surgical cases and astronomical phenomena.[9] Kitty tried to find a good home for the family's collection of books and music (recipients included Durham Cathedral and the city's newly founded university) and kept family memorabilia such as 'ArchBp Sharp's Gardening Book', 'Six parcels of Coins, collected by Dr John Sharp' and 'Koran belonged to Granville Sharp' in a special cabinet.[10]

Kitty's neat pencil annotations, explaining the authorship or circumstances of a particular document, are a familiar sight in the Sharp files. As the self-appointed custodian of family memory, Kitty almost certainly exercised control over the contents of the archive, fashioning it, consciously or unconsciously, to reflect her views as to how the family should be remembered. For this reason, the story of the Sharps is not a duplicate of the reality of their lives, but rather a representation mediated through the chance survival of certain documents over others, and also through the lens of Kitty's directorial eye.

In 1835 Kitty lost both her husband Andrew Bowlt and her mother Catharine, who died at Clare Hall at the age of ninety. Since her cousin Mary had died as a young woman in 1812, and Anne Jemima had not long outlived her, Catharine's death left Kitty as the only survivor of the thirteen Sharps who appear in the Zoffany painting. The richness of her family life, with its superabundance of aunts and uncles, their warmth, and unity, and the delight of their jolly doings, brought with it the pain of repeated bereavement, as one by one her beloved Sharps died. The slight figure on the canvas in a white sprigged dress is also Kitty Sharp at Clare Hall in June 1837, on the eve of Queen Victoria's accession to the throne, looking back at herself, and remembering.

Select Bibliography

Peter Ackroyd, *Thames: Sacred River* (Chatto & Windus, 2007)

Derek H. Aldcroft and Michael J. Freeman (eds), *Transport in the Industrial Revolution* (Manchester University Press, 1983)

Mark Argent (ed.), *Recollections of R J S Stevens: an Organist in Georgian London* (Southern Illinois University Press, 1992)

Joanne Bailey, *Unquiet Lives: Marriage and Marriage Breakdown in England, 1660–1800* (CUP, 2003)

Joanne Bailey, *Parenting in England 1760–1830: Emotion, Identity and Generation* (OUP, 2012)

Hannah Barker, *The Business of Women: Female Enterprise and Urban Development in Northern England 1760–1830* (OUP, 2006)

Hannah Barker, *Family and Business During the Industrial Revolution* (OUP, 2017)

Hannah Barker and Elaine Chalus (eds), *Women's History Britain 1700–1850* (Routledge, 2005)

Ilana Krausman Ben-Amos, *Adolescence and Youth in Early Modern England* (Yale University Press, 1994)

Stephen J. Braidwood, *Black Poor and White Philanthropists: London's Blacks and the Foundation of the Sierra Leone Settlement 1786–1791* (Liverpool University Press, 1994)

John Brewer, *The Pleasures of the Imagination: English Culture in the Eighteenth Century* (HarperCollins, 1997)

John Brooke, *George III* (Constable, 1972)

Christopher Leslie Brown, *Moral Capital: Foundations of British Abolitionism* (University of North Carolina Press, 2006)

David Brown (ed.), *Durham Cathedral: History, Fabric and Culture* (Paul Mellon Centre, 2015)

Jonathan Brown, *Farm Machinery 1750–1945* (Batsford, 1989)

Charles Burney, *The Present State of Music in France and Italy* (1771)

Charles Burney, *A General History of Music* (1789)

William F. Bynum, and Roy Porter (eds), *William Hunter and the Eighteenth-Century Medical World* (CUP, 1985)

Richard Campbell, *The London Tradesman* (1747)

Kathleen Chater, *Untold Stories: Black People in England and Wales during the Period of the British Slave Trade, 1660–1807* (Manchester University Press, 2009)

Ian R. Christie, *Wilkes, Wyvill and Reform: the Parliamentary Reform Movement in British Politics, 1760–85* (St Martin's Press, 1962)

Thomas Clarkson, *The History of the Rise, Progress and Accomplishment of the Abolition of the African Slave Trade, by the British Parliament* (1808)

Hugh J. Compton, *The Oxford Canal* (David & Charles, 1977)

Stephen Conway, *The British Isles and the War of American Independence* (OUP, 2000)

Brian Crosby, 'Private Concerts on Land and Water: The Musical Activities of the Sharp Family, *c.*1750–1790', *Royal Musical Association Research Chronicle* 34 (2001)

Brian Crosby, *A Catalogue of Durham Cathedral Music Manuscripts* (OUP, 1986)

David Brion Davis, *The Problem of Slavery in the Age of Revolution 1770–1823* (OUP, 1999)

David Brion Davis, *Inhuman Bondage: the Rise and Fall of Slavery in the New World* (OUP, 2006)

Francoise Deconinck-Brossard, *Dr John Sharp: An Eighteenth-Century Northumbrian Preacher* (St Mary's College, University of Durham, 1995)

H. T. Dickinson (ed.), *Britain and the American Revolution* (Routledge, 1998)

Patrick Dillon, *The Much Lamented Death of Madam Geneva: The Eighteenth-Century Gin Craze* (Headline, 2003)

Frank L. Dix, *Royal River Highway: A History of the Passenger Boats and Services on the River Thames* (David & Charles, 1985)

Seymour Drescher, *Abolition: A History of Slavery and Anti-Slavery* (CUP, 2009)

Peter Earle, *The Making of the English Middle Class: Business, Society and Family Life in London, 1660–1730* (Methuen, 1989)

David Eltis and David Richardson (eds), *Atlas of the Transatlantic Slave Trade* (Yale University Press, 2010)

Olaudah Equiano, *The Interesting Narrative of the Life of Olaudah Equiano* (1789)

Alexander Falconbridge, *An Account of the Slave Trade on the Coast of Africa* (1788)

Charles Feret, *Fulham Old and New* (Leadenhall Press, 1900)

Anthony Fletcher, *Growing Up in England: The Experience of Childhood 1600–1914* (Yale University Press, 2010)

Peter Freyer, *Staying Power: The History of Black People in Britain* (Pluto Press, 1984)

Christopher Fyfe, *History of Sierra Leone* (OUP, 1962)

Christopher Fyfe and Eldred Jones (eds), *Freetown: A Symposium* (OUP, 1968)

Mary Dorothy George, *London Life in the eighteenth century* (Kegan Paul, Trench, Trubner, 1925)

Mark Girouard, *Life in the English Country House: A Social and Architectural History* (Yale University Press, 1978)

Eliga H. Gould, *The Persistence of Empire: British Political Culture in the Age of the American Revolution* (University of North Carolina Press, 2000)

Carol Griffiths, *Bamburgh 'Ghosts': Voices from the Eighteenth Century* (Belford Bowen, 2014)

Paul Griffiths and Mark Jenner (eds), *Londinopolis: Essays in the Cultural and Social History of Early Modern London* (Manchester University Press, 2000)

Pierre Jean Grosley, *A Tour to London* (1765)

Charles Hadfield, *British Canals* (David & Charles, 1950)

Charles Hadfield, *The Canals of the West Midlands* (David & Charles, 1966)

Charles Hadfield, *The Canals of South and South-East England* (David & Charles, 1969)

Charles Hadfield, *The Canals of the East Midlands* (David & Charles, 1970)

Amy Harris, *Siblinghood and Social Relations in Georgian England: Share and Share Alike* (Manchester University Press, 2016)

J. R. Harris, *The British Iron Industry 1700–1850* (Palgrave Macmillan, 1988)

Olwen Hedley, *Queen Charlotte* (John Murray, 1975)

Christopher Hibbert, *George III: A Personal History* (Viking, 1998)

Bridget Hill, *Servants: English Domestics in the Eighteenth Century* (OUP, 1996)

Bridget Hill, *Women Alone: Spinsters in England 1660–1850* (Yale University Press, 2001)

Mary Hilton and Jill Shefrin (eds), *Educating the Child in Enlightenment Britain: Beliefs, Cultures, Practices* (Routledge, 2009)

Prince Hoare, *Memoirs of Granville Sharp*, 2 vols (1820)

Adam Hochschild, *Bury the Chains: the British Struggle to Abolish Slavery* (Macmillan, 2005)

Richard W. Hoyle (ed.), *Custom, Improvement, and the Landscape in Early Modern Britain* (Ashgate, 2011)

Margaret Hunt, *The Middling Sort: Commerce, Gender and the Family in England, 1680–1780* (University of California Press, 1996)

W. M. Jacob, *The Clerical Profession in the Long Eighteenth Century, 1680–1840* (OUP, 2007)

Peter M. Jones, *Agricultural Enlightenment: Knowledge, Technology, and Nature 1750–1840* (OUP, 2016)

Paul Langford, *A Polite and Commercial People: England 1727–1783* (OUP, 1998)

E. C. P. Lascelles, *Granville Sharp and the Freedom of Slaves in England* (OUP, 1928)

Susan C. Lawrence, *Charitable Knowledge: Hospital Pupils and Practitioners in Eighteenth-Century London* (CUP, 1996)

Richard Leppert, *Music and Image: Domesticity, ideology and socio-cultural formation in eighteenth century England* (CUP, 2009)

Eneas Mackenzie, *An Historical, Topographical, and Descriptive View of the County of Northumberland* (1825)

Simon McVeigh, *Concert Life in London from Mozart to Haydn* (CUP, 1993)

Simon McVeigh, 'Felice Giardini: A Violinist in Late Eighteenth Century London', *Music & Letters*, Vol. 64, No. 3/4 (July–October 1983), pp. 162–72.

H. Misson, *M. Misson's Memoirs and Observations in his Travels over England: with some Account of Scotland and Ireland* (1698)

H.-C Mui and L. Miu, *Shops and Shopkeeping in Eighteenth Century England* (Routledge, 1989)

Sheila O'Connell, *London 1753* (British Museum Press, 2003)

James Oldham, *The Mansfield Manuscripts and the Growth of the English Law in the Eighteenth Century* (University of North Carolina Press, 1992)

Richard Ovenden, 'Thomas Sharp's Library at Cambridge c.1748' (MA dissertation, UCL, 1987)

Mark Overton, *Agricultural Revolution in England: The Transformation of the Agrarian Economy 1500–1850* (CUP, 1996)

Janet K. Page, 'The hautboy in London's musical life, 1730–1770', *Early Music*, Vol. 16, No. 3 (August 1988), pp. 359–71.

W. M. Parson and W. M. White, *History, Directory, and Gazetteer, of the Counties of Durham and Northumberland* (1827)

John Peterson, *Province of Freedom: A History of Sierra Leone, 1787–1870* (Faber & Faber, 1969)

Nikolaus Pevsner, *Northumberland* (Yale University Press, 1992)

Hugh Phillips, *The Thames About 1750* (Collins, 1951)

Linda Pollock, *Forgotten Children: Parent–Child Relations from 1500–1900* (CUP, 1984)

Linda Pollock, *A Lasting Relationship: Parents and Children over Three Centuries* (University Press of New England, 1987)

Archer Polson, *Law and Lawyers; or Sketches and Illustrations of Legal History and Biography* (Longman, Orme, Brown, Green & Longmans, 1840)

Roy Porter (ed.), *The Cambridge Illustrated History of Medicine* (CUP, 2006)

Roy Porter and Dorothy Porter, *Patient's Progress: Doctors and Doctoring in Eighteenth-Century England* (Stanford University Press, 1989)

Norman S. Poser, *Lord Mansfield: Justice in the Age of Reason* (McGill-Queen's University Press, 2013)

Martin Postle (ed.), *Johan Zoffany RA: Society Observed* (Yale University Press, 2011)

William Henry Pyne, *History of the Royal Residences* (1819)

James Raine, *A Memoir of the Rev. John Hodgson*, 2 vols (London, 1858)

P. J. G. Ransom, *The Archaeology of the Transport Revolution 1750–1850* (World's Work, 1984)

Kate Retford, *The Art of Domestic Life: Family Portraiture in Eighteenth-Century England* (Yale University Press, 2000)

Aileen Ribeiro, *The Gallery of Fashion* (Princeton University Press, 2000)

Ian Campbell Ross, *Laurence Sterne: A Life* (OUP, 2001)

Marie B. Rowlands, *Masters and Men in the West Midlands Metal Trades before the Industrial Revolution* (Manchester University Press, 1975)

Charles Saumarez-Smith, *Eighteenth-Century Decoration: Design and the Domestic Interior in England* (Weidenfeld & Nicolson, 1993)

Simon Schama, *Rough Crossings: Britain, the Slaves and the American Revolution* (BBC Books, 2005)

Thomas Sharp, *The Life of John Sharp DD Archbishop of York* (1825)

J. Shuler, 'The Pastoral and Ecclesiastical Administration of the Diocese of Durham 1721–1771' (doctoral thesis, University of Durham, 1975)

F. O. Shyllon, *Black Slaves in Britain* (OUP, 1974)

Sir James Stephen, *Essays in Ecclesiastical Biography* (Longman, Brown, Green & Longman, 1850)

C. J. Stranks, 'The Charities of Nathaniel, Lord Crewe and Dr John Sharp 1721–1976' (Durham Cathedral Lecture, 1976)

Fred S. Thacker, *The Thames Highway: A History of the Inland Navigation* (David & Charles, 1968)

Hugh Thomas, *The Slave Trade: The Story of the Atlantic Slave Trade 1440–1870* (Simon & Schuster, 1997)

A. Tindal Hart, *The Life and Times of John Sharp, Archbishop of York* (SPCK, 1949)

Adrian Tinniswood, *The Polite Tourist: Four Centuries of Country House Visiting* (National Trust, 1998)

Penelope Treadwell, *Johan Zoffany: Artist and Adventurer* (Paul Holberton, 2009)

Jenny Uglow, *The Lunar Men: The Friends who made the Future* (Faber & Faber, 2002)

Amanda Vickery, *The Gentleman's Daughter* (Yale University Press, 1998)

Amanda Vickery, *Behind Closed Doors: At Home in Georgian England* (Yale University Press, 2009)

James Walvin, *Black Ivory: A History of British Slavery* (HarperCollins, 1992)

James Walvin, *The Zong: A Massacre, the Law and the End of Slavery* (Yale University Press, 2011)

Jessica Warner, *Craze: Gin and Debauchery in an Age of Reason* (Profile, 2002)

Mary Webster, *Johan Zoffany: 1733–1810* (National Portrait Gallery, 1977)

Mary Webster, *Johan Zoffany, RA, 1733–1810* (Yale University Press, 2011)

Anne Whiteman, J. S. Bromley and P. G. M. Dickson (eds), *Statesmen, Scholars and Merchants: Essays in Eighteenth-Century History presented to Dame Lucy Sutherland* (Clarendon Press, 1973)

Gareth Williams, *Angel of Death: The Story of Smallpox* (Palgrave Macmillan, 2010)

D. A. Winstanley, *Unreformed Cambridge: A Study of Certain Aspects of the University in the Eighteenth Century* (CUP, 1935)

Steven M. Wise, *Though the Heavens may Fall: The Landmark Trial that Led to the End of Human Slavery* (Pimlico, 2006)

Alun Withey, 'Medicine and Charity in Eighteenth-century Northumberland: The Early Years of the Bamburgh Castle Dispensary and Surgery, *c.* 1772–1802', *Social History of Medicine*, Vol. 29, No. 3 (August 2016), pp. 467–89.

Arthur Young, *A Six Months' Tour Through the North of England* (1770)

Philip Yorke (ed.), *The Diary of John Baker* (Hutchinson, 1931)

ARCHIVES

GRO: Gloucestershire Record Office. The Sharp papers are part of the Lloyd Baker archive, with the prefix D3549. In the Notes, only the document identification (e.g. 'GRO, 14/1/2') is given.

NRO: Northumberland Record Office. Most of the material relating to John Sharp's work at Bamburgh Castle is archived with the papers of the Lord Crewe Trustees at NRO 00452.

NoRO: Northamptonshire Record Office has archives relating to Elizabeth Sharp's stewardship of Wicken Park, including three estate ledgers.

TNA: The National Archives, Kew.

Notes

Overture

1   Martin Postle, 'Johan Zoffany: an Artist Abroad' in Postle (ed.), p. 32.

2   In the late 1750s, Zoffany was appointed as 'court and cabinet painter' to Johann Philipp Graf von Walderdorff, the Prince-Archbishop and Elector of Trier. See Postle (ed.), p. 20, and Clarissa Campbell-Orr, 'Six Courts & Four Empires: Zoffany as Courtier' in Postle (ed.), p. 76. Zoffany painted decorative schemes in the prince-archbishop's home in Koblenz, and also in Trier.

3   Postle (ed.), p. 24.

4   *The Tribuna of the Uffizi* (1772–9). The Tribuna is an octagonal room in the Uffizi Gallery, Florence, designed by Bernardo Buontalenti for Francesco de' Medici in 1584. Containing many of the treasures of the Medici collection, it was regarded as housing the greatest art collection in Europe.

5   Postle (ed.), p. 33.

6   Maya Josanoff, 'A Passage through India: Zoffany in Calcutta & Lucknow' in Postle (ed.), p. 125.

7   Postle (ed.), p. 32.

8   Ibid., p. 303.

9   *Self-Portrait with his Daughter Maria Theresa, James Cervetto and Giacobbe Cervetto* (c.1780).

10 See Jessica David, 'Zoffany's Painting Technique: The Drummond Family in focus' in Postle (ed.), pp. 168–9.

11 This represents an overview of Zoffany's palette generally, rather than the colours specifically used in his depiction of William Sharp. He also used yellow and red lakes, and ivory black – in fact most of the colours then available. See David in Postle (ed.), p. 168.

Chapter 1: Beginnings

1 Thomas to John, 28 November 1721, Palace Green Library, Durham, Add MS 956/2.

2 The term 'prebendal stall' refers to the seat in a cathedral reserved for a particular prebend. The holder of the 'tenth stall', for example, enjoys the endowments historically associated with that position. Thomas eventually had prebendary stalls at Southwell, Wistow and Durham.

3 John Sharp (1645–1714) was widely admired for his philanthropy, and for the 'plainness and unaffected simplicity' of his preaching. A man of deep personal piety, he enjoyed the particular confidence of Queen Anne.

4 See Shuler, pp. 195–7.

5 Stranks, p. 8.

6 'Saintly goodliness' at least as portrayed by Thomas in his three-volume biography of his father, *The Life of John Sharp DD Archbishop of York* (1825).

7 See Shuler, pp. 196–8; R. Ovenden, 'Sharp, Thomas (1693–1758)', *ODNB*. Thomas's publications were published compendiously in six volumes in 1763.

8 GRO 8/1/5. The 'Old Recipes of the Sharps Curious' is filed under Judith's name, but includes writing in different hands.

9 Clarendon, Hist. rebellion, 3.82.

10 This was in the early 1750s, when John was a young man of twenty-two or twenty-three.

11 V. Stater, 'Grenville, John, first earl of Bath (1628–1701)', *ODNB*.

12 Lord Macaulay, quoted in G. W. Kitchin, *Seven sages of Durham* (1911), p. 221. See William Marshall, 'Granville, Denis (1637–1703)', *ODNB*. This account of Denis Granville's treatment at the court of St Germain seems to be at variance with that suggested by Edward Corp in *A Court in Exile: The Stuarts in France, 1689–1718* (CUP, 2004). Corp makes no mention of ill treatment, and records that Granville received a pension from the exiled king.

13 Higgons wrote his most significant work, *The History of Isuf Bassa, Captain General of the Ottoman Army at the Invasion of Candia*, while serving as English envoy in Venice. See B. C. Pursell, 'Higgons, Sir Thomas (1623/4–1691)', *ODNB*.

14 W. P Courtney, 'Higgons, Bevil (1670–1736)', *ODNB*; E. Corp, 'Higgons, Thomas (1668/9–1733)', *ODNB*.

15 N. G. Wilson, 'Wheler, Sir George (1651–1724)', *ODNB*.

16 'Pele' towers were built in the Scottish and English borders between the middle of the fourteenth century, and the beginning of the

seventeenth century, as a defence against armed raids. A 'vicar's pele' was intended for the use of the whole community.

17 Pevsner, p. 629; Victoria County History, *Northumberland*, Vol. XV.

18 Victoria County History, *Northumberland*, Vol. XV.

19 With several of the children, sources suggest two possible dates of birth. In each case I have chosen the most likely.

20 Vickery, *Gentleman's Daughter*, p. 98.

21 Amy Harris, p. 33.

22 Vickery, *Gentleman's Daughter*, pp. 117–22; Pollock, *Forgotten Children*, p. 130.

23 Deborah Simonton, 'Women and Education' in Barker and Chalus (eds), p. 35.

24 Fletcher, pp. 6–7

25 Pevsner, p. 629; Victoria County History, *Northumberland*, Vol. XV.

26 GRO 14/1/2, 27 February 1758. GRO 14/1/2 contains Elizabeth Sharp's diary. Elizabeth did not keep a daily diary, in the manner of Samuel Pepys. Instead, she appears to have made contemporaneous records of significant family and personal events, and subsequently compiled them into a chronological narrative. This explains why some of the dating is rather haphazard.

27 Jacob, pp. 168–9.

28 David Brown (ed.), pp. 265, 279.

29 Ibid., p. 272. The Durham Cathedral statutes, sealed in 1554, required prebendaries to 'maintain a family and keep residence and hospitality'.

Chapter 2: Vocation

1   GRO 14/1/2, 16 March 1758.

2   GRO 13/1/S9.

3   Zacharias von Uffenbach, quoted in Winstanley, p. 204.

4   The Sharps' typical undergraduate day is partly based on that of Philip Yorke, an undergraduate at Cambridge in the 1770s, which he described in a letter to his uncle Lord Hardwicke. Quoted in Winstanley, p. 226. For further details of the teapots of punch, see ibid., p. 206.

5   Ovenden.

6   Jacob, p. 51, quoting Norfolk Record Office, Bradfer Lawrence Collection, 11b, Diary of Briggs Cary.

7   Earle, p. 89.

8   The standing army was very small in this period.

9   Earle, p. 90.

10   GRO 14/1/2, 1743.

11   Ben-Amos, pp. 63–4.

12   Earle, p. 94; Joan Lane, 'The Role of Apprenticeship in Eighteenth-
      Century Medical Education' in Bynum and Porter (eds), p. 67.

13   According to the Bank of England inflation calculator, £350 in 1743 is
      the equivalent of over £80,000 today, i.e. a substantial sum. It is possible
      that the relations who assisted in obtaining William the apprenticeship
      also contributed to the cost of the premium. This was a common
      occurrence at the time.

14   By the 1740s, a dressing room was not just for dressing, but also served
      as a private sitting room. See Vickery, *Behind Closed Doors*, pp. 147–50.

15   See Porter (ed.), pp. 217–18.

16   See for example, Porter and Porter, p. 66.

17   Lane in Bynum and Porter (eds), p. 75.

18   Ibid., p. 76.

19   Porter (ed.), pp. 217–18.

20   Ibid., pp. 218–19. See in particular the novelist Fanny Burney's extraor-
      dinary account of her operation for the removal of a breast tumour,
      without anaesthetic, in 1810.

21   Lane in Bynum and Porter (eds), pp. 77–8, 83, 101.

22   Amy Harris, p. 29.

23   Fletcher, p. 303. Fletcher explains: 'The closest and most intimate teenage
      relationships were … the friendships formed in the intense atmosphere
      of the schoolroom, between sisters.'

24   Barker and Chalus (eds), pp. 44–5; Fletcher, p. 98–9.

25   *Portia, The Polite Lady; or a course of female education. In a series of letters*
      (3rd edn, 1775), p. 153, quoted in Michele Cohen, 'Familiar Conversation:
      the Role of the "Familiar Format" in Education in Eighteenth and
      Nineteenth Century England' in Hilton and Shefrin (eds), p. 106.

26   The Sharp girls' notional timetable is based on historical examples, such
      as those set out in M. O. Grenby, 'Delightful Instruction? Assessing
      Children's Use of Educational Books in the Long Eighteenth Century'
      in Hilton and Shefrin (eds), pp. 181–98.

Chapter 3: London

1   Roy Porter, 'The Wonderful Extent and Variety of London' in O'Connell,
      p. 12.

2   Earle, pp. 17–18.

3   George, p. 161.

4   Ibid., p. 163.

5   Ibid., p. 202.

6   Ibid., pp. 202–4

7   Porter in O'Connell, p. 10.

8   Grosley.

9   Earle, p. 48; O'Connell, p. 257.

10 For details of the manufacture and trade of toys in this period see Uglow, p. 17.

11 George, p. 64, quoting William Petty, *Treatise of Taxes and Contributions* (1662).

12 Ibid., p. 73.

13 Ibid.

14 Ibid., p. 32.

15 Ibid., p. 42.

16 A trade card of 'John Smith, Map and Printseller' of Cheapside, from the 1750s, is in the collection of the British Museum. A pair of shoes meeting this description, dating from the 1760s, is in the collection of the Museum of London. The jewellery is based on a mid eighteenth-century flower spray ornament in the collection of the British Museum. A trade card of 'Martha Wheatland and Sisters, Milliners & Haberdashers', of Cheapside, from the Heal collection, is also in the British Museum. See O'Connell, pp. 60–3.

17 The street cries are taken from etchings by Paul Sandby, *Twelve London Cries Done from the Life, Part 1ˢᵗ, 1760*. 'All fire and no smoke!' is the cry of a man who sells flints and steels for creating sparks to light a fire. 'My pretty little ginny tarters' is the obscure opening of the cry of a man selling sticks for beating carpets, and continues 'for a ha'penny a stick or a penny a stick, or a stick to beat your Wives or dust your cloths'. The girl who sells James a memorandum book also appears in a print: according to O'Connell, 'Prints of street traders often hint that their bodies as well as their goods might be available to customers; and court reports and execution broadsides show that young women often moved between street trading and prostitution' (pp. 77–81).

18 For life as an apprentice, see Earle, pp. 100–5, and Ben-Amos, pp. 84–132.

19 J. R. Harris, pp. 51–3.

20 Rowlands, pp. 8–9.

21 J. R. Harris, p. 66.

22 Rowlands, pp. 26–32.

Chapter 4: Greeny

1   GRO 14/1/3.
2   Earle, p. 55.
3   GRO 13/1/S9.
4   Hoare, I, p. 100.
5   Lascelles, p. 3.
6   Hoare, I, p. 41.

Chapter 5: Water

1   The description is based on an image of the *Apollo* barge, one of several
     owned by the Sharp family, which forms part of a painting of the Sharp
     flotilla dating from *c*.1780. London ended abruptly at Millbank in this
     period. Until it was drained in the nineteenth century, this part of
     Westminster, and what is now Pimlico, was too marshy to be built on,
     and was used as farmland for producing fruit and vegetables for the
     London market. Tothill Fields spread westwards from Horseferry Road.
2   The description is based on contemporary prints of the riverside, and
     in particular those found in Phillips, pp. 144–73.
3   GRO 12/1/1.
4   Although The Boat Book is filed in James's section of the Sharp archive,
     the handwriting, and notes such as 'Jim, self' on 6 May 1753, suggest
     that it is the work of William. See Crosby, 'Private Concerts', pp. 10–11.
5   GRO 12/1/1.
6   Ackroyd, p. 190, with reference to Daniel Defoe's *A Tour Thro' the Whole
     Island of Great Britain*.
7   See, for example, Phillips.
8   Ackroyd, p. 126.
9   See Phillips, p. 173.

Chapter 6: Music

1   GRO 12/1/1; Crosby, 'Private Concerts', pp. 10–11. The meaning of 'bitts'
     is not known. 'Desks' presumably refers to some sort of music stand.
2   Crosby, 'Private Concerts', p. 75.
3   David Brown (ed.), p. 344.

4   GRO 7/2/15.
5   MM183–89 in Crosby, *A Catalogue of Cathedral Music Manuscripts* (also see Crosby, 'Private Concerts', p. 3).
6   Ibid. M185 contains this inscription.
7   Although there are seven part books, only five Sharp boys took part in the ensemble. The names: 'Francis Myddleton', 'James Mason' and 'John Wharton' also feature in the books. Myddleton was a relative of the Sharps, but the identity of the other boys is not known.
8   The flutes, which are now described as 'flageolets' in distinction to the modern form of the instrument, survive in the Bate Collection in Oxford, along with several of the other instruments depicted in Zoffany's portrait of the family.
9   Crosby, 'Private Concerts', p. 33; Argent (ed.), pp. 272, 10. See also Hoare, I, p. 218.
10 Hoare, I, p. 218.
11 GRO 17/5/13.
12 Raine, II, p. 337, unnumbered footnote.
13 McVeigh, *Concert Life*, pp. 86–7. Despite contemporary criticism of professional female violinists, McVeigh notes that Maddalena Sirmen and Louisa Gautherot 'achieved genuine celebrity for their performances of the most demanding violin concertos of the day'.
14 Crosby, 'Private Concerts', p. 20.
15 GRO 7/2/15.
16 Quoted in McVeigh, *Concert Life*, p. 4.
17 Ibid.
18 Burney, *Present State*, p. 95.
19 McVeigh, *Concert Life*, p. 219.
20 Crosby, 'Private Concerts', pp. 21–2.
21 Ibid., pp. 22–3.

Chapter 7: Priest

1   Shuler, p. 67.
2   Pevsner, p. 305.
3   Raine, II, p. 337, unnumbered footnote.
4   Pevsner, p. 305.
5   Judith's outfit is representative of female swimming costumes in this period.
6   Shuler, p. 62.

7   Quoted in Campbell Ross, p. 98. After his ordination in 1738, Sterne was appointed minister of Sutton-on-the-Forest in Yorkshire.
8   Pevsner, p. 305.
9   Jacob, p. 204.
10   Ibid.
11   Deconinck-Brossard.
12   In the eighteenth century, clerical appointments were made by patronage rather than by a formal process of competitive assessment, and the same system applied in the army, navy, law and civil service. See Jacob, pp. 74–7.
13   Shuler, p. 213.
14   Deconinck-Brossard.
15   Shuler, pp. 212–13.
16   Deconinck-Brossard.
17   Shuler, pp. 214–15.
18   GRO 9/1/15. John did in fact publish one sermon: *A sermon preached at St Nicholas's Church in Newcastle, before the governors of the infirmary, for the counties of Durham, Newcastle, and Northumberland, on Wednesday June 24, 1752* (1752).
19   GRO 9/1/4.
20   GRO 16/1/1.
21   Deconinck-Brossard.
22   Ibid.

Chapter 8: Letters

1   GRO 14/1/2, 1754.
2   Crosby, 'Private Concerts', p. 4.
3   Vickery, *Behind Closed Doors*, pp. 243–4.
4   Fletcher, p. 118.
5   See Vickery, *Behind Closed Doors*, pp. 231–56.
6   In one of his letters, Thomas gives a clue as to the nature of the letter-reading ceremony: 'I will allow of a Sister on either side, to put in her Head & read to herself'.
7   GRO 7/2/15, Some Extracts from the Common Letters of Family Correspondence of the Sharps between 1755 and 1763.
8   GRO 7/2/15, 28 February 1758.
9   Ibid., undated.

10 Ibid., 20 April 1756.

11 Crosby, 'Private Concerts', p. 13.

12 GRO 7/2/15, 23 December 1756.

13 The instrument is described in the Sharp's catalogue of music: 'A Chamber Organ with 3 Compleat Stops, viz, A Diapason throughout; a Flute Treble, & Flute Bass A Fifteenth Treble & Fifteenth Bass – made by Mess. Jordan, Byfield & Bridge.' See Crosby, 'Private Concerts', p. 15. Thomas's phrase '& like a second Amelia fell & bruised her lovely nose' is a reference to Henry Fielding's sentimental novel *Amelia* (1751), in which the eponymous heroine breaks her nose in a carriage accident.

14 Ibid.

15 Ibid.

Chapter 9: Upheaval

1 GRO 14/1/2, 1757.

2 Ibid.

3 Ibid., July 1757.

4 Ibid., 16 March 1758.

5 Crosby, 'Private Concerts', p. 63.

6 GRO 14/1/2, 1754.

7 Ibid., 16 March 1758.

8 Ibid., July 1759.

9 The description is based on a drawing in the Sharp archive, thought to be of William's music room in Mincing Lane. GRO 7/2/15. See also Crosby, 'Private Concerts', pp. 18–19.

Chapter 10: Marriage

1 GRO 14/1/2, 21 July 1759.

2 Ibid., 19 June 1780.

3 GRO 14/1/2, 1750. Elizabeth describes Hosier as a 'Gould Throster'.

4 Although Booth's conveyances 'enjoyed the highest possible repute in the profession' they were 'remarkably prolix'. Booth is said to have drafted George III's will. See J. M. Rigg, 'Booth, James Charles', *ODNB*; GRO 14/1/2, 1748.

5 GRO 14/1/2, 1750.

6 Ibid., August 1767.

7 Thomas Prowse was elected MP for Somerset on six occasions, and in 1761 declined the speakership. The couple were painted by Gainsborough.

8 The Prowses, as befitted their status as members of the landed gentry, lived in the fashionable West End, rather than the City. The family also owned land in Gloucestershire. See Briony McDonagh, '"All towards the improvements of the estate": Mrs Elizabeth Prowse at Wicken (Northamptonshire), 1764–1810' in Hoyle (ed.), p. 266.

9 GRO 14/1/2, 1757.

10 Ibid.

11 It is likely that the sisters met their brothers at the Angel, a popular inn and coaching house just outside London (which gives its name to the Underground station in Islington).

12 GRO 14/1/2, 1758.

13 Ibid., 9 May 1759.

14 Amanda Vickery, *Gentleman's Daughter*, pp. 13, 36.

15 GRO 14/1/2, 1762.

16 Tinniswood, p. 91.

17 Ibid., p. 74.

18 Ibid. The influence of Campbell can be seen in the views of tourists on houses that did not conform with his ideals: by the mid century for example baroque architecture was dismissed as beyond the pale. Hence Horace Walpole's acerbic commentary on Blenheim Palace, which he visited in July 1760, as 'execrable within, without, & almost all around'; on Burke, ibid., p. 84.

19 Ibid. p. 89.

20 Ibid., p. 88.

21 The Double Cube Room is the great centrepiece of Wilton House, created by Inigo Jones and John Webb *c*.1653.

22 Poem attributed to Mrs Knowles, 22 April 1776, GRO 12/1/6. See Amy Harris, p. 61.

Chapter 11: Invention

1 GRO 9/1/4. Chapman had retired.

2 'James Sharp: Common Councillor of London in the Time of Wilkes' in Whiteman et al. (eds), p. 278.

3 See for example, Vickery, *Gentleman's Daughter*, pp. 40–1.

4   GRO 14/1/2.

5   GRO 12/2/8.

6   Ibid., sale particulars, February 1792.

7   William Gladstone: 'Wedgwood was the greatest man who ever, in any age or country, applied himself to the important work of uniting art with industry.'

8   GRO 12/2/1.

9   GRO 12/2/3.

10   Based on the furnishings described in GRO 12/2/8, sale particulars, February 1792.

11   GRO 12/2/1.

12   Overton, p. 8.

13   Ibid., pp. 99, 101, 109–11.

14   See Jones, pp. 118–19.

15   Jonathan Brown, p. 20.

16   Overton, pp. 122–3; Jonathan Brown, pp. 26, 40.

17   The question was asked by George III, in the course of James's audience with the king in October 1770 (GRO 12/2/3).

18   Hoare, I, p. 34. James made the drawings on scraps of paper. Sketches and calculations on the subject of cogs, along with the note 'gone into the City but shall be back again Presently' (presumably left on his desk at the manufactory), are drafted on the reverse side of a piece of paper headed 'Office of Ordnance'. It is possible that Granville – who was an employee of the Board of Ordnance from 1758 – provided his brother with a regular supply of recycled paper from the office. GRO 12/2/5.

19   GRO 12/2/1. In fact nearly all early farm machinery developed as a process of constant adaptation.

20   Ibid., 'NB Books, with Plates and Descriptions of many of the above Articles may be had at the Several Booksellers above referred to. Price in English 3s. in English and French 3s 6d.'

21   Ibid.

Chapter 12: Wicken

1   GRO 13/4/2.

2   GRO 14/1/2, 8 February 1765.

3   William Pitt the Elder was created Earl of Chatham in 1766, the year after the Stowe dinner party. The Younger Pitt (1759–1806) and Grenville

(1759–1834) were first cousins – hence perhaps Elizabeth's 'see most of their family there'. Both boys were five at the time of the Stowe dinner. So it is possible that Elizabeth met the boys before or after dinner.

4   GRO 14/1/2, 1 October 1764.

5   Ibid.

6   McDonagh, p. 270.

7   Ibid., p. 273. A glebe is an area of land within a parish used to support the parish priest.

8   See RIBA Journal, XLVI (1939), p. 536.

9   GRO 14/1/2, 8 February 1765.

10 George and Elizabeth's imaginary interior decoration expeditions are based on Saumarez-Smith, pp. 132–3.

11 McDonagh, p. 270.

12 GRO 14/1/2, 19 September 1766.

13 *The Castle of Otranto* is regarded as the first Gothic novel. It spawned a literary genre.

14 GRO 14/1/2, 12 August 1765.

15 Ibid., 17 November 1766.

16 The Prowses travelled to France in 1763: Elizabeth gives an account of the journey in her diary.

17 Elizabeth does not record the details of her care for her father-in-law in this period. My description is based on her account of previous instances of Thomas Prowse's ill health, when she frequently nursed him during the night, and the warmth and patience of her character generally.

18 GRO 14/1/2, 1 January 1767.

19 Ibid., January–April 1767.

20 Ibid., 25 August 1767.

Chapter 13: Strong

1   Hoare, I, p. 42.

2   Ibid., I, p. 46.

3   A sinecure is 'a position that requires little or no work but yields position or honour' (*OED*).

4   Syriac is a dialect of Middle Aramaic. Along with Latin and Greek, it is thought to have been one of the three most important Christian languages of the early CE. Chaldean Neo-Aramaic originated in the Ninevah Plains and Upper Mesopotamia.

5   Hoare, I, p. 44.

6   Ibid.

7   Ibid., II, p. 357.

8   Granville Sharp MS, 'An Account of the Occasion which compelled Granville Sharp to study Law, and undertake the Defence of Negroe Slaves in England'.

9   Hoare, I, p. 49.

10   Shyllon, p. 19.

11   Hoare, I, p. 49.

12   Jane Austen, *Mansfield Park*, Ch. 21. Austen's third novel was published in 1814, seven years after Parliament abolished the slave trade in the British Empire. However, slavery itself remained legal in the empire until the 1833 Slavery Abolition Act. *Mansfield Park* postdates Granville's encounter with Jonathan Strong by fifty years – during which time, thanks to the efforts of abolitionists, there had been a widespread shift in public opinion against slavery. The 'dead silence' episode, though, remains characteristic of the views of the upper classes more generally in this period.

13   Hochschild, p. 194.

14   Walvin, *Black Ivory*, p. 7.

15   Hochschild, p. 86.

16   Ibid.

17   Christopher Leslie Brown, p. 155. In particular, the British liked to draw a comparison between what they perceived to be their own enlightened rule of the Americas, and the rapacious Spanish conquest of Mexico and Peru. Space constraints prevent anything more than a cursory examination of the issues surrounding Britain and the slave trade in this period.

18   Hochschild, p. 109.

19   Ibid., p. 16; Walvin, *Black Ivory*, pp. 26–31.

20   Hochschild, p. 31.

21   Walvin, *Black Ivory*, p. 16.

22   Hochschild, p. 32, quoting Equiano.

23   Hochschild, pp. 36–7, quoting Equiano.

24   Shyllon, pp. 3–4.

25   See Schama, pp. 31, 33, 411.

26   Hochschild, p. 118, quoting Clarkson, pp. 395–6; Walvin, *The Zong*, p. 43.

27   Shyllon, p. 6.

28   Ibid.
29   Ibid., p. 8.
30   Ibid. p. 9.
31   Ibid.
32   Ibid., p. 19.
33   Granville Sharp MS, 'An Account of the Occasion'.
34   Hoare, I, p. 50.
35   Stephen, p. 539.
36   Hoare, I, p. 50.
37   Shyllon, p. 20; Wise, p. 22.
38   William Smith, *State of the Gaols in London, Westminster, and the Borough of Southwark* (1776), p. 33.
39   Hoare, I, p. 51.
40   Wise, p. 23.
41   Granville Sharp MS, 'An Account of the Occasion'.
42   Hoare, I, p. 53.
43   Granville Sharp MS, 'An Account of the Occasion'.
44   Hoare, I, p. 54.
45   The circumstances of the Joint Opinion were that on 14 January 1729, legal representatives of the powerful 'West Indian' interest approached the senior law officers of the Crown – Attorney General Sir Philip Yorke and Solicitor General Charles Talbot – after dinner in Lincoln's Inn, with a view to clarifying the status of African slaves in Britain.
46   Granville Sharp MS, 'An Account of the Occasion'. Brion Davis (pp. 389, 392) explains that Granville adhered to a 'true law' founded on the maxims of common law and the law of God, which 'often merged in his mind', and which he believed had been 'obscured by centuries of encrustation'.
47   Hoare, I, p. 54.
48   Hoare, I, p. 69.
49   Ibid., p. 70.

Chapter 14: Old Jewry

1   GRO 9/1/4.
2   GRO 9/1/4, James to John, 9 January 1769; GRO 10/1/4 contains a plan of William's house in Old Jewry. In his letter to John, James reports that the 'Grand painted stair case [is] larger than that att St Bartholomews'.

He is referring to the grand staircase at St Bartholomew's Hospital in the City of London, designed by James Gibbs. The walls are painted with murals by William Hogarth.

3   GRO 23/1/6, John Owen (vicar of All Saints, Fulham), *A Discourse Occasioned by the Death of William Sharp Esq.* (1810).

4   Crosby, 'Private Concerts', pp. 32–4, 77.

5   Hoare, I, p. 32. Hoare knew both William and Granville personally.

6   Ibid., I, pp. 30–3.

7   Bynum and Porter (eds), pp. 20–21.

8   Ibid., p. 30.

9   GRO 23/1/16; GRO 10/1/18.

10   Porter (ed.), p. 218.

11   GRO 23/1/16.

12   GRO 10/1/6. Sir Richard Jebb was appointed physician to the king in 1786. The letter is not addressed to William (it begins 'Sir Richard Jebb is desired to come') – and he is not specifically mentioned in it. However, the presence of the letter in the Sharp archive could – conceivably – mean either that the letter was directed to William (i.e. on the outside) or that Jebb being unavailable for some reason, William went in his place. However, Sir Richard Jebb was a physician, rather than a surgeon – and William was not necessarily qualified to treat the king for a condition of this sort. The letter remains something of a mystery.

13   Princess Amelia (1783–1810), the youngest of the royal princesses.

14   There were limited exceptions, for example the care given under certain conditions to inpatients in a handful of London hospitals.

15   St Bartholomew's was run by a governing body of City politicians, merchants and bankers. The hospital was managed by a small steering committee. Lawrence, pp. 45–55.

16   Ibid., p. 57.

17   James Phillips, under whom William had served his apprenticeship in the 1740s, was a surgeon of St Bartholomew's between 1730 and 1749.

18   Lawrence, pp. 58–68.

19   The families were already connected, as Catharine's brother was married to the sister of James's wife (also confusingly called Catharine).

20   GRO 11/1/1.

21   Vickery, *Gentleman's Daughter*, p. 129.

22   GRO 11/1/11.

23   Vickery, *Gentleman's Daughter*, p. 135.

24   Ibid.

25   Ibid., p. 150.
26   GRO 14/1/2.
27   Ibid.

Chapter 15: Kew

1   The first Kew Bridge was opened on 1 June 1759. Its structure, which
     consisted of two stone arches at either end and seven timber arches
     between them, proved costly to maintain, and the bridge survived only
     thirty years.

2   According to James, rowing was the principal form of locomotion for
     the *Apollo*, 'except we are right before the wind with a common square
     sail' (GRO 12/2/1).

3   The aria is from Act 1 of *Agrippina* by Handel. John Crosdill (1751–1825)
     was one of the greatest violoncellists of his age. Redmond Simpson
     (1730–87) was famous for his virtuosity on the hautboy.

4   It was customary for the Prince of Wales to have his own residence,
     and George and Frederick lived in the house in Richmond Gardens
     from about 1765. The name and exact situation of the property is not
     known, but it is thought to have overlooked the river. See Hedley,
     pp. 97–8. They later moved to the Dutch House (now known as Kew
     Palace), possibly in 1773 though the date is uncertain. That the princes
     may already have been resident there in August 1770 is suggested by
     Elizabeth's use of the name 'the Prince of Wailes House', which was
     the name ascribed to the Dutch House in this period. See Hibbert,
     p. 100; Hedley, p. 106.

5   George and his younger brother Frederick were very close as chil-
     dren. The characterisation of William is based on his depiction by
     Zoffany in *Queen Charlotte (1744–1818) with members of her family*
     (c. 1771–2).

6   This description is based on the painting *The Dutch House, Kew* (1771–2)
     by Thomas Sandby. It would later be the princes' home. The Pagoda
     at Kew, designed by Sir William Chambers, was completed in 1762 as
     a gift for Princess Augusta, the founder of the gardens.

7   Originally a folk song, 'The Miller of Dee' was one of the most
     popular numbers in Thomas Arne's 1762 hit ballad-opera *Love in a
     Village*.

8 GRO 14/1/2, 5 August 1770.

9 Elizabeth reports that the owners of the accompanying boats 'had provided themselves with provition' (GRO 14/1/2).

10 GRO 14/1/2, 8 August 1770.

11 Charlotte had two brothers, Prince Charles and Prince Ernest, of whom one was the 'Prince of Mecklinbourg' referred to in Elizabeth's diary entry. It is known that both brothers were present in England in August 1771, the year after the Sharp water parties, when Zoffany painted them with their sister. See Postle (ed.), pp. 210–11. Elizabeth's description (a 'Bench under a large Tree' on the banks of the Thames) closely resembles the setting of the painting, and may refer to the same location. See Webster, *Johan Zoffany, RA, 1733–1810*, pp. 235–6.

12 GRO 14/1/2, 8 August 1770.

13 Ibid.

14 Ibid.

15 See McVeigh, 'Felice Giardini', pp. 162–72.

16 Hoare, Appendix, xii–xiii.

17 GRO 14/1/2.

Chapter 16: Canals

1 The description is based on *Richmond Lodge* (*c.*1770), a watercolour by Thomas Sandy, and on GRO 12/2/3, Transcript of audience with George III, 15 September 1770. Situated in the Old Deer Park, about 200 yards west of the newly built King's Observatory, Richmond Lodge was formerly a hunting lodge, before it came into the possession of the Hanoverian dynasty in the early 1700s. It was demolished in 1772. George III was keenly interested in a range of subjects that included agriculture, astronomy, scientific instruments and literature.

2 GRO 12/2/3, Transcript of audience with George III, 15 September 1770, p. 1.

3 GRO 14/1/2, 3 November 1770.

4 In her account of the concerts, Elizabeth notes: 'I think this was the first notis taken of us in Passing Richmond Gardens, by the Royal Family.'

5 Some of the credit for the coup of James's audiences with George III is due to the king himself. George was exemplary in his willingness to

make himself accessible to members of the public, and rarely refused a request for a private audience.

6   GRO 12/2/3, Transcript of audience with George III, 15 September 1770, pp. 16, 17.

7   GRO 12/2/3, Transcript of audience with George III, 27 October 1770, pp. 31–2.

8   Brooke, p. 302.

9   Ibid. The king played several instruments including the flute, harpsichord and pianoforte. George and Charlotte each had their own bands, some of whose members (including the queen's music master Johann Christian Bach) also performed at the Sharps' concerts at the Old Jewry and on the *Apollo*.

10   GRO 12/2/3, Transcript of audience with George III, 15 September 1770, pp. 15–16.

11   Ibid., pp. 12–13.

12   GRO 12/2/3, Transcript of audience with George III, 27 October 1770, pp. 29–30. In response to further questioning, James described the house as being 'ten feet long when shut up, and when drawn out double that length or any length between'.

13   GRO 12/2/3, Transcript of audience with George III, 15 September 1770, pp. 1, 6.

14   Prior to the construction of the Trent & Mersey Canal for example, the raw materials required by Josiah Wedgwood for his works at Burslem came by sea from Cornwall and Devon to the Mersey, then by barge up the Weaver to Winsford Bridge, and finally by pack horse to the potteries. See Hadfield, *British Canals*, p. 81.

15   Baron F. Duckham, 'Canals and River Navigation' in Aldcroft and Freeman (eds), p. 128.

16   Ibid., p. 131.

17   Compton, pp. 12–13, quoting Anon, *History of Inland Navigation* (1769). The construction of a canal led to an immediate and precipitate fall in the cost of coal to local markets. The urban poor would undoubtedly have been 'colder, hungrier, worst clad and more poorly housed if canals had not been created'. (Aldcroft and Freeman [eds], p. 132.)

18   The Trent & Mersey, which ran from the River Trent at Derwent Mouth in Derbyshire to the River Mersey, was completed in May 1777; the Stafford & Worcestershire, which ran from the Trent & Mersey at Great Haywood to the Severn at Stourport, opened in May 1772; the Coventry,

which ran from Coventry to the Trent & Mersey north of Lichfield, opened in stages from 1769; and the Oxford, from Oxford to the Coventry Canal at Bedworth, opened in stages from 1774.

19   Hadfield, *British Canals*, pp. 46–7; Aldcroft and Freeman (eds), pp. 109–10.

20   Hadfield, *British Canals*, pp. 46–7 quoting from Eliza Meteyard, *Life of Josiah Wedgwood* (1866).

21   *A Six Months' Tour through the North of England* was published in 1770. James explains that he extracted from the book, for the purposes of his own publication, 'so much as related' to the Bridgewater Canal.

22   Carne's cutting machine was used on a number of canals, including the Herefordshire & Gloucestershire. According to an advertisement for the machine, 'By this admirable contrivance the labour of removing the earth, which used to require a great number of hands with wheel barrows, is performed with much more expedition by a man and a horse.' See Hadfield, *British Canals*, p. 39.

23   James manufactured wheelbarrows specifically designed for canal construction. See Chapter 11, 'Invention'.

24   GRO 12/2/2, Address to the Common Council, December 1773.

25   GRO 12/2/3, Transcript of audience with George III, 15 September 1770, p. 16.

26   Ibid., p. 18.

27   Ibid., p. 1; James Brindley – the son of a Derbyshire crofter, and a former millwright who was employed by the Duke of Bridgewater to build the Worsley Canal, and later masterminded the construction of the Trent & Mersey, the Stafford & Worcester, the Oxford and the Coventry – was the outstanding engineer of his age. James Sharp described Brindley as 'the greatest natural Mechanick, perhaps, that was ever yet born' (GRO 12/2/2, Address to the Common Council, December 1773). GRO 12/2/3, Transcript of audience with George III, 15 September 1770, p. 16.

28   Ibid., pp. 1–2.

29   Hadfield, *Canals of South and South-East England*, p. 190.

30   Ibid., p. 192.

31   GRO 12/2/3, Transcript of audience with George III, 15 September 1770, p. 10.

32   GRO 12/2/2, Address to the Common Council, December 1773, p. 2.

33   Ibid., p. 4.

34   GRO 12/2/3, Appendix dated 29 January 1774.

35   GRO 12/2/2, Address to the Common Council, December 1773, p. 1.

36   GRO 12/2/3, Transcript of audience with George III, 27 October 1770, p. 25.
37   Ibid.
38   GRO 12/2/2, Address to the Common Council, December 1773, p. 1.
39   Aldcroft and Freeman (eds), p. 131.

Chapter 17: Radical

1   The description of the Presence Chamber is based on an aquatint by Thomas Sutherland (1785–1838) in Pyne, Vol. 3, plate 71. For George III's appearance, see for example Brooke, p. 288.
2   The speech is cited in full in John Noorthouck, *A New History of London including Westminster and Southwark* (1773), Book 1, Chapter 26.
3   See 'James Sharp: Common Councillor of London in the Time of Wilkes' in Whiteman et al. (eds), p. 286.
4   Ibid., pp. 283–5.
5   Peter D. G. Thomas, 'Wilkes, John (1725–1797)', *ODNB*.
6   'James Sharp: Common Councillor of London in the Time of Wilkes' in Whiteman et al. (eds), p. 285.
7   Ibid., p. 286.
8   Noorthouck.
9   GRO 14/1/2, 13 November 1770 .

Chapter 18: Absence

1   Ovenden.
2   Ibid.
3   GRO 7/2/15.
4   Crosby, 'Private Concerts', pp. 27–9. The King's Arms – formerly known as the Swan – was one of the two principal amateur music societies operating in the City in this period (see Chapter 6, 'Music').
5   Ibid., p. 75.
6   Ibid., pp. 4, 10.
7   See GRO 14/1/1; Crosby, 'Private Concerts', p. 4; Ovenden.
8   See the *Journal of St Bartholomew's Hospital, 1757–1770*.
9   GRO 12/2/5.

10   GRO 16/1/1, John to Judith, 14 May 1770.

11   Shuler, pp. 61–2. The figures date from 1736, but are unlikely to have altered significantly.

12   Although Elizabeth refers to Catharine as Mr Stevenson's 'daughter in Law', the evidence suggests that she was in fact his stepdaughter.

13   Catharine would receive 4% of the value of the bond as an annual income; GRO 14/1/2.

14   Ibid.

15   Ibid., 8 March 1771.

16   Ibid., 17 October 1771.

17   Ibid., 14/1/2.

18   GRO 16/1/1, 10 April 1761.

19   GRO 9/1/4, 2 February 1761.

20   Ibid., 6 December 1760.

Chapter 19: Children

1   GRO 14/1/2.

2   As we learn in Chapter 26, Jonathan Jackman was an elderly gardener who had worked at Wicken Park for nearly six decades.

3   GRO 14/1/2, 10 June 1769.

4   Fletcher, p. 61.

5   Vickery, *Gentleman's Daughter*, pp. 117–22; Fletcher, pp. 57–61.

6   Vickery, *Gentleman's Daughter*, pp. 117–22.

7   Pollock, *Forgotten Children*, pp. 129–30.

8   GRO 8/1/1, 25 May 1728. Grace died on 21 May 1728, a month after her second birthday.

9   Vickery, *Gentleman's Daughter*, p. 125.

10   Pollock, *Forgotten Children*, p. 139, quoting *The Remains of the Late Mrs Richard Trench* (1862), pp. 199, 201.

11   GRO 14/1/2.

12   Williams, p. 32.

13   Ibid.

14   Ibid., p. 24.

15   Ibid., p. 53. A similar procedure was practised in the village of Marloes in Pembrokeshire, where in the early eighteenth century the going rate for 'buying the smallpox' was threepence for the juice of twelve blisters.

16 Lady Mary's brother had died from smallpox and she herself bore the scars of the disease. Her interest in variolation appears to have been piqued when she noticed the absence of scarring amongst her Turkish acquaintances.

17 Williams, p. 138.

18 GRO 14/1/2.

19 Ibid., 14 October 1767.

20 Letters and journals from the period suggest the agony of the choice, with some like Benjamin Franklin tormented by their decision not to inoculate a child who later died from a natural incidence of smallpox.

Chapter 20: Somerset

1 My depiction of the court and Westminster Hall are indebted to Steven Wise's vivid descriptions in *Though the Heavens May Fall*.

2 Hoare, I, p. 61.

3 Steven Wise argues that it is 'unlikely' that the *Representation* had any intimidatory effect on Kerr's lawyers. See Wise, p. 57.

4 Shyllon, p. 39.

5 Hoare, I, p. 62.

6 Ibid.

7 Granville Sharp, *A Representation of the Injustice and Dangerous Tendency of Tolerating Slavery; or of Admitting the Least Claim of Private Property in the Persons of Men, in England*, p. 15.

8 Ibid., p. 12.

9 Ibid., pp. 37, 39.

10 Ibid., p. 79.

11 Ibid., pp. 104–5.

12 She was later to be a guest of Elizabeth's at Wicken Park (GRO 14/1/2, 10 July 1771) while her daughter, 'Miss Banks', had previously attended a Sharp water party (GRO 9/1/4). Sir Joseph himself was on friendly terms with the Sharps; see GRO 13/1/B3, Joseph Banks to Granville, 15 October 1777.

13 Shyllon, pp. 43–4; Wise, p. 60.

14 Shyllon, pp. 45–6.

15 James Oldham, 'Murray, William, 1st earl of Mansfield (1705–1793)', *ODNB*.

16 Wise, p. 74.

17   Shyllon, p. 50.

18   Oldham, p. 9. For a full account of Mansfield's life and career see Poser.

19   At the time of the Lewis trial, Dunning was both a leading barrister and Solicitor General in the Lord North administration.

20   In conversation with Sir Joshua Reynolds in later life, Dunning compared the experience of Mansfield's oratory with that of a painter seeing 'the finest painting by Titian or Raffaele', describing how 'Sometimes when we were leaving the court, we would hear the cry, "Murray is up" and forthwith we rushed back, as if to a play or other entertainment.' See Wise, p. 66.

21   On 6 April 1780, in the greatest triumph of his political career, Dunning carried his famous resolution 'that the influence of the crown has increased, is increasing, and ought to be diminished.' See William Cobbett, *The Parliamentary History of England*, Vol. 16 (1770), p. 898.

22   Polson.

23   Oldham.

24   The description is based on various well-known images of eighteenth-century London coffee houses, for example *Interior of a London coffee-house* (c.1690–1700) in the British Museum collection, and *A Mad Dog in a Coffeehouse* (c.1800) by Thomas Rowlandson.

25   Wise, p. 85.

26   *The Case of Lewis v Stapleton, His Master* (1771) in the archives of the New York Historical Society.

27   Lewis was born on the Gold Coast, where he was captured by a Spanish privateer and carried to Savannah, before working as a waiter in Cuba, and as a servant to a wine merchant in New York, before travelling to Jamaica, back to New York, and from there to England. Wise, pp. 89–91.

28   Shyllon, p. 53.

29   In the 1779 insurance case *Milles* v. *Fletcher*. See Oldham, p. 9.

30   *Lewis v Stapleton*.

31   Ibid.

32   Shyllon, p. 125.

33   Ibid.

34   Ibid.

35   'His exertions on a point of so deep and important an interest had begun not only to awaken the sympathy, but to attract the aid, of men of enlightened minds' (Hoare, I, p. 107).

36   The most senior of the counsel representing the claimant, and the first to be appointed, 'Bull' Davy had turned to law after his first career as

a druggist in Exeter had ended in imprisonment for bankruptcy. At the bar he developed a reputation as one of the few leading counsel able to joust with Lord Mansfield on terms of near equality. After his successful attack on the validity of general warrants in the John Wilkes litigation of the 1760s, Glynn became the counsel of choice for causes of a radical complexion, and also became involved in politics in his own right. The Somerset trial made Francis Hargrave's reputation, which he later enhanced with the publication of eleven volumes of state trials dating from the reign of Henry IV. James Mansfield acted as legal advisor to John Wilkes following his return to Britain in 1768. He was not related to Lord Mansfield.

37   In the margin of a page of the transcript of the Lewis trial, which records Dunning's thunderous declaration of the right to argue that slavery could not exist in England, Granville scrawled: 'When Mr Dunning spoke these word[s] he held in his hand G Sharp's Book on the illegality of tolerating slavery in England [printed in 1769], having one finger in the book to hold open a particular part: and after so solemn a declaration he appeared on the opposite side of the question against James Somerset the very next year. This is an abominable & insufferable practice of lawyers to undertake causes diametrically opposite to their own decided opinions of Law and Common Justice!!!' See Shyllon, p. 128.

38   The rule, which is currently set out in rC29 of the *Bar Standards Board Handbook*, was almost certainly recognised by the time of the Somerset trial. See Andrew Watson, 'Advocacy for the unpopular: The barristers' cab-rank rule in England and Wales, past, present and future', *Justice of the Peace*, Vol. 162, No. 25/26 (1998), 476–80, 499.

39   In a letter to a friend in America, dated 15 June 1772, Stewart described Dunning's performance as 'dull and languid', and that he 'would have made a much better figure on [Somerset's] side'.

40   *General Evening Post*, 13 June 1772; *Gazeteer*, 13 and 20 May 1772.

41   The roof was built in the fourteenth century, and is the largest medieval timber roof in northern Europe.

42   The Somerset hearing took place over six days, which did not follow consecutively but ranged over a period of five months. Though the delay is often blamed on Lord Mansfield's prevarication, the main cause of the various adjournments was the court's acknowledgement of the significance of the case, and its willingness to hear extended argument by counsel.

43 Wise, p. 125.

44 Ibid.

45 Yorke (ed.), p. 234.

46 Shyllon, p. 91.

47 Ibid., p. 92.

48 Wise, p. 143.

49 Ibid; Shyllon, p. 93.

50 Shyllon, p. 95.

51 Hoare, I, p. 135.

52 *Morning Chronicle*, 15 May 1772.

53 Wise, pp. 156–9.

54 Ibid., pp. 158–9.

55 Ibid.

56 Ibid., p. 170.

57 Ibid., p. 173.

58 There are various versions of the judgement. This is taken from the account which appears as an appendix to Granville's 1776 tract *The Just Limitation of Slavery in the Laws of God, compared with the Unbounded Claims of the African Traders and British American Slaveholders*, and which is identical to the reports of the judgement that appeared in the press in the days after the hearing.

59 *London Chronicle*, 22 June 1777; *London Packet*, 26 June 1772. See Shyllon, p. 110; Schama, pp. 60–1. Schama's account of the Somerset trial is at pp. 51–63.

60 Shyllon, p. 176.

61 29 August 1779, quoted in ibid., p. 165.

62 *Morning Chronicle*, 27 June 1772.

63 Shyllon, p. 136.

64 Space constraints prevent an adequate account of the impact of the trial on America. For a fuller account, see Wise.

65 Clarkson, pp. 66–7.

66 Hoare, II, p. 233.

Chapter 21: Welfare State

1 'De primo Saxonum adventu' quoted in Victoria County History, *Northumberland*, Vol. I, 'Bamburgh'.

2 John to John Ramsay, *Gentleman's Magazine*, 1793.

3   Lord Crewe named five trustees, all of whom were clergymen, and
     specified that future trustees should always hold a clerical position.

4   Stranks, pp. 9–10.

5   Ibid., p. 12.

6   NRO 452/J/36, Memorandum Book No. 81.

7   His work has since been criticised for its architectural infelicities. John
     defended himself by claiming that he had 'endeavoured to repair the
     Ruins as much in the Old Form and Style as I well could consistent
     with the Uses they were intended for' (Durham Palace Green Library
     Add MS 1014, John to Edward King, 4 March 1786). Pevsner's generous
     conclusion is that 'the pioneering social adventurousness' of the char-
     ities housed at Bamburgh 'outshone the rather ordinary architectural
     endeavours which went with them'. See Pevsner, p. 156.

8   Stranks, p. 10. Trustees were resident in the castle for certain periods
     of the year.

9   John to John Ramsay, *Gentleman's Magazine*, 1793.

10   Deborah Simonton, 'Women and Education' in Barker and Chalus (eds),
     p. 41.

11   NRO 452/J/36, Memorandum Book No. 81.

12   Ibid., 3 September 1762.

13   NRO 452/D/8/4/8/4, 'An Account of the Uses to which the Old Roman
     Tower in Bambrough Castle is at present appropriated' (undated, c.1780).

14   Ibid.

15   Ibid.

16   Griffiths, p. 76.

17   NRO 452/D/8/4/8/4, 'An Account of the Uses'.

18   NRO 452/D/8/4/8/16.

19   Parson and White, under 'Chatton'.

20   NRO 452/J/36, Memorandum Book No. 81.

21   NRO 452/D/8/4/8/4, 'An Account of the Uses'.

22   NRO 452/C/3/2/12/57, George Hall to John, 7 December 1782.

23   NRO 452/C/3/2/13/13, Ralph Dods to John, 24 February 1783.

24   NRO 452/D/8/4/8/4, 'An Account of the Uses'.

25   NRO 452/C/3/2/13/13, Ralph Dods to John, 24 February 1783.

26   NRO 452/D/8/4/8/4, 'An Account of the Uses'.

27   NRO 452/C/3/2/13/13, Ralph Dods to John, 24 February 1783.

28   NRO 452/D/8/4/8/4, 'An Account of the Uses'.

29   John to John Ramsay, *Gentleman's Magazine*, 1793

30   NRO 452/C/3/2/13/2.

31   NRO 452/C/3/2/13/47.

32   NRO 452/C/3/2/13/52.

33   NRO 452/J/36, Memorandum Book No. 81.

34   Ibid.

35   NRO 452/C/3/2/14/54. There is a similar report on 26 December 1785: 'Last Night being very stormy I sett out a patrole. Nedd Todd + John Carr at Beadnell Square they mett with a vessel in Great distress' (NRO 452/C/3/2/15/56).

36   NRO 452/C/3/2/10/26. On 3 June 1780, for example, Hall reported that 'yesterday we had 4 hours thick fog and 17 guns were fired all of the twopounder'.

37   NRO 452/J/36, Memorandum Book No. 81.

38   NRO 452/D/8/4/8/4, 'An Account of the Uses'.

39   NRO 452/C/3/2/67.

40   NRO 452/C/3/2/14/24.

41   NRO 452/J/36, Memorandum Book No. 81; NRO 452/D/8/4/8/4, 'An Account of the Uses'.

42   NRO 452/C/3/2/67.

43   NRO 452/C/3/2/13/12.

44   Through his emissary Henry Oxenden. In a letter from Oxenden to John dated 8 September 1788, he recounts his attendance at Lukin's workshop, and encloses a letter from Lukin to John.

45   Patent 1502, completed 1 December 1785.

46   NRO 452/C/3/2/13/2.

47   John to John Ramsay, *Gentleman's Magazine*, 1793.

48   NRO 452/J/36, Memorandum Book No. 81.

49   Ibid.

50   Ibid.

51   Ibid.

52   NRO 452/D/8/4/8/4, 'An Account of the Uses'.

53   George, p. 51.

54   Alun Withey, 'Medicine and Charity in Eighteenth-Century Northumberland: The Early Years of the Bamburgh Castle Dispensary and Surgery, c.1772–1802', *Social History of Medicine*, Vol. 29, No. 3, p. 469.

55   Ibid., pp. 468–70.

56   NRO 452/D/8/4/8/4, 'An Account of the Uses'.

57   NRO 452/C/3/2/17/6.

58   Ibid., Cockagne to John, 14 February 1787.

59   NRO 452/D/8/4/8/4, 'An Account of the Uses'.

60   Ibid.

61   Ibid.

62   Withey, p. 485.

63   Withey, p. 484, quoting NRO 452/D/5/2/1/1/65.

64   NRO 452/C/3/2/15/77.

65   NRO 452/D/8/4/8/4, 'An Account of the Uses'.

66   Withey, p. 482.

67   Ibid., p. 480 (the figures for Bamburgh relate to the slightly different period of March 1777 to March 1790).

68   GRO 24/1/2, 28 August 1799.

69   GRO 16/1/1, c.1770.

70   GRO 14/1/2, 26 January 1798.

71   NRO 452/C/3/2/12/54.

72   NRO 452/J/36, Memorandum Book No. 81, 29 July 1761. Perhaps this contributed to his indebtedness.

73   GRO 16/1/1. John to Judith, 14 May 1770.

74   NRO 452/C/3/2/5/51.

75   Withey, p. 475.

76   Ibid., p. 476.

77   Granville would have been very familiar with this building – the Board of Ordnance, where he worked, was based in the White Tower.

78   In his 'Account of the Uses', John is at pains to record that the 'best human precautions' have been applied to the safety of the castle inhabitants, with '15 Rooms out of 25' fireproofed, and a 'conductor with one Gold Point and 32 Iron Points' fitted with a view to safeguarding 'both the Castle and the Town of Bambrough from the effects of lightning' (NRO 452/D/8/4/8).

79   GRO 16/1/1, John to Judith, 14 May 1770. John also contributed his own funds to the castle charities. A memorandum dating from 1776 suggests that he and his brother Thomas together paid £1,030 towards the repairs to the castle, but family tradition suggests that John's overall contribution was as much as £10,000.

80   GRO 9/1/10 (lines from 'Bamborough Castle', a poem by John Ramsay. The original, in Latin, and an English translation on the reverse side of the page, is included in a bundle of letters and poetry sent by Ramsay to John, in the family archive in Gloucester).

81   GRO 16/1/1, 14 May 1770.

82   The bequest included 'the most valuable part' of the book collection
     of his grandfather, John Sharp (GRO 9/1/12). 'The Charities of
     Nathaniel Lord Crewe, Bishop of Durham, and Dr Sharp: Report of
     Mr Martin (D & C Office)'. For an account of the charities after 1792,
     see Stranks, pp. 18–24.

Chapter 22: Canal Voyage

1   See, for example, Hadfield, *Canals of the West Midlands*, p. 51. With
     reference to the Staffordshire and Worcestershire Canal: 'In August 1774,
     what was probably the first pleasure voyage on the canal was made by
     James Sharp's family of eight brothers and sisters, and a niece.'

2   GRO 14/1/2.

3   Ibid.

4   GRO 12/2/3, Transcript of audience with George III, 15 September
     1770.

5   GRO 12/1/11. The handwritten catalogue, titled 'Fleet of Boats belonging
     to 3 Brothers William, James & Granville Sharp', is almost certainly
     written by James's daughter Kitty. It appears to provide a key to a
     painting of the family flotilla still in the possession of the family, though
     Kitty does not explicitly say this.

6   GRO 12/1/4 and 12/1/6, 'Extract of a Letter from Bransdon, near
     Daventry, August 15' published in the *London Packet*, 19 August 1774.

7   GRO 12/1/1.

8   GRO 12/1/4 and 12/1/6, 'Extract of a Letter from Bransdon, near
     Daventry, August 15' published in the *London Packet*, 19 August 1774.

9   The engineer James Brindley had built this northerly section of the
     canal so that it followed the contours of the landscape, taking forty-
     four miles to cover a distance of sixteen as the crow flies. Facing
     the threat of a rival waterway in the early nineteenth century, the
     Oxford Company created a new route that cut eleven miles off the
     journey.

10   The Brinklow aqueduct cost an astonishing £112,000, and consisted of
     twelve arches connecting a 600-feet embankment at one end and a
     400-feet embankment at the other. See Compton, p. 21.

11   See Hadfield, *British Canals*, p. 85.

12   GRO 14/1/2, 19 August 1774.

13   This was the name given by Arnold Bennett to the towns making up the
      Potteries in his novels. Though in reality there were six 'Potteries' towns
      – Hanley, Burslem, Fenton, Longton, Tunstall and Stoke-upon-Trent.
14   Uglow, p. 87.
15   It is not known whether they bought the tea set in advance of the
      voyage, or at Etruria itself.
16   William Gladstone, 1863.
17   GRO 14/1/2, 20 August 1774
18   James's daughter Kitty later claimed that the Sharps 'were amongst the
      first to go through the Tonnel under Hare Castle Hill' (GRO 12/2/2).
      The tunnel was completed in 1777.
19   GRO 14/1/2, 23 August 1774.
20   Ibid., 26 August 1774.
21   Ibid., pp. 67, 68.
22   Ibid., p. 211.
23   GRO 14/1/2. 28 August 1774.
24   James Stuart based his design for the Doric temple on the Temple of
      Hephaistos in Athens. It was one of the first accurate Greek reproduc-
      tion buildings in the country. The Tower of the Winds was based on
      the Horologium of Andronikos, also in Athens. The cascade was washed
      away by a flood in 1795. The Ruin was composed from parts of the
      original manor house, and included a Gothic pigeon house. The design
      for the Chinese house was drawn from sketches made in Canton by
      Sir Percy Brett, who accompanied Thomas Anson's brother, Admiral
      Anson, during his circumnavigation of the globe. It is one of the earliest
      examples of oriental design in the country.
25   GRO 13/4/2, Extracts from Memorandum Book No. 1. Characteristically,
      Granville's account of the canal voyage is for the most part a record
      of the family's aristocratic engagements (e.g. 'Dined at Lord Dudley's').
26   GRO 14/1/2, 30 August 1774.

Chapter 23: America

1   GRO 13/4/2, Extracts from Memorandum Book No. 1, 28 July 1775. In
      March 1764, Granville had been made a 'clerk in ordinary' in the
      Minuting Branch of the Board of Ordnance. In January 1774 he succeeded
      to the place of 'second clerk' and acted as assistant to the secretary,
      John Boddington. See Hoare, I, p. 184.

2   'The Trumpet Shall Sound' from Handel's *Messiah* appears to have been a Sharp favourite, played for example in an Old Jewry concert on 13 March 1774. See Crosby, 'Private Concerts', p. 37.

3   As Granville makes clear in his memorandum entry, there were several letters requesting munitions.

4   Dickinson (ed.), p. 4.

5   Keith Mason, 'Britain and the Administration of the American Colonies' in Dickinson (ed.), p. 22.

6   Ibid., pp. 29–30.

7   Ibid., p. 35.

8   John Derry, 'Government Policy and the American Crisis 1760–1776' in Dickinson (ed.), pp. 49–52.

9   Ibid., pp. 56–9. The 1773 Tea Act permitted the East India Company to transport tea direct to America without paying English tea duty. The policy was conceived as a means of bolstering the fortunes of the East India Company, but it also had the effect of reducing the price of tea to American consumers. For this reason, the British government maintained that it would benefit the colonists.

10   Christopher Leslie Brown, p. 161.

11   Hoare, I, p. 257; Christopher Leslie Brown, p. 162; GRO 13/1/R4, Granville to the Duke of Richmond, 11 December 1777.

12   Christopher Leslie Brown, pp. 142–3. See Chapter 20, 'Somerset'.

13   As Hoare put it, though 'strangers, and far distance from one another', Benezet and Granville 'were alike earnestly labouring in the same benevolent attempt' (I, p. 143).

14   Christopher Leslie Brown, p. 165. Granville maintained the highest respect for the North American Quaker abolitionists, whose own anti-slavery activities predated his own by several decades.

15   Ibid., p. 154.

16   Ibid., p. 176.

17   Hoare, I, pp. 184–5.

18   Ibid.

19   GRO 13/4/2, Extracts from Memorandum Book No. 1.

20   Ibid.

21   'A Proclamation for Suppressing Rebellion and Sedition' was George III's response to the Battle of Bunker Hill. It declared the colonies to be in 'open and avowed rebellion'.

22   Hoare, I, pp. 185–6. An original draft of the letter at GRO 13/1/C18 has the relevant passage crossed out.

23 Ibid., I, pp. 189–90.

24 GRO 13/1/B27, John Boddington to Granville, 4 October 1775.

25 GRO 13/1/C18, Granville to Sir Charles Cocks (draft), 21 March 1776.

26 Hoare, I, p. 188.

27 Omai (his real name was Ma'i) was introduced into society by the naturalist Sir Joseph Banks, and met many of the well-known figures of the period including Lord Sandwich, Frances Burney and Samuel Johnson. Sir Joshua Reynolds's *Portrait of Omai* was painted in 1776, around the time that Omai received his English lessons from Granville. Omai stayed in England for three years before returning to Huahine in August 1777.

28 See Chapter 17, 'Radical'.

29 Christopher Leslie Brown, pp. 161–2.

30 John Cartwright, a military officer who had himself refused to fight in the American conflict, held Granville's conduct in particularly high regard. Cartwright and Granville joined forces to campaign against the wartime suspension of habeas corpus rights. See Christopher Leslie Brown, pp. 188, 190.

Chapter 24: Union

1 The description is based on *Windsor Castle from Eton Bank* (1801) by Paul Sandby; and also an image of the *Union* in a painting of the Sharp flotilla dating from about 1780, which is still in the collection of the family, and on drawings of the yacht in the Sharp archive.

2 GRO 12/1/10, 'Particulars and Conditions of Sale relating to the sale by auction of the *Union*, by Mr Christie, at his Great Room in Pall Mall, on Thursday, September 7, 1786', p. 1.

3 Ibid., p. 2. A comparison of the *Apollo* and the *Union* shows that whereas the *Union* was purpose-built with a deck over a row of cabins, the *Apollo* was a barge with a free-standing 'house'.

4 Ibid., pp 1–3.

5 Ibid., p. 3.

6 In GRO 12/2/7, 'Complete Plan of the Union Yacht', this is referred to as the 'Great Cabin'; *Morning Post* report quoted in Crosby, 'Private Concerts', p. 52.

7 GRO 12/2/7, 'Complete Plan of the Union Yacht'. Kitty appears to have written her pencil notes onto a much earlier plan of the *Union*.

8   GRO 12/1/10, 'Particulars and Conditions of Sale', p. 3.

9   Ibid.

10   Ibid.

11   GRO 12/2/7, 'Complete Plan of the *Union* Yacht'.

12   GRO 12/1/10, 'Particulars and Conditions of Sale', p. 3. Servants could
     be summoned to the cabins by application of 'bells and pulls'.

13   GRO 12/1/11, 'Fleet of Boats belong [*sic*] to the 3 Brothers William
     James & Granville Sharp'; this document, created by Kitty, appears to
     be a key to the painting of the Sharp flotilla still in the possession of
     the family.

14   GRO 12/2/7, 'Complete Plan of the *Union* Yacht'.

15   GRO 12/1/10, 'Particulars and Conditions of Sale', p. 2.

16   Apart from the *Union* and the *Apollo*, the only other vessel of any size
     in the painting is the *Proah*, which Kitty describes in her commentary
     on the painting as a 'double Keeled pleasure Barge'. The painting also
     shows five smaller boats which Catharine refers to as 'The *Challop*, or
     Jemima'; a 'Smaller Boat of the same kind the *Catharine*'; a 'Canoe the
     Mary'; 'the Yawl'; and 'the *Peter* Boat for Fishing'.

17   GRO 12/2/7. There are also sketches of a griffin, which can be seen
     indistinctly on the prow in the painting of the *Union*, and other deco-
     rative features such as a large parasol which were not included in the
     final design.

18   *Public Advertiser*, 9 September 1786.

19   GRO 12/1/10, 'Particulars and Conditions of Sale'.

20   GRO 12/1/8, Frances to Judith, 30 August 1777. Frances began her letter
     on this date, but as the events she describes include those of 1 September
     1777, she must have continued writing it in the days that followed.

21   GRO 12/1/9.

22   GRO 12/1/8.

23   Ibid.

24   GRO 12/2/7, sleeping accommodation described by Kitty.

25   Frances reports that the royal party 'went to the old place where we
     had music for an hour & half'. While Granville and Elizabeth refer to
     the location of the concert as 'the Queen's Oak', the allusion in all
     three cases is to the 'Bench under a large Tree' where the royal party
     sat to listen to Giardini's band on the *Apollo* in August 1770.

26   GRO 12/1/8, Frances to Judith, 30 August 1777.

27   Ibid.

28   Ibid.

29 Ibid.

30 GRO 12/1/9, 'Miss How, with her Umbrella in the rain, who went to her seat & sat some time whilst we played.'

31 GRO 12/1/8, Frances to Judith, 30 August 1777.

32 Frances does not mention it, but their new-found friend had another famous sibling: General Sir William Howe, head of the land forces in America. Both brothers had earlier joined a commission to attempt a reconciliation with the colonists.

33 GRO 12/1/9.

34 Ibid.

35 Ibid.

36 Ibid.

37 Lady Holland was the widow of Stephen Fox, the 2nd Baron Holland (1745–74). His younger brother was Charles James Fox (1749–1806). The Sharps would have approved of Charles's support for the American patriots, and abolitionist sympathies, but less so his private life.

38 GRO 12/1/9.

39 GRO 12/1/8.

40 GRO 12/1/9.

41 Ibid.

42 Ibid.

43 Ibid.

44 Ibid. Prince Henry, the Duke of Cumberland and Strathearn (1745–1790), was a younger brother of George III.

45 GRO 12/1/4, 10 September 1777.

46 GRO 14/1/2, 8 September 1777. First held in 1734, the Egham races became increasingly popular during the course of the eighteenth century. A coach service leaving from New Inn in the Old Bailey at 8 a.m. brought racegoers to Egham in time for the first race.

47 GRO 14/1/9.

48 Ibid.

49 The gardens of Garrick's villa at Hampton stretched down to the Thames. As the *Union* neared Hampton, Garrick's 'Temple to Shakespeare', which he erected in 1756, would have come into sight. See Zoffany's *David Garrick and his Wife by his Temple to Shakespeare at Hampton* (1762).

50 See Zoffany's *Garrick's Nieces in the Garden at Hampton* (1762).

51 GRO 14/1/9. The *Union* was moored 'by the City Navigation Barge'.

52 GRO 14/1/2.

53 GRO 12/1/4, 10 September 1777.

54 GRO 13/4/2, 22 August 1778.

Chapter 25: Elizabeth

1 GRO 12/1/4, *General Evening Post*, 4 October 1777. The letter is dated 2 October 1777.

2 Though the Northamptonshire gentleman refers to the player of the hautboy only as Mr S—n, it is almost certain that he is referring to Redmond Simpson.

3 The descriptions of the Harvest Home and *fête champêtre* are closely based on the account given by the Northamptonshire gentleman in his letter.

4 GRO 12/1/4, *General Evening Post*, 4 October 1777.

5 McDonagh, in Hoyle (ed.), p. 267.

6 Sir John Mordaunt, 7th Baronet (1734–1806). Groom of the Bedchamber from 1763–93 and MP for Warwickshire from 1793–1802. The family lived at Walton Hall in Warwickshire.

7 GRO 14/1/2 17 September 1778.

8 The three surviving volumes cover the periods 1768–71 and 1774–84.

9 NoRO, 364p/68, fo. 10. The ledgers record personal, household and estate expenditure. See McDonagh in Hoyle (ed.), p. 268.

10 Enclosure was a controversial measure as it deprived the poor of common rights. McDonagh argues that Elizabeth disapproved of some of the measures introduced by her predecessors, and that her social welfare activities were partially inspired by a sense of guilt. See McDonagh in Hoyle (ed.), pp. 278–9, 287.

11 NoRO, 364p/68, fo. 207.

12 McDonagh in Hoyle (ed.), p. 274.

13 Elizabeth also took steps to deal with two of the perennial problems affecting agricultural land in this region, by clearing anthills, and installing stone drains to alleviate the heavy clay soil. Ibid., pp. 274–5.

14 Ibid., p. 275.

15 GRO 14/1/2, June 1770 and 19 February 1774.

16 McDonagh in Hoyle (ed.), p. 275.

17 Ibid., p. 271.

18   GRO 14/1/2, July 1772.

19   NoRO, 364p/70.

20   McDonagh in Hoyle (ed.), p. 274.

21   GRO 14/1/2, 22 December 1774.

22   McDonagh in Hoyle (ed.), p. 281.

23   NoRO, 364p/70.

24   Ibid.

25   McDonagh in Hoyle (ed.), pp. 281–2.

26   GRO 14/1/2, September–October 1777.

27   NoRO, 364p/70.

28   Ibid. The cost of the song book is recorded in October 1776.

29   GRO 14/1/2, 26 May 1792.

30   NoRO 364p/68, May 1774 and 364p/70, June 1774.

31   Crosby, 'Private Concerts', p. 56.

32   GRO 13/4/2 13 August 1774.

33   GRO 14/1/2 September 1777.

34   Ibid., 21 June 1770.

Chapter 26: Zoffany

1   The description is based on Elizabeth's account of a visit paid by Zoffany to Wicken Park in December 1780, when the artist painted a portrait of her old gardener Jonathan Jackman (GRO 14/1/2). See also later in the chapter.

2   Webster, *Johan Zoffany, RA, 1733–1810*, pp. 114–15.

3   See Kate Retford, '"Peculiarly happy at taking Likenesses": Zoffany & British Portraiture' in Postle (ed.), pp. 104–5.

4   Webster, *Johan Zoffany, RA, 1733–1810*, p. 55

5   Ibid.

6   Ibid., pp. 115–16, 53.

7   See Retford in Postle (ed.), pp. 101. The term 'phiz mongering', meaning portrait painting, was used (or coined) by William Hogarth.

8   Webster, *Johan Zoffany, RA, 1733–1810*, pp. 605–6.

9   Postle (ed.), p. 260.

10   Webster, *Johan Zoffany, RA, 1733–1810*, p. 392.

11   GRO 14/1/2.

12   Ibid.

13 Ibid., December 1780. Though it is possible that the artist also relished the prospect of enjoying Elizabeth's hospitality in the rural idyll of Wicken Park.

14 Ibid. *Jonathan Jackman* (1780) by Zoffany. Inscribed on the reverse: 'Jonathan Jackman, 60 years gardener at Wicken Park. He sat for Mr Zoffany for his picture the day he completed his 80th year. He died April 29th, 1783, aged 82.' See Webster, *Johan Zoffany: 1733–1810.*

15 Webster, *Johan Zoffany, RA, 1733–1810*, p. 392.

16 John Kerslake, 'A Note on Zoffanys "Sharp Family"', *Burlington Magazine* (1978), p. 753.

17 Webster, *Johan Zoffany, RA, 1733–1810*, p. 391. My description of the costumes worn by the family in the painting is derived from Ribeiro, pp. 137–9; and Webster, *Johan Zoffany, RA, 1733–1810*, pp. 391–2.

18 GRO 12/1/2.

19 Family tradition suggests that the two Catharines did not share their husbands' enthusiasm for music, so this may be a gesture of solidarity in the face of yet another musical excursion.

20 Crosby, 'Private Concerts', p. 33. See Chapter 6, 'Music'.

21 According to the key to the painting created by James's daughter Kitty (GRO 12/1/2).

22 See Chapter 6, 'Music'.

23 Webster, *Johan Zoffany, RA, 1733–1810*, pp. 390–2.

24 Ibid., p. 392.

25 With the exception of the tower, the church was rebuilt in 1880–1.

26 Ibid., p. 390.

27 See Chapter 15, 'Kew'.

28 See Webster, p. 393. What the Sharps thought of these criticisms of their family portrait is not known.

29 Ibid.

30 See Kerslake, p. 753.

31 *Morning Herald*, 10 May 1781; Treadwell, p. 307; Kerslake, p. 754.

32 Kerslake, p. 754.

Chapter 27: Zong

1 The hawker's cry is one of Paul Sandby's etchings *Twelve London Cries Done from the Life, Part 1ˢᵗ, 1760* reproduced in O'Connell, pp. 79–80. 'This

man pushes a "machine from Italy" in which hot puddings are cooking. It is supported ... by straps from his shoulders, leaving his hands free to sprinkle sugar on the pudding before selling it.'

2 Olaudah Equiano, known as Gustavus Vassa in his lifetime, was a writer and abolitionist originally from what is now Nigeria. Enslaved in childhood, he later bought his freedom and became an influential member of the abolitionist movement in London in the 1780s. In 1789, he published his autobiography *The Interesting Narrative of the Life of Olaudah Equiano*. Its depiction of the horrors of slavery is considered to have played a role in the passing of the Slave Trade Act in 1807. Equiano was a leading figure in, and spokesman for, the black community in London, and was integral to the 'Sons of Africa', a small abolitionist movement consisting of free Africans in London. He worked closely with Granville on various abolition-related causes, including publicising the *Zong* massacre.

3 TNA T70/145, Minutes, Committee Meeting, 26 July 1784 p. 234.

4 Walvin, *The Zong*, p. 90.

5 Ibid., p. 95.

6 TNA, Documents in the Exchequer, E112/1528, 'The Answer of Colonel James Kelsall', 12 November 1783.

7 *Gregson* v. *Gilbert*, fols 33–40.

8 TNA, Documents in the Exchequer, E112/1528, 'The Answer of Colonel James Kelsall', 12 November 1783.

9 See John Weskett, *Digest of the Theory, Laws and Practice of Insurance* (1781), p. 525, and Walvin, *The Zong*, pp. 109–16.

10 TNA, T70/1695, 'Miscellaneous Letters to the African Committee', Captain William Llewellin, Gold Coast, 13 January 1780.

11 The log was lost or destroyed after the arrival in Jamaica. Walvin, *The Zong*, p. 95.

12 Shyllon, pp. 187–8.

13 See Hoare, I, pp. 352–3. Nothing seems to have come of this prosecution.

14 The hearing is covered in detail in Walvin, *The Zong*, pp. 139–55. All extracts are from the Sharp transcript of the hearing.

15 Sharp transcript, pp. 60–1, 76.

16 Ibid. pp. 89–90.

17 The full title is 'An Account of the Murder of 132 Negro Slaves on Board the Ship Zong or Zurg; with some Remarks on the Argument of an eminent Lawyer, in defence of that inhuman Transaction inclosed in the Letter of 2nd July 1783 to the Lord Commissioners of the Admiralty'.

See Anita Rupprecht, "'A Very Uncommon Case": Representations of the *Zong* and the British Campaign to Abolish the Slave Trade', *Journal of Legal History*, Vol. 28, No. 3 (December 2007), p. 334.

18   Hoare, I, pp. 361–5.
19   Rupprecht, pp. 334–5.
20   Hoare, I, pp. 360–1.
21   Walvin, *The Zong*, p. 177.
22   Rupprecht, pp. 336–7.
23   Ibid., p. 342.

Chapter 28: Glee

1   The description recreates a concert held at Old Jewry on 10 April 1783, attended by over 300 guests. A surviving programme specifies that the first glee sung was 'Amidst the Myrtles' by Jonathan Battishill (1738–1801) in five parts. The description of the room is based on the letter from James to John dated 9 January 1769, and (in the absence of any direct evidence about the internal decoration of the Old Jewry mansion) on the music room in Norfolk House, St James's Square, now in the V&A.

2   The programmes for the first and last concerts in the book were written in by William.

3   9 February 1777.

4   Crosby, 'Private Concerts', Appendix 8i.

5   See Crosby, 'Private Concerts', Appendix 5.

6   Ibid.

7   See McVeigh, *Concert Life*, p. 120.

8   McVeigh, 'Felice Giardini', p. 81, quoting Burney, *A General History of Music*, p. 896.

9   Giardini was the first of many celebrity European virtuosi to take London by storm. See McVeigh, 'Felice Giardini', p. 81.

10   The promoters of the Pantheon concerts distanced themselves from the Bach and Abel prototype by featuring English and Italian music in preference to a predominantly German programme (McVeigh, *Concert Life*, pp. 14–15). Intense rivalries such as existed between Bach and Abel and the Pantheon were common in this period. Founded in 1785, the 'Professional Concert' under Wilhelm Cramer achieved a reputation for instrumental virtuosity surpassing even that of Bach and Abel. In

late 1790, the violinist and impresario Johann Peter Salomon pulled off a major coup when he persuaded Haydn to visit London.

11 McVeigh, *Concert Life*, pp. 12, 101, 54. The supremacy of the orchestral concert, and the establishment of semi-permanent orchestras like the 'Professionals', was the most distinctive aspect of performance in this period.

12 Ibid., p. 223. McVeigh explains that 'A core symphonic repertoire had only just begun to be established by the turn of the century'.

13 Ibid., p. 8.

14 Crosby sets out the details of all six programmes, 'Private Concerts', pp. 36–8.

15 Ibid., p. 38.

16 Donald Burrows and Rosemary Dunhill, *Music and Theatre in Handel's World: The Family Papers of James Harris 1732–1780* (OUP, 2002), pp. 1008–9.

17 McVeigh, *Concert Life*, p. 22.

18 Crosby, 'Private Concerts', Appendices 9 and 10. The second glee concert in the Visiting Book is recorded as taking place on 10 March 1783. However, it is probable that it refers to a glee evening which is known to have taken place on 10 April 1783 – see later in the chapter.

19 In contrast to her account of the evenings of sacred music, when attendees fall under the headings 'Ladies', 'Gentleman' and 'Performers', Catharine's record of glee evenings merge the latter two categories.

20 Granville kept one of these in a commonplace book, where he refers to it as: 'A List of the Music performed to a very large Company near 400 people at Mr Willm Sharp's House in the Old Jewry 10 Apr. 1783' (GRO 13/4/1). The other three programmes are under GRO 12/1/2.

21 See Crosby, 'Private Concerts', pp. 40–4.

Chapter 29: Mortality

1 Bourne wrote a treatise on the subject, which James used as the basis for his own design.

2 GRO 12/2/3, Transcript of audience with George III, 27 October 1770. GRO 12/2/1, 'A Description of the Rolling Carts, as built by James Sharp, of Leadenhall-Street, London'. 'Society of Arts' refers to the Society for the Encouragement of Arts, Manufacture and Commerce founded in 1754 by William Shipley.

3 Though the spread of turnpike trusts, which used tolls to pay for repairs, had improved road transport, trusts provided only a partial solution to the problem. For one thing, not all roads were 'turnpiked', and for another, maintenance remained rudimentary.

4 GRO 12/2/1, 'A Description of the Rolling Carts'.

5 This scene is based on information given to George III in the course of James's interview with him on 27 October 1770 (he describes a successful trial in Tooley Street, where it 'answered very well, having no board or flags broke as we were used to have by narrow wheels', GRO 12/2/3); and letters written by James to his brother John. For example, on 9 January 1769 James reported that he had manufactured sixteen rolling carts, and was building more as fast as he could. One variety, the ironmonger explained, is constructed with three rollers to cover 'the whole surface for the purpose of Rolling parks and lawns'. He also referred to a contract with a dustman for the sale and repair of carts: 'I have also agreed with the Contractor or Dustman of the Holborn to supply him with Carts and repare them at twelve Pounds per annum each cart' (GRO 9/1/4).

6 Ibid., advertisement dated 1 December 1772.

7 To test the efficacy of his improvements, James carried out 'a fair Experiment in St John's Church' in Southwark, where two stoves were fitted. According to the promotional booklet, the results of the experiment vindicated James's alterations: 'the Air-box of the Stove on the North side is exactly agreeable to Dr Franklin's Pattern; but the Air-Box of the Stove on the South Side is so altered as to produce an amazing difference of Effect'.

8 James produced at least ten editions, in English and French, of a promotional booklet for the stoves, which were installed in public buildings such as the Common Council Room in Guildhall and Draper's Hall. See Whiteman et al. (eds), p. 280.

9 Whiteman et al. (eds), p. 280, quoting Leonard W. Labaree et al. (eds), *The Autobiography of Benjamin Franklin* (Yale University Press, 1964), p. 192.

10 GRO 12/2/9, 'Catalogue of the Neat and Genteel Household Furniture, Plate, China, Books, Pictures, Prints ... and Other Valuable Effects, of Mrs Sharp (Retiring from Business) at her Late Residence, No. 15 Leadenhall Street ... Which will be Sold by Auction ... on Wednesday the 29th of February 1792'.

11 Whiteman et al. (eds), p. 286. Parliamentary reform was another cause on which the brothers acted in concert. James was a member of the

City of London branch of Christopher Wyvill's Yorkshire Association (founded in 1779). On 6 April 1780 Granville drafted a 'Warning' against the dangers of triennial parliaments, which James read to the City association, prompting a resolution in favour of annual parliaments.

12 Ibid., p. 287.

13 GRO 14/1/2, 10 July 1783.

14 GRO 13/4/2.

15 GRO 14/1/2, 10 July 1783.

16 Ibid., September 1783.

17 Ibid., 10 September 1783.

18 Ibid., 26 September 1783.

19 Ibid.

20 GRO 13/4/2, 31 October–2 November 1783.

21 Ibid.

22 Ibid.

23 Ibid., 5 November 1783.

24 GRO 14/1/2, 6 November 1783.

25 GRO 13/4/2.

26 GRO 14/1/2, 5 November 1783.

27 The obituaries appear to have been transcribed by James's daughter Kitty.

28 Hoare, II, p. 144.

Chapter 30: Independence

1 GRO 14/1/2, 3 February 1792, 'Sisr. James gave up her business in Leadenhall Street'.

2 Hoare, II, p. 186.

3 Earle, p. 161.

4 This is in fact the subtitle of a collection of 'essays, or rudiments for young beginners, in twelve articles' written by 'One of that sex' (1678).

5 See Barker, *The Business of Women*, p. 133; and Barker, *Family and Business During the Industrial Revolution*, and in particular pp. 103–5 (though with the caveat that the families studied by Barker were in most cases of a lower social class).

6 GRO 9/1/4, Granville to John, 3 November 1783.

7 GRO 14/1/2.

8   Ibid.

9   In later life Granville was a keen member of a London madrigal society.

10   Vickery, *Behind Closed Doors*, pp. 188–92.

11   GRO 14/1/2, 26 April 1792.

12   Ibid., 2 January 1763.

13   GRO 8/1/4, David Hastings to Judith, 15 October 1757.

14   GRO 8/1/6.

15   GRO 21/1/30. Unmarried women (as opposed to girls) were still some-
     times, confusingly, referred to as 'Mrs' in this period.

16   GRO 12/1/2, Kitty's key to the painting. None of the artworks survive.

17   GRO 16/1/1, John to Judith, 14 May 1770. Though Judith's letters have not
     survived, the force and tenacity of her argument is implicit in John's replies.

18   Frances also remained unmarried; however, there is no evidence that
     she was ever proposed to.

19   GRO 14/1/2, 1757.

20   Ibid., 28 March 1772.

21   Amanda Vickery, *Behind Closed Doors*, p. 210.

22   Ibid.

23   There were only 325 divorces between 1670 and 1857, and of these a
     mere four were initiated by women. It was also theoretically possible
     to obtain a separation in the Church courts, but to do so required a
     wife to prove the double charge of adultery and life-threatening cruelty.

Chapter 31: Visionary

1   Granville's correspondence reveals numerous examples of his acts of
     private charity.

2   Hoare, II, p. 230, quoting from Clarkson, Vol. I.

3   Ibid.

4   Clarkson, I, p. 282.

5   Hoare, II, p. 234–5, quoting from Clarkson.

6   Hoare, II, p. 403.

7   GRO 13/1/S8, Granville to John, March 1779.

8   See Christopher Leslie Brown.

9   Davis, *Problem of Slavery*, p. 389.

10   GRO 13/1/C26, Granville to Sir G. Onesiphorus Paul, 11 May 1780.

11   Christopher Leslie Brown, p. 196.

12   Stephen, II, p. 314.

13   Hoare, I, p. 36.

14   Ibid., II, pp. 328, 329.

15   GRO 13/1/S8, Granville to John, 19 July 1787.

16   Clarkson to 'T Harrison, Esq.', quoted in Hoare, II, p. 403.

17   Ibid., I. p. 5.

18   Peterson, pp. 17–20.

19   Ibid., p. 20.

20   Ibid., pp. 20–1.

21   Ibid., pp. 26–7.

22   This was in retaliation for the destruction of one of his own towns by sailors from a British warship.

23   Ibid., pp. 28–9. Though conditions for the settlers improved during the early 1790s, complaints by the Nova Scotia contingent that the Company had reneged on promises regarding land ownership and taxation soured relations between the emigrants and their newly appointed governor.

24   Ibid., pp. 30–6.

25   Absolute reliance was placed on the advice of Henry Smeathman, even though he had previously counselled against establishing a penal colony in Sierra Leone on grounds that it was 'unhealthy'. See ibid., p. 18.

26   'The Enlightenment and the Founding of Freetown: An Interpretation of Sierra Leone History, 1787–1816' in Fyfe and Jones (eds), pp. 13–14.

27   Ibid., pp. 15–16.

28   Ibid., p. 44. When the possibility of supporting the colony by agriculture proved illusory, the emigrants turned to trade, and Freetown became an important entrepot for European goods. See also Fyfe and Jones (eds), p. 9. Schama provides a detailed account of the founding of Sierra Leone from p. 182.

29   Such as 'Remarks on the Uses of the Definitive Article in the Greek Text of the New Testament' (1798).

30   'An Answer to an anonymous Letter [dated September 1777] on Predestination and Free-Will' (1801).

31   1786, 1773, 1771 and 1791 respectively. *An English Alphabet for the Use of Foreigners, wherein the Pronunciation of the Vowels is explained, in twelve short Rules, with their several Exceptions* (1786) was a sequel to *On the Pronunciation of the English Tongue, in French and English; and the same in English only* (1767).

32   Hoare, I, p. 31.

33   Ibid. pp. 31, 298–9, 301. David Brion Davis (p. 391) argues that 'the role of the eccentric' allowed Granville 'to expose the moral compromises of his society without being branded a rebel'.

34   Lascelles, p. 130.

Chapter 32: Fulham

1   See Phillips, p. 172.

2   Defoe quoted in O'Connell, p. 11.

3   *London Evening Post*, 14 March 1741, quoted in Feret, p. 111.

4   Ibid.

5   Ibid., p. 112. This later became a favourite resort of Granville, who worked in an upstairs room overlooking the river.

6   GRO 14/1/2, 24 October 1786.

7   Ibid., 8 November 1786.

8   It was apparently 'first observed after a very painful and critical operation which he performed upon a lady, when, upon being directed to look at some excellent pictures from which the room was hung, he found his sight utterly fail[e]d him'. See GRO 23/1/6, John Owen (vicar of All Saints, Fulham), *A Discourse Occasioned by the Death of William Sharp Esq.* (1810), p. 14.

9   He was apparently 'gifted with the rare endowment of being able to extract his pleasures from what was nearest at hand', and could find 'a recreation and repast, where persons of fastidious minds would have pined in listlessness, or sickened with disgust'. Ibid., p. 26.

10   GRO 16/1/1.

11   The description is based on Mary's diary for the period 1798–9, and a letter written by William to his sister Judith dated 18 February 1799 (GRO 16/1/1) in which he describes the Fulham social whirl. 'Lines Written a Few Miles above Tintern Abbey' was published as part of the *Lyrical Ballads* in 1798. *Artaxerxes* by Thomas Arne is an opera in three acts, first performed at the Theatre Royal Covent Garden in 1762, and regularly revived thereafter.

12   GRO 16/1/1, William to Judith, 18 February 1799.

13   GRO 14/1/2.

14   Fletcher, p. 223.

15   GRO 24/1/2, Extracts from the diary of Mary Lloyd Baker (née Sharp), 1798–9.

16   Ibid., 2 September 1798, 24 September 1798 and 19 September 1798.

17   Ibid., 17 September 1798.

18   GRO 24/1/1.

19   GRO 24/1/2, 23 August 1799.

20   GRO 24/1/1.

21   GRO 13/4/2, Extracts from Memorandum Book No. 1, 9 July 1785, 19 August 1785.

22   Ibid.

23   Ibid.

24   GRO 17/5/2.

25   Ibid. The Sharps' hosts at Brizlee were Hugh Percy, 1st Duke of Northumberland (1714–86), and his second son, Lord Algernon Percy, 1st Earl of Beverley (1750–1830). The summer 1785 drought broke several records. According to Kitty, 'The party afterwards Dined at Alnwick Castle from where a large Company went in the Even to the Play in a stable or Barn in Alnwick – accompanied by Lord Algernon Percy (Lord Beverley)' (GRO 17/5/2).

26   GRO 13/4/2, Extracts from Memorandum Book No. 2, April 1792.

27   Ibid., 3 May 1792.

28   GRO 14/1/2, 26 April 1792.

29   GRO 17/3/2, Title deeds of 'Miss Sharp's House in the South Bailey, Durham'.

30   GRO 14/1/2, 12 October 1804.

31   Ibid., 23 August 1799, 2 September 1799.

32   Ibid., 23 March 1809. Elizabeth reports that it took her '9 days' to reach Durham 'with my own horses & 3 servts'. This was considerably longer than it had taken Granville to reach Durham by stage coach in 1792, on the eve of John's death, but still an improvement on journey times in the 1740s, when William and James journeyed to London to start their apprenticeships.

33   GRO 14/1/2, 1 April 1809.

34   Ibid., 23 April 1788.

35   Ibid., 23 May 1809.

36   GRO 23/1/6, John Owen (vicar of All Saints, Fulham), *A Discourse Occasioned by the Death of William Sharp Esq.* (1810), pp. 31–2.

37   Ibid.

38   Hoare, II, pp. 314–15.

39   Christopher Leslie Brown (p. 161) argues that Granville's tract *A Declaration of the People's natural Right to a Share in the Legislature; – against*

the attempts to tax America, and to make Laws for her against her Consent (1774) represents 'one of the first attempts in England to make a case for colonial legislative autonomy'.

Coda

1   GRO 12/1/2. The three documents referred to in this passage survive in the Sharp archive. They are all in Kitty's handwriting, and are pasted together on a piece of thick linen. The date of the earlier documents – i.e. the pages removed from behind the painting – is not known.

2   'Reminiscences of Barwick Lloyd Baker' quoted in Whiteman et al. (eds), p. 283.

3   GRO 12/1/2. As well as her musical gifts, Kitty was also an exquisite dancer. In extolling Kitty's talents, during their tour on the *Union* yacht in August 1777, George III and Queen Charlotte praised the little girl's 'Dancing' as well as her 'singing'.

4   'Reminiscences of Barwick Lloyd Baker' quoted in Whiteman et al. (eds), p. 283.

5   Ibid. It is particularly noteworthy that Kitty was the only amateur soloist recorded as performing in the sacred music concerts detailed in the Visiting Book.

6   This appears to be Clare Hall Manor in Potter's Bar, built *c.*1754 incorporating an existing early seventeenth-century range, by Thomas Roberts. The house became a convent in 1886, a hospital from 1896 to 1976, and is now part of a laboratory campus.

7   Bowlt grew up near Bamburgh, apparently of relatively humble stock (GRO 17/1/11). He was clearly something out of the ordinary, for by the age of seventeen, John had appointed him to the position of deputy bailiff at the castle. By 1782 he was working as an assistant curate at Bamburgh, and living in the archdeacon's household. See Griffiths, pp. 8, 75.

8   GRO 17/1/11. The auction took place between 3 and 11 August 1835. Following the marriage, Bowlt changed his name to Sharp, and adopted the family coat of arms.

9   GRO 17/5/11.

10 NRO 00452/C/3/1/90/102 and GRO 6/5/11. This particular donation was made – under cover of a letter to the Venerable Archdeacon Thorp – in July 1835. The university was founded in 1832.

Picture Credits

Page 1: *The South West View of the City of Durham* (1776) © archivist 2015/ Alamy Stock Photo; page 35: Charles White, *View of the River Thames from Chelsea* (1750) © Guildhall Library & Art Gallery/Heritage Images/Getty Images; page 115: Michael Angelo Rooker, *A View of the Princes House at Kew* (1776) © The Print Collector/Getty Images; page 209: Robert Laurie, *View of Fulham from the White Lion Inn, Putney* (1783) © Guildhall Library & Art Gallery/Heritage Images/Getty Images.

Plate 1

Johan Joseph Zoffany, *The Sharp Family* (1779–81), from a private collection; on loan to the National Portrait Gallery, London.

Plate 2

(Top left) Johan Joseph Zoffany, *Self-Portrait with His Daughter Maria Theresa, James Cervetto, and Giacobbe Cervetto* (1780): Yale Center for British Art, Paul Mellon Collection; (Top right) Engraving of Thomas Sharp, from *The works of Thomas Sharp, D.D. Late Archdeacon of Northumberland, and Prebendary of Durham, in six volumes* (1763), shelf mark Bamburgh K.7.17. Reproduced by permission of Lord Crewe's Charity and of Durham University Library; (Bottom) Line drawing of Whitton Tower during Thomas Sharp's residency: http://whittontower.com/history.html

Plate 3

(Top) Thomas Bowles, *The South West Prospect of London, from Somerset Gardens to the Tower* (1750): Yale Center for British Art, Paul Mellon Collection; (Bottom) Letter from Granville Sharp to his sisters dated 18 October 1757 (D3549 7/2/15), from the Lloyd Baker archive. Reproduced by kind permission of Gloucestershire Archives.

Plate 4

(Top) 'James Sharp, manufacturer of agricultural impliments', eighteenth-century advert © Culture Club / Getty Images; (Bottom) 'Two views of a bladder stone' (D3549 10/1/3), from the Lloyd Baker archive. Reproduced by kind permission of Gloucestershire Archives.

Plate 5

(Top left) Charles Turner, after J. Abbot, *William Sharp* (1784) © National Portrait Gallery, London; (Top right) 'Portrait of English abolitionist, scholar and philanthropist Granville Sharp (1735–1813)', from *Encyclopaedia Londinensis* (1827) © The Print Collector/Alamy Stock Photo; (Bottom) Steel-engraved antique print of Wicken Park, Northamptonshire (1847), from a drawing by J. P. Neale.

Plate 6

(Top) Johan Joseph Zoffany, *Queen Charlotte (1744–1818) with members of her family* (c. 1771–2) © Royal Collection Trust/Her Majesty Queen Elizabeth II 2020; (Bottom) Johan Joseph Zoffany, *George III (1738–1820)* (1771) © Royal Collection Trust/Her Majesty Queen Elizabeth II 2020.

Plate 7

(Top) 'Bamburgh Castle, in Northumberland', from *The Antiquities of England and Wales* by Francis Grose © Antiqua Print Gallery/Alamy Stock Photo; (Bottom) James Hayllar, *Granville Sharp (1735–1813), The Abolitionist, Rescuing a Slave from The Hands of His Master* (1864) © Victoria and Albert Museum, London.

Plate 8

(Top) Johan Joseph Zoffany, *A View in Hampton Garden with Mr and Mrs Garrick Taking Tea* (1762). Courtesy of the Garrick Club, London; (Bottom) The Sharp family flotilla, from a painting in the private collection of the Lloyd-Baker family, reproduced by kind permission of the Lloyd-Baker Estate.

Acknowledgements

My first thanks go to Polly Morland whose generosity of spirit in introducing me to my agent Patrick Walsh made this book possible. I owe a great debt of gratitude to Patrick himself, for his expert guidance in the preparation of the proposal, and for his unfailing help and support in the later stages of the project. John Ash at PEW Literary similarly played a key role at the proposal stage, and has continued to make excellent suggestions as the book developed.

I am keenly aware of my good fortune in finding a publisher in Chatto & Windus, and in Clara Farmer in particular, whose enthusiasm for the Sharps, and vision, have been hugely important to me. I am also immensely grateful to Alex Russell, who has guided me through the process of creating this book with patience, sensitivity, tact and wisdom, devoting long hours to help me hone *The Good Sharps* to its final form.

From a research point of view, I am indebted to the staff of the Gloucester Archives, who with kindness and patience assisted me in mining the treasures of the Sharp archive; and also to the staff of the London Library, for their unflagging help and support. A special thank you must go to Carol Griffiths, whose research on the Bamburgh Castle papers was invaluable in my own presentation of the subject, and who has been generous in her advice and guidance. I am also indebted to Françoise Deconinck-Brossard, who has shared her expert knowledge of John Sharp, as well as providing guidance on the family more generally. My final, and most resounding, words of thanks in this section belong to the late Brian Crosby, whose work on the musical life of the Sharps provided much of the inspiration, and much of the source material, for this enterprise.

In writing this book, I have been aware of my responsibility both to the memory of the Sharp family itself, and to their descendants.

For this reason, I feel particularly lucky in the support of Victoria Murray-Browne, the great-great-great-great-great granddaughter of William Sharp – who by chance works at Vintage. I have been touched by her kindness and enthusiasm for the scheme, and also for the support of her wider family, and in particular Henry and Jude Lloyd-Baker who welcomed me into their home to view their personal Sharp archive.

Space does not permit me to list all the friends who have supported me in this project, but without them it would have been a far more lonely, difficult and unrewarding experience. Two exceptions must be made in the form of Cybele Hay, who read the first draft of the book and provided helpful criticism and advice; and India Jane Birley, who with an artist's eye, illuminated my understanding of Zoffany's painting of the family. And finally, and most importantly, I thank my children, who with characteristic good nature have put up with their mother's almost constant state of distraction; and my beloved husband Tom, who has been a beacon of warm-heartedness, enthusiasm, tolerance and support.

Index

356 INDEX